The Global Limits of Competition Law

Global Competition Law and Economics

Ioannis Lianos and D. Daniel Sokol, editors

The Global Limits of Competition Law

Edited by Ioannis Lianos and D. Daniel Sokol

STANFORD LAW BOOKS
An Imprint of Stanford University Press
Stanford, California

Stanford University Press
Stanford, California

Printed in the United States of America on acid-free, archival-quality paper

Library of Congress Cataloging-in-Publication Data

The global limits of competition law / edited by Ioannis Lianos and D. Daniel Sokol.
p. cm.—(Global competition law and economics)
Includes bibliographical references and index.
ISBN 978-0-8047-7490-1 (cloth : alk. paper)
1. Antitrust law. I. Lianos, Ioannis. II. Sokol, D. Daniel.
K3850.G59 2012
343.07'21—dc23 2011048548

Designed by Bruce Lundquist
Typeset by Westchester Book Composition in Bembo, 10.5/14

Contents

Preface vii

Contributors xi

Introduction 1
Ioannis Lianos and D. Daniel Sokol

PART I. THE COMPETITION LAW PROCESS

1. *The Limits of Antitrust* and the Chicago School Tradition 15
George L. Priest

2. Competition Law and Human Rights: Striking a Balance Between Business Freedom and Regulatory Intervention 22
Arianna Andreangeli

PART II. THE ECONOMIC LIMITS OF COMPETITION LAW

3. Limits of Imports from Economics into Competition Law 39
Anne-Lise Sibony

4. Complications in the Antitrust Response to Monopsony 54
Jeffrey L. Harrison

5. Antitrust and the Close Look: Transaction Cost Economics in Competition Policy 66
Herbert Hovenkamp

PART III. COMPETITION LAW AND ITS SYNERGIES WITH OTHER AREAS OF LAW

6. Anticompetitive Government Regulation 83
D. Daniel Sokol

7. A Global Perspective on State Action 99
Damien M. B. Gerard

8. IP's Advantages over Antitrust 117
Daniel A. Crane

9. Competition Law and Consumer Protection Against Unfair Commercial Practices: A More-than-Complementary Relationship? 127
Paolisa Nebbia

PART IV. COMPETITION LAW AND INSTITUTIONAL DESIGN

10. Judicial Scrutiny and Competition Authorities: The Institutional Limits of Antitrust 141
Javier Tapia and Santiago Montt

11. Competition Authorities: Independence and Advocacy 158
Frédéric Jenny

12. Competition Law Remedies: In Search of a Theory 177
Ioannis Lianos

PART V. COMPETITION LAW AND CULTURE

13. How Culture May Change Assumptions in Antitrust Policy 205
Thomas K. Cheng

14. Promoting Convergence of Competition Policies in Northeast Asia: Culture-Competition Correlation and Its Implications 221
Ki Jong Lee

15. The Limits of Competition Law in Latin America 236
Julián Peña

Notes 253

Index 283

Preface

The Global Limits of Competition Law is the first book in the Stanford University Press series Global Competition Law and Economics. The series is aimed at one of the most central questions to the study of competition law (known as antitrust in the United States)—how law, economics, and institutions respond to an increasingly global and interconnected antitrust community. Over time, the use of economic analysis in competition law has become the most important development globally in this area of law. The universalist concepts of economics might serve as a common vocabulary enhancing exchange and dialogue between various competition law systems, a sort of *tertium comparationis* or metalanguage facilitating any effort of comparative analysis. Yet, the same economic inputs do not always lead to similar legal outputs, as other variables may interfere, most notably institutional and cultural factors. It is therefore important to integrate the economic analysis of competition law into the broader economic, political, social, and institutional settings of each competition law system. Although there is some excellent comparative work in this area, we believe that a discussion of the interaction of all these factors from a global perspective has been lacking. Similar issues on the implementation and the scope of competition law come up in a number of jurisdictions. Too often policy makers merely reference the ready-made solutions adopted by more established competition law systems, such as the United States and the European Union, without due regard to local factors. This gap in the literature is particularly important in view of the expansion of competition law globally.

The aim of the series is to create a well-developed set of books that will address the broader context in this dynamic area of law and policy. Indeed, the geographic coverage of the competition law enterprise has expanded considerably during the last two decades. More than 120 countries have now enacted competition law statutes and many apply them regularly. Newspapers globally cover important competition cases, and competition law has become a prominent field of law with its own army of practitioners and academics. Yet, despite the valuable efforts of the International Competition Network with regard to competition authorities and some recent academic initiatives, there is little work in competition law and economics addressing, from a global perspective, common challenges faced by a variety of competition law systems. There is an emerging global competition law community, employing a common vocabulary, that of industrial economics, and proceeding to similar legal classifications, influenced by the two major competition law systems in the United States and Europe, but there are very few outlets for advancing a global discussion on the issues raised by the implementation of competition law in different economic and social settings. The aim of the series is to provide exactly this thinking space by involving academics from around the world.

The topic examined by the first volume in the series is "the global limits of competition law." Over the past three decades, the competition law enterprise has witnessed a profound transformation of its psyche. One of the most effective challenges came from Chicago, where a number of law and economics scholars had cast doubt on policy makers' "overconfidence" on the competition law tool and advocated its "rationalization." We used the twenty-fifth anniversary of the publication of Frank Easterbrook's seminal article *The Limits of Antitrust*[1] to frame a broader discussion about what procedural, substantive, and institutional limits there are to the effective use of antitrust. Easterbrook raised the issue of litigation costs for business, suggesting that judges should develop a filter or presumptions approach that would provide some legal certainty to firms and would limit the ever-expanding sphere of competition law. In Easterbrook's case, his concern was to respond to the doctrinal problem of the era in which he wrote the work. Antitrust was primarily an American enterprise and the combination of low procedural hurdles for private plaintiffs, high litigation costs, and the significant potential for mistaken prosecution suggested the need to create filters to "limit" antitrust. The discussion over the limits of antitrust illustrates the impact of the Chicago approach in U.S. antitrust law but also, in variable degrees, in other competition law systems reaching maturity. This debate over the limits of competition law is still ongoing.[2] However, its context and content have evolved. The debate does not only focus on the issue of economic reasoning in competition law but also integrates other factors such as the institutional, cultural, and legal background of each competition law system. A different conceptualization of the "limits" of competition law has emerged, drawing more on practical considerations, empirical findings, and theoretical metaprinciples. We hope that the first volume in the series will provide useful and original perspectives on this important topic and that it will enhance a global discussion over the adequate "limits" of the competition law enterprise in each jurisdiction.

The authors would like to thank the Centre for Law, Economics and Society at University College London; the University of Florida; the chapter contributors; our research assistants, Kevin McGarry, Leigh Anne Siddle, Jay Strader, and Christine Wang; Kate Wahl at Stanford University Press; John Donohue at Westchester Book Services; and our families for their support.

Contributors

Arianna Andreangeli is lecturer in competition law at Edinburgh Law School, University of Edinburgh. Her publications include *EU Competition Enforcement and Human Rights* (Elgar, 2008), "The Public Enforcement of Articles 101 and 102 TFEU Under Council Regulation 1/2003: Due Process Considerations," in *Research Handbook on EU Competition Law and Policy* (Ioannis Lianos and Damien Geradin, eds., Elgar, 2011), and "Interoperability as an Essential Facility in the Microsoft Case—Encouraging Competition or Stifling Innovation?," in the *European Law Review*.

Thomas K. Cheng is an assistant professor at the Faculty of Law of the University of Hong Kong. He specializes in antitrust law, especially international and comparative antitrust. He has published a number of articles and book chapters on competition law in Hong Kong and the interface between patent and antitrust in developing countries.

Daniel A. Crane is professor of law at the University of Michigan and counsel at Paul, Weiss, Rifkind, Wharton & Garrison LLP. He is the author of *The Institutional Structure of Antitrust Enforcement* (Oxford University Press, 2011) and various other books and articles on antitrust law. He was previously professor of law at the Benjamin N. Cardozo School of Law, visiting professor at NYU and the University of Chicago, and a Fulbright Scholar and visiting professor at the Portuguese Catholic University.

Damien M. B. Gerard is a research fellow affiliated with the Charles de Visscher Centre for International and European Law (CeDIE) of the University of Louvain (UCL, Belgium), and a consultant with Cleary Gottlieb Steen & Hamilton LLP (Brussels). His scholarship focuses on EU competition law enforcement and the theory of European integration. Recent representative publications include a contribution to the ongoing debate on the due process implications of the transformation of EU antitrust enforcement in the *European Law Review*, the chapter on judicial review in the leading treatise on cartel law in the European Union (Mario Siragusa and Cesare Rizza, eds., 2nd ed. 2011), one of the first comprehensive articles published on EU state aids rules applied to the financial crisis in *Concurrences*, and an account of possible remedies to protectionist threats to cross-border mergers in the EU in the *Common Market Law Review*.

Jeffrey L. Harrison is the Stephen C. O'Connell Chair at the University of Florida College of Law. He received his PhD from the University of Florida and his JD from the University of North Carolina. He has taught at the University of Texas, the University of North Carolina, the Sorbonne (Paris), and the University of Houston. He writes in the areas of antitrust, contract, copyright, and law and economics and has written a number of books including *The Law and Economics of Monopsony* (Cambridge University Press, 2010, with Roger Blair) and *Understanding Antitrust and Its Economic Implications* (Lexis, 2008, with E. Thomas Sullivan).

Herbert Hovenkamp is the Ben V. & Dorothy Willie Professor of Law at the University of Iowa. He is a fellow of the American Academy of Arts and Sciences and recipient of the Justice Department's John Sherman Award. His principal books are *Antitrust Law* (20 volumes, with the late Phillip E. Areeda and Donald F. Turner), *Creation Without Restraint: Promoting Liberty and Rivalry in Innovation* (2011, with Christina Bohannan), *The Antitrust Enterprise* (2006), and *Federal Antitrust Policy* (4th ed. 2011).

Frédéric Jenny holds a PhD in economics from Harvard University, a doctorate in economics from the University of Paris, and an MBA from ESSEC Business School in Paris. He is professor of economics at ESSEC. He is also a judge on the French Supreme Court (Cour de cassation), chairman of the OECD Competition Committee, non executive director of the Office of Fair Trading, and visiting professor at University College London Law School. He was previously vice-chair of the French Competition Authority (1993–2004) and chair of the WTO Working Group on Trade and Competition (1997–2003). He has written extensively about trade, competition, and economic development and has served as an adviser to many developing countries on competition issues.

Ki Jong Lee is professor of law at Sookmyung Women's University, Korea. He serves as secretary general of the Asia Competition Association, a non-governmental, international competition forum in Asia. He has investigated the correlation between national cultures, or citizens' values, and competition policies by applying the methodologies of cross-cultural psychologists. The result of his earlier research, "Culture and Competition: National and Regional Levels," was published in the *Loyola Consumer Law Review.*

Ioannis Lianos is the City Solicitors' Educational Trust Reader in European and Competition Law at the University College London, Faculty of Laws and Gutenberg Research Chair at the École Nationale d'Administration, France. His primary research interest lies in comparative (EU, U.K., French, U.S.) competition law, international competition law, European Union law (internal market, external relations), comparative administrative and regulatory law (public-private partnerships, public utilities law, judicial review of economic regulation), law and economics, empirical legal studies, and economic sociology.

Santiago Montt has worked at Universidad de Chile Faculty of Law as director of the Center of Regulation and Competition, and since April 2011 works as senior legal manager at BHP Billiton Base Metals. He teaches state liability and an introductory course on regulation at the undergraduate level at Universidad de Chile, as well as competition law and investment protection at the graduate level.

Paolisa Nebbia is a case handler at the Italian Competition Authority, having previously worked as a reader in competition law at the University of Leicester and, prior to that, as a fellow in law at St. Hilda's College, University of Oxford (2005–2007). She has published in the areas of EC law, competition law, and consumer law. Her publications include, in addition to several articles in major European law journals, the chapter on vertical agreements in *Law of the European Union* (David Vaughan and Aidan Robertson, eds., Oxford University Press, 2008) and *Unfair Contract Terms in European Law* (Hart Oxford, 2007).

Julián Peña is a partner in charge of Allende & Brea's antitrust and trade department in Argentina, and is founder and moderator of *ForoCompetencia*, a discussion group on competition issues with members from over twenty countries. He is professor of competition law at the Graduate Program of the University of Buenos Aires and was visiting professor at the University of Florida. Peña is the author of *Merger Control—Legal Framework and Case Law* (Rubinzal, 2002) and of numerous articles and chapters.

George L. Priest is the Edward J. Phelps Professor of Law and Economics and Kauffman Distinguished Research Scholar in Law, Economics, and Entrepreneurship at Yale Law School. One of the nation's foremost antitrust scholars, he is also the author of a wide number of articles and monographs on the subjects of product liability, tort law, insurance litigation, and settlement.

Anne-Lise Sibony is professor of European law at the University of Liège (Belgium), where she teaches EU law and law and economics. She also teaches EU competition law at the University Paris II (France). Her main research interest is in how law absorbs insights from sciences such as economics or psychology. She is the author of *Le juge et le raisonnement économique* (2008), which analyzes legal techniques incorporating economic reasoning into judicial decision making.

D. Daniel Sokol is associate professor of law at the University of Florida Levin College of Law. His research focuses on U.S., comparative, and international antitrust. He is series coeditor of Stanford University Press's Global Competition Law and Economics book series. He is the author of articles, coeditor of *Latin American Competition Law and Policy* (Hart Oxford, 2009, with Eleanor M. Fox) and coeditor of the *Oxford Handbook of Antitrust Economics* (Oxford University Press, forthcoming, with Roger D. Blair).

Javier Tapia is the head of Research and Advocacy Division, FNE (Chilean Competition Agency). He has taught at the University of Chile.

The Global Limits of Competition Law

Introduction

Ioannis Lianos and D. Daniel Sokol

We brought together a set of authors from law and economics to present ideas on various "limits" to antitrust law (broadly defined) in a more global context. The issues that the chapters in this book raise suggest a broader set of limits, some intrinsic to antitrust, others extrinsic. Our starting point was the intrinsic limits of competition law that Judge Frank Easterbrook highlighted in his seminal article *The Limits of Antitrust*. We consider, however, that Judge Easterbrook's points related to his concern about overenforcement of antitrust law and the risks raised by the specificity of the U.S. enforcement system, which combines a relatively centralized, easily controllable public enforcement system with a largely decentralized private enforcement system that provides important incentives for litigation of competition law disputes, sometimes with the sole aim to extract rents from the alleged competition law infringers. Such a combination is rarely the case in other jurisdictions, even in the European Union, where private enforcement of competition law is still nascent and, in any case, lacks the instruments facilitating the choice of litigation in the United States, such as treble damages, contingency fees, class actions, and extensive discovery. A proper discussion regarding the limits of antitrust should therefore aim to examine an array of circumstances, not exclusively institutional, that might affect the scope of the competition law exercise. We start from the traditional limits imposed by the antitrust law process before addressing other, broader limits of competition law relating to competition economics, synergies with other areas of law, institutional design, and culture.

Part I: The Competition Law Process

Far from being just an area of economics, competition law should pay close attention to the process rules that constitute the backbone of its legal system and ultimately define its reach. In Chapter 1, George Priest provides historical context for Easterbrook's writing. Priest places Easterbrook's article within the Chicago School antitrust tradition. In particular, Priest suggests that two Chicago School thinkers, Aaron Director and Ronald Coase, laid the intellectual foundations for Easterbrook in two critical areas. The first was in the emphasis on conceptualizing the market, rather than more active antitrust enforcement, as a default mechanism for economic organization. That is, the market could self-correct for monopolistic behavior. The second foundation regarded the expectation of judicial error. The concern with judicial error focused on the fact that judges were more likely to make errors based on false positives ("Type I" errors of mistaken prosecution) than false negatives ("Type II" errors of insufficient prosecution). The complexity of competition law and the prospective nature of some of the analysis performed create some uncertainty over the extent of Type I and II errors.

In Europe, the limits imposed by process have taken on a new twist that is foreign to how antitrust has been practiced in the United States and extrinsic to competition rules as such. In Chapter 2, Arianna Andreangeli discusses Council Regulation No 1/2003, which conferred pervasive investigative powers upon the European Commission and also bolstered the cooperation between the European Commission and the National Competition Authorities. The regulation enlarged the array of tools at the Commission's disposal for competition matters. However, the stronger competition enforcement in recent years by the European Commission raises a number of issues about the position of the investigated parties as well as, more generally, their freedom to choose how to conduct themselves in the market. For a number of years, a lively and often strongly worded debate has been taking place as to the fairness of the European Commission's application of the competition rules. Some argue that the current mechanisms for competition enforcement would not secure compliance with the concept of "due process" as enshrined in European human rights standards and especially in Article 6(1) of the European Convention on Human Rights (ECHR). Andreangeli notes that the potential tensions between freedom of enterprise and the protection of genuine competition have become especially evident in the aftermath of the *Microsoft* case. In *Microsoft*, the Commission and the Court of First Instance were prepared to impose considerable limits on the freedom to contract and on the exercise of intellectual property rights enjoyed by a dominant undertaking. Given this position, Andreangeli addresses where to draw the boundary between, on the one hand, the pursuit of competition through administrative action and, on the other, the effective protection of business freedom and of freedom from disproportionate interferences with the undertakings' rights. The first part of her chapter focuses on the procedural aspects of this issue and considers the extent to which the current safeguards, prescribed by Council Regulation No 1/2003 and interpreted by the European Court of Justice, are sufficient to fulfill the standards of due process enshrined in the ECHR. The second part addresses the substantive question of whether the restrictions on the freedom of contract, and more generally on market freedom, imposed upon dominant firms by competition enforcement agencies are compatible with the rights contained in the ECHR.

Part II: The Economic Limits of Competition Law

Economic analysis drives competition law. To what extent, however, is economics a limit to antitrust? That is, has the competition law doctrine internalized advances in economics? The integration of economic analysis into competition law raises important questions on the extent to which it is possible to use in a legal context the existing economic methodology that developed in response to the internal economic discipline concerns. Economic analysis may set limits to the ability of competition law to come up with optimal legal rules that are administrable. The next few chapters explore issues within this theme.

In Chapter 3, Anne-Lise Sibony reflects on factors that limit imports from economics into competition law. Leaving aside well-known limitations that are inherent in economic science as well as practical limitations that stem from unavailability of data, this contribution focuses on limits that characterize the importing process itself. Taking the view that there are generally several different ways of importing any given economic insight into the law, Sibony looks at the technical choices that an importer of economics (court, competition authority) faces. Going back to basic legal categories of interpretation and proof, this analysis highlights trade-offs that have to be made between different importing techniques, each with its own limitations.

In Chapter 4, Jeffrey Harrison highlights the complexity of integrating economic concepts in legal outputs with a study of the application of competition law to monopsony. To some extent the U.S. monopsony antitrust law analysis is the mirror image of the analysis of monopoly and collusion among sellers. Two particular problems, however, complicate monopsony analysis. The first is the possibility that sellers can be forced onto an all-or-nothing supply curve. The outcome is exploitation of input providers without losses in allocative efficiency. The second problem is identification of the proper parties to bring private actions when they are permitted. In these respects, Harrison argues that the concepts of antitrust injury and standing must be applied in the context of sellers and not the more typical case of buyers.

In Chapter 5, Herbert Hovenkamp emphasizes the diversity of economic theory by addressing the role of transaction cost economics (TCE) within antitrust. He identifies at one extreme the "structural" school, which saw market structure as the principal determinant of poor economic performance. At the other extreme was the Chicago School, which also saw the economic landscape in terms of competition and monopoly, but found monopoly only infrequently and denied that a monopolist could "leverage" its power into related markets. Since the 1970s, both the structural and Chicago positions have moved toward the center, partly as a result of TCE. As Hovenkamp notes, a distinctive feature of TCE is that transactions occur with a limited range of partners depending on limits of knowledge and previous technological commitment, or asset specificity. The question of who trades is at least as important as the terms of trading. TCE analysis of contractual restraints also recognizes that one threat to consumers is double marginalization, which can occur when market power is held by separate firms with complementary outputs.

Antitrust is relevant in two ways. First, private arrangements can minimize double marginalization, justifying practices such as tying in markets characterized by single-firm dominance or product differentiation. Both tying and bundled discounts operate as a kind of "reverse leveraging," benefiting consumers. Second, transaction costs sometimes explain why private contracting is inadequate for addressing double marginalization problems and, thus, they justify antitrust intervention.

Hovenkamp then explains how TCE has also reinvigorated the link between conduct and exclusion, as illustrated by the Williamson/Areeda-Turner dispute over predatory pricing and the rise of the antitrust literature on raising rivals' costs (RRC). The RRC literature has attempted to restore a meaningful conception of anticompetitive exclusion without a return to the excesses of the structuralist school. Nevertheless, Hovenkamp suggests that one comparative advantage of both structuralism and the Chicago School was their simplicity. For the structuralists, concentration explained everything and inferences were drawn in favor of condemnation. Within Chicago School analysis the impossibility of leveraging and the mobility of resources explained everything and inferences were drawn in favor of exculpation. Hovenkamp concludes that TCE analysis is more specific to the situation, however, demanding close scrutiny when significant market power either is present or realistically threatens.

Part III: Competition Law and Its Synergies with Other Areas of Law

This part explores the interaction of competition law with other areas of law that pursue different objectives and in some instances may limit or expand its scope. These chapters explore the characterization of competition law as separate from regulation. In some cases competition law may be a substitute and in other cases it may be a complement. In yet another set of cases, other forms of regulation may create constraints on the effective functioning of competition law.

In Chapter 6, D. Daniel Sokol notes that Easterbrook focused only on competition problems that were specifically within the realm of antitrust law. In doing so, Easterbrook overlooked government-created restraints on competition. This, Sokol argues, was a mistake, as the real limit of antitrust is that antitrust enforcement (particularly public enforcement) may not reach the type of conduct that is most harmful to economic growth and development—anticompetitive government regulation. Sokol's chapter explains the causes and dynamics of anticompetitive government regulation. He then explores both the potential and the limits of antitrust to address the behavior. His chapter concludes with suggestions for how competition authorities might want to prioritize the kinds of competition advocacy interventions that have a high likelihood of success to reduce the anticompetitive impact of government restraints.

Damien Gerard (Chapter 7) also focuses on government restraints. His chapter's more narrow focus is on state action. He argues in the European context that the key test in assessing the legality of public restraints (as opposed to private practices) ought to be whether they infringe the internal market provisions rather than the competition law rules of the Treaty on the Functioning of the European Union (TFEU). Indeed, he writes that the internal market provisions are best suited to achieve the right balance between the pursuit of allocative efficiency and the necessary deference to Member States' (albeit limited) sovereignty. In turn, they effectively prevent protectionist behaviors while preserving Member States' ability to pursue redistributive objectives. Hence, he argues that it is time to depart from the state action doctrine as developed by the EU courts and thus to consider public restraints through different lenses other than private practice. To reach this conclusion, Gerard undertakes a three-stage analysis. First, he provides an overview of the state action doctrine as developed in the EU and contrasts it with the position adopted in the United States. Second, he highlights the main pitfalls of the state action doctrine and their origins. Third, Gerard suggests a new approach to public restraints and tests it against past cases.

In Chapter 8, Daniel Crane suggests a significant change from existing antitrust practice. The limit of antitrust may be antitrust law itself. Thus, Crane suggests shifting some of antitrust's responsibility to intellectual property law in areas where there is overlap. Much of the judicial retrenchment of antitrust liability norms in the United States in the last quarter century has been motivated by concerns over antitrust's institutional and remedial structure. Treble damages, lay juries, attorney-fee shifting, and other features create a concern that overly zealous antitrust enforcement will chill beneficial competition, as Easterbrook noted. There is also a perception that courts are ill equipped to police dominant firm behavior, for example, by limiting the prices a monopolist charges or the quality of its service, or by imposing the terms and conditions upon which it must deal with rivals. Crane argues that intellectual property law can address many of the issues that antitrust cannot (or will not) address in IP-intensive industries. For example, by shifting from property rules to liability rules for intellectual property rights, courts can police market power without imposing an affirmative obligation to deal or (usually) directly engaging in rate regulation of dominant firms.

One natural area of overlap in competition and regulation is in the area of consumer protection. Indeed, many competition agencies also have a consumer protection function. In Chapter 9, Paolisa Nebbia argues that while the assumptions and the aims of competition and consumer protection laws are substantially different, parallel remedies under each set of rules may, in some cases, be available. Her chapter identifies a number of situations where a claim may be couched in terms of both a competition law and an unfair commercial practice. She then examines whether, in practice, any similarity between the two types of claims can justify common approaches at the enforcement level.

Part IV: Competition Law and Institutional Design

By now it should be clear that the economic sophistication of competition law, the complexity of its enforcement, its interaction with other areas of law, and the process limits imposed by the legal system should be taken into account in designing appropriate institutions for an effective implementation of competition law. The chapters of this part examine that design.

Focusing on institutional design, Javier Tapia and Santiago Montt (Chapter 10) discuss the allocation of power within a competition system between the enforcement body with primary jurisdiction over competition matters on the one hand and the reviewing courts or tribunals on the other. First, they address the basic set of questions that emerge from an institutional analysis. At the most basic level, institutional design must answer whether there should be a unified administrative decision maker, or if there should be separation between enforcement and adjudicatory functions. As a corollary, if there is a separate body in charge of deciding competition law violations, should the adjudicatory body be a specialized tribunal, or should it be the courts of general jurisdiction? Second, what are the characteristics that the reviewing court should have?

Based upon these questions, the chapter identifies four models of judicial scrutiny that fit well in comparative practice. The remainder of the chapter focuses on two of those models in more detail based upon a case study of the Chilean competition law system. Tapia and Montt conclude that despite a still-limited knowledge of institutional design, judicial review would benefit from a deferential standard of review applied by courts in relation to a competition authority's expert decisions.

Frédéric Jenny (Chapter 11) also focuses on institutional design. During the 1990s, competition law expanded in a great number of countries, and major efforts have been undertaken in the context of various international organizations (such as the Organisation for Economic Co-operation and Development and the International Competition Network) to promote a convergence of views on the goals of competition law and to define best practices for competition authorities. Because the 1990s were a period of rapid economic expansion, deregulation, and privatization, a generally held view was that competition authorities should be independent of both businesses and governments. It was also commonly accepted that competition authorities should have a dual role: the role of competition law enforcers and the role of competition advocate. Jenny notes that this model worked reasonably well until the middle of the first decade of this century as competition authorities became respected enforcers of competition laws. Nevertheless, this model had some critics in countries where there was a concern that the government itself, either through direct intervention as a supplier of goods or services or as a drafter of restrictive regulations, was a major source of competition problems. When the economic and financial crisis hit, Jenny argues, government intervention became much more widespread and ubiquitous than before. Government interventions included fiscal stimulus packages and grants of state aid, the promotion of bank mergers or recapitalization schemes, the reinforcement of financial regulations, and the adoption of restrictive international trade measures. Jenny notes that the concern about competition shifted somewhat from anticompetitive practices by business firms to unwarranted and shortsighted government interventions in market mechanisms.

Jenny suggests that the model of competition authorities as institutions independent of the executive branch of government focused mostly on anticompetitive practices of firms. Indeed, under such models, competition authorities, not being part of the government, have been largely left out of the policy debate. In some countries, the competition authority, even though it is independent, may provide public opinions and, therefore, has some ability to let government or parliament know which general direction it considers the most compatible with competition law and policy. But being outside of government means that competition authorities are not consulted on a range of issues that may affect the competitive environment and are not in the drafting room when restrictive policies are being finalized. Whether this is a good or a bad thing is open to debate, and the answer partly rests on an assumption about the respective roles of law enforcement and advocacy in shaping a more competitive environment for the future. Jenny concludes that the model of a competition authority independent of the executive, but in charge of both antitrust enforcement and competition advocacy, may need to be revised. Therefore, according to Jenny, a better model would separate the functions and include an independent enforcer and an administrative body in charge of competition advocacy.

In Chapter 12, Ioannis Lianos highlights a less-examined limit to competition law—that of implementing effective and proportional remedies. The focus is not, as in Easterbrook's article, on the definition of the scope of liability and process rules that limit the discretion of competition authorities, but on the remedial phase of competition law enforcement. There is an inherent tension between the objective of efficiency in competition law enforcement and the limited power competition authorities have to adopt far-reaching remedies that would appear disproportional with regard to the competition law violation identified. The recourse to economic analysis offers a flexible tool to competition authorities eager to redesign the market process so as to promote effective competition. However, the rule of law and basic requirements of corrective justice may limit the discretion of competition authorities to adopt remedies and may consequently limit the scope of competition law. Lianos examines the application of what he terms "discretionary remedialism" to EU competition law, in particular by focusing on the enforcement of Article 102 TFEU on the abuse of dominant position. He defines "discretionary remedialism" as the view that courts (or competition authorities) have discretion to award the "appropriate" remedy in the circumstances of each individual case rather than being limited to specific (perhaps historically determined) remedies for each category of causative events. He notes that principles of discretionary remedialism separate the issue of liability from that of remedy. Lianos opposes this view. His chapter begins with an examination of the relationship between the liability and the remedy phases of an Article 102 proceeding in general. He then integrates the issue of discretionary remedialism and the distinction between the liability and remedial phase with the broader debate on the relation between efficiency and distributive justice from one side and corrective justice from the other side. Next, he examines the importance of discretionary remedialism in the context of antitrust. In this context, he illustrates why it is important to limit discretionary remedialism's effects by exploring the objectives pursued by competition law remedies. He argues that a coherent theory of competition law remedies is incompatible with a sharp dichotomy between liability and remedy. The emergence of a remedial proportionality test in EU competition law demonstrates also the necessary logical connection between the remedy and the liability phases. The final part of the chapter explores whether and how the remedial proportionality test will operate in the context of an "effects-based approach" under Article 102 TFEU.

Part V: Competition Law and Culture

In Chapter 13, Thomas Cheng questions whether economic concepts that underpin competition law doctrines are culture-specific. Most microeconomic and industrial organization theories have been developed in Western countries. It is possible that the validity of these concepts diminishes when economic actors behave differently across cultures. Cheng notes that divergence across cultural norms means that firms and consumers may behave differently from country A to country B. Cheng focuses his analysis on two areas of competition law—cartels and vertical restraints. After explaining how some traditional assumptions about behavior in each setting may vary based upon culture, Cheng suggests that cultural considerations may require fine-tuning of competition analysis and enforcement under some limited circumstances. In doing so, he explains that cultural variations may undermine the feasibility of a one-size-fits-all approach to antitrust that some scholars and policy makers have embraced in recent years.

Also on the topic of culture, Ki Jong Lee (Chapter 14) examines the role of culture in competition law within an Asian context. His chapter examines the correlation between national cultures and competition policies in searching for measures to promote convergence of competition policies in Northeast Asia. Lee's chapter presents evidence on culture-competition correlation. He then discusses the implications of the correlation for the convergence of competition policies. He concludes with some suggestions to promote competition law and policy convergence within Asia. He advocates the promotion of competition-friendly values at a regional level to push for the convergence of competition policies. In the long run, Lee argues, competition authorities need to undertake measures directly focusing on citizens' values beyond the traditional scope of competition advocacy.

In Chapter 15, Julián Peña points out some common limits to the development of competition law in Latin America. These common limits are cultural, political, economic, and institutional. Peña analyzes each of these limits to assess the challenges faced by implementing competition laws and policies designed for a different context without making the necessary adjustments to the reality of each country (or the region as a whole). His chapter is a cautionary story of good intentions that have created ineffective policies because competition law has not been calibrated to the reality of Latin America.

Overall, we believe that this book reflects a broader understanding of what limits there are to competition law. Indeed, titling the book *The Global Limits of Competition Law* reflects the reality that after over one hundred years of operation in the United States, "antitrust" has become global. The context and dynamics of competition law and policy share some common themes around the world but also suggest some differences based on a number of different assumptions about legal regimes, economics realities, and institutional designs.

Part I

The Competition Law Process

1

The Limits of Antitrust and the Chicago School Tradition

George L. Priest

The Chicago School Antitrust Tradition

As is well known, putting aside a few stray endeavors that had no abiding influence, law and economics as a field began with the work of Aaron Director and Ronald Coase centered on papers published in the *Journal of Law & Economics*, which began publication in the late 1950s. Looking back on those efforts, law and economics as developed by Director and Coase was not exactly ideological, but derived from what might be called a deeply held belief system that political interference in market activities interfered with freedom and reduced societal welfare. The phrase "reduced societal welfare" is a modern, technocratic concept. The opposition of Director and Coase to governmental interference in market activities was much deeper. Director was one of the founding members (along with Milton Friedman, Frank Knight, Ludwig von Mises, and George Stigler, among others) of the Mont Pelerin Society, organized by Friedrich Hayek in 1946. Hayek had published *The Road to Serfdom* in 1944. Following themes of *The Road to Serfdom*, the Mont Pelerin Society was, and to some extent still is, dedicated to the proposition that political interference with market activities is harmful to freedom—though the Society avoided a purely libertarian approach—and to broader individual and societal goals. Coase was not present at the first meeting of the Society but became a member two years later, in 1948, and at some later point, a Life Member.

The early volumes of the *Journal of Law & Economics* illustrate the commitment of the editors—first Director, succeeded by Coase—to the belief in the superiority of the market to political allocation of resources. The first issues contain some articles that might be regarded as economic science, but they also contain numerous articles that are essentially essays in political economy—market-oriented political economy: in volume 2 of the *Journal*, Hirshleifer's articles *Capitalist Ethics—Tough or Soft?*[1] and *The Sumptuary Manifesto*,[2] and Buchanan's *Positive Economics, Welfare Economics, and Political Economy*;[3] in volume 3, Jacob Viner's *The Intellectual History of Laissez Faire*;[4] in volume 4, Stigler's *Private Vice and Public Virtue*.[5] Though these early volumes of the *Journal* do not ignore the scientific application of economic analysis, they resemble more closely a high-level journal of promarket political philosophy than a journal of economic science.

The political philosophy, however, would not entirely generate the law and economics movement; the philosophy combined with empirical work would. From the earliest issues, the editors—Director and Coase—encouraged articles of an empirical nature critical of specific governmental interventions in the market, first to complement, later to completely supplant, the essays on political economy.

Antitrust law and economic regulation were particular subjects of criticism, though articles in the *Journal* also addressed the effects, economic and otherwise, of the minimum wage,[6] unionization,[7] licensing,[8] and even the British National Health Service,[9] among others. In the first issue of the *Journal*, Director published John McGee's reanalysis of the *Standard Oil* case, showing that the basic theory of predatory pricing underlying the Supreme Court's opinion had misunderstood the economic practices at issue entirely.[10] Rockefeller and associates had created the Standard Oil monopoly not by predatory practices such as undercutting prices or through railroad rebates (hard to distinguish from volume discounts), but by buying out rivals, giving them a share of potential monopoly profits. Note that the point of McGee's argument is not that the Standard Oil monopoly was not a monopoly and perhaps ripe for dissolution (McGee expressly put aside that question), but rather that the economic analysis of predatory pricing adopted by the Supreme Court and in popular understanding was naive, if not idiotic. McGee's point, surely encouraged by Director,[11] was to demonstrate that the justification given by the Court and accepted in popular opinion for governmental interference in this famous case was basically nonsense.

Most of the other articles criticizing antitrust law solicited or encouraged by Director and Coase were of this nature: Telser's study of resale price maintenance, criticizing the Supreme Court's *General Electric* opinion;[12] Ward Bowman's[13] and, later, Ken Dam's[14] work on tying arrangements; Stigler's article on the *U.S. Steel* case;[15] John Peterman's studies of *Brown Shoe* and *International Salt*.[16] Although these articles generated substantial new learning concerning industrial practices, the underlying aim of the antitrust program was only partially scientific advance; more centrally, it was to ridicule the grounds upon which courts interfered with the marketplace.

The deep Chicago School belief in the superiority of markets and in the mistaken views of courts is reflected in the most famous article in the *Journal* (as well as in the history of law and economics), Ronald Coase's *The Problem of Social Cost*.[17] The article is well known, but the political dimension of Coase's analysis and how his article fits within the Chicago School tradition are often unappreciated. The article is remembered today as vastly changing our understanding of the effects of legal rules. But I do not believe that it was drafted with that ambition in mind, and the article does not remotely pursue the implications for the effects of tort law or even more generally of property law, though his examples come from property law cases. That work was later accomplished by Harold Demsetz, Richard Posner, and others. Coase's article instead was directed at attacking Pigou and Pigou's purported demonstration that government, including the courts, could and should intervene in multiple markets to correct what we now call externalities.[18] The point of the article was to show that Pigou's analysis of correcting externalities was unsupportable.

The political or ideological dimension of the Coase Theorem is often ignored. To Coase, the implication of the proposition that "in the absence of transaction costs, the assignment of liability will have no effect on the allocation of resources" is that courts and the government can do no good by interfering in markets. If government action can somehow reduce transaction costs, that may enhance welfare; otherwise, courts and the government are fooling themselves by attempting to improve upon market outcomes and should stay out. Coase's ambition was to deflate arguments for more intrusive government, not—as it happened—to revolutionize our understanding of the operation of the legal system. As a demonstration of Coase's academic program, it is not often remembered that the academic project to which Coase turned after *The Problem of Social Cost* was not the extension of the Coase Theorem to the analysis of legal rules, but an attack on one of the last major institutional vestiges of socialism in Western societies, the post office.[19]

At the time, the character of Coase's insight seemed and, to some extent, still seems today an incredible demonstration of extraordinary genius. I remember thinking then, "How could a person generate such a counterintuitive idea?," and discussing the question with Dick Posner and, later, Harold Demsetz, among others. The extraordinary nature of the intuition led many to look back at Coase's earlier writings to attempt to discover possible precursors of the idea. Important in this respect was Coase's early article *The Nature of the Firm*[20]—an article upon which *The Limits of Antitrust* importantly relies to show the difficulty courts face in evaluating contractual arrangements in comparison with firm integration, and which influences Easterbrook's other corporate work. In that article, Coase identifies the transaction costs of using the price mechanism, in contrast to direct ordering within a firm. Many, including the Nobel Prize Committee, have regarded Coase's early focus on transaction cost reduction as an explanation for the creation of a firm as at one with the recognition of the importance of transaction costs in determining the effects of legal rules.

I am skeptical of this explanation for two reasons. First, Coase's work after *The Nature of the Firm* did not generally focus on the implications of transaction costs. Second, there is a more direct source of the analysis in *The Problem of Social Cost*, consistent more broadly with Coase's and Aaron Director's beliefs. Again, the principal ambition of *The Problem of Social Cost* was to show that Pigou's rationalization of broad governmental, including judicial, intervention in the marketplace was both foolish and ineffectual. The Coase Theorem follows directly from a belief system that sees market transactions as inherently superior to and dominant over government interventions. If one sees a problem, an externality, that government intervention is attempting to solve, but believes deeply that the market will solve the problem more effectively, the analysis of *The Problem of Social Cost* becomes more apparent. Market transactions can serve to solve problems among conflicting property uses that governmental interventions cannot hope to equal. The Coase Theorem fits squarely within the Chicago School tradition that views markets as superior means of allocating resources and that, conversely, views governmental interventions as lacking analytical support and harmful in effect.[21]

These two propositions of the Chicago School tradition—(1) that markets are superior to any form of governmental, including judicial, intervention, and (2) that judicial interventions generally have no coherent analytical basis—are central, I believe, to understanding the background of *The Limits of Antitrust* and the nature of the contribution of that article.

That these two propositions are central to Chicago School analysis is clear. As is well known, Aaron Director, the first editor of *The Journal of Law & Economics*, did not publish very much. In 1964, however, when Ronald Coase succeeded Director as editor of the *Journal*, Coase published as the lead article of his first issue, clearly as a tribute to his predecessor, a memorandum that Director had written in 1953 but never published, which (I presume) Coase entitled *The Parity of the Economic Market Place.*[22] That article makes many points, in particular about the different treatment that U.S. liberals give to freedom of speech versus market freedom (which Coase would later pursue), but two stand out:

1. "Laissez faire has never been more than a slogan in defense of the proposition that every extension of state activity should be examined under a presumption of error;"[23] and
2. "It is not essential to demonstrate that there is only one road to serfdom or that a particular road must inevitably lead to a specified destination [distancing himself from Hayek]. Some institutions are more flexible than others. We must choose those which minimize the risks of undesirable consequences."[24]

These are ideas that I believe served as the basis for the extension achieved in Easterbrook's *The Limits of Antitrust.* Though skeptical of governmental and judicial interference, the Chicago School never advocated abandoning antitrust law in the Armentano libertarian way. The Chicago School tradition sought to constrain antitrust law—chiefly by ridiculing its excesses—but accepted antitrust enforcement as an underlying background condition of market activity.

Easterbrook's *The Limits of Antitrust* in the Chicago School Tradition

Easterbrook's analysis in *The Limits of Antitrust* builds upon the foundations of the Chicago School tradition in two important ways. First, the article extends the idea that markets are more effective than governmental intervention in correcting the impact of anticompetitive action. Thus, the article makes the important point that, with respect to what are now known as Type II prosecutorial errors—false negatives—the marketplace will correct them through enhanced competition. In contrast, again in the Director–Coase tradition, antitrust prosecution should avoid committing Type I errors—false positives—where the effects, such as with the operation of per se rules, may be irreversible.

This point does not extend as far as, but is similar in spirit to, Coase's analysis in *The Problem of Social Cost.* The point, however, derives from a much clearer understanding of the effects of legal rules than Coase's analysis. In *The Problem of Social Cost*, there were no rules resembling per se rules under the Sherman Act. Even the important article by Calabresi and Melamed, *Property Rules, Liability Rules and Inalienability*,[25] did not exactly address per se rules in antitrust. They are a form of an inalienability rule, but a peculiar form. A firm cannot—as in the Coasian world—negotiate around per se rules to achieve allocative efficiency.[26] Easterbrook saw this point and flagged the much greater danger of false positives in antitrust, a point not previously recognized in the literature.

Second, Easterbrook's article builds importantly upon the idea that courts will make erroneous judgments. Here, his distance from the Chicago School tradition is greater, which should be acknowledged. As explained, the Chicago School antitrust tradition had no doubt that judges commit errors. Indeed, in the earlier literature of the School, the term "error" does not capture the phenomenon. The Chicago School tradition held up judicial opinions in antitrust and other areas to ridicule them as laughingstocks. The underlying ambition was to delegitimize judicial and governmental interference in the market.

The Limits of Antitrust, in contrast, accepts judicial error as an underlying fact and, without ridicule, addresses, as science, the implications of inevitable judicial error for the fashioning of effective antitrust rules. This is an extraordinary extension for which Easterbrook should be given great credit, especially as it undoubtedly affected the ultimate adoption of the Chicago School approach to antitrust by the Supreme Court. Most of the articles by the Chicago School analyzing the great Supreme Court antitrust cases are hostile and dismissive of the Court's analysis. Robert Bork's important book *The Antitrust Paradox* was effective in providing a legal blueprint for the adoption of the Chicago School analysis but still possesses (and Bork has admitted this and has apologized for it) a sarcastic tone, largely dismissive of the ability of the Supreme Court or other courts to understand industrial organization.

The Limits of Antitrust, in contrast, explains why courts as well as businesspeople are unlikely to be able to understand complex issues in industrial organization and why—given that inability, not to be ridiculed, but to be adjusted to—the rules and methods of decision making in antitrust cases must be amended. The article then proceeds to fashion a set of filters to inform antitrust prosecution and antitrust analysis. This insight and the development of working rules for antitrust policy are achievements beyond those of the preceding Chicago School tradition. Those achievements importantly brought the Chicago School tradition within the mainstream of American legal analysis.

. . .

The lessons of *The Limits of Antitrust* are currently under attack. The current (2011) chief of the Antitrust Division has declared, "there is no such thing as a false positive . . . . I think, the more people in the bar start rejecting this idea of false positives, the better off we're going to be."[27] And she appears to be jettisoning quite broadly the sensible filters that Easterbrook's analysis puts forth. However provocative rhetorically, her point is analytically vacant and provides no guidance on appropriate antitrust enforcement. The history of the development of Sherman Act jurisprudence since *Trans-Missouri Freight* has been the successive elimination of false positives. And that will remain the course of antitrust law thanks, in large part, to Easterbrook's important article, *The Limits of Antitrust*.

2

Competition Law and Human Rights

Striking a Balance Between Business Freedom and Regulatory Intervention

Arianna Andreangeli

The protection of genuine competition represents a key objective for policy makers and law enforcers both at European Union (EU) and domestic levels. However, the more proactive and incisive approach adopted by the European Commission toward enforcement raises several issues for the position of the parties affected by competition investigations. For a number of years, a lively and often strongly worded debate has been taking place about the "fairness" of competition proceedings before the Commission. Tensions between freedom of enterprise and the protection of genuine competition have also become apparent in light of the considerable limits placed on the exercise of intellectual property rights enjoyed by a dominant undertaking. Consequently, an underlying question emerges: where should a line be drawn between the pursuit of competition through administrative action and the effective protection of business freedom?

Prelude: Competition Enforcement Between Effectiveness and Procedural "Fairness"

Preliminary Observations

Competition policy lies at the core of the tasks of the EU and requires the establishment and operation of an effective framework for its implementation. For this purpose, the Commission enjoys extensive fact-finding and sanctioning powers.[1] In addition, Council Regulation No 1/2003 provides an express legal basis for the imposition of antitrust remedies. The 2003 reform also has pushed toward the decentralized application of Articles 101 and 102 TFEU to individual cases, thus boosting the involvement of national competition agencies and national courts,[2] and strengthening cooperation among the competent agencies.[3]

Regulation No 1/2003 enshrines an obligation to provide information on new cases (Article 11) and confers on the Commission and the National Competition Authorities (NCAs) the power to exchange and use as evidence information gathered in the course of investigations (Article 12) and to carry out investigative measures each on behalf of other agencies. To ensure the smooth operation of these features, the Member States envisaged the creation of the European Competition Network (ECN). Established via an informal declaration in 2003, the ECN provides an "unofficial" space for the circulation of information and the resolution of issues arising from parallel investigations.[4] However, due to its very nature, it does not act as a "clearinghouse" in the event of conflicts arising from multiple investigations pending in two or more jurisdictions or operate according to a uniform set of binding rules on the collection and transmission of evidence.[5] According to Council Regulation No 1/2003, each NCA is only subject to the law in force in its own jurisdiction.[6] It follows that once evidence has been gathered in compliance with the applicable evidentiary rules, it can be transmitted to and used by a different authority regardless of any different, perhaps more protective, legal standards in force in the receiving jurisdiction.[7]

Six years since the full entry into force of the Modernisation Regulation, a number of successful antitrust decisions have been adopted by the Commission.[8] However, they have not quelled the debate concerning how to reconcile the current structure for the enforcement of Articles 101 and 102 TFEU with the observance of the human rights rules enshrined in the general principles of EU law.[9] That the Commission acts as investigator, prosecutor, and judge in the cases it deals with and that its decisions are subject to only limited review as regards their substance, in accordance with Article 263 TFEU, have prompted a number commentators to argue that the existing procedural rules would threaten the effective protection of the rights of "due process" enjoyed by the investigated parties and should consequently be radically reformed.[10] How far can these powers of investigation and sanction actually go to achieve a "fair balance" between the exercise of public power and respect for the fundamental guarantees enjoyed by the investigated parties?[11] These questions will be addressed in the following sections.

The European Convention on Human Rights and EU Competition Proceedings: Brief Remarks

The Court of Justice has elaborated autonomous human rights safeguards as part of the general principles of EC/EU law and has acknowledged that instruments such as the European Convention on Human Rights (ECHR) play a significant role in inspiring the interpretation of these principles.[12] The central position of the ECHR was confirmed by the EU Charter of Fundamental Rights, which is now legally binding on the Union institutions as well as on domestic authorities when they act within the scope of EU law.[13]

The primary aim of the ECHR was to protect natural persons against state abuses. Nonetheless, some suggest that the reliance on the part of the ECHR on the rule of law as a "cluster of principles" encompassing democracy, human dignity, and personal freedom can provide a justification for the extension of some of its rules to corporate actors involved in commercial activities.[14] Although public authorities, including supranational bodies, remain entitled to intervene in the private activities of individuals or corporate entities, they can do so only within precise limits.[15] According to Hayek, the rule of law dictates that each expression of public power affecting the rights of individuals or legal entities must have a legal basis provided by sufficiently precise, clear, and accessible rules and must be constrained in accordance with canons of proportionality, equality, and nonarbitrariness.[16]

Yet, despite being compatible with personal freedom and with the values of a democratic society, the market could not be left completely unbridled but should be subject to "carefully thought out legal frameworks" aimed at steering competition toward the public interest.[17] Indeed, the presence in the ECHR of due process rules, provisions defending the privacy of the home and of correspondence, and the protection of property rights, albeit within limits dictated by the public interest and assessed in each case by the competent public authorities, are fully compatible with the "objective values" enshrined in the rule of law.[18]

This conclusion has very important consequences for commercial actors[19] who, due to their involvement in the market within "welfare states," are exposed to the impact of the operation of potentially pervasive regulatory frameworks.[20] However, the case law of the European Court of Human Rights suggests that the intensity of the protection afforded to entities active in the commercial arena must be carefully assessed and framed in such a way as to avoid irremediably hampering the effectiveness of these regulatory structures.[21] In this context, the Court took the view that the Convention would allow for a somehow more "lenient" approach to be applied with respect to the protection of rights enjoyed by commercial entities.[22] At the same time, it emphasised that these constraints are legitimate only if they have a clear, foreseeable, and accessible legal basis and are imposed in accordance with principles of nonarbitrariness and proportionality and after a procedure allowing those affected by them an opportunity to present their views and objections.[23]

In the light of the above analysis, the ECHR provides for the protection of a number of fundamental safeguards to corporate entities engaged in commercial activities, in accordance with the rule of law. However, the remit of the ECHR cannot be determined "in isolation," but must always take into account the context in which its application is invoked and the values and principles affected by the alleged interference.[24] Consequently, a question emerges on how to strike a balance between effective regulation of economic activities and the respect for those human rights that, thanks to the "objective values" on which the ECHR is based, are enjoyed by commercial actors. Some of these issues will be examined in the following sections.

Human Rights Protection in Antitrust Procedure: Between Effective Enforcement and Due Process Standards

Protecting the Rights of the Defense in Competition Investigations: The Example of the Privilege Against Self-incrimination

Human rights considerations play an even more important role in competition proceedings. These proceedings, despite being conducted in "administrative frameworks" and not before the courts, are criminal in nature, given both their general applicability in the public interest and the deterrent and punitive nature of the sanctions that can be imposed for their infringement.[25] Accordingly, the proceedings leading to their application should be subjected to stringent standards as regards the hearing of the suspected infringers and the adoption of the final decisions.[26] However, to what extent the needs of effective competition enforcement and more generally of the efficient functioning of regulatory structures can be balanced against the respect of due process guarantees compatible with the ECHR in similar cases remains an open question.

This tension is particularly apparent regarding the different approaches adopted with respect to the protection of the right not to incriminate oneself in "criminal cases" before the European Court of Human Rights and the Court of Justice of the EU. The right to remain silent was recognized by the Strasbourg court in *Funke* as one of the "international standards that lie at the heart of the concept of a fair trial" primarily to protect the integrity of the will of an accused against forms of improper compulsion in the taking of evidence.[27] Statements taken from the accused on pain of sanction for failure to cooperate and therefore "in the defiance of the will of the suspect"[28] could not later be used against him in separate criminal proceedings since the evidence had been obtained by coercion.[29]

In the recent *O'Halloran and Francis* case the European Court of Human Rights emphasised that while the right to a "fair trial" was in itself absolute, what actually made a fair trial, i.e., its features, including the right to remain silent, should be assessed in each case in light of the legal context in which they are to operate.[30] The circumstances of the case, the nature and the objectives of the proceedings and the intensity of the coercion exercised in taking the evidence would have to be carefully appraised.[31]

Particularly for evidence obtained in the course of "regulatory" proceedings, the Strasbourg court emphasised that individuals choosing to perform specific activities may be required to submit to "responsibilities and obligations as part of [a] regulatory regime," which could also involve the duty to provide the authorities with potentially self-incriminating information and a corresponding restriction of their right to remain silent.[32] To conform to the ECHR, the contracting states' competent authorities would have to demonstrate that the applicable rules respected the "essence" of these rights.[33]

By contrast, the Court of Justice of the EU held in *Orkem*[34] that firms affected by competition proceedings, despite not being entitled to "evade the Commission's investigations," enjoyed a limited degree of protection against self-incrimination in the course of their preliminary stages to avoid impairing irremediably their rights of defense.[35] Even though the Commission officials could compel the investigated parties to provide all the factual information that might be known to them, regardless of the circumstance that it could be used as evidence against them,[36] they could not oblige the undertakings to give "answers which might involve an admission . . . of the existence of an infringement which is incumbent on the Commission to prove."[37] To adopt a more extensive reading of the privilege would pose an unjustified obstacle to the Commission's performance of its function.[38]

Whereas the Strasbourg court focuses on the nature and intensity of the coercive powers exercised to extract the evidence and on the procedural safeguards assisting that exercise, to ensure that the investigated parties' right to a fair trial is not tainted by improper forms of oppression on their will,[39] the Court of Justice of the EU restricts the scope of the privilege to evidence taken as a result of direct coercion (e.g., financial penalties) and takes as its "starting point" the substance of the questions directed at the investigated parties, i.e., whether they are merely of a "factual nature" or can lead to the admission of responsibility for the alleged infringement.[40]

Consequently, once a question concerns the existence of facts—even though the answer may allow the investigating officials to draw strong inferences of the undertakings' responsibility—the Commission officials may demand an answer to it.[41] Can the approach adopted in EU law be reconciled with the human rights standards enshrined in the Convention? It could be argued that after the *O'Halloran* judgment the Strasbourg court appears more open to the idea of adopting a more "nuanced" view of the components of the right to a "fair trial" in the regulatory arena.[42] However, even taking into account the need to avoid jeopardizing the effectiveness of these regulatory structures and the circumstance that competition investigations tend to involve legal entities,[43] the approach to the privilege adopted by the Court of Justice of the EU may not be entirely capable of striking a "fair balance" between the public interest and the need to preserve the essence of the undertakings' rights of defense, and it may therefore have to be restrained to adhere more closely to the Convention.[44] The scope of the right to remain silent should prevent the disclosure of self-incriminating information when it appears from the circumstances of the case that the degree of coercion exerted on the investigated parties was excessive or the safeguards attending the investigations have not been observed.[45]

The different principles and objectives characterizing the EU and the ECHR legal systems have led to the adoption, in the respective jurisdictions, of different standards for the protection of human rights within regulatory frameworks. However, it is beyond doubt that although the effective enforcement of the Treaty competition rules constitutes a primary objective, its implementation should not go as far as to defy the essence of the undertakings' rights of defense and should ensure that appropriate limitations to the Commission's powers are in place to avoid procedural abuses, in accordance with the principles enshrined in the rule of law, to which the EU institutions are committed.

The Decentralized Application of Articles 101 and 102 TFEU and the Need for "Foreseeability" in Competition Enforcement

According to Article 5 of the Regulation, NCAs are now empowered to apply the Treaty competition rules to individual cases.[46] However, they do so in a radically changed landscape, characterized by their cooperation with the Commission and with one another within the ECN.[47]

Since practices covered by Treaty antitrust rules have (or are likely to have), by definition, an impact on trade between Member States, they are capable of adversely affecting competition in markets falling within the jurisdiction of more than one NCA, and therefore the framework established by the Modernisation Regulation is characterized by the possibility of parallel proceedings.[48] However, although cases are likely to be taken on by the authority or authorities that are "well-placed" to deal with the allegations[49] and may be "seized" by the Commission only, in accordance with Article 11(6) of the Regulation,[50] parallel jurisdiction raises a number of issues on protection of the rights of defense and especially on respect for the principle of *ne bis in idem*.

Article 4, Protocol VII of the ECHR enshrines this principle and recognizes it as belonging to the general principles of Community law by the Court of Justice.[51] Article 50 of the EU Charter of Fundamental Rights also confirms this principle.[52] Nonetheless, Regulation 1/2003 does not expressly protect *ne bis in idem*. Regulation 1/2003 not only is based on the principle of parallel jurisdiction, but also reiterates that a decision adopted by NCAs will not preclude the Commission or another national agency from taking action with respect to the same infringement.[53] The rationale behind this difference is that since EU and domestic competition rules fulfill different policy objectives and their application addresses only those anticompetitive effects that occur within the jurisdiction of each individual authority, the principle of *ne bis in idem* would not be applicable to prevent double prosecution on the part of the Commission.[54] It would only apply to the Commission's duty to take into account any earlier penalty in assessing the fine it wished to impose on the entity.[55]

However, the European Court of Human Rights has taken the different view that the principle of *ne bis in idem* aims to prevent the repetition of criminal proceedings that have been concluded by a final decision.[56] Consequently, according to the European Court of Human Rights, this rule should be read as containing a right not only not to be sanctioned twice, but also not to be investigated and prosecuted twice for the same infringement.[57] Against this background, one may doubt that the possibility of parallel investigations envisaged by Council Regulation No 1/2003 could be regarded as being consistent with the ECHR[58] or with Article 50 of the EU Charter of Fundamental Rights, according to which no one may be tried and punished twice for the same offense "within the Union"[59] and regardless of whether its effects may be felt within the jurisdiction of different enforcement authorities.[60]

The needs of the meaningful enforcement of the Treaty antitrust rules require effective enforcement action.[61] However, even taking into account these important objectives, the very notion of parallel jurisdiction appears to fall short of the requirements of the rule of law[62] since it would not allow the investigated parties to identify the competent authority[63] and would expose them to the risk of later prosecution "elsewhere" within the ECN.[64]

The Commission can, whenever a case raises issues of "Community interest" and has a clear "transnational dimension," seize jurisdiction over it and thus preempt other agencies from examining its merits or inflict sanctions on the firms found to be responsible for the antitrust infringement in question. However, it has no obligation to take this action. Consequently, it is unclear whether the current rules are capable of eliminating any of the concerns for the respect of the *ne bis in idem* rule outlined above.[65]

Accordingly, Council Regulation No 1/2003 should be reformed so as to preclude NCAs from launching further investigations with respect to allegations of anticompetitive behavior that have already been "disposed of" by other enforcement agencies and a fortiori by the European Commission,[66] unless the alleged second offense does not have "essential elements" in common with the one already being dealt with.[67]

The very system of parallel competences characterizing the Modernisation Regulation raises concerns about the protection of the investigated parties against double jeopardy[68] and seems to depart from the principles of foreseeability and legal certainty enshrined in the rule of law. The system should provide a rule of "administrative" res judicata precluding NCAs from taking action with respect to infringements that have already been investigated and sanctioned in other jurisdictions.

Human Rights Protection and Antitrust Remedies: Limiting Economic Freedom for the Purpose of Promoting Genuine Competition? The Case of Article 102 TFEU Remedies in Intellectual Property Cases

The right to enjoy one's property, despite not being absolute, is protected by the Convention.[69] It is therefore indispensable to confine the discretion of public authorities to "alter property rights in unpredictable ways" in the public interest.[70] According to Article 1, Protocol I of the ECHR, everyone has the right to the "peaceful enjoyment" of his or her possessions,[71] i.e., tangible and intangible goods,[72] including intellectual property rights[73] and, albeit within limits, legal claims.[74] This right may be either forfeited altogether or constrained or "controlled" in its exercise.[75]

However, these constraints should have an express legal basis, pursue a legitimate aim in the public interest, and bear a relationship of proportionality between the needs of the public at large and the protection of the rights of the individuals or legal entities concerned in the exercise of the public power in the circumstances.[76] The presence of appropriate procedural rights, and the availability of compensation for the deprivation of property or of adequate remuneration in case of constraints being placed on its use, are key aspects in this assessment.[77]

In relation to interferences with intellectual property rights, the Strasbourg court held in *Balan* that the respondent state infringed the Convention by making repeated use of the applicant's copyrighted work despite his opposition and without paying any remuneration.[78] The Court held that the public interest could have equally been served by paying the applicant reasonable royalties.[79] The now defunct Human Rights Commission in the *Smith Kline and French Laboratories v. the Netherlands* case,[80] which was the subject of a friendly settlement,[81] examined the compatibility of forced copyright licenses.

The Commission held that the grant of a "compulsory licence" constituted a form of "control on the use of property" of the patent holder[82] since it constrained "the sole right of exploitation" of the invention granted to its owner.[83] Consequently, it was indispensable to assess whether a forced license was consistent with the Convention, i.e., whether it was "prescribed by law" and sought to achieve "a legitimate aim in a proportionate manner."[84]

The Commission pointed to the circumstance that patent rights were limited in many contracting states and that the latter enjoyed a significant margin of appreciation.[85] It emphasised, however, that forced licenses could be granted only to "encourage technological and economic development" and if as a result of the disclosure of the invention it could be expected that a "new product or process . . . capable of industrial application" could have been developed and supplied on the market.[86]

On the merits, the Commission found that the license was limited in scope to what was necessary to allow the party requiring it to employ its own invention[87] and that the holder of the "primary" patent had been entitled to royalties, thus establishing a reasonable link of proportionality between that legitimate aim and the restriction imposed on the applicant's rights.[88] Therefore, the Commission, after declaring the application admissible, expressed the view that the respondent state had not infringed the applicant's right to enjoy its intellectual property.[89]

The above analysis supports the view that the Convention rules will apply to intellectual property (IP) rights. However, it also identifies several issues that are peculiar to this type of property. As the Human Rights Commission recognized in *Smith Kline*, one of the key attributes of IP rights is the conferral of a de facto monopoly on their holder with respect to the possibility to duplicate a valuable "product" as a means of rewarding the investment made by the owner. Nonetheless, this "monopoly could over time hamper the creativity" of third parties and therefore justify imposing limits on it to further genuine innovation.[90]

However, the rules governing these restrictions must be sufficiently clear and foreseeable. Each decision must also be adopted after having given the owner of the right a reasonable opportunity to be heard and must provide for adequate compensation in the form of reasonable royalties. Perhaps most importantly, the parties seeking to exploit the patent at issue must demonstrate that the compulsory license would be likely to further innovation, by allowing them to manufacture a product displaying sufficiently "novel" features.[91]

Consequently, although the ECHR protects property rights, including those concerning patents, trademarks, and copyright, there may be a number of reasons why it is legitimate for the contracting states to limit their scope in order to further other objectives of public interest. These limits must comport with the principles provided by Article 1, Protocol I of the Convention.

Economic Freedom, Competition Enforcement, and Antitrust Remedies: How to Strike a "Fair Balance" Against Powerful Undertakings When Framing Behavioral Remedies

A number of questions may be raised in relation to the power enjoyed by the European Commission to "bring an infringement to an end" by imposing significant limits on the right of "powerful" firms to choose how to conduct themselves on the market.[92] In several decisions, especially concerning the application of Article 102 TFEU, the Commission has obliged dominant undertakings to "share" their own tangible property such as transport infrastructures,[93] to enter into supply relations with other firms even if that may prima facie be incompatible with their commercial interests,[94] or ultimately to grant IP licenses to their competitors in order to ensure that the latter may remain active in a relevant market in which their own proprietary technology has become "essential" to operate profitably.[95]

According to Article 7 of the Modernisation Regulation, the Commission enjoys the power to impose on the undertakings responsible for an antitrust breach such remedies as may be necessary to terminate the infringement and are proportionate to it.[96] Thus, the Commission can, after having found a violation of the Treaty antitrust rules, require the undertaking or undertakings responsible for it to modify their future behavior or, in exceptional cases, their structure in order to restore the status quo ante the competition infringement.[97] Paramount to the framing of antitrust remedies is the application of principles of "necessity" and of "proportionality." The concept of necessity requires the antitrust authorities to design each remedy in the light of the type of infringement, as determined by the relevant substantive rules.[98] Compliance with the principle of proportionality, instead, demands that the remedy constitute the only suitable means to bring the infringement to an end and that there be no less burdensome alternative to it.[99]

It is clear from its text that Regulation No 1/2003 uses language that, at least on its face, is very similar to that adopted by the Strasbourg court. However, what is not clear is whether the standards adopted in the EU are as exacting as those enshrined in the ECHR.[100] The Court of Justice had been reluctant to impose on dominant companies an obligation to grant IP licenses to their rivals.[101] Refusals to license would only infringe Article 102 in "exceptional circumstances," i.e., when the refusal related to inputs that were "indispensable" (because they could not be objectively duplicated, due to objective legal, technical, or economic obstacles[102]) for operating in a distinct market, it prevented the undertaking requesting that access from supplying a "new product,"[103] and it was not "objectively justified."[104]

The Court emphasised that the "new product" criteria would be the crucial factor in striking a balance between maintaining competition versus protecting and fostering investment.[105] Consequently, at least in earlier cases, the Court identified only those inputs without access to which the requesting undertakings could not "produce new goods or services not offered by the owner of the rights and for which there was potential consumer demand."[106] A more extensive view could "upset" the careful balance between effective competition and the legitimate interest of the IP owner to exploit her inventions and foster investment.[107]

Regarding the approach adopted with respect to "controls on the use of property" by the ECHR,[108] the view adopted in these relatively less recent judgments appears to be consistent with the Convention standards. It could be argued that the Court of Justice, just as the Convention organs, aimed to ensure that the interests of effective competition would prevail over the exclusivity of IP rights only if the interference with the latter led to genuine technical advancement.[109]

However, it is questionable whether the above reading remains compatible with the current interpretation of Article 102 TFEU in relation to "exclusionary abuses." More recent case law and especially the 2007 *Microsoft* judgment have heralded an approach that seems to privilege, at least in part, the interests of rivals over the incentive to innovate of the industrial leader.[110]

The Commission stated in its 2009 Guidance on the application of Article 102 to exclusionary abuses (hereinafter referred to as 2009 Guidance) that a refusal to grant an IP license is likely to infringe the competition rules if the input covered by IPRs is "objectively necessary to compete effectively" in a related market, either because it cannot be duplicated or, perhaps more importantly, because the input is of "significant competitive importance" for the undertakings operating in that market.[111]

Consequently, the shift from the concept of "indispensability" to the "objective necessity" test now requires the Commission only to prove that without the license, rivals would not be able to compete with the same "ease" as the firm owning the IP right.[112] As to the other requirement that the refusal to license lead to "likely consumer harm," the Commission stated that this concept should be read to encompass cases in which not only does the refusal prevent the undertakings seeking access from offering products or services that are not a "duplicate" of what is already available on the relevant market,[113] but also if it prevents rivals from supplying "improved goods or services for which there is a potential demand" or which "contribute to technical development."[114]

As a result, the Commission moved away, at least in part, from the "innovation driven" concept of "new product" to a less-stringent view of technical development that would also cover forms of "follow on" innovation.[115] It may not be that this relatively more generous approach confirms to the need to strike a "fair balance" between genuine competition and encouraging and rewarding investment.[116] It is also telling that so far the Commission and the EU Courts have been reluctant to accept that the concern for maintaining the integrity of investments made by dominant companies could constitute an "objective justification" for a refusal to license.[117] Importantly, the 2009 Guidance does not even acknowledge the possibility for a powerful firm to refuse to grant or to limit the scope of an IP license in order to recoup its costs and thereby protect the value of its inventions.[118]

I argue that the Commission relied perhaps too readily on the General Court's conclusions in the *Microsoft* judgment to justify its views in the 2009 Guidance.[119] However, in doing so the Commission may have overlooked the "exceptional" nature of the merits of that case and not given sufficient consideration to the concerns for long-term innovation which, up to the *IMS Health* preliminary ruling, had been at the forefront of the EU courts' jurisprudence.[120]

Additionally, the 2009 Guidance, by emphasising the importance of follow-on innovation did not wholly capture the impact of a forced license on the long-term incentive to innovate of individual firms. The Guidance thus appears inconsistent with the concept of "proportionality" resulting from the ECHR.[121] With respect to the concept of "likely consumer harm," it could be argued that by referring generally to products "contributing to technical development" the Commission has not resolved the evidentiary difficulties already characterizing the "new product" condition.[122] Therefore, one may legitimately doubt whether the current EU approach meets the requirements of "clarity" and "foreseeability" enshrined in the rule of law.[123]

Against this background, the "transition" from the restrained approach to prima facie abusive refusals to license developed by the Court of Justice to the more "lenient" criteria for the assessment of these practices adopted by the General Court in *Microsoft* and perhaps more dramatically by the Commission's 2009 Guidance has led to results that are inconsistent, at least in part, with the principles enshrined in Article 1, Protocol I of the ECHR. The standards contained in the 2009 Guidance have not only been diluted so much that they are no longer capable of striking a "fair balance" between the common interest of protecting genuine competition and the protection of the rights of individual IP owners. They have also become so opaque that they do not allow dominant companies to foresee the antitrust law consequences of a refusal to license IP rights.[124]

Thus, with respect to the concept of "likely consumer harm," the approach adopted by the 2009 Guidance[125] not only deprives this criterion of any "critical" function in the appraisal of these practices,[126] but also appears to have significantly increased the uncertainty characterizing the assessment of the legality of a refusal to license, a development that does not appear consistent with the "prescribed by law" conditions required by the rule of law principles.[127] If it was already difficult to assess whether the "offshoot" of the exploitation of a given invention was genuinely "novel," it would be even more complex to predict, in substance, the direction of the technical development of a specific industry as well as the impact of the refusal to license on its course.

By contrast, the "new product" requirement established in the *IMS* decision,[128] despite presenting some evidentiary difficulties, provided a sufficiently precise paradigm for proving the degree of "novelty" of any prospective product.[129] However, in light of the Commission's views contained in the 2009 Guidance, it is doubtful that a "move backward" to the old *IMS* test may be forthcoming.

Economic Freedom: An Engine as Well as a Limit for Genuine Competition?

The nature of antitrust proceedings as "criminal in substance" has raised a number of concerns about their compliance with standards of due process laid down by Article 6 of the ECHR.[130] The examination of the current approaches adopted by the Court of Justice and the Commission in relation to the privilege against self-incrimination casts doubt on whether the level of protection afforded by EU law to the right to remain silent in the course of the Commission investigation is consistent with, ultimately, the rule of law.[131]

In relation to the parallel jurisdiction at the basis of the Modernisation Regulation, the framework for the enforcement of the Treaty antitrust rules, while being aimed at ensuring an efficient allocation of cases and the prompt investigation and sanction of competition infringements, may be inconsistent with the protection of individual undertakings against double jeopardy within the ECN as a whole.[132]

As to the power of the Commission to impose antitrust remedies, the case law of the European Court of Human Rights demonstrates that the Convention allows for limitations on the scope of the right of "everyone" to peacefully enjoy their property as well as for restrictions on their freedom of contract, subject, however, to several conditions dictated by Article 1 of its Protocol I.[133] With respect to the power of the Commission to impose on the holder of an intellectual property right a duty to grant licenses to other firms, the Human Rights Commission illustrated in its Smith Kline report that the need for innovation and the concern for strengthening the drive toward further technological development should be at the forefront of the assessment of whether a duty to license constitutes a "proportionate" remedy to terminate an infringement of Article 102 TFEU. However, the European Court of Human Rights doubted that the 2009 Guidance on the priorities in the enforcement of Article 810, as influenced by the 2007 *Microsoft* decision, could be compatible with the standards governing the application of Article 1, Protocol I of the ECHR to compulsory licenses and especially with the principle of proportionality.

. . .

More generally, discussing the compliance of antitrust remedies with human rights standards seems to question whether the current directions of antitrust enforcement have been appropriately set and whether the standards governing unilateral exclusionary conduct are "fit for purpose," i.e., capable of reconciling the apparently diverging goals of competition and technical innovation. The past ten years have seen considerable success in uncovering anticompetitive behavior, albeit not without criticism. One hopes that the commitment to the ECHR expressed with the Lisbon Treaty will prompt a rethinking of the rules governing competition proceedings and remedies.

Part II

The Economic Limits of Competition Law

3

Limits of Imports from Economics into Competition Law

Anne-Lise Sibony

A "more economic approach" to EU competition law is generally considered progress. Competition authorities[1] and scholars alike find competition rules based on "sound economics" desirable. Yet economics does not always provide ready-to-use solutions to problems faced by enforcement authorities and courts. This is why more economics does not always mean better law. At the very least, improvement of the law through economic import is not automatic. This is particularly true of economic discourse on the goals of antitrust. Stressing that the sole goal of antitrust should be consumer welfare, for example, does not necessarily help clarify the law or make antitrust enforcement more administrable. This is not to say that economic discourse on goals should be discarded. Rather, it means that economic input in the legal process—whether it consists of a discourse on the goal(s) of antitrust rules or whether it pertains to other more detailed aspects of antitrust such as the legal test for a particular type of anticompetitive conduct—is only a starting point. Economic insights are not, in and of themselves, soluble in the law. Importing elements of economic discourse into the law requires some analytical work, if only because there may be several different ways to bring those elements to bear on a legal decision-making process. In other words, choosing the best importing technique for a given economic insight calls for careful analysis.

This chapter aims at describing these choice-of-importing-technique issues. It deliberately focuses on legal techniques available to import economics and does not seek to make value judgments on the imported economic wisdom. Of course, these value judgments need to be made and are made by courts and competition authorities. Clearly, the question of how best to import any given suggestion stemming from economics only arises when the suggestion is deemed worthy of being imported. These necessary and preliminary value judgments are outside the scope of this chapter, which focuses instead on the next and less often explored step in the process of importing economics into the law. It aims at describing the technical choices courts and authorities face when they want to import insights from economics. More precisely, this chapter describes the importing techniques law offers and distinguishes among them, with a focus on the limits of each technique.

Interpreting the Law in Light of Economics

Competition law is par excellence an area in which interpretation of the law is sometimes modified in order to take into account insights from economics. Judicial interpretation of the law may incorporate elements borrowed from economics in several different ways. One reason why it is useful to try to distinguish them is that different interpretive techniques may display different properties with relation to legal certainty, flexibility, and administrability and therefore lend themselves to trade-offs.

While a general theory of importing techniques and their properties is outside the scope of this chapter, it may be useful, for each importing technique used in the field of competition law, to look at the following three properties: the degree of legal change it implies, the flexibility it affords, and its fidelity to economic reasoning. The degree of change a new, more economic interpretation brings, as compared with a previous, less economic interpretation of the same legal provision, may be defined as the capacity of the new interpretation of the law to change the outcome of a case. As courts do not envisage large changes lightly, it seems fair to assume that this dimension matters. The greater the change brought about by a new economics-based interpretation, the more thorough the scrutiny it will (or at least should) be subject to before it is adopted.

The degree of flexibility of an economics-based interpretation is the second factor to bear in mind when a new, more economic interpretation is considered. In the present context, flexibility refers to the relative ease with which it will be possible to change the new interpretation if, after some time, economics produces an even better insight on the same question. Third, various ways in which a given economic insight is incorporated into legal construction may differ in terms of fidelity to the original economic reasoning. Partial transplant may, for example, result in low fidelity.[2]

With these aspects in mind, incorporation of economic insights by way of interpretation will be analyzed in four steps. The first step is concerned with the most basic of imports from economics, namely when an economic insight translates as a mere statement of legal relevance of certain facts. The second step deals with an important intermediary operation in the process of applying a legal concept, namely regrouping various relevant facts. The third step analyzes a final product of interpretation—a legal test inspired by economic analysis. This three-step analysis leads to a fourth step, the understanding of how a fact that is both economically and legally relevant may be linked to several different legal categories. The analysis proposed here uses predation to illustrate a discussion of choice of interpretive technique.

The simplest and single most significant contribution of economics to interpretation of competition law provisions happens when economists call the attention of courts to the relevance of certain facts. For instance, economists say (in essence), "Judge, if you are interested in 'dominant position' you ought to pay attention to 'barriers to entry.'"[3] The European Court of Justice (ECJ), early on in its jurisprudence, had been confronted with the question of what other factors, besides market shares, were relevant to establish the existence of a dominant position.[4] Economists helped to name such factors. More generally, economists introduce statements in the competition law discourse about the relevance of certain facts, which they call by an economic name. What matters is not so much the name, but the attribution of relevance itself. If courts rule that the facts to which economists refer are indeed relevant for legal purposes, they borrow from economics, even though they might use different names.[5]

This elementary importing technique is apt to incorporate fundamental elements of economists' viewpoints, such as "consumers matter"[6] or "incentives matter."[7] Yet, in itself, this technique does not guarantee any particular degree of fidelity to economic reasoning. Indeed, as long as courts only admit the relevance of certain facts without stating in the grounds of the judgment *how* the relevant facts must be taken into account or *why* they are relevant,[8] legal reasoning remains open ended. It may coincide with or differ from the economic reasoning underlying the very suggestion, which is incorporated into legal interpretation.

Market definition is a case in point. Courts in the EU have learned to admit the relevance of cross-price elasticity for the purposes of defining a market, but they keep requiring, as a matter of law, that markets be defined even where it does not make economic sense to do so, because market power is not at stake.[9] Legal relevance (of cross-price elasticity) is assigned in conformity with the teachings of economics but the overall reasoning (about why markets need to be defined) is lost.[10]

Admission of legal relevance, as an importing technique, displays a variable degree of flexibility. One essential factor in this regard is whether courts deem the facts to which economists draw attention merely as *relevant* or whether they are considered as constituting a *necessary condition* for applying a particular legal idea.[11] If courts deem relevant a fact that economists stress, for example recoupment in predation cases, it will be up to the parties to discuss it, and if they choose to discuss it, courts will have to hear this discussion. This is much more flexible than if the economically relevant fact is made, by means of interpretation, a fact that as a matter of law must be established in all cases.

Considered from the vantage point of legal change, admission of relevance presents two noteworthy characteristics. First, it is a very ordinary legal technique; indeed, assigning relevance to facts is what courts routinely do when they interpret a rule. Because the technique is so common, it represents an easy and convenient way to incorporate economics into the law. If a suggestion emanating from economists that certain facts are relevant seems convincing to a court of law, the court will face no technical difficulty in accepting it. Second, this technique may result in varying degrees of legal change. Adding one relevant fact, like barriers to entry, to an already long list of criteria considered relevant for assessing dominant position may alter the outcome in only a few cases, especially if factors already taken into account capture part of what economists call barriers to entry. Yet the additional precision of naming relevant facts also may result in considerable change of the rule. If, for example, in order to make a case of financial predation, what a party needs to establish is not that the alleged predator has deeper pockets than the alleged prey, but rather that it has unequal access to financing,[12] it clearly makes a difference, as courts will have to look at a different set of facts altogether (such as how firms interact with banks). Thus, one crucial element in assessing how much a new admission of relevant facts changes the law is how the various relevant facts are linked.

Rearranging Different Relevant Facts

Knowing which facts are relevant for the purpose of applying a legal idea is only one part of interpreting a rule. How law rearranges and combines the various relevant facts is essential to further describe the legal reasoning leading to a particular outcome. Some ways of grouping relevant facts are very familiar. For example, under EU law, in any abuse of dominance case, courts divide their appraisal in two steps: they will first examine whether the firm holds a dominant position in a relevant market and only then will they consider whether the firm has committed an abuse. At least this is how courts present the reasoning. Economists had suggested an alternative way of rearranging facts: look first at whether there is a restriction of competition (this would take market power into account) and then at whether the conduct at stake may be justified.[13] Essentially the same facts were to be taken into account under this proposal and under the then and current legal approach. Yet it is beyond doubt that rearranging the same relevant facts in a way that departs from the traditional and familiar two-step approach would have been regarded as a radical change had this part of the proposal been adopted.[14]

However, translating economic insights by adopting a particular way of rearranging relevant facts does not necessarily upset legal categories. It only does so when, as in the previous example, courts call into question an established structure of legal reasoning. When, on the contrary, courts weakly structure legal assessment, intermediary notions borrowed from economic analysis contribute to enhancing legal certainty by giving a better defined structure to legal assessment. The phrase "intermediary notions" used here is not intended to suggest that some notions possess an intrinsic characteristic of intermediariness; it aims at describing a particular legal use of some notions as marking intermediate steps in an overall assessment.[15] Examples include "margin squeeze," "leveraging effect," or "overlap." These are notions that are not to be found in the legal provisions themselves but may command a step—modest in the case of overlap, very substantial in the case of margin squeeze—in the appraisal of a unilateral conduct or of a merger.

Incorporating an element of economic analysis as an intermediate step in a legal decision is of practical significance not only because there are many examples of economic notions used in this way in competition law but also because legal disputes are organized around intermediate findings. Such findings constitute the pressure points on which lawyers concentrate their argument when a case is litigated. When economic notions are used in this way, they therefore provide the very structure of legal argument.

This importing technique is characterized by a good degree of fidelity to economic reasoning, precisely because it helps focus the legal debate on economically significant points. Its main limit is low flexibility. Once a certain structure of legal argument becomes enshrined in legal practice, it solidifies as law and becomes hard to change. As noted above, in terms of intensity of legal change, initial adoption of a new way to rearrange facts inspired by economic analysis will represent a fundamental, and possibly unacceptable, legal change if traditional distinctions are upset. On the other hand, it may be perceived as a small change and a clear improvement if it helps order multiple relevant facts in an assessment method that is more structured than current court practice.

Legal Tests

Coining a legal test is the ultimate importing technique—it builds on the two techniques previously outlined and constitutes an improvement on both of them. A legal test based on economic analysis incorporates statements of relevance about all economically relevant facts and explicitly regroups those facts in meaningful bundles tied around intermediate economic notions. It also does more, in that it explicitly ties the bundles together. In other words, a legal test is a structured and complete statement of relevant facts. The test gives the structure of a correct answer to a legal question (such as "is this predation?").

Legal tests are a first-best among importing techniques. Because they consist of an articulated set of questions, they usually translate economic reasoning with a good degree of fidelity. A legal test also offers a good degree of legal certainty as it makes assessment of facts more predictable. However, precisely because adoption of a new, more precise, economic-based legal test is generally considered progress (although there may be disagreement about the best test), legal tests may not be changed easily. One limit of this technique is, therefore, that it is characterized by a low level of flexibility.[16] This is why it is essential to get the test right in the first place. A second limitation of legal tests is that, once adopted, they lend themselves to mechanical application, without regard to *why* specific facts are legally relevant. It is of course the specific virtue of legal tests to act as a checklist for the fact finder. Yet this may result in the reasoning underlying the test being lost and, if the test is less than perfect, in unsatisfactory outcomes.[17]

This risk of crystallization may be overcome by active attention of courts to the meaning of their findings in the specific context of the case, as opposed to a box-ticking attitude. For example, in its *Impala* judgment, in which the Court of First Instance (CFI) had to assess whether the Commission erred in finding that a merger did not strengthen a collective dominant position, the court had regard to the test for collective dominance established in *Airtours*[18] but also stated that

> in the context of the assessment of the existence of a collective dominant position, although the three conditions defined by the Court of First Instance in *Airtours* v *Commission* . . . , which were inferred from a theoretical analysis of the concept of a collective dominant position, are indeed also *necessary*, they may, however, in the appropriate circumstances, be *established indirectly* on the basis of what may be a very mixed series of indicia and items of evidence relating to the signs, manifestations and phenomena inherent in the presence of a collective dominant position.[19]

In this judgment, the CFI did not depart from the *Airtours* test. It ruled, however, that this test should not be applied literally. Flexibility is infused in the test by holding that, if the relevant facts and links between these facts can be established through an analytical detour, due to the circumstances of the case, there is no point in insisting that all three cumulative *Airtours* conditions be established separately. It is enough to establish the analytical equivalence between the necessary conditions of that test and the facts of the case. This is somewhat like saying that, even though the necessary ingredients for a cake, according to a case law recipe, are flour, sugar, and eggs, the existence of a cake may be established even though it has not been proven that flour, sugar, and eggs were in the kitchen. Those three ingredients may be *necessary* for the cake to have been baked, but cake crumbs will also be *sufficient* evidence that a cake was there. The reason why the court in *Impala* can leave the *Airtours* test aside is that it does not consist of necessary and sufficient conditions, as would be the case in a perfect test.

Because it is generally hard to identify sufficient and necessary conditions for a conduct (or a merger) to restrict competition, there are not many full-fledged legal tests based on economic analysis.[20] Economics produces building blocks for legal tests but only rarely ready-made ones. This is not necessarily a bad thing, as conformity with sound economic analysis is not the only requirement for a good legal test. It is equally important that economically relevant facts be linked to existing legal categories, preferably with the right ones.

Linking an Economically Relevant Fact to the Right Legal Category

Economists, like everyone else, tend to think in their own categories. This is why the link between their reasoning about competition issues does not always have an obvious translation in legal terms. To overcome this difficulty, one possibility is to import economic categories into legal language. There are many examples of this. Originally, notions such as barriers to entry, substitutability, or margin squeeze neither were a part of statutory language nor belonged to common legalese. They were imported from economics into case law. But adding new words to the (legal) thesaurus is a translation technique that should only be used as a last resort. Even where it is appropriate to use it—i.e., when no legal term is adequate to express an economic idea worth importing—it will not stop the need to explicitly link the novel legal category to existing ones. Law is a system, and new additions need to be connected to the backbone formed of statutory language and existing case law. Such connection may take many different forms, such as creating a new distinction (e.g., between several types of predation), reversing established case law (e.g., holding that *ex ante* possibility of recoupment does need to be established to prove predation), and considering an economically relevant fact (e.g., recoupment) as an indication that a legally relevant fact (e.g., predatory intent) has been established.

Such translation issues do not always receive the kind of attention they deserve from economists or legal scholars. An example illustrates the type of discussion needed regarding translation. Intent is a legal category that economists and economically minded antitrust lawyers do not like much. Richard Posner gave a well-known expression to the criticisms directed against intent as a legally relevant fact for the purposes of assessing monopolization under Section 2 of the Sherman Act.[21] Exclusionary intent should not matter, so goes the argument, because exclusionary intent is indistinguishable from competitive intent.[22] An additional argument against including intent among legally relevant facts is that evidence of intent is easy to manipulate. Well-counseled dominant companies will leave no paper trail containing aggressive language, while less careful ones will be likely to do so. Punishing intent thus will unfairly discriminate in favor of polite corporations while not catching harmful conduct.

While this argument concerning direct documentary evidence of intent is convincing, it may not be decisive. Arguments against intent need to be balanced against the benefits of allowing intent to matter. One strong argument in favor of intent is that this legal category is apt to capture economic analysis when it is framed in terms of strategy. Taking firms' strategies better into account was precisely one of the key recommendations contained in an economist's report commissioned by the European Commission when preparing the "Reform of [its interpretation of] Article 82."[23] It seems hard to find a better legal vehicle than the category of intent to do this. Both strategy and intent refer to what a firm aims at doing, its objectives, and the means it deploys to reach them. In this sense, they are close enough. Another good reason not to discredit intent, from a European perspective, is pragmatic. Under EU law, intent does matter, whether economists like it or not, and it is so enshrined in the case law that it is hard to imagine a reversal from EU courts on this point.[24] Although the solution may be second best (Posner's criticisms have some validity), using intent in abuse cases as the legal locus of where to incorporate economic reasoning relating to strategy may be the best we can do, taking legal constraints into account.

Giving a legal umbrella to economic reasoning by linking an economic category such as a firm's strategy to a legal one such as intent is a technique that makes legal change smooth, as, by definition, economics is imported through an existing legal category that already has its place in legal reasoning. Were it not for the inappropriate warfare connotation, it could be compared to a Trojan horse method for economic content to penetrate the legal sphere without alerting the guardians of the legal fortress.

Fidelity to economic reasoning when using this technique depends on the choice of a suitable legal category to incorporate one particular line of reasoning. This may be illustrated by considering, for example, the typical economic reasoning on the role of recoupment in predation cases. Without a reasonable expectation of recoupment, it is argued, it is not rational for a firm to engage in predation. There are at least two ways to link this reasoning to legal categories. First, one can infer that, in the absence of a reasonable expectation of recoupment, a predation strategy is unlikely (this assumes firms behave rationally). In other words, predatory *intent* is unlikely. Second, one can argue that, if recoupment is improbable, so is *consumer harm*. Economists would probably consider that the second link displays a higher degree of fidelity to the original reasoning. However, fidelity to economic reasoning is not the only dimension that counts. Arguably, it is more useful to link economic reasoning to a legal category that carries greater weight. If, for example, the recoupment argument is linked to effects, but effects do not matter in actual decisional practice,[25] fidelity will go hand in hand with the ineffectiveness of an economic argument. In other words, when choosing to which legal category an economic argument should be linked, there may be a trade-off between fidelity to the original economic reasoning and the actual bearing of the economic import on legal outcomes.

Flexibility of this importing technique will depend on how structured the economic content imported into a legal category is. If, for example, a court rules that predation is one category of abuse and that there are three kinds of predation, it will be impossible to prove a case of predation without proving that it fits in any of the three categories. Such rigidity is inherent in importing a typology. When, however, the imported content is more loosely structured, linking economic insights to a particular legal category does not necessarily entail a rigid legal outcome.

Choice of Importing Technique: The Example of Predation

Predation has been mentioned in this chapter several times, as it is the example of choice to illustrate how different importing techniques described thus far may constitute alternative means when a court considers importing a particular economic idea or reasoning into the law. In EU law, the landmark case on predation is *AKZO*.[26] In this ruling, the Court adopted a price/cost test. In the Court's words:

> Prices below average variable costs . . . by means of which a dominant undertaking seeks to eliminate a competitor must be regarded as abusive[27] [and] prices below average total costs, that is to say, fixed costs plus variable costs, but above average variable costs, must be regarded as abusive if they are determined as part of a plan for eliminating a competitor.[28]

This test has been considered good law ever since *AKZO*. What is more, it has been applied as the only valid test for predation. The CFI ruling in *Wanadoo* is a case in point. The CFI applied the test literally. It took the test to mean that, when prices are below average variable cost, price/cost comparison is the sole criterion; when prices are above average variable cost but below average total costs, there are two separate criteria for predation: (1) the price/cost comparison and (2) an additional element of intent.[29]

One reason to disagree with this reading of *AKZO* is that it does not make logical sense. Contrary to what the CFI held, intention and price/cost comparison should not be treated as two distinct and cumulative elements, both at the same level in the reasoning. As is apparent in the first prong of the

AKZO test, price/cost comparison is an *indication* of intent (and a decisive one in the case of prices below average variable costs). It follows that under *AKZO*, however regrettable this may be, intent is the sole legal criterion. *AKZO* may be read to say that, in one case (prices below AVC), intent is inferred from price/cost comparison, while in the second case (prices above AVC but below ATC), the indication of predatory intent, which may be inferred from the price/cost comparison, is not conclusive and needs to be complemented by additional evidence of intent. In the CFI reading of *AKZO*, the price/cost comparison, borrowed from Areeda and Turner,[30] is an autonomous legal criterion, while in the reading we suggest, the same economic import only has the value of a presumption, as it is (implicitly but essentially) linked to the legal category of intent. The judgment of the Court on appeal in the *Wanadoo* case does not choose between these two readings,[31] but it illustrates in another manner how a given economic argument may be given several different legal translations.

On appeal, France Télécom (the dominant undertaking accused of predation) argued that the CFI had erred in law because it failed to recognize that the possibility of recoupment is part of the legal test for predation. In essence, the appellant invited the Court to align EU law with the U.S. Supreme Court in *Brooke Group*.[32] In spite of support of advocate general Mazák for this proposition, the Court stuck to its previous case law and refused to hold that the possibility of recoupment had to be established in all cases of predation.[33] It ruled however that the possibility of recoupment was a *relevant* fact.[34] Interestingly, the ECJ did not see the relevance of this fact in the same light as the U.S. Supreme Court. Indeed, it did not link it with the same legal category. In the court's judgment, the relevance of recoupment is not linked with the assessment of the effects of conduct on consumer welfare. Rather it seems to be linked, again, with the appraisal of exclusionary intent.[35] The economic argument according to which it is not rational for a firm to engage in predation if it cannot reasonably expect to recoup its losses is not seen under EU law as an argument on which a dominant undertaking may rely to deny predatory conduct. It is, on the contrary, an argument on which the Commission may rely to exclude rationales other than predatory intent that may be put forward by an alleged predator.[36]

Some readers of the *Wanadoo* judgment may think the ECJ turned a sound economic argument on its head. Certainly, the Court did not follow the Organisation for Economic Co-operation and Development (OECD) recommendation to use the possibility of recoupment as a "filter," i.e., a preliminary step to assess whether there is a prima facie predation case that deserves further analysis.[37] Instead, the Court tried to incorporate the assessment of an *ex ante* possibility of recoupment in the existing EU legal framework for predation, where it does not readily fit.[38] The new admission of relevance does not modify the existing legal test, it merely opens more refined discussions on the likelihood of predatory intent.

Whatever opinion one may have on the better rule for predation, it follows from the above that all interpretive techniques that may be used to incorporate an economic argument are not equivalent to one another. Holding that a fact must be established or judging it merely relevant, linking it with one legal category or another, adding it as a new prong to an existing legal test, or leaving it outside the existing test are choices that lead to vastly different policy implications.

While interpretive techniques are rich and versatile, they do not constitute the whole range of possible legal techniques for importing economic elements. Creating a presumption is a technique that constitutes a distinct category and can sometimes, though not always, serve to import economic input into the law.

Presumptions

Presumptions are to be distinguished from interpretation of the law in that they relate to proof. Questions of proof arise only once the law is interpreted and *what* needs to be proven has thereby been made clear. Only then does it make sense to ask *how* required facts may be proven and whether a presumption will lighten the burden of proof bearing on one party.

In competition law, presumptions may act either as barriers to economic imports or, on the contrary, as vehicles for importing economics. EU case law on abuse of dominance offers a good illustration of the first phenomenon. Economically minded commentators have long insisted that consumer harm should be established for a unilateral conduct to be found abusive and have now been heard by the Commission.[39] The Court, for its part, has ruled that consumer harm may be inferred from alteration of the structure of the market,[40] and this presumption is still good law.[41] Even where consumer harm is required (i.e., under Article 102, subparagraph b),[42] it is, according to the case law, enough to show competitor's harm. Such a presumption spares competition authorities and parties the burden of a fact-based assessment of consumer harm.[43] While this may make practical sense, due to the considerable difficulties of such an assessment, it also clearly denies any relevance to economic arguments on consumer harm, which firms are particularly keen to develop. In this sense, the presumption goes against the introduction of a more sophisticated economic approach of consumer harm.

In other instances, on the contrary, presumptions may serve to import economic wisdom into the law. Even in those cases, presumptions create an evidentiary shortcut and keep some economic evidence out of the courtroom. This is the nature of a presumption. But unlike the presumption of consumer harm based on competitor's harm, some shortcuts are based on economic consensus. This is particularly the case where the element imported from economics is a perception of what is economically normal (rather than a statement of relevance, an inference, or any other element of economic reasoning). For example, in *Tetra*, the CFI relied on economic scholarship to hold that conglomerate mergers do not *normally* harm competition.[44] It should be noted that economic scholarly consensus, as used by the CFI in this ruling, plays exactly the same role as any statement based on common perception of causality in other areas of the law. Indeed, the perception of what is normal generally constitutes the basis for a presumption. For example, courts will presume that someone who has been convicted of controlling prostitution for gain, and who proves unable to account for the origin of his revenues, derives part of his revenues from his illegal activities. In much the same way as a general rule based on common (or judicial) experience, a statement about what *normally* happens with conglomerate mergers is used as a basis for a presumption. The only difference is that, instead of being rooted in common sense, the statement about normalcy that is being incorporated in the judgment is based on economic literature.

This part of the *Tetra* ruling has given rise to much discussion because it has been read, initially by the Commission, to relate to standard of proof. This is probably due to the fact that the CFI, after stating that conglomerate mergers normally do not harm competition, went on to rule that "the proof of anti-competitive conglomerate effects of such a merger calls for a precise examination, supported by convincing evidence, of the circumstances which allegedly produce those effects."[45] On appeal, the Court confirmed the CFI judgment and held that, contrary to what the Commission argued, the CFI had not raised the standard of proof. According to the Court, it had "merely [drawn] attention to the essential function of evidence, which is to establish convincingly the merits of an argument."[46] In other words, the standard of proof being constant (and not named in EU law), it takes more evidentiary effort to establish a fact that is held to be intrinsically improbable, such as the harmful character of a conglomerate merger, than it would to prove to the same standard a fact that is intrinsically more probable, such as the harmful effect of a horizontal merger. This distinction between a variation of the standard of proof and a variation of evidentiary burden under a constant standard of proof has been aptly captured by Lord Hoffman in a now much quoted opinion.[47] As Lord Hoffman explained, it takes more evidence to convince a court that one has seen a lioness in Regent's Park, than to convince it to the same standard that the animal seen in that urban park was an Alsatian.[48] In much the same way, it takes more convincing evidence to prove to the requisite standard that a conglomerate merger harms competition than to prove that a horizontal or vertical merger has the same effect.

Tetra is therefore not about the standard of proof. It is about a presumption that alleviates the evidentiary burden of a party and, conversely, increases that bearing on the Commission. This presumption is based on a perception of economic normality. More generally, presumptions as an importing tool seem particularly suited to incorporating exactly this kind of statement, relating to what *normally* happens.[49] When a presumption is, as in this case, based on economics, one can observe that economic theory (rather than empirical observations) plays the same role that common knowledge does for ordinary presumptions, namely that of authority for a judgment on normality or on causality. As there is no common experience of economic causality, this does raise questions about how courts are satisfied that something really is "normal" economically.

The natural advantage of presumptions as compared to other importing techniques is that a true presumption is rebuttable. If a presumption based on economics is at odds with facts that can be established, it may, like any presumption, be reversed. This possibility to check against the facts of a case a general statement borrowed from economics (i.e., economic theory more often than empirical observations) avoids complete crystallization of possibly false economic consensus. In this respect, it displays more flexibility than a substantive rule. This being said, it will often be hard to prove against a presumption. Some presumptions may be so enshrined in judicial practice that one may wonder if they are still rebuttable. In EU law, the presumption already mentioned, that consumers are harmed when market structure is altered, is a case in point. This example also shows that, in order for presumption to be based on sound economics, or what is generally considered sound economics at any given point in time, there ought to be a way to challenge presumption and introduce state-of-the-art scientific—or, better still, empirical—argument into the courtroom. This may be facilitated where provisions for *amicus curiae* to intervene exist, which is not currently the case before EU courts.

. . .

There are various legal techniques to import insights from economics into the law. Most of them relate to legal interpretation, but economics may also be incorporated into the legal decision-making process at the stage of proof through presumptions. While economists who advocate a particular idea often consider that it should translate to a new legal test, there are several different ways for a court or competition authority to take economic insights into account. Not all techniques are interchangeable. For example, creating a presumption is particularly suited when the borrowed element is a judgment on economic normalcy or economic causality. For other types of imports, such as statements of relevance or other elements of an analytical framework, several importing techniques may be available. As the discussion on the case law on predation illustrated, the choice between these competing techniques is neither obvious nor always explicit. The purpose of this chapter is to highlight some of the issues at stake in these technical choices. These issues have received less attention than choices between Type I and Type II errors. They deserve more attention from scholars and courts, as choices of importing technique influence the magnitude of legal change caused by an import, as well as future flexibility of legal rules, which is an important dimension when economics is the source from which the law borrows. On a more theoretical level, these technical choices also factor into the interaction between the law on the one hand and economics as a science on the other, as they display different levels of fidelity of the legal transplant to the original economic element. As there is only a limited set of legal techniques, choices faced by courts when they consider adopting an element of economic analysis may boil down to trade-offs between the respective limitations of available importing techniques.

4

Complications in the Antitrust Response to Monopsony

Jeffrey L. Harrison

There is a tendency among antitrust scholars, judges, and practitioners to focus on practices by single sellers or groups of sellers. Increasingly, however, the importance of possible anticompetitive actions by buyers has been recognized. This recognition is long overdue. Actions by buyers, or monopsonists,[1] have many of the same negative economic impacts as those by sellers. In addition, whether it is in the form of competing buyers of the services of physicians or professional athletes, or of agricultural commodities, the use of monopsony power has far greater impact on markets than most would expect. In this sense, a limit of antitrust is the inability of academics and judges to understand certain economic complexities that do not fit within tradition frameworks of analysis.

The new level of consciousness about monopsony is explained, in part, by the 2007 decision of the Supreme Court in *Weyerhaeuser Co. v. Ross-Simmons Hardwood Lumber Co.*[2] The Court noted "close theoretical connection between monopoly and monopsony."[3] In fact, in many respects monopsony is the mirror of monopoly. Monopsonists use buying power to lower prices while monopolists use seller (or market power) to raise them. In both instances, there is likely to be lower output and higher prices of the final output.[4] In fact, it is tempting to take all of the antitrust analysis that is applied to sellers and apply it to buyers. For example, just as there is seller-side price fixing, boycotts, and mergers, buyers can engage in the same practices.

Economic theory generally supports the idea of comparable treatment but is somewhat more complicated when one attempts to apply existing legal standards. The focus in this chapter is on some of the stickier issues that arise when antitrust is applied to monopsony. In a real sense they represent limitations on antitrust as it exists because they require policy makers to examine issues with which they are unfamiliar and formulate new approaches to some of those issues. This analysis starts with a short review of monopsony theory. The purpose of this review is to provide a context for the specific issues that are addressed in the following sections. The first complication concerns what is called the "all-or-none supply curve." This amounts to an argument that in some circumstances, monopsony may not be harmful. The discussion then explores questions left open by *Weyerhaeuser,* issues of antitrust standing (a decision about those eligible to bring a private action based on a monopsony theory), the treatment of cooperative buying, and the treatment of monopsony in the context of some practices to which the application of United States antitrust law is currently somewhat muddled.

A Brief Look at Monopsony Theory

This overview will inform some of the complications explored in the next section. The starting point for most price theory is basic price and output determination in the context of perfectly competitive conditions. This is depicted in Figure 4.1. Demand and supply intersect at an equilibrium price Pc and equilibrium quantity Qc. This same analysis applies to all goods and services that are sold under competitive conditions, whether they are outputs or inputs. When applied to inputs, demand is determined by the amount of revenue that will be generated by use of that input when it is converted to outputs that are sold. Supply, as in all cases, will be a function of the costs of production of the input or output.[5] The graph also shows the lowest price acceptable to sellers for each level of sales. On the left side of the equilibrium quantity, the marginal revenue product exceeds the cost of producing the unit (and it is profitable to purchase the unit). To the right of that point, the cost of production, as indicated by the supply curve, exceeds the marginal revenue product, as indicated by the demand curve, and those units will not be purchased.

Under monopsony conditions, the analysis changes dramatically. First, under competitive conditions, no single buyer has the ability to affect price. In particular, if a buyer attempted to pay less than the equilibrium price, no

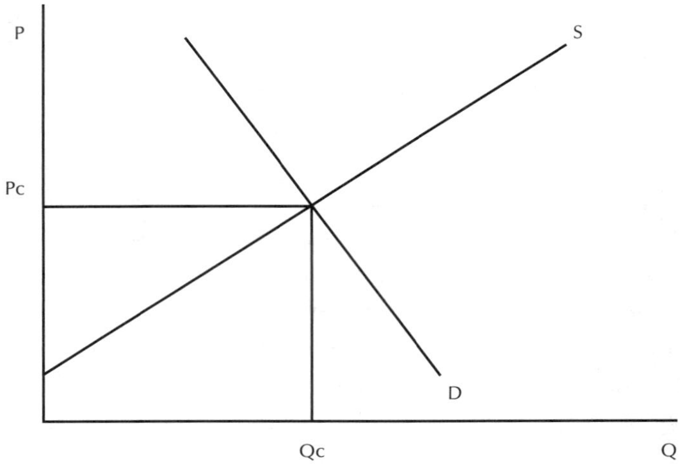

Figure 4.1 Competitive conditions

supplier would sell to that buyer. The essence of monopsony power is the ability to pay a lower price and still make purchases. A firm must determine the optimal price for it to offer given that some suppliers will still sell at a lower price and that some will not. This means the relevant comparison is between the marginal revenue that each *additional* unit of input will generate and the additional cost of hiring each unit.[6]

To understand the change in the analysis, it is important to note that the quantity of input offered for sale will increase with the price offered. The cost of moving up the supply curve, however, is not just the price of each unit of input because the new higher price applies to all units purchased.[7] For example, suppose a monopsonist is buying 2 units of an input for $2 each for a total of $4. Now, it would like to buy 3 units but this means paying $3 each. The total cost is $9. The extra or marginal cost of the third unit is actually $5. Thus in Figure 4.2, the relevant comparison is between the marginal revenue product curve (demand) associated with the purchase of one more unit of output and the extra cost of that unit of input. That second curve lies above the supply curve and is labeled marginal factor cost (MFC).

As Figure 4.2 indicates, the monopsonist will purchase Qm inputs. It will pay the price that is the lowest consistent with that level of purchases. This is found on the supply curve at Pm. Comparing Figures 4.1 and 4.2 illustrates that the monopsonist pays a lower price and purchases fewer units of the input than a firm in a competitive market.

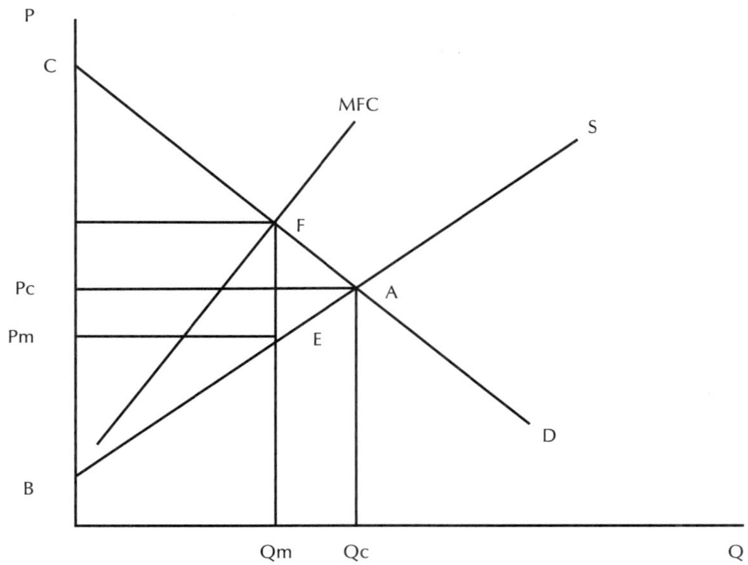

Figure 4.2 Monopsony conditions

Does the fact that the monopsonist pays less mean consumers are better off? One line of thinking is that since a monopsonist pays less, buyers from the monopsonist in output markets will pay less and there is no damage to consumers.[8] In fact, the opposite effect is more likely. If the monopsonist purchases fewer units of input, it will produce a lower level of output. Restricted output, in turn, leads to higher prices in output markets.

A comparison of the graphs illustrates addition losses. When the quantity is Pc and the quantity Qc, an allocatively efficient level of the input is purchased. The triangle ABC show the level of social welfare generated. Some accrues to buyers (area CAPc) and some to producers of the input (BAPc). Under monopsony conditions, sales of the input are restricted and the total welfare to producers is EBPm and to the monopsony buyer is CFEPm. The sum of these is less than ABC. In effect, there has been an overall loss in welfare.

The All-or-None Supply Issue

The standard analysis above illustrates why monopsony does not benefit buyers in output markets. The idea that the lower price paid by the monopsonist is "passed on to" output buyers has been accepted by courts in some instances.

This idea is mistaken.[9] The error in this analysis is that the monopsonist may control the *price* it pays for an input but cannot control the *quantity* of the input offered for sale at that price. Hence, if the competitive price is, for example, $5 and the monopsonist uses its power to lower prices to $3, the quality offered for sale in output markets will decrease.

Suppose, however, that the monopsonist can control both price and quantity. If this is the case, the monopsonist can force suppliers onto the all-or-none supply curve. The all-or-none supply curve does not indicate how much sellers will offer to sell at each price but what would be offered at each price *if* the alternative would be to sell nothing at all.[10] When the monopsonist has the power to push sellers onto the all-or-none supply curve the amount purchased of the input does not decline. Consequently, the monopsonist's output does not decline and consumers are not worse off. Moreover, since the quantity of the input purchased remains the same, there is no the effect on *overall* welfare, as described above. There is, nevertheless, an impact on how social welfare is distributed. What the all-or-nothing context creates is a situation in which the monopsony buyer captures the surplus that had initially accrued to the sellers.

The all-or-none supply curve creates a number of complexities for antitrust law. The first is whether it is always easy to detect when sellers have been forced onto their all-or-none curve. The day-to-day dickering between firms may not be conclusive on this issue. More importantly, even if the all-or-nothing case is detected, what should the antitrust response be? In the case of a collusive monopsony, the answer is that it is probably per se unlawful as horizontal price-fixing. In the case of a single firm (a monopsonist), there is good reason to believe from case law that there will be no antitrust response at all.[11] What is awkward is that in neither case is there harm to consumers, at least in the short run. Thus, are the distributed consequences alone enough to warrant an antitrust response?

The final complexity is whether there are long-term effects that are harmful to consumers. In other words, a firm or firms with monopsony power may be able to push sellers to their all-or-none supply curves in the short run, but it does raise the possibility that producers of these inputs will exit the industry in the long run with the result being eventual harm to consumers.

The *Weyerhaeuser* Problem

Weyerhaeuser was the Supreme Court's first extensive and express consideration of predatory pricing by a monopsonist.[12] The Court claims to treat monopsony predation in the same manner as monopoly predation. As this chapter will explain, in a way it does and in a way it does not. In order to understand why, a slight digression into the more commonly discussed matter of seller predatory pricing will be useful. Although there is disagreement on whether it occurs and whether it is potentially harmful enough[13] to devote resources to eliminate the conduct, the basic idea is that a firm could lower prices below its costs in an effort to eliminate competing sellers. The losses incurred during this period would be recovered once competitors had exited and the successful predator raised its prices for at least long enough to earn a profit on its below-cost pricing "investment." In 1993, the Supreme Court, in *Liggett v. Brown and Williamson Tobacco,*[14] announced a difficult (for plaintiffs) two-part test for those relying on a predatory pricing theory of liability. First, the price must be below some measure of cost.[15] The idea here is that it makes little sense to deliberately lose money on a sale if it is not part of an overall plan to regain it in the future.[16] Second, it must be shown that there is a high likelihood of recoupment.[17] In short, this means that competitors would not reenter the market at a rate that would interfere with the predator's ability to earn a return on its investment.

If the analysis is flipped to monopsony or the buying side of the market, a similar two-step process could be applied. First, the buyer must offer more for an output than would seem to make sense if it were just attempting to maximize profits. In effect, the price offered for the input would be compared with the marginal revenue product of that input since the marginal revenue product is the additional revenue generated by the use of that input. Logically, it is irrational to pay more for an input than it generates for the firm in terms of revenue. Such a pricing strategy is consistent with driving the prices of competing buyers up and eliminating them as buyers. Of course, as *Brooke Group* notes, the threat is not of great concern unless the predatory buyer is able to eliminate competing buyers and then lower the price offered for inputs far enough below the marginal revenue product and for long enough to recoup the losses incurred during the predatory buying period. In short, the firm would establish itself as a monopsonist.

Although the logic seems to work both ways and the *Weyerhaeuser* Court acknowledged the similarity between the predatory seller and predatory buyer, it veered from establishing a parallel standard for the predatory buyer. Thus, it announced the two-part standard. First, "[a] plaintiff must prove that the alleged predatory bidding led to below-cost pricing of the predator's outputs. That is, the predator's bidding on the buy side must have caused the cost of the relevant output to rise above the revenues generated in the sale of those outputs."[18] Second, "A predatory-bidding plaintiff also must prove that the defendant has a dangerous probability of recouping the losses incurred in bidding up input prices through the exercise of monopsony power."[19]

In effect, the Court did not establish a standard that was *parallel* to the more conventional seller predatory pricing, it established the *same* standard. This standard, when applied to the predatory monopsonist, is underinclusive. That is, firms causing the same type of harm as a monopsonist that is caused by the predatory monopolist will escape antitrust exposure. This may be a little hard to understand at first. After all, by raising the price of inputs, the predatory monopsonist raises the prices of inputs to itself and competing buyers. The increase in the price of inputs will raise the price of output perhaps to the point that those prices exceed the costs of production.

What is missing from the analysis is that there are actually two sources of benefit to the predatory monopsonist. The first requires, as illustrated above, that the predatory monopsonist charge below-cost prices in the output markets. This may not be the case. If so, does this mean the predatory monopsonist causes no harm? The answer to this is no. The buyer who pays more than the marginal revenue product for one of its inputs may still be able to sell its output at a price that is above cost. For example, it may have monopsony power in other input markets, which means lower than competitive prices are paid for those inputs. This may reduce the cost of production to the point of offsetting the losses it suffers by "overpaying" in another input market. In fact, if it has monopoly power in the output market, it may be able to sell its output at a price higher than its costs despite paying more than marginal revenue product for the input market in which it is pricing predatorily. The key question is, thus, not the final output price but whether the prices above marginal revenue product in input markets make sense except as a way to eliminate competing buyers.

What this means is that the predatory monopsony story may not be finished yet. The Court's opinion does not reveal whether it deliberately left more leeway for predatory bidding than for predatory pricing. How important this is depends on one's perspective. If one believes that predatory efforts are rarely likely to succeed or even be tried, then a narrow definition of what it means to be a predatory monopsonist is to be applauded. On the other hand, if one favors a more economically consistent approach without regard for the likelihood of suits based on predatory buying or selling, it appears the Court has favored predatory buyers without a sound economic rationale.

Antitrust Standing and Injury

The Supreme Court has developed a number of policies that are not directly about defining antitrust offenses. Instead they are about which private parties are eligible to bring private antitrust actions. The Count's development of these doctrines took place in the context of buyers. The same concerns that led to this evolution in antitrust law are also applicable to monopsony. First, however, it is useful to briefly review these developments. In the first of its opinions, the Court established that indirect purchasers from price-fixing firms may not recover. Later the Court addressed what it meant to suffer an antitrust injury and the concept of antitrust standing. A firm suffers antitrust injury when the harm incurred is something the antitrust laws were designed to avoid. Standing has more to do with one's proximity to the anticompetitive activity. It is possible to have suffered an antitrust injury but not have antitrust standing. A good example of this might be indirect purchasers. Although not initially described as a standing analysis, it is clear that the disqualification of indirect purchasers is comparable to a standing decision. No doubt the increased prices paid when a firm purchases from a purchaser who purchased directly from price-fixing firms are something the antitrust laws were designed to avoid. Yet the purchases are, in essence, not sufficiently proximate to the price-fixing, and those affected lack antitrust standing.[20]

In the case of a collusive monopsony or oligopsony, it is clear that those selling directly to the price-fixers are direct sellers and suffer antitrust injury. It seems equally clear that a seller one level up from those sellers would not have standing. Consequently, if a fertilizer manufacturer sold its output to farmers who sold their output to a colluding group of buyers of, say, tomatoes, the fertilizer sellers would be indirect sellers or, depending on the label one prefers, they would not have standing even though they had been negatively affected.

What is more puzzling is the situation in which the colluding buyers of tomatoes, due to the lower prices they offer, acquire and resell less in the output market. As a consequence, they raise their own prices in the output market but not because they have agreed on those prices with other sellers. If they had fixed the prices they will pay for tomatoes, the sellers clearly have the ability to bring an action. What about the *buyers* of the tomatoes who now are charged higher prices? The higher price is not a consequence of price-fixing by resellers of tomatoes while acting as resellers. Instead it is the result of price-fixing among those same parties when acting as buyers of tomatoes.

Nevertheless, those harmed by higher tomato prices are buying directly from parties involved in an anticompetitive activity, and the harm suffered seems like the type the antitrust laws were designed to avoid.

What makes this question interesting is examining it from the more conventional perspective involving price-fixing sellers. Here the sellers restrict output and reduce sales. This means suppliers of inputs to those firms sell less, and since demand for their output has dropped, they receive lower prices. Here too there is a direct transaction and a harm the antitrust laws were designed to prevent. Yet at this point there appear to be no reported actions by those who supply price-fixing sellers.

Nor do there appear to be any cases in which customers of a collusive monopsony have sought damages stemming from the higher prices they may pay as a result of the conspiracy. The logic for barring suits by the sellers of inputs to those who fix prices on the selling side of the market or buyers from those who fix prices on the buying side of the market is not readily evident unless it is based on the belief that antitrust remedies can be formulated to encourage efficient levels of various activities. In other words, this would be the assumption that both upstream and downstream liability would mean inefficient levels of deterrence. This avenue of thought will not be explored further here other than to observe that a *fixed* punitive amount of treble damages hardly seems consistent with efforts to adjust damages based on a desired level of deterrence.

Cooperative Buying

If an antitrust scholar proposed allowing a group of sellers to agree on prices so they could get "better" prices by using their monopoly power, most readers would think something was seriously amiss. On the other hand, the proposal that buyers be permitted to join together in order to use their "buying power" in order to bargain for better prices does not sound as absurd. In fact, it is tempting to argue that the antitrust law is really focused on consumer welfare and that buying co-ops are beneficial for consumers. The premise of this statement is itself debatable.[21] As the brief theoretical discussion above demonstrates, there is no guarantee that savings by buyers, including members of a buying co-op, will be passed on to consumers.[22]

Nevertheless, buying co-ops are often legal while collusive monopsonies are not. Moreover, for the most part the Supreme Court has not addressed the issue of how to distinguish presumptively cooperative buying from collusive monopsony. Its most detailed analysis is found in *Northwest Wholesale Stationers, Inc. v. Pacific Stationery and Printing Co.*[23] The case concerned the expulsion of a member from a cooperative buying group. The Court thus did not address the illegality of a buying co-op itself but provided some insights into the legality of cooperative buying. Most importantly, it observed:

> Wholesale purchasing cooperatives such as Northwest are not a form of concerted activity characteristically likely to result in predominantly anticompetitive effects. Rather, such cooperative arrangements would seem to be "designed to increase economic efficiency and render markets more, rather than less, competitive." The arrangement permits the participating retailers to achieve economies of scale in both the purchase and warehousing of wholesale supplies, and also ensures ready access to a stock of goods that might otherwise be unavailable on short notice. The cost savings and order-filling guarantees enable smaller retailers to reduce prices and maintain their retail stock so as to compete more effectively with larger retailers.[24]

Clearly the Court is not suggesting that combining for the purpose of increasing monopsony leverage is permissible. On the other hand, combining in order to take advantage in ordering or storage seems to be fair game. In some measure these advantages relate to reducing transactions costs and are hardly likely to draw antitrust fire.

As an economic matter, though, it is not clear that all uses of monopsony leverage are harmful. In fact, in the context of monopoly, the use of monopsony power may be economically beneficial. Thus, a rule against combining for the purpose of acquiring monopsony (or monopoly power) cannot be justified on the basis of being uniformly consistent with social or even consumer welfare. The process of attempting to distinguish different types of monopoly and monopsony, however, requires a great deal of fine-tuning and the possibility of false negatives.[25] Perhaps a more sensible approach is to exempt certain entities from the usual scope of the antitrust laws. For example, in recent years extreme increases on the buying side of medical care markets have led some states to permit collective bargaining by physicians.[26]

Monopsony and Some General Antitrust Issues

There is uncertainty in antitrust law about three specific types of practices that seem generally to concern sellers. Obviously, this lack of clarity is even more pronounced when buyers undertake similar or the same practices. For example, tying arrangements have been regarded as per se offenses. They have only rarely been treated in the same manner as other per se offenses in that an assessment of market power is required. Now the per se rule is perhaps only nominal, even if that.[27] A second practice falling into the uncertain area is group boycotts. In these instances firms agree to boycott a supplier or a customer that is selling to or buying from a firm competing at the same level as the boycotting firms. This level can involve either buying or selling.[28] At one point, group boycotts were thought to be per se unlawful, but in 1978 the Court noted that it had not applied that label except in circumstances in which the firms involved occupied dominant market positions.[29] A third practice that seems to fall in a gray area is a horizontal division of a market. The key case here is *United States v. Topco*[30] in which the practice was declared unlawful per se. This view was echoed as recently as 1990 in *Palmer v. BRG of Georgia, Inc.*[31] Still, in the past thirty years, the Court has been receptive to procompetitive justifications for practices that were once per se unlawful.

There can be monopsony versions of all these practices. For example, a firm could buy from another firm only on the condition that the selling firm also sells it a product that it would prefer to sell in an alternative market. In this context, the buying firm would have buying power in what might be called the "tying product" market. Second, a group of buyers may agree not to buy from a supplier who is selling to a competing buyer. The objective would be to increase or protect buying power. There is no reason to believe that the uncertainty with respect to this practice and any eventual clarity will not be applied equally to those designed to increase monopoly and monopsony power. Finally, in the instance of territory divisions, competing buyers could agree to divide the market. For example, wood processors might divide up portions of a state or the nation and agree which ones will be the sole buyers in each segment.

The uncertainty with respect to the selling-side or more conventional versions of these practices surely carries over to their buying-side counterparts. In the case of tying, the most important arguments against illegality are that the arrangements actually result in efficiencies and that purchasers of the tied product are often not forced to buy it. Typically this is because it is more economical to supply the two products as a package and this offsets any harm by virtue of the possible foreclosure of those selling only the tied product.

In the case of the tying buyer, four questions would be relevant: does the buyer requiring the seller to sell the two products actually experience any economies by doing so, is the seller actually forced to sell the so-called tied item, is there foreclosure of firms who would like to purchase only the tied item but cannot, and is there any significant likelihood that the buyer will gain monopsony power in the tied product market? The complexities of the analysis suggest that the trend toward rule of reason treatment in typical tying cases is also appropriate for buying-side tying.

The treatment of buying-side territorial divisions may not parallel selling-side cases. The principal criticism of *Topco* is that a territorial division may be, on balance, procompetitive if it results in the creation of a new product. In that case, firms agreed not to compete in the sales of a brand of food (Topco) that they had agreed to develop. Their agreement could be viewed as a way to keep one seller from free riding on the promotional efforts of others. Without that protection the product may not have existed at all. In the case of territorial divisions by buyers, a similar procompetitive justification is much harder to imagine. What this suggests is that territorial divisions by sellers may eventually fall into the rule of reason category while territorial divisions by buyers are likely to continue to be per se unlawful.

. . .

Monopsony is the mirror image of monopoly from the perspective of economic theory. One would expect its treatment to be the same under the antitrust laws as the treatment of monopoly. This is a good rule of thumb, but what it actually means to treat monopsony in the same manner is not always obvious. In the *Weyerhaeuser* case the Supreme Court was either unable to discover what seems to be obvious or declined to afford parallel treatment to those accused of predatory buying. In other instances, like tying and territory divisions, the likely contexts in which the cases arise may require a slightly different analysis than is found in the typical selling-side case. Most clearly, the final chapter of the antitrust treatment of monopsony is far from completed.

5

Antitrust and the Close Look

Transaction Cost Economics in Competition Policy

Herbert Hovenkamp

Since the 1970s, transaction cost economics (TCE) has become an increasingly powerful tool in antitrust analysis. At that time the reigning but embattled school of antitrust in the courts was structuralism, or the structure-conduct-performance (S-C-P) paradigm, which saw market structure as the principal determinant of anticompetitive behavior and poor economic performance.[1]

Within that model, which was closely associated with Harvard's economics department and law school, structure entailed conduct of a certain kind and this conduct entailed poor performance. As a result, conduct dropped out as a variable of interest and one could reason directly from structure to performance. S-C-P's promoters tended to believe that monopoly power and its exercise were widespread.[2] Building on a neoclassical model in which sellers placed their goods on an anonymous market and purchasers bought them in single-shot transactions, they were suspicious of deviations from common law contract models for distribution. The result was elevated fears of both ownership vertical integration and vertical contractual practices such as tying, exclusive dealing, resale price maintenance, or related restraints. Antitrust policy became hostile toward all of them. At its core lay the "leverage" theory, which feared that a monopolist could easily "exploit . . . his dominant position in one market to expand his empire into the next."[3]

At the other extreme was the Chicago School position, whose theory of vertical integration began with the collapse of the "leverage" theory in the

1950s,[4] and developed into a more general argument that most vertical ownership and contract integration should be lawful per se.[5] The Chicago School also tended to see the economic landscape in terms of competition and monopoly, but they saw far fewer situations where monopoly could be created or maintained for long periods.

The critique of the leverage theory showed that in a basic tying situation a firm with market power and the ability to charge prices above cost could not increase its overcharge by tying or other forms of vertical integration. To the contrary, in the case of successive or complementary firms with market power, combining two products or process stages into a single firm would actually increase output and reduce price by eliminating double marginalization. Tying was thought mainly to be a form of price discrimination, which permitted a monopolist to extract more profits but also typically increased output. As a result there was no reason based on economic welfare grounds for condemning ties.

Since the 1970s both the old Harvard and the traditional Chicago positions have moved from opposite directions toward the middle. To say that the rise of TCE is solely responsible for this realignment of antitrust policy is an exaggeration. However, TCE has helped antitrust develop a new "center," which has influenced both the case law and the academic literature. TCE's analytic tools serve to critique both the leverage theory and the belief that pricing and vertical practices are virtually never anticompetitive. The result has been to position antitrust analysis somewhat closer to Chicago's "benign" position than to the inherent hostility position reflected by structuralism and the traditional leverage theory.

Perhaps the single most important historical source for TCE is Ronald Coase's *The Nature of the Firm*, which was published in 1937. Coase argued that the costs of using the market determine the boundaries of the firm.[6] A firm intent on maximizing its value chooses internal production up to the point that the marginal cost of producing internally equals the marginal cost of external procurement and vice versa. Firms in a bargaining relationship that have specialized commitments to a common technology or resource do precisely the same thing. They maximize value by bargaining with each other to the point that the marginal payoff of reaching a bargain equals the marginal payoff of moving on.

Following Coase, TCE generally assumes that business firms organize their activities so as to maximize their value, which they can do both by economizing and also by obtaining higher prices. Sensible antitrust policy recognizes that both advantageous contracting and monopoly can be profitable to a firm, and a firm can be expected to pursue both when they are available. Nevertheless, the opportunities for economizing are many, while those for monopoly are relatively few.

Further, firms always evaluate alternatives from their present perspective, which necessarily includes the consequences of past decisions. The movement of resources from the current position is costly, and one of these costs is that of relying on the market.[7] One of the first choices firms must make is whether to use internal production or external procurement for a particular input or process. When products and distribution are specialized, many of a firm's contractual arrangements with others must necessarily be long term and somewhat open ended, in the sense that they do not anticipate every conceivable circumstance. Product differentiation tends to produce specialization at all levels. This has two effects. First, it tends to increase vertical integration, because the cost of internal production is relatively lower and the cost of market procurement relatively higher. Secondly, insofar as a firm uses external procurement its contractual relationships become more durable and more complex because the parties must often make substantial commitments to the technologies and product designs of their trading partners.[8] While all participants are rational, they do not have perfect information and they almost always know more about themselves than about others. A rational firm anticipates that, to the extent uncertainty exists, everyone in the market will try to use new situations to their own advantage, itself included.

Transaction cost economics builds on these insights, which determine not only what a firm's boundaries will be but also who are likely to be its bargaining partners in outside markets and what those bargains will look like. For example, an exclusivity provision in a contract permits a firm to retain some of the control and disciplinary advantages of internal production, while sharing investment costs and risk. TCE also fully explains the decision to engage in commons rather than individual production in situations where individual boundaries are costly to define or defend (e.g., fisheries or grazing rights). To the extent that boundaries are ambiguous and defending them is costly, a firm invests in the protection of individual boundaries only to the extent that the payoff exceeds that of producing in a commons. As a result firms often use commons production for some portion of their output (e.g., fishing) and individual production for other portions (e.g., processing of caught fish). The analysis helps explain the use of traditional common pool resources of rivalrous goods, such as grazing or irrigation rights but also common production of nonrivalrous goods, as in patent pools.[9]

Finally, one of the many costs of resource movement is the administrative cost of the cumbersome and imperfect machinery antitrust uses to analyze and deter anticompetitive practices. To the extent that the goal of competition policy is to increase wealth, administrative costs may counsel that certain practices be left unchallenged because the gains from enforcement will not exceed losses when enforcement costs themselves, including error costs, are included.[10]

This framework generally produces antitrust rules that are more benign than the old "hostility" tradition, but somewhat more aggressive than the Chicago School promoted. Transaction costs and other resource movement costs provide benign explanations for many practices that the hostility tradition condemned. But transaction costs also can create entry barriers or make other forms of market movement sticky and thus increase both the possibility and duration of monopoly. In a well-functioning market, a manufacturer and its dealers will bargain to the maximizing position, which is typically the position that benefits consumers as well. In the real world, however, transaction costs may enable dealer cartels or powerful individual dealers to impose restraints that are competitively suboptimal for both the manufacturer and consumers.[11] In that case, antitrust has a role to play.

The fundamental unit of analysis for TCE is the transaction, rather than the much broader set of goods or servies that constitute a market in ordinary economic analysis.[12] Equally important is the question of *who* transacts with *whom*. A distinctive feature of TCE is that it does not assume that each trader has a range of trading partners that is coextensive with the product and geographic market at issue. Rather, transactions occur in a setting that limits the range of trading partners depending on knowledge, previous investment, or technological commitment and past history. This limited range in turn affects the types of contracts that the partners make with one another.

By virtue of previous commitments (asset specificity), pairs of firms are thrust into positions where the potential net payoff of reaching a further bargain is greater than the payoff of abandoning this position and starting over.[13] What makes these situations interesting is that firms seek them out because there are gains to be had from joint specialization. Bargaining in such markets typically yields arrangements and practices that seem inconsistent with perfect competition—transfer prices that are above cost, price discrimination and nonlinear pricing, exclusivity provisions, tying and bundling, and contractual impositions on the prices, locations, and practices of trading partners. In classical political economy, goods were generic and distribution was unspecialized. As a result, everyone traded with everyone else. Building on this premise, the leverage theory was inclined to be suspicious of situations where specific buyers and sellers in the distribution process were locked in to one another by long-term contractual requirements. This suspicion accounts for many of the harsh rules that antitrust applied to vertical contractual practices as well as vertical ownership integration through the 1970s.[14]

Historically, Chicago School writers understood that these practices are perfectly consistent with general competitive conditions, but their focus on the impossibility of leveraging inclined them not to see any opportunities for harm whatsoever. That is, they tended to believe that no contract a monopolist or dominant firm made, other than collusion with rivals, would enable it to reduce output profitably more than it was already doing.

The dedicated vertical relationships whose analysis has been a centerpiece of TCE often behave like bilateral monopolies in the sense that within them price is indeterminate and bargaining complex. For example, if a manufacturer with market power has costs of $4, distribution costs of $3, and the profit-maximizing price is $10, there are $3 in economic profits to be made. If the manufacturer can sell efficiently through a competitive dealer network it will retain the markup for itself, permitting the dealers only a competitive return. However, if dealers are specialized and their market is limited, the dealers themselves may have power to bargain with the manufacturer over how the overcharge is distributed among them. In an unstructured setting this lack of a determinate price can produce high transaction costs, double marginalization, or both.[15]

In most vertical business contracting settings, however, the contractual form establishes a "hierarchy" that imposes stability, although not necessarily joint maximization. For example, in the typical franchise setting the franchisor establishes a contract form and strikes a deal with each franchisee individually. The franchisees may have little opportunity to collaborate with each other or cycle through counteroffers. In this respect the structure of the franchise arrangement resembles a business firm more than a market. Retail dealers often make investments that are specific to a particular manufacturer's product, and manufacturers for their part make investments in these dealers. This is how bilateral monopoly relationships get started, but both manufacturers and dealers embrace such opportunities. Indeed, the entire principle behind the development of modern contractual distribution systems is that the gains more than offset any transaction problems that arise from this form of co-investment. The same thing applies to supply agreements. For example, General Motors and Fisher Body Works were once two highly specialized firms whose production was "locked" together by previous design commitments.[16]

Simple bilateral monopoly is not an antitrust problem, even if it increases transaction costs, unless the firms committed to such relationship have market power in at least one external market. Costly bargaining and advantage taking might implicate contract or perhaps tort law. But no arrangement that they make has antitrust significance as long as they lack market power; external prices will not be affected. This was the error that the Supreme Court majority made in the 1992 *Kodak* case. The customers' purchase of durable Kodak photocopiers placed them into a bilateral monopoly relationship with Kodak to the extent that the customers needed aftermarket parts that only Kodak could supply. In his dissent Justice Scalia likened the situation to a bilateral monopoly—one in which a swimming pool contractor discovers a five-ton boulder buried in the customer's yard after excavation is well under way.[17] Transaction costs will be magnified if such problems are not specified in advance, at the time of initial contracting. However, residential back yards and swimming pool contractors are both competitive, and the resolution of this dispute will have no impact on the market price or output of homes, homes with swimming pools, contracting services, or any other antitrust market that might be relevant to the dispute.

When at least one firm in a distribution market has serious market power, however, the welfare of consumers depends more on well-functioning distribution markets. At that point, if bargaining breaks down, antitrust may have a role to play. For example, suppose that *A* is a monopoly manufacturer of a product and *B* is its monopoly dealer or *B* represents a cartel of all of *A*'s dealers in a particular retail market. In a well-functioning market *A* and *B* should be able to negotiate to the profit-maximizing output. The division of the profits is indeterminate, but consumers would be indifferent to that outcome as well because the final price would be the same. The extent of monopoly will not be greater because the firm in question uses restrictive contracts to distribute its product, provided that the dominant firm and its dealers reach the joint maximizing agreement.

If the manufacturer and the dealer(s) both have market power in their respective output markets, however, the bilateral monopoly situation threatens double marginalization, which does injure consumers. To illustrate, a gasoline refiner with market power might face a double-marginalization problem if a gasoline retailer downstream or a cartel of retailers have market power in the retail market as well. The manufacturer would sell to the dealer(s) at a price that the manufacturer determines by equating its own marginal cost and marginal revenue; that is, it would take a monopoly markup. The dealer with market power of its own would then accept that price as given and add its own monopoly markup. The price is suboptimal for everyone concerned. Both the manufacturer and dealer would be better off if they could agree on a "joint maximizing" output and price level, which would be the same one as if there was only one monopoly in the distribution chain. Consumers would also be better off under a single monopoly.

Double marginalization problems occur in both vertically related markets and markets for complements. The transaction cost problem is typically more serious for complements than vertically related firms because producers of complementary products, such as computers and printers, often are not in a position to deal with each other.[18]

Double marginalization is fundamentally a transaction cost problem.[19] That is, with zero transaction costs, vertically related firms with market power would agree on the joint maximizing output, but in fact they frequently do not. A precondition to double marginalization is that both firms have some market power and that one firm is not in a position to avoid the power of the other at low cost by dealing with someone else. In cases of oligopoly there might be more than one firm at each level, but each of the firms has some market power. Since pricing in excess of marginal cost is common in product-differentiated markets,[20] double marginalization is common as well.

As a general proposition firms faced with double marginalization have three choices:

1. Accept the consequences of double marginalization, which might be the best alternative if internal production is costly and alternative (3), a "bargaining" solution, is unavailable; for example, a manufacturer selling to a market-dominating local dealer may have no choice but to accept that dealer's high markups as a cost of doing business; everyone involved including consumers are injured.
2. Integrate by ownership into the other production level, whether by merger or new entry.
3. Use the "bargaining" solution, which is to enter into one of many types of contractual arrangements under which the two vertically related firms increase output and cut price toward the joint maximizing level.

Recognizing that both options (2) and (3) can result in lower prices and higher output, antitrust would respond with a more benign attitude toward vertical new entry, vertical acquisitions, and vertical contracting, although not necessarily with per se legality. This of course requires examination of the economics of various types of distribution contracts. Perversely, antitrust policy has been counterproductive to the extent that it has prohibited the parties from reaching a bargain that will maximize their joint profits.

An easy case is maximum resale price maintenance, which is readily explained by double marginalization concerns. The manufacturer limits the dealer's markup to an approximation of the competitive level. Assuming that the dealer cannot enlarge its markup in other ways, such as by reducing valuable services, the manufacturer can get back to its optimal monopoly price level. If the manufacturer is a monopolist, that price will reflect no more than the amount of power that it has. If the manufacturer is a competitor, then the output price should be competitive as well. For example, in the *State Oil* case, which adopted a rule of reason for maximum resle price maintenance (RPM), the individual dealer may have had power in its local retail market but there was no reason to think that State Oil, a relatively small player in the much larger supply market, had significant market power.[21]

The same thing is true of quantity and loyalty discounts, which can enable a manufacturer and dealer to share the gains that result from increasing output to the joint-maximizing level. The discount operates like an economy of scale, enabling the dealer to achieve lower costs by selling more of the manufacturer's product.[22]

A loyalty, or market share, discount differs from a quantity discount in that the discount is fixed to a percentage of the reseller's purchases rather than an absolute quantity or dollar amount.[23] Loyalty discounts are often better than quantity discounts for both manufacturers and consumers when the downstream market is concentrated. Quantity discounts discriminate against smaller firms that are unable to purchase in the same volume as larger firms. As a result, quantity discounts can give larger firms a price umbrella or in extreme cases even drive smaller firms out of the market altogether. Once again, the concern is essentially of double marginalization—the manufacturer wants to keep the downstream market as competitive as possible, and keeping smaller firms in the market facilitates this goal. Otherwise the price reduction for purchasing more will be offset by increased market power given to the larger dealers as the smaller dealers are denied the discount.

Transaction cost analysis also explains many tying arrangements and bundled discounts, which occur when a seller offers a discount to one who purchases two or more different products together.[24] Many famous old tying cases involved tied products that were commodities sold in highly competitive markets, such as dry ice in the *Carbice* case or salt in *International Salt*.[25] In those cases price discrimination rather than controlling double marginalization very likely explained the tie. The typical tied products today, however, are manufactured products sold in product-differentiated markets.[26] The one exception is fast-food franchises, where the tied product is often food items or supplies that are almost certainly sold in highly competitive markets.[27]

Tying almost always involves complementary products—that is, products that are more valuable if they are used together. As noted previously, the double-marginalization problem for complements, often called the "Cournot complements" problem, is similar to the one for vertical distribution.[28] The complementary goods problem might involve something like a computer and a printer, an MP3 digital music player and downloaded music, or a computer operating system and software applications. In such cases the printer manufacturer will charge its profit-maximizing price for the printer and the cartridge manufacturer will do the same for its cartridge. The two separate markups can be significantly higher than the combined markup that would be taken by a firm that sold both products together. Further, profits would be higher for the single firm than for the two firms separately and consumers would be better off because output would be higher and prices lower. Complementary rights in intellectual property sold by separate firms can lead to the same result, such as the "royalty stacking" that occurs when different firms own patents that are essential to the production of some good or process.[29] In such cases welfare would be increased if a single firm sold the complementary goods.

Assume that firm *A* makes a computer while firm *B* makes a compatible printer. Most but not all customers purchase one of each and they are both sold in oligopoly markets at prices above cost. Given that these prices maximize individual profits, neither firm wishes to cut the price of its own product. At this point firm *A* would have an incentive to acquire firm *B,* or vice versa, or perhaps it would enter the printer market on its own. Firm *A*'s profit-maximizing price for a computer/printer combination would be lower than the sum of the prices charged by the separate firms. Firm *A* would also earn more, output would be higher, and consumers would benefit as well.

Firm *A* could accomplish this in two ways. It could simply tie computers and printers, refusing to sell the two separately. That would benefit those consumers who wanted one of each, but it would injure those who needed only one of the two products, perhaps as a replacement. Alternatively, it could charge the single product profit-maximizing price for each product separately but a lower price for the combination—that is, it would use a bundled discount to eliminate double marginalization for those buyers who regarded the goods as complements at the time of purchase.[30]

But why should we not force the firm simply to offer the computer and the printer separately at the lower prices? For example, suppose that the individual profit-maximizing prices of the computer and printer are $1,000 and $400, respectively, while the profit-maximizing price for the package when sold by a single firm is $1,200. Would it not be preferable on policy grounds to require the manufacturer to sell the two products separately at, say, $900 and $300? This would eliminate the double marginalization and it might satisfy those who find the tie unacceptable on some other ground.

First of all, if none of the rival printer companies cut their price to match, then the result would be the same as tying in any event. That is, the buyer would take both from firm *A*. Second, however, if one or more of the other printer companies *did* cut the printer price to $300, then firm *A* would not capture all of the printer sales. A premise of the double-marginalization story is that the price cut on the printer is profitable *because* the manufacturer obtains the higher output that accrues to both the computer and the printer. If it cannot tie and be assured of getting all of the printer sales, then it will not cut its price.

The double-marginalization explanation of tying and related practices is robust and has broad application in markets characterized by single-firm dominance or product differentiation. Tying and bundled discounts can operate as a kind of "reverse leverage" in cases where both the bundled products are sold in less than perfectly competitive markets.

The other side of the double-marginalization problem is that high transaction costs may interfere with manufacturers' efforts to control it by contract. A good example is vertical price and nonprice restraints, an area where the TCE literature has made important contributions. The free rider explanation for these restrictions, which dates to the 1960s, is but one example.[31] Manufacturers use resale price maintenance and nonprice restraints in order to achieve some of the efficiencies of intrafirm distribution while preserving the risk-sharing and incentive features of contractual distribution mechanisms. For example, a firm distributing its own product would ordinarily provide the optimal level of distribution services. By using RPM it can emulate this level when using independent dealers and alternative enforcement mechanisms are too costly or ineffectual. By the same token the self-distributing manufacturer would sell its full product line through each store. In a contractual distribution network it may have to offer inducements to dealers to carry the full line, often by using RPM in order to guarantee margins on the more popular goods so as to prevent "cream skimming" by other retailers.[32] Alternatively, a single firm engaged in self-distribution would place the optimal number of stores in a community and a firm engaged in contractual distribution would try to replicate that allocation by using territorial restrictions or other limits on dealer location.

However, there may also be situations in which vertical agreements exacerbate double marginalization and high transaction costs prevent efficient solutions from emerging. For example, antitrust legitimately has an interest in the problem of dealer cartels or powerful individual dealers.[33] Well-placed local dealers may be in a position to exercise market power in their individual retail markets. Depending on their power vis-à-vis the manufacturer, they may be able to extract RPM on competing dealers for their own benefit but to the detriment of an efficient distribution system. The cost of moving resources being what it is, it may be less costly for the manufacturer to comply than to set up alternative equally satisfactory dealerships. The result will be higher local prices.[34] Once again, this is fundamentally a problem of transaction costs. If bargaining worked perfectly, a manufacturer and its dealers would agree on the joint maximizing output level and negotiate over the division of profits. But when a powerful established dealer can frustrate this by insisting on higher local markups, a manufacturer may be powerless to resist, particularly if vertical integration into retailing is not possible on account of the need for distribution by multiproduct retailers. *Dr. Miles* itself was such a case, involving RPM instigated by a cartel of retail druggists.[35]

Another area where transaction cost analysis has led to changes in antitrust analysis is price discrimination, which occurs when a firm obtains higher ratios of price to marginal cost from some buyers than from others. Systematic price discrimination does not occur under perfect competition because, by definition, some prices are not at marginal cost. So price discrimination presupposes at least some power to set a price above marginal cost to particular customers. The amount of power is not substantial, however, and sufficient market power to have antitrust consequences cannot be inferred from the existence of price discrimination alone.

While price discrimination is often unrelated to market monopoly, it may result from bilateral monopoly. For example, a firm about to enter the fast-food industry as a supplier can profit by sharing risk, and self-employed franchisees may have stronger incentives to do well than widely scattered employees would. If the firm built its own restaurants it would expect to earn from them in proportion to their relative success. Franchising is an attractive alternative to the extent that it replicates this opportunity, while permitting franchisees to share the risk as well as part of the reward. For its part, the nascent franchisee receives a method of doing business, a recognized name and product, and the promise of high returns proportional to its level of success. So it willingly puts up its share of the capital (the franchisee fee), opens an outlet, and pays either a recurring fee proportional to sales or an overcharge on various tied consumable products used in the franchised business, or some combination. *Ex ante*, the franchisee knows that its payments are proportional to sales and one certainly cannot say that the prospect of high sales and accompanying high franchise fee is a deterrent. Once entered, these arrangements are profitable and also durable, even in competitive markets, because the value of a successful franchise is high and extraction is too costly in relation to the available alternatives. For example, a high-volume McDonald's franchise is highly profitable and desirable to its owner, notwithstanding that it is also highly profitable to the franchisor and at little more expense than it incurs with the less successful franchisee.

In sum, the phenomenon that makes price discrimination possible in such cases is not monopoly but rather the fact that assets are specialized and that transferring to attractive alternative arrangements is not costless. Down the road a highly successful franchisee may become resentful that its franchisor is earning high returns on this particular franchisee's business with no greater effort than it puts into the business of less successful franchisees. But that outcome is a feature of joint risk taking. In any event, resentment in this case is odd because the prospect that a particular franchisee would become highly successful would have acted *ex ante* as an inducement rather than a deterrent to entry.

The case of price discrimination in aftermarket products is similar. Many price discrimination ties involve arrangements in which the seller charges a below-market price for a tying product[36] but overcharges on a tied product whose use varies with the intensity of use of the tying product. A printer plus a subsequent stream of replaceable ink cartridges is one example.

The aftermarket price discrimination tie is simply a conditional sale that may lead to a bilateral monopoly, depending on what is specified in advance. Going in, if the underlying market is competitive a customer may be able to choose between a more expensive printer with less costly cartridges or vice versa. In *Kodak* the Supreme Court was aware of this and made something of the fact that Kodak may have changed its policy late in the copy machine's life cycle. As a result customers may have gotten a different and less attractive bilateral monopoly deal than the one they had bargained for at the beginning. But that change in policy is not an antitrust problem, although it may involve contract law or tortious misrepresentation.

Already in the 1950s, Chicago School writing on variable-proportion ties saw them as price discrimination devices[37] and the case law had seen them as such far earlier.[38] This Chicago School story was not about transaction costs, however, but rather about the profitable ways in which a monopolist might extract its overcharge. The TCE story is, if anything, even more benign because it starts out with a seller who is not necessarily a monopolist at all. As a result, the welfare gains from the output increases that attend price discrimination still apply, and competition in the underlying market offers even further protection for consumers. For example, the *Chicken Delight* franchise tying arrangement, which the Ninth Circuit condemned, involved a nondominant franchisor who required franchisees to purchase various food items and cooking supplies from itself.[39] The franchise fee was zero and the franchisor obtained its return entirely from the supplies.[40] The tie very likely produced an increased number of franchises, increased product sales, and increased welfare by both general welfare and consumer welfare measures. But if for some reason it did not, customers could always go across the street to Kentucky Fried Chicken or McDonald's. In sum, TCE has extended the Chicago School analysis to the ubiquitous situations in which price discrimination ties are imposed by nonmonopolists.

Price discrimination ties, even by a monopolist, are rarely candidates for condemnation on that ground because in the great majority of cases they improve consumer as well as general welfare. In general, such ties involve second-degree price discrimination, which is typically more benign than third-degree price discrimination.

In a third-degree price discrimination scheme a seller is able to identify *ex ante* customers who exhibit differential willingness to pay for some good and charge them different prices. For example, a seller might charge commercial users of its stereo equipment $100 and residential users $60.[41] This type of discrimination creates a discontinuity in marginal valuation that transfers some sales from high-value to low-value customers. Consumer welfare can be reduced even if output remains constant. In this illustration, for example, a commercial user who valued the stereo at $90 would be denied the sale. Rather, that unit would be sold to someone for $60 even though she valued it at far less than $90. As a result, economists have known for nearly a century that third-degree price discrimination reduces welfare unless it results in an output increase.

By contrast, in the typical variable-proportion tying case the seller reduces the price of the tying good and increases the price of the tied good; however, the latter price is the same for all. For example, a manufacturer might cut the price of its printer from the stand-alone amount of $400 and instead charge $200, but it would raise the price of tied cartridges from $25 to $40. In that case the seller would earn more from buyers who used the printer more intensely, because they consume more ink cartridges. The distortions come from the reduced price for the printer, which favors consumers and brings more of them into the market, but also from the increased price of the cartridge, which raises per use variable costs.[42] Significantly, however, the higher cartridge price is the same for everyone. Such ties can benefit consumers in a wider variety of circumstances, even in the rare case where output falls as a result of the tie.[43] Further, such arrangements are common even in competitive markets. In that case when consumers find them unfavorable they can always substitute away.

This analysis also suggests that vertical restraints that segregate buyers can be more harmful price discrimination devices than ties are. While variable proportion ties represent instances of second-degree price discrimination, segregation restraints discriminate in the third degree. For example, the manufacturer who uses vertically imposed customer restrictions to segregate customers by class or the patentee who uses field-of-use restrictions for the same end is engaged in third-degree price discrimination.[44] Welfare harm is more likely, although even here it should not be presumed.

TCE has also informed our understanding of exclusionary practices by dominant firms. One example is the well-known debate between Areeda and Turner against Oliver Williamson over the proper test for predatory pricing. Williamson believed that the Areeda-Turner predatory pricing test was too lenient and did not adequately address the threats imposed by longer-run strategic behavior.[45] Another area in which TCE has reinvigorated the analysis of exclusionary practices is raising rivals' costs (RRC), which begins with the premise that many exclusionary practices are more easily rationalized as devices for increasing rivals' costs than as mechanisms for excluding them from the market altogether. In general, the RRC literature has attempted to restore a meaningful conception of anticompetitive exclusion without a return to the more severe apprehensions of the structuralist school, which tended to view rivals and smaller firms as anesthetized patients rather than as vigorous competitors who could respond in kind.[46] Some Chicago School writers have been very critical.[47] Resources are in fact quite mobile, but transaction costs and the other attendant costs of resource movement must be taken into account as well.

"Exclusionary" distribution agreements can present analogous problems in transaction cost analysis. For example, interbrand free riding can be a particular problem for manufacturers dealing through multibrand retailers.[48] Ordinarily a manufacturer engaged in self-distribution would not have an incentive to retail the products of rivals in addition to its own. Exclusivity arrangements imposed on dealers can make the manufacturer-dealer relationship behave more like a single firm would behave. Nevertheless, in a few cases exclusive dealing and foreclosing ties can also impair competition.[49] Other things equal, a dealer and its customers are best off when supply markets are competitive and unreasonably exclusionary arrangements can prevent such competition from developing.

. . .

TCE has served to limit antitrust analysis from the structuralist expansionism of the 1970s and earlier, but also as a corrective for those inclined to see the movement of resources as essentially costless. Both are extremes that antitrust policy should avoid.

Part III

Competition Law and Its Synergies with Other Areas of Law

6

Anticompetitive Government Regulation

D. Daniel Sokol

Frank Easterbrook's article *The Limits of Antitrust*[1] focused on the concern of false positives and the overly large role of private rights of action in antitrust cases dealing with monopoly power. The concern with private rights within the United States at the time was unique relative to the rest of the world. At the time that Easterbrook wrote his article, the problems of private antitrust made up over 90 percent of all antitrust actions in the United States. Given a court system that had a weak filter for the use of these rights at the summary judgment and pleading stages, Chicago School thinkers viewed overly broad private rights as a significant problem to effective antitrust. In addition, with the small number of other jurisdictions that had antitrust law at the time, let alone enforced it (with private rights under these other systems minimal, especially given the lack of treble damages), Easterbrook may not be entirely faulted for thinking that the core issue in antitrust enforcement was American in nature and focused on the overly broad use of private rights.

The problem with Easterbrook's article is that it assumed away the competition problems that were not specifically within antitrust law. The larger problem of creating a competitive market requires a broader examination of competition policy rather than just competition/antitrust law. Easterbrook overlooked one key area in which monopoly power may in fact be both durable and harmful to competition across the globe—government-imposed restraints on competition. Indeed, the real limit of antitrust is that antitrust enforcement (particularly public enforcement) may not reach the type of conduct that is most harmful to economic development—anticompetitive government regulation.

Particularly surprising about Easterbrook's emphasis on private rights of action is that he wrote his article during a period of significant regulatory change in the United States to remove anticompetitive government regulation. One of the mantras of the Reagan administration was that regulation might be used as an anticompetitive restraint. As President Reagan famously declared in his first inaugural address, "government is not the solution to our problem; government is the problem."[2] Yet Reagan was not the first to note that government might allow rent seeking by interest groups in the form of government restraints. Indeed, Easterbrook's colleagues at the University of Chicago in the economics department and business school, such as Stigler, Peltzman, and Becker (among others), pioneered work involving public choice and regulation, including public choice and antitrust.[3]

Government may restrain competition for welfare-enhancing reasons. This might be because of market failure, such as a situation of natural monopoly or certain situations of information asymmetries. Competition policy does not concern itself with these types of restraints, except to determine in the first instance when such a restraint promotes competition. Rather, competition policy is concerned with those restrains that limit competition.[4]

This chapter explains the causes and dynamics of anticompetitive government regulation. The chapter suggests both the potential of antitrust to address the behavior and the limits of antitrust in this regard. It then details the types of action that agencies around the world undertake against anticompetitive government restraints. Unlike other areas of antitrust action by competition agencies, action against public restraints may not take the form of enforcement in all cases. Indeed, in some cases an antitrust agency may undertake competition advocacy when there is no way under competition law to litigate against such conduct. This chapter concludes by suggesting how competition agencies should prioritize the kinds of advocacy interventions that may prove to be more successful in terms of addressing this set of limits of antitrust.

The Nature of Government Restraints

In *The Limits of Antitrust*, Easterbrook noted that competitors could use antitrust laws to raise rivals' costs. He wrote:

> Antitrust litigation is attractive as a method of raising rivals' costs because of the asymmetrical structure of incentives. The plaintiff's costs of litigation will be smaller than the defendant's. The plaintiff need only file the complaint and serve demands for discovery. If the plaintiff wins, the defendant will bear these legal costs. The defendant, on the other hand, faces treble damages and injunction, as well as its own (and even its rival's) costs of litigation. The principal burden of discovery falls on the defendant. The defendant is apt to be larger, with more files to search, and to have control of more pertinent documents than the plaintiff. . . . The books are full of suits by rivals for the purpose, or with the effect, of reducing competition and increasing price.[5]

Easterbrook was correct in this analysis. However, this chapter argues that government may be more effective in raising rivals' costs than a private plaintiff. Firms may undertake strategic behavior to shape the nature of opportunities in the market to better increase profits.[6] One way that firms may behave strategically is through the creation of various barriers to entry.[7]

There are a number of ways that firms can get government to create barriers to entry or other strategies to raise rivals' costs. Government may favor firms through a process of "competitive neutrality." Other factors that may allow government involvement to raise rivals' costs may be direct or indirect subsidies or regulatory schemes that affect a particular market participant (such as exclusive rights or grandfather clauses that impact only new entrants). Moreover, governments can create direct and indirect subsidies for favored firms. The worldwide impact of state aids and subsidies is significant. In one study such support represents 3.6 percent of the world GDP.[8]

Firms might use government regulation as a means to block innovation if such innovation was to facilitate new entry. Similarly, interest groups might create barriers to entry for new firms and new modes of competition or seek to create immunities to antitrust laws by sector or to create state-sponsored monopolies. Indeed, new cross-country research finds that large firms with market power are the ones most likely to successfully lobby government.[9]

In another strategy for raising rivals' costs, government might create anticompetitive regulation to support state-owned enterprises (SOEs). In an area with increased nationalizations due to the financial crisis and the increased global reach of sovereign wealth funds and Chinese SOEs, the impact of SOEs on antitrust is significant and will continue to be for some time. Government may provide SOEs certain anticompetitive advantages when such SOEs compete against private firms. Indeed, government has certain incentives to create an uneven playing field in those markets where its SOEs compete with private firms. These government restraints might result in direct preferences, such as below-market rates for loans or subsidies. Some of the preferences might be indirect, such as implicit loan guarantees (that the government will bail out an SOE in case of potential bankruptcy) for favorable lending, regulatory preferences such as the creation of a statutory monopoly position, limitations on foreign ownership, implicit subsidies through a lack of taxation, or more lax corporate governance requirements vis-à-vis private firms. These anticompetitive government regulations impact the ability of private firms to compete with SOEs.[10]

Why Public Restraints?

The economic theory of regulation (ETR) provides insights into the nature of how anticompetitive regulation occurs and the motivations for such restraints.[11] ETR is a subset of public choice. ETR assumes that political players are rational actors who seek to maximize their utility. Political actors, therefore, may use the coercive power of the state to benefit producers over consumers. Producer interests are more powerful in that they are more highly concentrated and more targeted. This allows producers to use regulation for a wealth transfer to themselves from consumers. Though scholars have made a number of contributions to creating complex models of ETR,[12] this chapter uses a simple ETR model to explain why public restraints come about and why they are so resistant to attack by competition agencies.

Firms can make a decision to benefit from private or public restraints. Whereas the market can self-correct when there are competition problems (at least theoretically), public restraints are far more durable. For example, for firms that seek to collude, it is more effective to have the government create a cartel than for firms to do so privately. A government-sanctioned cartel means that cartelists need not worry about cartel defection. The government serves as the cartel manager. As a result, the cartel will be long lasting. Moreover, because of the immunity from antitrust, firms in a government-sanctioned cartel do not need to concern themselves with civil or criminal penalties for their cartel participation because of the cartel's immunity. The cartel members also do not have to expend additional resources to prevent detection of the cartel, as the cartel activities are public with government sponsorship.

Types of Restraints

The nature of the limitations of antitrust law due to immunities, whether explicit or implicit, set the parameters for the types of antitrust enforcement that can be used in a given country. Thus, immunities serve to limit the scope of action that antitrust agencies can undertake.

There are a number of ways in which immunities to antitrust may be introduced. Certain immunities might be included in the antitrust law at the time that the law comes into effect. These may be introduced as a function of ETR because of sector regulators who push to keep certain areas of regulation exclusive to themselves for turf-related reasons instead of concurrently through antitrust law or through the court system.

One set of immunities is through the substitution of sector regulation for antitrust enforcement. Sector regulators may view antitrust as an encroachment of control in that sector. As such, the antitrust agency is a potential threat for funding, control, and prestige vis-à-vis the sector regulator. Therefore, the sector regulators may defensively attempt to limit the role of antitrust law in the sector. One reason for the substitution of competition oversight by a sector regulator may be benign, such as industry experience. However, ETR suggests that a reason for the choice of exclusive sector oversight may be that sector regulation is more prone to capture by interest groups. Sector regulators have more concentrated interest groups than antitrust, which is a law of general applicability.

Historically, sector regulators have served a different role than antitrust enforcers. Many sector regulators around the world preceded antitrust agencies. During a time of greater state control over the economy, sector regulation served a market replacement function rather than a market facilitation function. Consequently, the nature of the legal inquiry for sector regulation tends to be broader. Whereas antitrust embraces efficiency as its goal either explicitly or implicitly around the world, oftentimes sector regulators have a broader set of objectives. This may include fairness, supply or quality of service, diversity of participants, job preservation, or things that might fit into the broad notions of "public good" or "public interest," which include efficiency with these other concerns.

Such broad legal criteria allow for more direct political considerations to be taken than would be the case by antitrust enforcers, who overall tend to be more technocratic and isolated from concentrated industry pressures. The concentrated industry pressure also increases the chance of capture of the sector regulator by its regulated industries and those legislators interested in that sector.[13]

In some cases, ineffective courts can create entry barriers. Courts may be overwhelmed by complexity, particularly in industries where there is a high level of specialization, such as telecommunications. However, it is not only with complex regulatory areas that courts may create public restraints. United States case law development provides an example of how courts can create and expand public restraints. As Damien Gerard's chapter in this volume explores in greater detail, the United States has a state action exemption to antitrust. This judicial public restraint has its origin in the Supreme Court case *Parker v. Brown*.[14] In *Parker*, the competition issue involved mandatory state government restraints in California that controlled the marketing and sale of agricultural products.[15] The product in question was raisins, where 90 percent of California raisins were shipped out of state.[16] The effect of *Parker* was to shield the anticompetitive California law that imposed additional costs on out-of-state consumers. More generally, *Parker* allowed for state laws to be used by private parties in an anticompetitive way to benefit themselves through state action at the expense of consumers. In later Supreme Court jurisprudence, the Supreme Court created a two-pronged test in *California Retail Liquor Dealers Ass'n v. Midcal Aluminum, Inc.*,[17] to determine the limits of the exemption for state supervision. The two-pronged test required a party to show that its conduct was (1) "clearly articulated and affirmatively expressed as state policy;" and (2) " 'actively supervised' by the State itself."[18] While on its face the test would seem to limit the state action exemption, in reality in over a quarter century since *Midcal*, courts have allowed the scope of the state action exemption to grow.

Advocacy

Oftentimes, competition agencies cannot bring enforcement actions against public restraints because the behavior in question has immunity from competition law. Therefore, the primary method by which antitrust agencies reduce public restraints is through competition advocacy. There are a number of elements to competition advocacy. Advocacy may take the form of an *ex ante* competition regulatory impact assessment of proposed legislation. This can be either formal, as part of the legislative process such as submissions and testimony, or more informal through letters, legal briefs, studies, or discussions with legislators or regulators. In the long term, competition advocacy also entails constituency development of procompetitive business regulation and market studies by the antitrust agency of current measures undertaken by the state that may negatively impact competition.[19]

Advocacy starts from a presumption that market competition is superior to government-created regulation. Only when there is a market malfunction might there be a justification for government regulatory intervention. The danger that the competition agency seeks to overcome is that the regulatory process may be hijacked by interest groups who might use government power to create anticompetitive restrictions through the coercive nature of government power.

Competition advocacy will never be able to eliminate rent seeking entirely. However, it can increase the costs of rent seeking so that certain rent-seeking legislation or regulation may never be introduced, may be modified to become less anticompetitive, or may lead to overturning certain existing laws and/or regulations. Additionally, taking Easterbrook's error/cost analysis into consideration, the difference between advocacy and other areas of antitrust is that the risk of false positives is much smaller regarding advocacy against government restraints than with enforcement.

The International Competition Network (ICN) has noted three factors that seem to impact the likely success of a competition advocacy intervention. The first factor is the information asymmetry between the competition agency and those that push the restraint. Antitrust agencies may not always know that an anticompetitive restraint has been proposed. Thus, it is important when in the time line of a proposed government restraint the competition agency becomes aware of its impact on the ability to prevent (or in a second-best scenario, to minimize the impact of) the restraint. The more time an agency has, the greater the likelihood that it can take action against the restraint. A second factor is whether the antitrust agency's consultation on legislation is compulsory or noncompulsory. In this sense, can the competition agency undertake advocacy on its own initiative or must another part of government request the recommendations that the competition advocacy work would provide? The third factor is how binding the recommendation of the antitrust authority is for changing policy. The more binding the recommendation is, the greater the chance that the advocacy will be effective.

In practice, measuring the success of competition advocacy is difficult to do. Does one measure based on a change in regulatory outcome? Does one include the amount of time spent and the political capital expended? Does one measure success based upon the improvement in consumer welfare? Does one look to the number of times interventions are made or in particular sectors in the economy? What is the time frame used to measure success? Does one measure success by surveys, agency statements, independent experts, and/or by self studies? However one decides to measure the effectiveness of competition advocacy, there do not seem to be any easy answers. Most agencies merely list successful advocacy efforts or a list of all advocacy attempts. This suggests the need for better and more consistent measurements to create metrics for "success."

In the United States, there have been two studies to try to quantify the effects of advocacy. Both suggest only limited inferences can be reached on the effectiveness of the advocacy efforts. The first study addressed Federal Trade Commission (FTC) advocacy from 1987 to 1989. It found that in 40 percent of advocacy interventions for which recipients provided feedback, "the governmental entity's actions were totally or in large part consistent with at least some of the FTC's recommendations and that any action taken was largely or partly because of those recommendations."[20] Whether or not the FTC interventions actually influenced the outcome was unclear. The second study of FTC efforts came in the form of an FTC submission to the Organisation for Economic Co-operation and Development Competition Committee. That study found a stronger connection between FTC advocacy efforts and regulatory outcome. The study noted:

> Ninety-four percent of respondents said that the FTC's comments were considered during deliberations, and 54 percent of respondents—and 79 percent of those who had an opinion—answered that the FTC influenced the ultimate outcome. Only 11 percent of respondents did not believe the FTC's comment had an influence on the ultimate outcome. More specifically, the survey also suggests that when an outcome is consistent with the FTC position, the advocacy likely played some role in achieving that outcome. Of those who responded that the outcome was consistent with FTC recommendations, 79 percent of respondents believed that the advocacy influenced the outcome.[21]

How much influence the advocacy had in the outcome was not clear, as the impact of advocacy is one of a number of factors that influenced the final outcome. Thus, there are endogeneity concerns in drawing inferences from such surveys and each of the surveys presented potential bias in the responses. Moreover, what the FTC did not measure was whether the resources expended on the advocacy interventions were worth the costs relative to other areas in which such resources could have been expended.

Public Choice Pushback from Government

ETR teaches that concentrated groups have more power than more diffused groups. Antitrust agencies, in effect, take over the advocacy function of society as a whole against special interests. In this sense, antitrust agencies face an uphill battle in convincing other regulators and legislators about the importance of competition. Other government units, regulated firms, industry associations, civil society groups (including bar associations), and the public at large all possess political power that might be harnessed in favor of advocacy. However, these same stakeholders may try to thwart advocacy efforts by the antitrust agency.

Competition agencies must overcome voter ignorance and information asymmetries. Voters may be rational, but rationally ignorant in their choice of political views when it comes to economic impact of certain policies.[22] Competition advocacy can alter the information asymmetry to provide information to voters about the true costs of various public restraints. An approach that reaches the broader voting population can embed a larger competition culture that will support the reform goals of competition advocacy. These grassroots efforts for the creation of a competition culture change the balance of power for a competition agency in its efforts. Less voter ignorance means that a competition agency can create a broader constituency to support advocacy efforts.

One broad issue with attacking government restraints is that it takes competition law and policy away from the more technocratic decision-making issues such as determining the efficiency of a particular merger (for which there is little political interference) to issues of industrial policy (where there is significantly greater political interference). Unlike a merger that can be decided on the merits, attacking what are political decisions of industrial policy opens up competition authorities to potential retaliation by other branches of government and other interest groups. Interest group theory helps to explain case selection within antitrust agencies.[23] ETR calculations impact the priorities of an agency to undertake advocacy work by subject or by particular type of advocacy. Indeed, antitrust agencies (and antitrust law) may be subject to capture in various forms.[24] This can take the form of less funding for the agency, the removal of certain powers from the competition agency, or the creation of an additional agency that has some competition-related functions that haswith a broader mandate of a "public interest" that looks beyond notions of economic efficiency to guide policy.[25]

Other governmental actors, producers, or consumers at large, in their own ways, may seek to influence the goals of an antitrust agency. Should an antitrust agency not come out with the "right" finding in its advocacy work, it may face a loss of prestige, a reduction in funding for the agency, or other potential penalties such as a different organizational structure that might make it less independent. The mere threat of such changes might be enough to limit the potential scope of agency-level decision making on advocacy or other issues.

Antitrust policy and antitrust law themselves are functions of the larger institutional context of law and policy in a given country. The institutional context provides the parameters for action for particular policy choices and agency discretion. That is, antitrust agencies must determine when and how to take action based on political economy factors in their advocacy work. The same types of capture and ETR concerns that impact other parts of government also may affect antitrust agencies.[26] An agency may be constrained in the types of advocacy work that it may undertake because of concerns of the external interests potentially impacted by competition advocacy. An agency's attempt at competition advocacy may expose the agency to attacks from these interest groups both inside and outside of government.

Perhaps one reason that agencies are unwilling to spend significant resources on advocacy work is that the private interests of staff within the agency are not in favor of advocacy. Limited agency resources constrain advocacy efforts. Antitrust agencies allocate limited funding for advocacy in part because advocacy work takes away from resources devoted to enforcement, and lawyers, in particular, may favor bringing cases (and not necessarily the right sort of cases).[27] Competition advocacy work for antitrust lawyers does not bring the personal rewards that litigating cases would in terms of long-term career prospects. Hence, lawyers will tend to prioritize cases over advocacy because of the rewards for internal promotion and for financial remuneration outside of the agency in private practice.

Not all public choice concerns regarding limits on an agency to fight against public restraints are based upon interest group theory. Popular sentiment (because of voter ignorance) may need to be combated as well. For example, during a period of high energy prices, the impulse on the part of the population as a whole (to be sure aided by interest groups that would benefit from such a policy) may be to create legislation against price gouging even when there are explanations of the behavior based upon the economics of the industry such as supply and demand.

Majoritarian interests make the competition agency subject to greater political pressures. Sometimes there needs to be a political safety valve, and the least bad outcome for a competition agency may not be to eliminate the restraint (because it will fail and also lose political capital) but to make it the least harmful restraint possible. In other cases, a successful intervention may result in the creation of a sunset provision for the regulation. In yet other circumstances, a competition agency may formulate an advocacy intervention through a market study. If managed correctly, an agency's market study on such topics can provide political cover against a majoritarian backlash. The competition agency may well know the answer to a particular increase in price for a certain industry, but may undertake a more comprehensive report with which to provide political cover to curtail far more anticompetitive effects that a proposed law could create.

A breakdown on how authorities apportion their time suggests that advocacy work has been undervalued at competition agencies (see Table 6.1). A 2009 ICN report[28] reveals the low percentage of the total competition budget.

Overall, the report states that agencies estimated that their competition advocacy work was between 1 and 15 percent of budgetary allocations. The agencies in Table 6.1 provide a sample of this allocation range. It seems that a number of the competition agencies of the more developed countries spend a smaller total percentage of their resources on advocacy work. It is not clear why this is the case. Is it because the competition message is more effective because the regulatory environment is more promarket? Is it because agencies in the developed world have more tasks and can take on tougher cases that are resource and time intensive, such as monopolization cases? Given

Table 6.1 Spending on competition advocacy

Competition authority	*Percentage of resources devoted to advocacy*
European Commission	10
Honduras	2.26
Japan	1.5
Korea	0.3
Mexico	3
New Zealand	2.7
Russia	10
Spain	8.5
Switzerland	10
U.K. Office of Fair Trading	6
U.S. Federal Trade Commission	1–2
Zambia	10–15

that the European Commission spends 10 percent of its budget on advocacy work and developed country agencies in Spain and the United Kingdom spend 8.5 and 6 percent respectively, whereas the U.S. Federal Trade Commission spends 1 to 2 percent, New Zealand 2.7 percent, and Japan 1.5 percent,[29] the possibility that more advanced agencies require fewer advocacy resources is not entirely explanatory. It may be that some agencies expend fewer resources because they are more efficient with their allocation of budgetary resources according to how such agencies measure success. The other alternative is a troubling one—that agencies significantly underspend on competition advocacy, because of both internal and external public choices.

Next Steps

Agencies seem to want the power to undertake *ex ante* regulatory impact assessments. One theory (beyond that of bureaucratic creep) is that *ex ante* interventions are easier to achieve and may have bigger cost savings given the amount of effort necessary to reach an advocacy objective. There are costs and benefits to granting a competition agency the power to provide *ex ante* impact assessment. A regulatory impact assessment is a significant use of resources. On the one hand, if the competition agency runs the regulatory impact assessment, it risks using its scarce resources on regulatory matters instead of other matters such as private restraints, like cartels. On the other hand, if the competition agency runs the impact assessment, it is more likely able to focus on government restraints and to take more control over the impact assessment than if it merely submits nonbinding comments on the regulatory impact. In most countries, legislators do not have a binding legal obligation to incorporate comments by a competition agency made as part of a regulatory impact assessment of a particular law.[30]

The ultimate goal for many competition agencies is to have a set of *ex ante* and *ex post* powers akin to those in South Korea. In South Korea, the Korean Fair Trade Commission (KFTC) chairman has ministerial rank in the government. This means that informal procompetitive interventions can be made at the highest level of policy discussions. The ministerial rank also potentially has a greater impact in terms of the persuasiveness of other forms of competition advocacy. Additionally, Korean law (Article 63 of the Monopoly Regulation and Fair Trade Act) mandates that other government ministries that seek to enact new law or amend existing laws must consult with the KFTC and a Regulatory Reform Committee (headed by the chairman of the KFTC) *ex ante*.[31]

These *ex ante* consultations seem to impact the scope of new government restraints being introduced. From 2006 to 2009, for example, 63 new anti-competitive regulations were prevented from enactment.[32] These ranged in practice from entry restrictions, restrictions on business activities, price controls, to regulations that served to undermine consumer interests and creation of government facilitated cartels and other types of cases.[33] Similarly, Korean law mandates that new regulations pass through a competition regulatory impact assessment that analyzes the competitive effects of such regulations.[34] Because of the success of the program, what is difficult to quantify is the number of laws and regulations that do not even get introduced because of the knowledge that the KFTC will be able to limit the anticompetitive effect of such laws.

The U.S. experience with health care and financial reforms provides examples of the very limited role that *ex ante* competition advocacy plays without the powers that the KFTC has. In both areas of reform, the U.S. competition agencies played a minor role in shaping the debate. Both President Obama and the U.S. Congress framed health care reform as one of competition and lowering costs. However, decision making happened at more senior levels of government than with the competition authorities. What input the agencies provided was marginal, and very little time at the agencies was spent on providing speeches, workshops, and presentations on what competition meant in health care. Likewise, in the overhaul of financial regulation, the U.S. competition agencies played a very minor role. Indeed, the FTC even lost some of its consumer protection power as Congress created a new stand-alone financial services consumer protection agency and reassigned some FTC staff to it.

An alternative strategy (or one done in conjunction with *ex ante* review) is to focus on *ex post* assessment of laws and regulations. The KFTC took stock of various regulations over a ten-year period to modify or eliminate fifty-six, fifty-one, twenty-three, and sixty-eight anticompetitive regulations in 2004, 2005, 2007, and 2008 respectively.[35] Similarly, Australia undertook a comprehensive review of its laws and regulations for anticompetitive effect.[36] This review, as part of Australia's National Competition Policy launched in 1995, took ten years and identified hundreds of laws and regulations that limited competition. After prioritizing policies for review, Australia revised most of the anticompetitive policies.[37]

This chapter takes the viewpoint that the priority for an agency in its advocacy should be to undertake *ex post* reviews of public restraints. Ultimately, this alternative focus may prove to be more politically palatable and effective (regardless of the increased cost of overcoming more *ex post* competition advocacy) because benefits can be quantified. Even though an agency may get a bigger bang for the buck with *ex ante* advocacy, it is difficult to prove to both the political class and the public at large the cost savings of public restraints never created. Moreover, this battle over the prevention of public restraints occurs with other interest groups that may seek a reduction of funding from the competition agency. A focus on the removal of existing public restraints illustrates real cost savings to the overall population and to the political class. It creates the political capital necessary to eventually push for the powers of a regulatory impact assessment.

For an *ex post* approach to be successful, there are a number of factors that a competition agency must embrace. First, there must be a political backing of the advocacy program by the top echelons of government. This is a problem with competition law and policy generally. *Ex post* assessment requires a sell at the "retail level" of what competition law and policy actually does for the population as a whole and for a country's political leadership. To create a competition culture means often linking competition policy to improving country competitiveness, reducing government waste, and providing concrete (rather than theoretical) justifications that the removal or reduction of anticompetitive government restraints will lead to economic gains. Similarly, it requires that any restraints that continue are the least distortive of competition possible. Creating a competition culture is more difficult in the post–financial crisis world, where a significant proportion of legislators and voters have lost faith in the market. However, *ex post* analysis allows for quantification of savings to consumers. A second criterion for the successful elimination or reduction of government restraints is to create a set of financial incentives (rewards) for those parts of government that undertake such a review. A third criterion that creates success is the process that evaluates the review of public restraints. A final criterion is to provide adequate resources to create institutional machinery to get through such comprehensive review.[38]

An example of where to focus *ex post* review is in procurement, which may be a significant overcharge for governments—some studies suggest a conservative estimate of over 20 percent.[39] Procurement is an area in which advocacy can be linked to broader cartel enforcement. In many countries, budgetary expenditures on public procurement make up a significant part of a government's total budget. To the extent that private companies can collude in procurement through bid rigging, a competition authority can assist through advocacy by better designed bidding rules that prevent bid rigging and detect it when it occurs. Advocacy in the area of procurement may include suggesting bidding rules for government contracts that make the possibility of collusion less likely, such as auction design or tender rules.

Overall, the emphasis on removing barriers to effective government procurement not only aids improved societal welfare, but the impact improves the standing of competition authorities in a country where the potential political backlash for this sort of advocacy will be relatively minimal as compared to other areas of advocacy where there might be concentrated interests or other values that the government might want to support over increased competition (such as industrial policy). An emphasis on making procurement more efficient and effective saves the government money. Moreover, it does so in a way that develops goodwill and credibility for the competition agency with other parts of government. Bid rigging affects not just the market but is also a crime upon the government. As such, the prevention of bid rigging through advocacy efforts creates goodwill for the competition agency that allows for greater development of its political capital. The agency can then use this political capital when it undertakes advocacy with more contentious issues of public restraint that might involve sector regulators or legislators.

Two brief examples on the effect of advocacy on procurement provide stories of tangible benefits. The Canadian Competition Bureau has linked advocacy on procurement with cartel enforcement. Since the outreach program began in 2005, the Competition Bureau has trained over 3,000 procurement officials in issues related to cartel offenses that emerge in the procurement context. As a result of this advocacy training, detection of bid rigging has increased.[40] Similarly, Chile has also undertaken advocacy work in the area of procurement. The Chilean competition agency has issued over 300 reports on municipal bidding documents.[41] These efforts have raised the agency's standing within government and given it increased political capital.

. . .

The real limit to antitrust is in public restraints. Competition agencies should shift more resources to attacking such restraints in lieu of money focused on traditional enforcement against dominant firms. With the advocacy function of a competition agency to attack public restraints, agencies should respond to public choice concerns and attack existing regulations where there is not strong political support. Such an approach will allow competition agencies to build their political capital. This in turn will allow competition agencies to undertake more advocacy against public restraints where the political resistance to such change will be stronger.

7

A Global Perspective on State Action

Damien M. B. Gerard

In industrialized countries, state intervention is often presented as a major source of interference with the market. As former Federal Trade Commission (FTC) Chairman Timothy Muris once famously put it: "[A]ttempting to protect competition by focusing solely on private restraints is like trying to stop the flow of water at a fork in a stream by blocking only one of the channels. Unless you block both channels, you are not likely to even slow, much less stop, the flow. Eventually, all the water will flow toward the unblocked channel."[1] The focus of this chapter is with the "other" channel—that of government-erected barriers to competition, i.e., public restraints or "state action"—and on the appropriate means to discipline it. While acknowledging that those restraints carry the potential of harming allocative efficiency as much as private anticompetitive practices do, this chapter raises a question of principle: should public restraints be considered through the same efficiency lenses as private practices? In contrast, should government be allowed to interfere with competition for reasons of public policy? Consequently, should state action be subject to the discipline of competition law—i.e., antitrust—or to another system of analysis and, in the latter case, which one?

The argument developed hereinafter is rooted in three basic premises. First and foremost, while public restraints that protect "special interests at the expense of society" must be disciplined, they should also be distinguished from those restraints whereby governments pursue legitimate redistributive objectives, notably to "reduce the societal strains that increased efficiency and globalization may cause."[2] The search for the relevant criteria on which to draw that distinction constitutes the central inquiry of the present chapter. Second, disciplining state action requires some form of hierarchical relation between the public authority that is at the source of the distorting measure and the one endowed with the power to assess the validity thereof, i.e., a central, federal or supranational authority empowered to review regional, state, or national choices. A variety of factors, such as the degree of proximity between the relevant authorities, can of course affect the legitimacy of that hierarchical assessment. Third, competition law, like any discipline, embodies a particular rationality that focuses on the protection of the process of competition. Its reach is therefore constrained to ensure a level playing field between market actors conducive to efficient outcomes.[3] Likewise, its effectiveness depends on a precommitment to the free market, rooted in a willingness to allow private initiatives to flourish and the contestability of markets to prevail.

In turn, this chapter argues that the discipline of competition law does not accommodate well the variety of redistributive objectives pursued by public authorities. As a result, it does not appear particularly well suited for distinguishing between legitimate and other public restraints. Conversely, when competition law attempts to do so, it often finds itself constrained to stretch the boundaries of its own rationality, which entails a risk of inconsistencies and double standards. This is notably because the assessment of public restraints requires consideration for a broad range of public interest justifications, which competition law does not allow. Subsequently, this chapter explores the opportunity of submitting public restraints to an alternative ubiquitous discipline, that of trade law as applicable either within or between sovereign states, and it endeavors to determine the conditions necessary to ensure the sustainability of such an approach. The underlying rationale lies in the fact that both competition and trade disciplines pursue the same overarching allocative efficiency objective. Because competition and trade law address different actors, namely private economic entities on the one hand and public authorities on the other hand, their respective systems of analysis factors in different variables. Provided that the scope of the notion of obstacle to trade is defined sufficiently broadly, trade law appears more promising to achieve the right balance between the pursuance of allocative efficiency and the necessary deference for governments' sovereign choices and, hence, to address public restraints. In other words, its system of analysis appears better suited to distinguish between the protection of parochial interests and genuine concerns to achieve redistributive objectives.

State Action and the Limits of Competition

As noted, this section discusses the opportunity of submitting the assessment of the legitimacy of public restraints to the competition law system of analysis, i.e., efficiency-related standards. Conversely, it questions whether competition requirements constitute the proper criteria for determining the justified or unjustified character of state measures affecting market actors' freedom to compete. In doing so, it draws on the respective experience of three jurisdictions, namely the People's Republic of China (PRC), the United States, and the European Union.

PRC: Integrating the Control of Public and Private Power?

A peculiar feature of the PRC's Anti-Monopoly Law (AML) consists of the coexistence of provisions prohibiting private anticompetitive practices on the one hand and abuses of administrative powers by provincial and local governments on the other hand. The latter, set forth in Chapter V of the AML,[4] target a broad range of practices such as: (1) requirements to deal, purchase, or use commodities provided by designated local undertakings (Art. 32); (2) discriminatory charges and technical barriers to trade (Art. 33); (3) discriminatory bidding requirements (Art. 34); (4) restrictions on investment or establishment by businesses originating from outside the relevant region (Art. 35); and (5) the prohibition of regulations or practices compelling businesses to engage in prohibited monopolistic activities or otherwise eliminating or restricting competition (Arts. 36 and 37). A number of those provisions (Arts. 32, 33, and 35) address protectionist obstacles to the circulation of goods and to corporate investment and establishment within the PRC, which constitute "a chronic problem that is found throughout China."[5] In effect, they enshrine principles similar to those of the U.S. Commerce Clause and of the EU internal market provisions, i.e., free trade principles. Other provisions (Arts. 36 and 37) amount to a particularly far-reaching restatement of the so-called state action doctrine, as conceived by the European Court of Justice and *a contrario* by the U.S. Supreme Court, whereby practices (mandated) by public authorities are not immune from the discipline of competition law.

Even though the means provided for the enforcement of the provisions on abuses of administrative power appear particularly weak, Eleanor Fox praised the AML's attempt at integrating the control of abusive public and private power because, in her view, the "problems are integral" so that "they are helpfully placed under one legal roof."[6] Since "market-blocking public abuses have a natural home in antitrust," she further argued, the PRC has "designed a modern law" by giving private and public restraints "one home."[7] While that proposition is certainly appealing, questions remain: (1) Should public interest justifications not form an integral part of the assessment of the abusive character of the exercise of administrative power? (2) Does the AML allow for such justifications? (3) In the affirmative, isn't there a risk that such justifications could interfere with the strict discipline to which private restraints ought to be submitted according to other AML provisions, such as Arts. 13 or 17? and (4) Given those risks, in particular in a jurisdiction where the competition law discipline is relatively nascent and the rule of law remains vulnerable, is it sound to advocate a merger of the standards applicable to public and private restraints or to allow different standards to coexist under the AML label, even though they belong to proximate yet distinct disciplines? Given the AML's early stage of development, the practice of other jurisdictions that have a long-standing tradition of competition law enforcement, notably the United States and the European Union, can assist in answering these questions.

United States: State Action as a Limit to Competition?

In the United States, competition law requirements as embodied in the Sherman Act have been referred to by the Supreme Court as the "Magna Carta of free enterprise."[8] Interestingly, the Sherman Act is also "neutral" as to its addressees: it targets "[e]very contract, . . . , or conspiracy, in restraint of trade" and "[e]very person who shall monopolize, or attempt to monopolize, . . . any part of the trade or commerce among the several States, or with foreign nations."[9] As an exception to those general rules, the Supreme Court has developed in various opinions what is commonly referred to as the "state action exemption doctrine" whereby states are shielded from the antitrust law discipline when they engage in *bona fide* exercises of their sovereign regulatory powers. Moreover, under this doctrine, private entities are immune from antitrust liability when they act in furtherance of a "clearly articulated" state policy and under "active supervision" by the state.[10]

The two leading cases in that respect are *Parker v. Brown* (1943) and *California Liquor Dealers v. Midcal Aluminum* (1980). In *Parker v. Brown*, the Supreme Court upheld a program initiated by the California state legislature aimed to limit competition among raisin growers by allowing them to jointly set prices and output levels, i.e., to operate a cartel.[11] The Supreme Court thus found that the Sherman Act did not prohibit restraints imposed by states acting as sovereigns. Put otherwise, despite the all-encompassing wording of the Sherman Act, the Court created an exception to the supremacy of federal over state laws pursuant to the U.S. Constitution, in deference to states and in that particular case in favor of a piece of legislation enacted in the aftermath of the Great Depression.[12] In *Midcal*, the Supreme Court rejected claims that another regulatory scheme set forth by the California legislature, whereby the state compelled wholesalers and retailers to sell wine according to price schedules or fair trade contracts filed with the state by wine producers or wholesalers, was immune from liability under the state action exemption. In essence, the Court found that the California law provided for a system of resale price maintenance in violation of the Sherman Act and that the state's involvement in the system, by merely enforcing prices established by private parties, was insufficient to satisfy the requirements of *Parker v. Brown*.[13] Those two cases have inspired many others and triggered countless commentaries.[14] In 2003, the FTC undertook a comprehensive assessment of the state action exemption doctrine and found that the interpretation of both the "clear articulation" and "active supervision" criteria was relatively unsettled and had resulted in an expansion of the doctrine,[15] to the point of shielding significant anticompetitive behavior by specific state authorities or in the form of broad regulatory regimes.[16]

However, in the United States, public restraints are also subject to the alternative discipline of the Commerce Clause of the U.S. Constitution. The Supreme Court has interpreted the Commerce Clause *a contrario* as depriving the states of the power to impede interstate commerce; that interpretation is known as the "dormant" Commerce Clause. Over time, the dormant Commerce Clause has been applied to discriminatory state measures, either "facially" or at least *de facto*. Its system of analysis provides for the consideration of legitimate local interests justifying the restriction of trade as it embodies a balancing test between the effect on trade and the local interest whose protection is sought, the outcome of which is typically influenced by the nature of that interest and the proportionality of the means used in pursuance thereof. In spite of its limitations, the dormant Commerce Clause has proved to be effective in addressing a range of parochial and protectionist restraints originating in government. In fact, it appears that "apart from the Commerce Clause, control of parochial administrative restraints is difficult to achieve" in the United States.[17]

European Union: Competition as a Limit to State Action?

Despite—or because of—the long history of European welfare states' interferences with the market, the European Union has adopted and implemented since its inception a range of provisions aimed to address public restraints in the framework of the market integration process among its member states. Traditionally, direct state interferences with the EU common market in the form of tariffs, equivalent measures, or other nontariff barriers have been subject to the trade law discipline of the internal market provisions of the former European Community Treaty, now Treaty on the Functioning of the European Union (TFEU),[18] which have been referred to by the European Court of Justice (ECJ) as the "foundations of the [Union]."[19] Those provisions entail a similar system of analysis based on the following sequence: (1) the determination of the existence of an "obstacle to trade," (2) the pursuit of a public interest objective, and (3) the assessment of the proportionality of the measure in view of the objective pursued. Thus, if member state measures can be justified by a recognized public interest and are proportionate to the interest protected, they ought to be upheld. Indirect interferences with the common market, on the other hand, whereby member states grant special rights or subsidies to private economic actors, or enact laws or regulations aimed to shield them from competition or to limit the freedom to compete, are subject to, respectively, Articles 106 TFEU (special rights), 107 TFEU (state subsidies), and a judicially construed "state action doctrine" combining Articles 101 (and 102) TFEU with Article 4(3) of the Treaty on European Union (TEU) (principle of loyal cooperation). The law on state aids has developed into a full discipline in its own right and falls therefore beyond the scope of this section, which focuses instead on Article 106 TFEU and the "state action doctrine."

Article 106 TFEU is the only provision of the EU treaties referring expressly to state measures that restrict competition. It provides, generally, that member states cannot enact or maintain in force legal provisions that would shelter public undertakings and undertakings to which member states have granted special or exclusive rights, from the rules of the EU treaties and in particular those on competition. It also introduces one important limitation, namely that the application of the rules on competition to those undertakings cannot obstruct the performance of the tasks of general economic interest assigned to them.

Article 106 TFEU is enforced directly by the European Commission[20] and indirectly by the ECJ by means of preliminary rulings issued pursuant to

Article 267 TFEU, at the request of national courts.[21] The application of Article 106 TFEU, when combined with the EU competition rules, follows generally the same pattern. First, the Commission or the ECJ assesses the existence of a "special or exclusive right," which has been broadly defined as any "protection . . . conferred by a legislative measure on a limited number of undertakings which may substantially affect the ability of other undertakings to exercise the economic activity in question in the same geographical area under substantially equivalent conditions."[22] Second, since the grant of special or exclusive rights often results in the forming of a dominant player, most cases entail a combination of Articles 106 and 102 TFEU and the conditions for a finding of dominance need then to be established. Logically, the third step in the application of Article 106 TFEU entails the assessment of the existence of an abuse of dominant position.[23] In that respect, the ECJ has consistently held that "the mere creation of a dominant position through the grant of special or exclusive rights within the meaning of Article [106(1) TFEU] is not in itself incompatible with Article [102 TFEU]" but that "[a] Member State will be in breach of the prohibitions laid down by those two provisions only if the undertaking in question, merely by exercising the special or exclusive rights conferred upon it, is led to abuse its dominant position or where such rights are liable to create a situation in which that undertaking is led to commit such abuses."[24] The fourth step consists of identifying whether the beneficiary of the special or exclusive right is endowed with the task of operating services of general economic interest, so that the application of the rules of competition to its activities would unduly harm the performance thereof. A broad range of services can be considered of "general economic interest" and the ECJ, in particular, is generally deferential to the claims of defendants or Member States in that respect. However, such claims are subject to a proportionality test pursuant to which the Commission or the ECJ assesses whether the exclusive right granted to the relevant undertaking is necessary to enable it to perform the task of general interest that it has been assigned to, "under economically acceptable conditions."[25]

Addressing public restraints, in the form of special rights or otherwise, by resorting to the discipline of competition law, however expedient, is not immune to risks. Article 106 TFEU offers a good illustration of some of those risks. Indeed, experience shows that the notion of abuse is loosely defined in Article 106 TFEU cases; practices or "situations" are held abusive whereas they would not be labeled as such in pure Article 102 TFEU cases, i.e., if encountered on the part of a dominant undertaking to which no special or exclusive right had been granted by a Member State. Thus, for example, the ECJ has considered as being abusive in various cases the mere fact of "not being able to satisfy demand," of charging "unfair and disproportionate" service fees, or of entering a neighboring or ancillary market.[26] Such holdings imply that the mere fact of "dealing" as a dominant player and thus possibly charging monopoly prices and/or limiting output, in the absence of established exploitative or exclusionary practices, could contravene Article 102 TFEU. In turn, they suggest that Article 102 TFEU could prohibit monopolization in the absence of abusive practices. This is problematic because it leads to double standards in the application of Article 102 TFEU and, as a result, creates legal uncertainty in the interpretation of the scope of that provision, which is already complex and difficult to ascertain. This uncertainty also influences significantly the commercial behavior of numerous undertakings.

The EU provisions on competition, prominently Articles 101 and 102 TFEU, are designed as "rules applying to undertakings."[27] Interestingly, the Court of Justice has endeavored since the late 1970s and the *INNO/ATAB* case to give them vertical effect by using the principle of loyal cooperation enshrined in Article 4(3) TEU as a sort of incorporation clause with the view of constraining Member States not to impede the effectiveness of the EU rules on competition in the exercise of their regulatory powers.[28] This judicial construct is commonly referred to as the "state action doctrine" even though its ambition is not to exempt state action from the discipline of competition law but, to the contrary, to submit government measures restricting competition to such discipline.

In state action cases, the ECJ carries typically a three-pronged analysis.[29] First, it starts by acknowledging that the EU rules on competition "read in isolation" relate only to the conduct of undertakings and do not cover measures adopted by Member States in the form of legislation or regulation. In the second stage, the ECJ states that the principle of loyalty embodied in Article 4(3) TEU still "requires the Member States not to introduce or maintain in force measures, even of a legislative or regulatory nature, which may render ineffective the competition rules applicable to undertakings." Third, the ECJ considers that the principle of loyalty, combined with the rules on competition, are violated where

> a Member State requires or favours the adoption of agreements, decisions or concerted practices contrary to Article [101 TFEU] or reinforces their effects, or

> deprives its own legislation of its official character by delegating to private traders responsibility for taking economic decisions affecting the economic sphere.

In practice, the scope and limits of that judicial construction combining Articles 4(3) TEU and 101 TFEU (more rarely 102 TFEU) are far from clear. Each case applying the doctrine gives rise to controversy, even within the ECJ between judges and prominent (former) Advocates General. The two main points of contention raised by that case law echo, once again, the difficulty of subjecting public restraints to the discipline of competition law. They relate to the two categories of cases that have been decided by the ECJ under the state action doctrine and raise issues as to, respectively, the completeness and the consistency of the test applied.

The first category comprises cases where defendants in front of national courts were prosecuted pursuant to a state measure that they viewed as limiting their freedom to compete and considered contrary to EU requirements. This was the case in *Meng* and *OHRA*, which involved German and Dutch laws prohibiting insurance brokers to either pass on their commissions or to offer discounts to their clients, or more recently in *Doulamis*, which involved the prohibition of advertising by dentists under Belgian law. The ECJ upheld the state measures in those cases because, under the state action doctrine as construed by the ECJ, a state measure is illegal only if it is linked with an anticompetitive conduct, e.g., in the form of an anticompetitive agreement, on the part of private undertakings. In other words, not every state measure limiting the freedom to compete is subject to Articles 4(3) TEU and 101 TFEU. In particular, those state measures making "corporate behavior of the type prohibited by Article [101 TFEU] superfluous" fall "outside the scope of the state action doctrine,"[30] which is a key difference from the approach followed by the U.S. Supreme Court in *Midcal*. However, as Advocate General Léger observed in *Arduino*, there are various state measures entailing an appreciable restriction of competition that are not rooted in an anticompetitive conduct on the part of economic operators.[31] Accordingly, (1) the state action doctrine does not provide a suitable framework to assess their validity; whereas (2) private actors acting pursuant to those measures are effectively "immune" from liability under the EU rules on competition.

The second category consists of those cases linked with anticompetitive conduct on the part of economic operators, e.g., a price-fixing or market-sharing agreement. However, echoing one of the central criticisms voiced by the 2003 FTC State Action Task Force Report in relation to the U.S. state action exemption doctrine, they often rest on a convoluted, inconsistent, and sometimes naive analysis of the "active supervision" criterion, i.e., whether the state "retains the last word" in the decision-making process translating the conduct into law. In effect, multiple criteria appear to guide such determination, according to the case law, including whether (1) the measure is subject to the final approval of a government authority, e.g., a minister, possibly after consulting with other independent public bodies, with little consideration given to whether such approval amounts in practice to pure rubber-stamping or not; (2) the measure has been elaborated by a committee composed of a majority of members independent from the industry actors or associations, without regard for the fact that the natural asymmetry in information allows those industry actors to retain a preponderant influence in spite of their mathematical representation; or (3) industry representatives must take into account statutory criteria, which does not prevent them, however, from acting in the interest of their "national" industry or according to criteria that the industry has previously "inspired."

In addition to their formal and somewhat speculative character, the ECJ has applied those requirements in a somewhat inconsistent manner. In *Arduino* and *Hospital Consulting*, the ECJ appears to have relied mainly, if not exclusively, on the necessary "Minister's approval" for the tariffs elaborated by the National Bar Council to enter into force, whereas it transpires from *CIF* that such approval was found insufficient to immunize a market allocation and price-fixing scheme in place among matches manufacturers.[32] In *Reiff*, the ECJ was satisfied that representatives of the relevant branches of the German long-distance haulage industry acting as "independent experts" set exclusively the road transport tariffs, whereas in *Centro Servizi Spediporto*, the ECJ insisted that road transport tariffs in Italy were set by a committee composed of "17 representatives of the public authorities and a minority of 12 representatives of associations of economic agents."[33] In *Arduino*, the ECJ acknowledged that the National Bar Council was not bound by public interest criteria in setting up tariffs without such finding affecting its final position, whereas in *Reiff* it put a lot of emphasis on the need for the Tariff Board to fix tariffs on the basis of considerations of public interest and in particular to "take account of the interests of the agricultural sector and of medium-sized undertakings or regions which are economically weak or have inadequate transport facilities." Conversely, in *CNSD*, the ECJ quashed an Italian scheme that allowed representatives of professional customs agents to set service fees "in the exclusive interest of the profession."[34]

Moreover, in addition to the inconsistencies highlighted above, might not Member States have legitimate reasons to merely codify or legitimize measures proposed by industry actors, which, on their face, the ECJ may deem to restrict competition? This is particularly so, given the growing complexity of many industrial sectors and the difficulty for governments to cope with such complexity. Thus, as Advocate General Jacobs in *Pavlov*, Advocate General Léger in *Arduino*, and Advocate General Maduro in *Cipolla* all observed, what matters ought to be the aim pursued by the state, i.e., whether the measure at issue is justifiable on public interest grounds.[35] However, Article 101 (and 102) TFEU does not (and ought not to) allow for public interest grounds to justify anticompetitive conduct, in particular those that are so "by object," e.g., price-fixing or market-sharing practices.[36] Likewise, Article 4(3) TEU, which is not a substantive provision, can hardly be construed to allow for such justification. As a result, the state action doctrine appears to place the ECJ in an uncomfortable position and to force it to stretch both the facts of the cases and its own case law and to resort to inconsistent findings, in order to reach acceptable solutions.

The above overview of the treatment of public restraints under the respective competition laws of the PRC, the United States, and the European Union illustrates how current the state action issue is and how problematic its treatment under competition law can be. In particular, the U.S. experience reveals the relative ineffectiveness of the U.S. antitrust laws to discipline state measures affecting competition, partly as a result of a lenient interpretation of the "active supervision" criterion. In contrast, resorting to the internal trade discipline of the Commerce Clause seems to offer better outcomes. Yet, the limitations applied to the interpretation of that provision of the U.S. Constitution, inasmuch as it tackles predominantly discriminatory measures, also raise the concern of its underinclusiveness. The EU experience, on the other hand, illustrates the risk of double standards that arise from the application of competition law principles to public restraints, as well as the difficulty to accommodate, in the competition analysis, the broad range of public policy choices inherent in the exercise of government prerogatives. Indeed, the tendency of the ECJ to limit the scope of the state action doctrine, to sometimes "cherry pick" the facts and twist the boundaries of its own state action principles, may be due to the lack of room in the competition law system of analysis for the consideration of public interest justifications. As a result, the next section explores the opportunity of submitting public restraints to an alternative discipline, that of trade law, and attempts to identify the necessary conditions for ensuring the sustainability of such an approach.

Exploring the Possibility of Submitting State Action to the Trade Law Discipline: The EU Case

An alternative to the competition law approach would be to submit the control of public restraints to the alternative discipline of trade law, whether at national/federal or supranational/global level. This proposition is rooted in five intuitions. First, trade law and competition law pursue converging objectives; both aim in essence to protect market participants by empowering them to challenge impediments to the opportunity to compete on a particular territory. Second, trade law is naturally geared toward the assessment of public restraints, whether in the form of tariffs, equivalent measures, or other non-tariff barriers. Thus, trade law could, at limited cost, expand its scope to those public restraints affecting competition. Third, the system of analysis of trade law, whether under the U.S. Commerce Clause, the EU internal market provisions, or World Trade Organization (WTO) law, embeds a balancing exercise allowing expressly for the consideration of a broad range of public interest justifications, tempered by proportionality requirements. Fourth, most government initiatives affecting competition are likely to force outsiders to incur additional costs to access the local/regional/national domestic market and thus may constitute an obstacle to trade, depending on the criteria used to define the notion of obstacle under the relevant legal regime. Fifth, competition and trade law, with their respective system of analysis, might well act, with respect to public restraints, as "communicating vessels" so that the broader the scope of the trade requirements, the narrower the residual need to submit public restraints to competition requirements. The following paragraphs endeavor to verify those intuitions and, generally, to assess the opportunity of exploring the trade law route for disciplining public restraints at state, national, regional, or global level by revisiting the law of the European Union, as presented hereinabove, and drawing a number of tentative general conclusions therefrom.

Revisiting Article 106 TFEU in Light of the Trade Law Discipline

The grant of exclusive or special rights by nature affects the freedom to compete, with a particular impact on market entrants and outside competitors. As a result, both the Commission and the ECJ have in the past combined Article 106 TFEU with the EU internal market provisions, i.e., trade law. The most recent formal decision adopted by the Commission pursuant to Article 106 TFEU, for example, involved the compatibility of exclusive rights granted by the French government to three French credit institutions for the offering of special tax-free savings accounts (so-called livret A and livret bleu), with the freedom of establishment (Article 56 TFEU, then 49 EC).[37] In turn, when looking at other recent cases where the Commission or the ECJ applied Article 106 in conjunction with Article 102 TFEU, i.e., dominance, one wonders why there has not been a pairing with the EU free trade/movement provisions.

In the German "mail preparation services" case,[38] for instance, could the Commission not have construed the regulatory framework putting Deutsche Post's competitors at a competitive disadvantage as an obstacle particularly affecting out-of-state commercial mail preparation service providers? Indeed, in addition to being prevented from incurring the benefit of earning savings on postage, those hypothetical market entrants did not typically have at their disposal the local infrastructure necessary to benefit from the exceptions to the reserved postal monopoly of Deutsche Post. In *Carra*,[39] could the ECJ not have considered that the limitation put on the number of authorized placement intermediaries was likely to affect in particular the nationals of other Member States seeking employment in Italy, who, by definition, had little direct access to the Italian employment market? In *Sydhavnens Sten & Grus*,[40] the ECJ itself admitted that the municipal rules at issue prevented qualified intermediaries from participating in the collection of waste with a view to reselling it in other Member States, in contravention of Article 40 TFEU (ex. 34 EC) on the freedom to export. It also cleverly refrained from finding the existence of an abuse of dominance by jumping directly to the assessment of the possible justification for the special rights and the proportionality thereof. In *Ambulanz Glöckner*,[41] could the ECJ not have construed the monopoly granted to medical aid organizations over patient transport services as affecting particularly out-of-state ambulance transport providers and thus creating an obstacle to trade? Indeed, the special rights granted to medical aid organizations were intrinsically linked to their responsibility for emergency ambulance services, which in turn required the maintenance of aid and rescue resources throughout the relevant territory, twenty-four hours a day, which is by definition a difficult task for a "foreign" service provider.[42]

In fact, virtually all special rights caught under Article 106 TFEU that affect trade between Member States, which is a precondition for the application of both the competition and internal market rules of the EU Treaties, could be construed as hindering "market access" and are thus likely to amount to an "obstacle to trade" within the meaning of the free movement provisions of the TFEU. This is because the current test applied in the EU to establish the existence of such an obstacle goes beyond discriminatory measures targeted at outsiders and extends to measures applying de jure in the same way to domestic and foreign actors.

Revisiting the EU State Action Doctrine in Light of the Trade Law Discipline

In *INNO/ATAB*, the ECJ hinted that national measures compelling anticompetitive practices generally would be incompatible with the EU internal market/trade rules.[43] Recently, some prominent Advocates General have further highlighted the shortcomings of the state action doctrine and displayed a preference for assessing public restraints according to the EU internal market rules. However, they have not necessarily drawn all consequences from such preference. Advocate General Maduro, in *Cipolla*, considered that, based on a thorough reasoning, the scale of lawyers' fees—which had been upheld by the ECJ in *Arduino* on state action grounds—was on various grounds restrictive of the freedom to provide services.[44] Likewise, Advocate General Bot in *Doulamis*, after finding that a Belgian law prohibiting advertising by dentists did not fall within the ambit of the state action doctrine as construed by the ECJ, undertook to assess its compatibility with the freedom of establishment and the freedom to provide services and found it justifiable, eventually, for public health reasons. Interestingly, the ECJ had already followed a similar approach in the early *Leclerc* case,[45] which also involved a government measure affecting competition—*in casu* the prices of books, while lacking a direct link with or refraining from mandating anticompetitive conduct on the part of economic operators. Hence, one may wonder whether in other such cases, like *Meng* or *OHRA*, the ECJ could not also have considered that the prohibition imposed on insurance brokers to pass on commissions or offer discounts to their clients affects the freedom to compete of would-be entrants on the German or Dutch market, thus restraining their freedom of establishment?[46]

Subsequently, could the same reasoning apply to those cases where the ECJ actually found its state action doctrine to be applicable? In *Reiff* and *Centro Servizi Spediporto*, for example, which involved the setting by law of compulsory road transport tariffs, could the ECJ not have found that such limitations on the freedom to compete on prices affected in particular out-of-state competitors willing to access the German or Italian road transport market?[47] In *CNSD*, the ECJ itself hinted at the fact that the regulatory scheme allowing customs agents to collectively set their service fees affected the free movement of goods "because of the various types of import or export operations within the Community [that] make it necessary for an independent registered customs agent to be involved" and, in particular in relation to Italy, because of "a large proportion of goods dispatched from regions in the north-east of the country to Germany and the Netherlands."[48] There is also a strong argument that a state-organized cartel impedes the freedom to provide services by out-of-state service providers and/or their freedom of establishment. This was clearly the case in *CIF*, for example, where the market-sharing and quota allocation arrangements in effect foreclosed access to the Italian market by "foreign" match manufacturers. The case arose out of a complaint from a German manufacturer who alleged difficulties in distributing its products in Italy.[49]

Generally, it appears that favoring an assessment of the compatibility of government measures restricting competition with the EU free trade/movement provisions could produce convincing results and would appear, in effect, hardly revolutionary. Indeed, it would amount to little more than bringing to the surface the analysis already underlying many state action cases, where the ECJ appears to be searching for the aim actually pursued by the relevant public authority in limiting competition and concerned to reach an acceptable solution at the end of its often convoluted reasoning. At the same time, it could bring significant added value in terms of consistency and legal certainty, to the benefit of private actors and public authorities alike, as well as greater deference to Member States' regulatory powers within clearly defined boundaries. Indeed, the system of analysis applicable under the EU free trade/movement rules entails that, once a state measure is deemed to constitute an "obstacle to trade," it may still be justifiable based on public interest grounds. As a result, an approach based on the EU internal market rules would leave greater room for public interest justifications and thus greater deference to Member States than one based on the competition rules, which ought to recognize only efficiency justifications.

Eventually, such a move from the competition to the trade discipline would be made possible by the evolution of the interpretation of the notion of "obstacle to trade" under EU free trade/movement law toward a market access standard. This standard virtually encompasses all state measures likely to affect in any material respect the freedom to compete and particularly that of market entrants or out-of-state competitors. In other words, the notion of obstacle to trade in the EU has been increasingly interpreted as including all measures that, "even though they apply *without distinction*, affect the conditions for pursuing the activity concerned and have the effect of depriving an economic operator of an effective means of competing with a view to penetrating a market" (emphasis added).[50] Interestingly, that evolution in the interpretation of the notion of obstacle is now common to all four components of the EU free trade/movement discipline (goods, services, establishment, and capital).[51]

Conditions for a Trade Law Approach to Disciplining Public Restraints

In view of the EU experience, submitting public restraints to the discipline of trade law rather than to that of competition law appears sustainable and no less effective. It would carry added value in terms of consistency and legal certainty. Such a shift would imply that a limitation to competition is subject to either set of rules depending on whether it originates in a government measure or in a private practice. More importantly, it would entail greater consideration for the various interests underlying the sovereign choices of government authorities and would thus seem better equipped to distinguish between those restraints serving purely parochial interests and those pursuing legitimate redistributive objectives. Still, at least two factors characterizing the EU framework may not be present in other settings or at the global level.

First, the system of analysis of EU free trade/movement law embodies a particularly broad definition of the notion of obstacle to trade. This definition extends to those measures that apply indistinctively to foreign and domestic actors but are merely "burdening" outsiders to a material extent. Arguably, this is not the case in the United States under the dormant Commerce Clause, at least not to the same extent, or at global level under WTO law.[52] Yet, this broad definition might well constitute a key condition to regard competition and trade as alternative (but not interchangeable) disciplines for public restraints. Such a broad understanding is then balanced in the sequence of analysis by due consideration for an equally broad range of public interest justifications. In turn, the proportionality assessment of the means used in furtherance of those objectives and thus potentially affecting competition is governed by a margin of appreciation mechanism that allows for local variations, particularly in those cases characterized by great regulatory diversity (e.g., health/welfare policy) and/or in areas marked by profound moral, religious, or cultural considerations.

Second, as a corollary, the far-reaching trade discipline applicable within the EU, as reflected in the broad understanding of the notion of obstacle to trade, is conditioned on a great substantive convergence among EU Member States and an altogether large consensus as to the legitimacy of the EU institutions in reviewing national/domestic choices (even if they are not immune to criticism). In effect, EU Member States are bound by a "basic constitutional charter" in the form of the EU Treaties and by a "kind of surrogate, or shadow, Constitution" in the form of the European Convention on Human Rights.[53] Second-guessing government choices necessarily entails constitutional implications and legitimacy considerations. Arguably, such a level of convergence and consensus hardly exists at the global level. It is doubtful that the WTO, for example, could at present develop a system of analysis to catch nondiscriminatory measures, let alone a quasi state action doctrine rooted in a competition discipline where it would face similar, if not greater, constraints. In contrast, a degree of convergence and consensus similar to (and often greater than) the one present in the EU could be found at the level of regional trade agreements and/or federal/national states, which therefore could implement a review of public restraints anchored in an internal trade law system of analysis. Such an approach would accordingly allow for the factoring of public interest justifications in determining the validity of local/regional policy choices.[54]

. . .

This chapter discussed the limits of competition law in addressing public restraints, from a global perspective. Those limits can be crudely summed up by a lack of room in the competition system of analysis for public interest considerations. For that reason, the chapter explored the opportunity of submitting public restraints to an alternative ubiquitous discipline, that of trade law. The trade law system of analysis appears better suited to achieve the right balance between the pursuit of allocative efficiency objectives and the necessary deference for governments' sovereign choices. In other words, the trade approach appears capable of tackling parochial interests effectively while preserving the ability of public authorities to pursue legitimate redistributive objectives.

The public/private divide has loomed consistently in the background of the above discussion. As Odudu suggested, "[D]ifferential treatment of public authorities and private (corporate) citizens can be justified to reflect the differing roles played by citizens and the state in a constitutional democracy," the underlying assumption being that "public power is exercised in the public interest and the public interest is determined through democratic representation" so that "the exercise of public power needs distinctive substantive and procedural rules that take account of the nature of the activity engaged in [and] the legitimacy of those activities."[55] Arguably, all public participants in the global arena do not abide by the same democratic standards. Yet all those participants are endowed with a certain form of legitimacy, even if contested and/or contestable. The public/private divide justifies, fundamentally, the application of different disciplines to restrictions of competition caused by private parties or public authorities. Even though allocative efficiency is the common overarching objective, specific rules factoring different variables are required to reflect the different nature and missions of private and public entities. Hence the proposition of submitting public restraints, irrespective of their nature, to the discipline of trade law allows for the consideration of a broad range of public interest justifications. Conversely, it would limit the scope of competition law to private practices justifiable on economic efficiency grounds. In turn, that proposition is informed by a currently deep political concern—even if sometimes poorly articulated—toward the reliance on economic efficiency principles to constrain the implementation of public policies and the perception that such trend has largely been driven by "globalization," which cannot be ignored.

As a corollary, this chapter is also concerned, fundamentally, with the lasting legitimacy of competition law, conditioned on an acknowledgment of its limits and on the consistency of the assessments carried out according to its own efficiency-driven rationality. Competition law may well set the default rules for the market economy. It has great resources because of its broad formulation and its often effective remedies. Still, its scope is limited. It cannot address each and every market failure and appears ill-equipped to assess the legitimacy of sovereign choices. Eventually, as Odudu put it, again: "[N]o claim is made that wider goals should not be pursued; rather the wider goals must be pursued outwith competition law adjudication."

8

IP's Advantages over Antitrust

Daniel A. Crane

A quarter century ago, Frank Easterbrook taught us that antitrust law has its limits.[1] Easterbrook convincingly argued that the error costs associated with false positives were likely to exceed the error costs associated with false negatives given the institutional characteristics of U.S.-style antitrust enforcement and the workings of the market. Easterbrook advocated various "filters" courts could use to screen out weak antitrust claims, thus confining antitrust to grave disruptions of competitive forces.

The rising post-Chicago riposte to Easterbrook and his fellow Chicagoans paints a portrait of Chicago's antitrust as not merely "limited" but "lifeless."[2] Post-Chicagoans articulate a number of ways in which Chicago's simplifying assumptions can be importantly misguided.[3] The academic pendulum, if not its tailing judicial analogue, appears to be swinging back toward intervention.

As the antitrust pendulum swings, the domain of problematic technologies and practices is shifting too. In particular, the share of the economy characterized by intellectual property (IP) has grown exponentially over the last quarter century. According to one estimate, the total value of U.S. intellectual property is now between $5 and $5.5 trillion, or about 45 percent of U.S. GDP.[4] Not only has the IP-intensive sector of the economy grown exponentially relative to the overall economy, but IP-intensive industries raise many of the most interesting and difficult questions that gave Easterbrook pause about antitrust interventions a quarter of a century ago and give post-Chicagoans fodder for a renewed push. Questions surrounding network effects, duties to share bottleneck technologies, predatory innovation, technological integration of complementary goods, abuse of technological standardization, and pooling of patents or copyrights dominate competition policy. Bricks-and-mortar industries show up still, but because they often involve homogeneous goods they appear in the relatively uncontroversial domain of cartel enforcement.[5] The "hot" issues of intervention or nonintervention belong to the world of Microsoft, Apple, Intel, Google, IBM, Merck, Novartis, and Schering-Plough.

Many of the salient questions about antitrust's limits concern antitrust's application to IP or IP-intensive industries. As to this domain, the choice between limited and vigorous antitrust requires not merely a comparison between market failures and government failures. It requires an assessment of the relative competence of antitrust and intellectual property as discrete, but cognate, disciplines to manage problems of market power. Antitrust's limits seem stronger if IP can deal more effectively with the same problems.

In this chapter, I argue that antitrust may be optimally limited as to IP-intensive industries if IP itself can perform some of the functions necessary to control market power. In particular, I argue that IP has three advantages over antitrust that render it the preferable regulatory tool. First, whereas antitrust law requires a search for a violation of a norm—essentially a crime or a tort—IP can address issues of market power by molding substantive IP rights prospectively. Second, whereas antitrust's remedial structure is heavy artillery that can chill innovation and competition, IP's remedial structure is more finely tuned to address complex problems of market power. Finally, the presentation of issues in IP cases provides some natural fault lines that allow superior substantive resolution of issues relating to access to IP. Recognition of these advantages permits governmental interventions to correct market failures and promote competition even while recognizing the limits of antitrust.

Molding Substantive Rights

Intellectual property sometimes, but certainly not always, creates persistent and strong market power. One should not overstate the scope of the problem, since by no means every patent, copyright, or trademark creates anything approaching market power. As Edward Chamberlain observed as far back as 1932, one must distinguish between legal monopoly—the exclusive right granted by intellectual property law—and monopoly in an economic sense.[6] For example, 95 percent of all patents have no economic value at all, much less monopoly value.[7] This essay will be copyrighted, but I have little hope that it will bring me monopoly riches.

Still, many intellectual property rights do create entrenched market positions. Even here, one has to be careful not to express hostility to all monopoly rents returned by the grant of intellectual property rights, since some monopoly profits may be necessary to incentivize the creation of new technologies and works. Ideally, however, antitrust, IP, and other regulatory instruments would work conjunctively to make sure that the IP system grants just enough incentive for the creation of socially desirable innovations.

Which regulatory levers should courts and regulators prefer to pull in order to limit market power in IP? Roughly speaking, the two choices are (1) grant broad IP rights *ex ante* but then police their abuse *ex post* by invoking antitrust principles or (2) grant more-limited IP rights *ex ante* out of solicitude to competition values but then allow free exercise of the IP rights granted, unharassed by antitrust interventions, *ex post*. In my view, all else being equal, courts and regulators should incline toward the latter option.

The reason lies in the vastly different legal cultures, requirements, limitations, and costs surrounding the distinct enterprises of molding prospective entitlements and condemning past violations of social norms. It is the difference between criminal and tort law on the one hand and adaptive modifications in a licensing regime on the other. In order to find a violation of antitrust law, a court needs to establish the violation of a legal norm—some sort of "bad" conduct.[8] This enterprise necessitates a large investment in formal legal "build up"—enunciating the liability principle, ensuring that it was sufficiently predictable to be foreseen *ex ante*, and establishing formal burdens of proof, safe harbors, and other mechanisms to safeguard the defendant's procedural and substantive interests. On the other hand, regulators making decisions on prospective licensing need not worry about all of these legal formalisms, retroactivity concerns, due process protections, burdens of proof, and so forth. They can simply consider the optimal bundle of rights to be granted given particular instrumental goals and adjust the bundle over time as instrumental goals change or learning about those goals change.

To see an outworking of the different IP and antitrust approaches to controlling market power in IP, consider two cases—one decided by the U.S. Supreme Court and the other by the European Court of Justice—concerning the right to exclude competitors from rote information.[9] The American case, *Feist Publications v. Rural Telephone Services*,[10] was decided as a copyright case, although it initially raised antitrust issues as well.[11] The Supreme Court held that a local phone service provider that was required by state regulation to issue an annually updated telephone directory did not have a copyright in the alphabetically ordered listing of names since that composition did not involve a "minimal degree of creativity."[12] The upshot was that the telephone company could not exclude its competitor from producing a complementary product to that of the monopoly telephone service.

In the European case, *Magill*,[13] the European Court of Justice (ECJ) held that three television stations that had copyrights under Irish and British law on the listing of their programs abused their dominant position by refusing to license their listings to a company that wanted to create TV guides. The European Commission had ordered a compulsory license, and the ECJ affirmed.

Both *Feist* and *Magill* were ultimately about the invocation of property rights in database collections to exclude rivals from a complementary service. In *Feist*, the Supreme Court did not have to worry about accusing the telephone company of wrongdoing or about specifying the contours of an awkward and potentially problematic duty to deal. It simply rejected the copyright, thus freeing competition in phone books. By contrast, in *Magill* the ECJ turned an excessive intellectual property right into a generalized duty to deal by dominant firms—a duty hard to justify as a generality and difficult to administer in practice.

Feist's location of the decision internally within copyright seems the preferable choice. Recall that the competitor originally asserted an antitrust claim as well—a claim that, if accepted, would have required enunciating a duty to license IP. A generalized duty to deal in IP creates a variety of conceptual and administrative problems and may erode incentives to innovate. It is particularly troubling when antitrust duties to deal are created in cases of weak IP, such as *Magill*, and then extended without modification to cases of much stronger IP, like *Microsoft* and *Intel*. A far preferable solution is simply to consider competition values when deciding whether to accord IP protection in the weak case.

Of course, IP only enjoys this advantage over antitrust if the relevant institutional decision makers are able to substitute between antitrust and IP policy levers. The contrast in policy lever choice between *Feist* and *McGill* reflects in part the fact that the European Commission and European courts (the General Court and the European Court of Justice) have relatively little role in specifying the contours of intellectual property rights but play a strong role in defining antitrust norms. By contrast, the U.S. Supreme Court has the power to mold both antitrust and IP norms and hence can substitute between them depending on the comparative advantage of invoking one norm or the other.[14] It will often turn out that this flexibility is advantageous and that deciding the issues as IP issues rather than antitrust issues improves the decision in the particular case under consideration and prevents unintended doctrinal side effects. Perhaps if, in the future, EU member states begin to shift more IP functions to the European Commission and the European courts, they will observe that European antitrust law begins to appear less interventionist in IP-intensive industries and that IP law picks up some of the slack. From at least the perspective of controlling market power in IP, this would be a desirable exchange.

Well-Tailored Remedies

A second substantial IP advantage lies in the remedial differences between IP and antitrust. Antitrust law is generally structured for punitive remedies—fines in Europe and criminal liability or treble damages in the United States. The possibility of injunction against future misbehavior is also available but is usually employed by negotiation rather than unilaterally imposed by the courts in complex circumstances involving intellectual property rights. The far-reaching structural decrees imposing future obligations with respect to intellectual property—such as the BMI and ASCAP, AT&T, Microsoft, and Intel decrees—have almost all been consent decrees, reflecting tailored decision making with the input of the parties.

By contrast, IP remedies oriented toward controlling market power come essentially in two flavors: (1) stripping intellectual property rights (IPR) altogether, or (2) allowing the IPR holder to exploit the IP right but limiting the amount it can charge. For example, in cases of patent misuse, the usual remedy is to provide the alleged infringer with a defense against patent infringement until the misuse is cured.[15] In other instances, however, a court or agency may permit the patentee to continue to enforce its patent, but capped by a maximum rate it may charge.

To some extent, these two forms of IP remedy parallel an injunction remedy following the finding of an antitrust violation. For example, in the FTC's ultimately unsuccessful enforcement action against Rambus,[16] the Commission first found that Rambus had violated Section 5 of the Federal Trade Commission Act by misleading the JEDEC standard-setting organization as to its patents and patent applications relating to the computer memory technologies that were being standardized. The Commission then turned to the question of remedy. A majority of three commissioners voted to allow Rambus to continue to enforce its patents, subject to a maximum royalty rate consisting of a figure low in the probability distribution of the rates it could possibly have charged if the patents had been properly disclosed.[17] Two other commissioners dissented on remedy and voted to require Rambus to license its patents to anyone seeking to practice the standard at a zero royalty rate.[18] In some sense, these two views represent the two remedial possibilities when market power is considered as an IP problem rather than an antitrust problem.

But there is an important difference when royalty caps, in particular, are considered in an IP rather than an antitrust concept. In some circumstances in the IP context, it is possible to focus on remedy without first finding liability for a "violation." To the extent that courts or agencies have the option of sometimes treating IP rights as liability rights rather than property rights, slippery questions of abuse or violation may disappear altogether.

Since Calabresi and Melamed's groundbreaking article,[19] the vocabulary of "property rules" and "liability rules" has been part of IP and antitrust's lexicography.[20] The essential feature of a property rule is that the IPR holder has the right to exclude others from use of its invention or work, typically by refusing to license and calling in the aid of a court to issue an injunction against infringement. By contrast, under a liability rule, the IPR holder has no right to exclude others from its invention or work, but may seek to collect a royalty from anyone who uses the invention or work.

Whether a particular IPR is characterized as a liability or property right is important for purposes of controlling market power. Property rights give the IPR holder a strong holdout position, since he can charge an unlimited rate and refuse to deal altogether. By contrast, under a liability regime, the IPR holder has no right to refuse another access to his invention and hence cannot hold out at all. Further, to the extent that he is entitled to collect a royalty, the rate (or at least the upper bounds of the rate) is determined by some impartial third party, such as a judge, regulator, or arbitrator.

There is a voluminous literature on whether liability rules or property rules should govern intellectual property.[21] The current status quo is a mixed regime with some rights sounding in property and others sounding in liability and perhaps a gradual drift toward less property and more liability.[22] At present, however, relatively few courts or commentators have made an explicit connection between the remedial possibility of converting an IPR into a liability right and controlling market power in IP.

Converting an IPR from property to liability may be an attractive means of controlling market power when the conversion allows the IPR holder to retain other, more valuable rights in its bundle. As Louis Kaplow has shown, the optimal resolution to the antitrust/patent intersection would involve ordinally arranging various "practices," such as additional years of patent life and permissions to engage in various forms of potentially anticompetitive behavior, and permitting the patentee to retain those practices with the most favorable ratio between incentive-reward benefit and social cost up until the point that the patentee had a sufficient amount of incentive to create the invention.[23] This process might require, for example, allowing the patentee to engage in price discrimination through tying—since that would generate a high level of incentive to the patentee at relatively low social cost—but not to engage in price-fixing with rivals, since engaging in that practice would only provide a weak reward to the patentee (because the reward would have to be shared with rivals and hence would be diluted) and entail a high social cost. One extension of Kaplow's model is to treat the right to exclude—the central distinction between liability and property rights—as a practice that the IPR holder would forfeit if it wanted to retain other more valuable and socially beneficial rights.[24]

For example, suppose that a patentee wishes to participate in standard-setting organizations (SSOs) without predisclosing its patents or patent applications.[25] Apart from the desire to obtain a monopoly holdout position by springing the existence of its patents on those seeking to practice the standard after everyone is locked into the standard, there may be legitimate reasons for not wanting to predisclose patents. The patentee may be concerned that its competitors will seek to reposition their own patent portfolios or otherwise oppose a particular standardization option simply to harm the patentee's interests. One way to allow the patentee to retain its right to participate in the SSO without predislosure, without entailing the socially costly risk of post-standardization hold-up, is to treat the right to participate in an SSO as a prospective waiver of property rule treatment for any patents ultimately infringed by practicing the standard. As a matter of IP law, the patentee could simply be deemed to have exchanged one right for the other. Poststandardization, the patentee would be required to license its patents on reasonable and nondiscriminatory terms to anyone seeking to practice the standard. In the event that a licensee was dissatisfied with the rates offered by the patentee, it could seek the aid of some neutral third party—such as a court, regulator, or arbitrator—in setting the rate.

This suggestion is not novel, since many SSOs already require that all participants precommit to reasonable and nondiscriminatory ("RAND," or fair, reasonable, and nondiscriminatory, "FRAND") terms if they wish to participate in the SSO.[26] The added value in embedding such a principle in IP law rather than leaving it up to contract is that the contract claim is difficult to enforce. For example, there have been circumstances where patentees have made RAND commitments to SSOs and subsequently assigned their patents to third parties, who then have resisted judicial enforcement of the RAND commitment on the ground that they were not parties to the original promise and that the licensees seeking to enforce the promise were not third party beneficiaries.[27] Contract law is not sufficiently robust to ensure the consistent enforcement of RAND commitments.

Antitrust law could do the job, but much more cumbersomely than IP, as evidenced by the FTC's failure to persuade the federal court of appeals for the D.C. Circuit that Rambus had committed an antitrust violation.[28] IP has the advantage of already embedding equitable considerations into the question of whether to accord property or liability rights. Under *eBay v. MercExchange*,[29] courts are supposed to take a variety of equitable factors into account in deciding whether to issue an injunction against permanent patent infringement. In the event that the court does not issue the injunction, it treats the patent right as a prospective liability right and sets a royalty rate that the patentee may collect. It would not be a stretch of existing principles to police more issues of market power by considering the sorts of trade-off decisions suggested in the SSO cases and, more generally, embedded in Kaplow's model.

This is not to say that IP law should prospectively adopt a rule of categorical denial of property treatment to any patentee that has participated in an SSO, or otherwise begin jettisoning property protection for IP helter-skelter out of fear of market power. Rather, the point is that *if* there is a need to address concerns about market power in IP in a particular case, there is an advantage in many cases to considering an IP bundle-of-rights trade-off analysis instead of casting the issue as antitrust "violation" or "competitive on the merits." IP's remedial flexibility and its existing familiarity with rights trade-off decisions give it an advantage over antitrust in addressing a range of market power issues.

Finding Natural Fault Lines

A final advantage of IP lies in its superior ability to locate natural fault lines suggestive of where mandatory sharing of IP should end. When IP law holds that a patent or copyright must be "shared" with rivals in order to avoid consolidating excessive market power in the patentee or copyright holder, it partially satisfies antitrust's occasional demand for compulsory dealing by dominant firms in possession of strategic bottlenecks to essential facilities. Yet, by merely allowing self-help infringement by those that can infringe the intellectual property right and not affirmatively requiring dealing by the dominant firm, it avoids most of the administrative difficulties that have pushed the U.S. courts and agencies to back away from an antitrust duty to deal.

Consider the U.S. Supreme Court's explanation for essentially eliminating a duty to deal under Section 2 of the Sherman Act. Citing an article by Phillip Areeda, the Court explained in *Trinko*: "No court should impose a duty to deal that it cannot explain or adequately and reasonably supervise. The problem should be deemed irremedia[ble] by antitrust law when compulsory access requires the court to assume the day-to-day controls characteristic of a regulatory agency."[30] The disturbing image the Court has in mind here is of a district court daily determining the scope and parameters of the monopolist's obligation to license and policing the monopolist's compliance with the court's mandatory injunctions. Courts have long been reluctant to issue mandatory (as opposed to prohibitory) injunctions precisely because of these sorts of fears that ordering affirmative compliance entails intractable judicial entanglement in the parties' affairs.

The IP approach largely avoids this problem. Far from compelling "firms to reach out and affirmatively assist their rivals,"[31] the IP liability rule approach merely denies the dominant IPR holder the affirmative aid of the court in fencing out the trespasser. Indeed, the burden shifts to the dominant firm to seek the aid of the court in establishing the relevant royalty rate that it may charge infringers. The only injunctive undertaking by the court is a possible negative injunction in the event that the infringer fails to pay the royalty. But that sort of injunction is no more intrusive than the ordinary "cease and desist" injunction employed in all sorts of IP cases.

To be sure, this IP advantage has the arguable disadvantage of failing to go far enough in solving problems of market power in IP. Christina Bohannan and Herbert Hovenkamp have argued that a court's refusal to issue an injunction under *eBay* is not a reliable way of implementing an antitrust duty to deal, since "it does not apply to ex ante requests for dealing only to remedies once an infringement is found."[32] One could also add that merely transitioning an IPR from property to liability fails to satisfy the need of the competitor who cannot adequately help himself, because he needs more than just permission to use the IPR but also affirmative logistical help from the IPR holder. For example, under the Microsoft consent decree, Microsoft was not merely required to relinquish certain of its intellectual property claims, but affirmatively to cooperate with rivals to ensure compatibility with the Windows operating system.[33] If Microsoft had merely lost the right to enforce its copyrights and not been affirmatively obligated to cooperate with its rivals via the intermediation of a Technical Committee, it is doubtful that the consent decree would have been successful in restoring competition.

It is quite true that the denial of a permanent injunction against infringement does not solve the full set of problems ostensibly necessitating a duty to license intellectual property, but it does solve the subset of problems most amenable to a legal solution. It also helps to explain which problems legal systems should try to solve through compulsory dealing duties and those that they should not try to reach, defaulting instead to imperfect, but superior, market solutions. Thinking about any potential duty to deal in IP as an infringer's self-help remedy alleviates one (but certainly not all) of the objections to ever requiring a dominant firm to share its intellectual property. It rewards those firms that take initiative and actually use existing technologies over those who sit back and claim that they were stymied by the IPR holder's monopolistic refusal to deal. The self-help line is not a perfect one, but it is probably the best one available.

. . .

IP's advantages over antitrust are to be found in its superior ability to shape substantive rights, its greater remedial flexibility, and its acuity in locating natural fault lines for the duty-to-deal questions. This is not to say that IP can solve all market power problems in its own domain—that we don't need antitrust interventions in IP because IP can take care of itself. Rather, it is a call for a light antitrust hand with respect to IP and a consideration whether IP-specific mechanisms may be available as an alternative to antitrust intrusion.

9

Competition Law and Consumer Protection Against Unfair Commercial Practices

A More-than-Complementary Relationship?

Paolisa Nebbia

From a broad theoretical perspective, there is a profound difference between consumer law and competition law. The former addresses market failures affecting the consumer's subjective ability to choose: these market failures are "internal" to the consumer, or "inside his head," in the sense that they make the consumer unable to choose effectively among the available options.[1] Consumer law seeks to ensure that consumers' critical faculties remain unimpaired by preventing the use of unfair terms,[2] aggressive or misleading selling techniques, and, in general, unfair dealing. Competition law, on the other hand, ensures that the marketplace remains competitive so that a meaningful range of options remains open to consumers, unimpaired by restrictive practices such as price-fixing agreements; it addresses market failures that are "external" to the consumer and lead to an objective inability of the market to provide sufficient options to the consumer.

Further differences can be found in the fact that competition law operates at the level of market structure by prohibiting any conduct that restricts, distorts, or impedes competition and uses economic analysis to determine whether an agreement has anticompetitive effects and whether such effects are appreciable. Accordingly, competition law ensures consumer protection by "indirect" means, by encouraging firms to innovate by reducing slack, putting downward pressure on costs, and providing incentives for the efficient organization of production. Consumer law operates at the level of the relationship between individual traders and consumers and aims at making sure that the trader's conduct does not impair the consumer's ability to choose or does not bring an unfair advantage to the trader by introducing a direct form of control on individual transactions. Put differently, consumer law addresses distortions at the level of demand, while competition law addresses distortions at the level of the offer.[3]

In spite of their different approaches, consumer protection law and competition law are commonly considered to be complementary tools to ensure consumer welfare on the basis of two sets of reasons, which economists would probably sum up as follows.[4] From an efficiency point of view, as economic theory shows, perfect competition ensures that allocative and productive efficiency are simultaneously achieved by forcing firms to offer the most attractive combination of prices and qualities technologically available. Consumers are thus able to find the price/quality that best suits their preferences, thus maximizing the sum of producers' and consumers' welfare. While perfect competition assumes that consumers are able, absent any legal or regulatory standards and remedies, to discipline untrustworthy or otherwise undesirable firms by simply shifting expenditure, even a fervent believer in the market forces would admit that in some cases this is not a realistic assumption.[5] In the case, for example, of products that are purchased infrequently or of credence goods for which an individual consumer cannot usually rely on personal experience to evaluate the truthfulness of a seller's claims, there may be a need to ensure disclosure of information that the trader would otherwise have no incentive to make public. Also, reputation and repeat sales may not deter fly-by-night or scam operators whose only aim is to cheat consumers, grab the revenues, and disappear from sight, often to reemerge in another guise to steal again.

When market forces cannot overcome these threats to consumer welfare, because some sellers are unconcerned about repeat business and reputation or because information asymmetries make deception difficult to detect, rules and remedies in contract, tort, and criminal law may sanction duress, fraud, and breach of contract. They are, however, of limited use for a number of reasons, ranging from the mere fact that certain conducts are not caught by the traditional remedies to the fact that *ex post* monetary sanctions in individual cases are inadequate to effectively curb unfair conduct. In these circumstances, there is a role for regulatory requirements on firms' behavior toward consumers, affecting communication, advertising, sales promotion, contracting and precontracting conduct, and so on, to increase consumer surplus in the firm-consumer relationship.[6]

The other commonly acknowledged point of intersection between consumer and competition law has to do with market manipulation. Behavioral economics has highlighted several cognitive and behavioral biases in people and accordingly has detected marketing techniques that trigger a significant departure from the standard model of consumer behavior typically assumed by neoclassical economic analysis. Advertising, promotion, and price setting are commonly used, to varying degrees, to alter the process of formation of consumers' preferences, which constitutes the key assumption of competition law.

In the specific European context, competition and consumer law share one other objective, that of furthering market integration. Most consumer law measures adopt as their legal basis the Treaty provisions on the establishment of an internal market and expressly set out as their goal the creation of a "level playing field," i.e., an area where competition between firms within the EU is no longer distorted by the different legal frameworks that regulate business-to-consumer relationships. Similarly, the goal of market integration has always played a major role in European competition policy, as the Community institutions' assessment of territorial protection in vertical agreements well proves.

The aim of this chapter is to further investigate the different facets of the relationship between consumer and competition law by reviewing some practical cases, drawn mainly from the experience of the Italian Competition Authority (ICA). These will reveal that the correlation between the two sets of rules may be understood as complementary not only in a strict sense—i.e., one tool may be used to tackle conduct that is harmful to consumers but does not fall within the scope of application of the other—but also in a broad sense, i.e., one tool may be used to enhance the effectiveness of the other, even in the presence of significant overlaps between the two. There are good reasons to entrust the enforcement of the two sets of rules to the same authority, or at least to ensure smooth channels of communication between the two.

Unfair Commercial Practices and Competition Authorities: The Italian Case

Directive 2005/29 concerning unfair business-to-consumer commercial practices in the internal market lays down rules aimed at an EU-wide standard of protection against unfair commercial practices. The objective, as set out in Article 1, is to deliver a high degree of consumer protection and to facilitate the functioning of the internal market.

The directive applies to all business-to-consumer transactions whereby the consumer is influenced by an unfair commercial practice that affects decisions on whether to purchase a product, on the freedom of choice in the event of purchase, and on decisions as to whether to exercise a contractual right. A general clause defines all practices that are unfair and therefore prohibited, but the vast majority of practices that are considered unfair would fall under one of the two categories set up by the directive, the misleading or the aggressive practices. Misleading actions are the ones that

1. contain false information and are therefore untruthful; or
2. in any way, including overall presentation, deceive or are likely to deceive the average consumer, even if the information is correct; and
3. cause or are likely to cause the average consumer to take a transactional decision that he would have otherwise not taken.[7]

The directive includes unfair competition in the notion of misleading practice (to the extent that it causes consumer detriment), as the directive expressly states that a commercial practice shall also be regarded as misleading if, in its factual context, taking account of all its features and circumstances, it causes or is likely to cause the consumer to take a transactional decision that he would not have taken otherwise. The directive also covers any marketing of a product, including comparative advertising, that creates confusion with any products, trademarks, trade names, or other distinguishing marks of a competitor.

The directive considers a practice aggressive if in its factual context, taking account of all its features and circumstances, by harassment, coercion (including the use of physical force), or undue influence it significantly impairs or is likely to significantly impair the average consumer's freedom of choice or conduct with regard to the product and thereby causes or is likely to cause him or her to take a transactional decision that he or she would not have taken otherwise.

The directive sets out two nonexhaustive lists of practices that are regarded as unfair. If a practice falls within one of the lists, it is ipso facto considered unfair and is banned in all circumstances, without applying the average consumer test. The two lists can be found in Annex I to the directive.

In enforcement matters, the directive leaves considerable leeway to the Member States, and simply requires them to ensure that persons or organizations regarded under national law as having a legitimate interest in combating unfair commercial practices, including competitors, may take legal action against such unfair commercial practices and/or bring such unfair commercial practices before an administrative authority competent either to decide on complaints or to initiate appropriate legal proceedings.

In Italy, the ICA is the designated enforcer for the implementation of Directive 2005/29 (Articles 18 to 27 of the consumer code). The ICA set up a Consumer Protection Directorate, which is specifically aimed at fulfilling that task and whose structure and procedures are similar to those of the Competition Directorate.[8] The ICA has taken such competence very seriously. In 2009, the ICA carried out 272 investigations. Of these, 246 ended with a declaration of infringement, and infringers paid a total of €35 million in fines.[9]

Sanctioning Unfair Commercial Practices as a Means to Enhance the Effectiveness of Competition

Evidence gathered by the ICA in different industries seems to suggest that unfair commercial practices, if adopted on a large scale, can actually be used to prevent the development of effective competition in markets that are not characterized by the presence of a dominant player and in the absence of any anticompetitive agreement or practice.

The major example lies in the telecoms sector. Since 1998, the ICA has called for the introduction of mobile number portability (MNP) as a means to ensure that new entrants can access the market.[10] In an opinion adopted in 2001, the ICA noted that the Italian market was saturated, which meant that operators were unlikely to be able to gain new customers who had never used mobiles before, but could only "steal" customers from their rivals. Under these circumstances, MNP would be

> a powerful tool to increase the competitive pressure on the larger operators, capable of producing significant effects on the market structure as it decreases barriers to entry to new operators. The removal of the barrier arising out of the fact that the customer had to change his phone number is likely to increase the amount of competition as it would trigger a redistribution of market shares in favour of the more efficient operators, with a decrease in prices and, accordingly, an increase of consumer welfare.[11]

In the *Telecom* decision (Telecom being the former State monopolist),[12] an action brought by consumers and small competitors (new entrants) highlighted the following allegedly unfair commercial practices on behalf of Telecom:

approaching customers over the phone and seeking retention by providing incomplete or obscure information about Telecom's new offers and tariffs; making defamatory statements against the recipient operators, particularly the Mobile Virtual Operators; and setting up practical obstacles to migration so as to discourage consumers, such as requests to fill in various forms several times, unjustified delays in dealing with the request, lack of cooperation with the recipient operators for the solution of technical problems that may arise from the transfer.

The ICA found that Telecom operated a mass campaign that involved unfair practices carried out against a large number of migrating customers, and the distortion of the decision-making process of the consumer had effects that were not limited to the individual case.[13] Hence, the conduct was considered to be particularly offensive since it interfered with the decision-making process of a large number of customers.

Interestingly, conduct similar to that condemned in the Italian Telecom case triggered a fine of €27.6 million by the French Competition Authority against France Telecom (the former state monopolist) for having abusively hindered the development of new competing operators in the overseas departments.[14] Using the files in its possession as the manager of virtually all local loops, France Telecom focused its commercial efforts on subscribers who had migrated to a competing operator, in an effort to bring them back as customers. The conduct sanctioned included encouraging competitors' customers to fill out predrafted cancellation forms, denigrating competitors, and provoking major malfunctions to the lines that would deceptively appear to consumers to be the result of their decision to switch to an alternative operator. The negative effect on alternative operators was compounded by the fact that these practices, applied in territories of relatively small size, quickly contributed to creating a poor brand image of newcomers in the market.

As opposed to the Italian case, which could not be tackled under competition law for lack of dominance, France Telecom's position as an incumbent in the overseas territories made it possible to resort to Article 102 of the Treaty on the Functioning of the European Union (TFUE). If one considers that the factual background to the Italian and the French cases is almost identical, the difference in the tools used by the authorities to address the relevant conduct reveal that consumer law can be used to tackle the behavior of operators that, while no longer dominant following the opening up of the market to competition, still retain the ability to unduly influence consumer choice. In the cases described above, it is clear that the impact of a mass-scale implementation of an unfair commercial practice may well go beyond the individual, business-to-consumer relationship and may prevent the effective operation of competition.[15]

Along the same lines, the ICA also addressed problems concerning obstacles to customer migration in the Italian banking sector by sanctioning as an unfair commercial practice the conduct of several banks that aimed to prevent money borrowers from transferring their mortgage to another lender.[16] As in the previous case, firms adopted unfair commercial strategies to prevent a large number of customers from switching from one operator to another, but the requirements of neither Article 101 nor Article 102 could be fulfilled, so as to sanction the contested conduct. Yet, in light of the fact that a large number of banks and branches were involved in the infringement, the cumulative effects of the unfair practice prevented effective competition in the banking sector.

The lesson to be drawn is that in cases that fall short of competition law, consumer law may enhance consumer choice. It is not accidental that in all the decisions described above the unfair practices occurred as a follow-up to measures that aimed to introduce or increase competition in sectors where competition law remedies by themselves were not fully successful.

One caveat is that no cross-fertilization between competition and consumer law may occur in the absence of an ongoing, open dialogue between competition and consumer enforcement agencies. This dialogue is essential for markets to operate smoothly. The following French case illustrates this point. In February 2008,[17] France Telecom (which also provides Internet and TV services under the brand Orange) had been granted the exclusive right to retransmit three of the twelve sets of Premier league football matches on its channel Orange Foot.[18] The contested practice consisted of requiring that the subscription to Orange Foot be subject to the subscription to the Orange Internet service. The decision of first instance by the Tribunal de Commerce in Paris declared this practice illegal under Article L. 122 of the French Consumer Code, which prevents certain forms of tying.[19]

The Paris Cour d'appel overturned the decision and found, after declaring Article L. 122 inapplicable to the extent that it introduced a prohibition on a selling method that was not contained in Directive 2005/29,[20] that the contested offer could not fall within the definition of an "aggressive practice" in accordance with Article 8 of the directive. In particular, the court established that the mere fact that access to Orange Foot was associated exclusively with the Internet service could not "impair the average consumer's freedom of choice" within the meaning of Article 8. It reasoned that the average consumer who wished to subscribe to an Internet service, in making his choice, also would consider the ancillary service associated with it and would be able to differentiate it from the competing offers. The court did not address, however, the parallel issue, i.e., that the consumer who wishes to watch football matches on Orange Foot was unable to make any choice at all. In a sense, it was a forced double exclusive relationship (distribution exclusivity, resulting in a subscription to the television service itself, and transport and access exclusivity that required payment for a subscription to the Internet service provider's offer to access the contents) because Orange required consumers to purchase Internet service, as well as the subscription to Orange Foot, even though consumers might not be interested in Orange Foot.

The court's reasoning, in failing to take into account all implications of the contested practice, is hard to reconcile with a later opinion of the French Competition Authority,[21] which also tackled the issue of "double exclusivity." The French Competition Authority examined the opportunities and risks resulting from the double exclusivity model (such as possible opening of the pay-TV market, as against likely foreclosure of the high and very high-speed market) and concluded that the consumer might end up being locked in a "closed ecosystem," where he would remain with an operator solely or mainly because of the content that this operator may acquire on an exclusive basis. Adopting a similar reasoning would have brought the Cour d'appel to conclude that forcing consumers to purchase the Internet service in order to watch the Orange football matches might impair the average consumer's freedom of choice and, therefore, constitute an aggressive commercial practice. Had it applied such reasoning, the Cour d'appel would have grasped a perfect chance to ensure effective consumer choice while, at the same time, pinpointing the critical issues involved in double exclusivity from a competition point of view.

Unfair Practices, Dominant Position, and Public Service Obligations

In cases where the competition- and consumer-based remedies totally overlap, the latter may provide a speedier and simpler means of redress for the aggrieved parties. One example is in the transport industry. The recent introduction of high-speed trains in Italy has allegedly prompted the only rail operator in Italy, former state monopolist Trenitalia, to put in place a number of unfair practices, mainly affecting commuters' lines. The conduct in question includes unjustified increases in prices, increased delays, and the unavailability of certain commuters' routes during peak hours. Trenitalia runs two types of service. It runs the commercial, high-speed route, which it manages directly as a profit-making business. It also runs the commuters' routes via a concession by the regions (or in some cases, the state) on the basis of "public service contracts," is subject to public service obligations, and realizes no significant profits (Trenitalia actually receives state subsidies to cover its losses). The poor service on the commuters' routes could be ascribed to the fact that Trenitalia, shortly after starting its profit-making, high-speed service, appeared to have allocated to it the most attractive routes, while leaving the worst slots for the commuters' service and increasing their prices. According to the complaints, Trenitalia also purposely failed to ensure punctuality in the commuters' lines, in an attempt to prompt customers to switch from the cheaper service to the expensive high-speed trains. These practices may alternatively be classified as an abuse of dominant position, unfair commercial practices, or a failure to discharge public service obligations.

As far as public service is concerned, although the public service contracts list all obligations imposed on Trenitalia in running the service, there are no means for consumers to enforce such provisions. Accordingly, if the conduct qualified as "failure to discharge public service obligations," no means of redress would be available to the victims of Trenitalia's conduct. Against this background, the two sets of remedies that can usefully tackle this type of conduct are based in either competition or consumer law. However, the advantage of couching the claim as an unfair commercial practice lies in the fact that, while unfair conduct would need to be proved, it is not necessary to identify the relevant market and to establish dominance. The need to resort to such competition law notions, still unfamiliar to the average European lawyer, may constitute a significant hurdle to bringing a claim in the case of a private action, for example if the claim were to be brought by commuters' associations. Hence, the consumer law route may be a more appropriate tool to tackle conduct that is both anticompetitive and unfair in cases that may not be factually complex but may involve private claimants who are not willing to undertake antitrust litigation, commonly perceived as complicated and expensive.

. . .

This chapter has examined how consumer law may be used to complement and enhance the effectiveness of competition law. This occurs in at least two sets of cases: first, when markets have been opened up to competition but the conduct of the major player(s) prevents its development; second, where consumer-based remedies appear to be a more viable route to tackle anti-competitive conduct for claimants who are not willing to undertake antitrust litigation.

Yet, it is pretty obvious that consumer and competition law view consumer welfare from a significantly different perspective. Consumer law does not consider "consumer welfare" as a tool for its decision-making processes and simply aims to grant a set of rights to a well-defined group of individual entities that can be singled out on the basis of the fact that they act in order to satisfy personal and family needs and, for that reason, they deserve protection in their relationships with businesses: from this point of view, the protection of even one single person may justify the application of consumer law. Competition law, on the other hand, perceives consumers as "purchasers," i.e., not as a group of rightholders but simply as the counterpart to producers in a universe that is divided into "buyers" and "sellers"; against this background, "consumer welfare" (whatever meaning one wants to ascribe to it)[22] is simply a standard for deciding whether a certain conduct increases the efficiency/well-being of buyers of a specific product and, hence, for detecting anticompetitive behavior.

In spite of such differences, in practical terms, the two disciplines may well assist one another. While the European Commission is currently devoting significant time and energies in planning a European tool to encourage the private enforcement of competition law,[23] it must be pointed out that, at the level of remedies, several of the issues that arise in this context may also be relevant to the effective enforcement of consumer law, thus suggesting that, at least as far as consumer collective redress is concerned, it may be appropriate to introduce common measures to facilitate both types of claims.[24] One similarity, for example, has to do with competition between enforcers. Where enforcement (of either consumer or competition law) has been entrusted to a public body, mechanisms would have to be envisaged to enhance cooperation between the private and the public actors (e.g., ensuring that the decision of the public authority is binding), so as to facilitate private actions. A second similarity concerns the quantification of the loss suffered by the victim of anticompetitive or unfair conduct. This is relatively simple where, for example, the consumer is a direct buyer, or there is a clear failure to comply with one of the promises contained in an advertisement. However, it may be more complicated where the consumer is an indirect purchaser or in the case of agreements concluded between companies to boycott another company, or where the consumer alleges that he has been the victim of an aggressive practice, such as repeated unwanted phone calls.[25]

Such problems have never been seriously addressed as far as the private enforcement of consumer law is concerned, on the assumption that individual consumer losses are considered to be too insignificant to prompt any damage claims on behalf of the aggrieved customer. This, however, will change remarkably should any form of collective consumer redress be introduced. Directorate General Health and Consumers Affairs (DG SANCO) has recently published a green paper on collective consumer redress[26] that explores the options that are available in relation to consumer collective redress and proposes possible initiatives at EU level. The idea is that consumer-based and competition-based claims are to be kept distinct, "because of the specific nature of antitrust law and the wider scope of victims which includes also SMEs claims." Yet, consumer claims based on consumer and competition law have several features in common, which may suggest that the two types of claims may be enforced by means of a single tool.

This issue has attracted the attention of Competition Commissioner Almunia, who has launched a public consultation, commencing at the end of 2010, that will gather views on collective redress rules across the EU. The intention of the public consultation is to cover collective redress in antitrust and other policy areas, such as consumer protection and environmental law. Based on this consultation, the Commission would prepare a general legal framework on EU collective redress and would subsequently draw up specific legislative initiatives for the different policy areas. If the Commission sticks to its agenda, the relationship between consumer and competition law may be enriched by one further nuance.

Part IV

Competition Law and Institutional Design

10

Judicial Scrutiny and Competition Authorities

The Institutional Limits of Antitrust

Javier Tapia and Santiago Montt

There can be little doubt that an effective mechanism of judicial scrutiny of competition law decisions is an essential part of any competition regime. Competition authorities' powers and discretion (which may generally refer to questions of fact and law, including policy)[1] find their internal limit in the different levels of intervention that reviewing courts may be prepared to apply in the process of judicial scrutiny.

In *The Limits of Antitrust*, Judge Frank Easterbrook remarked that unless courts know the "right" balance between competition and cooperation in each market, they do not know in which direction to proceed.[2] His belief was that, in fact, judges know very little about business practices and their knowledge regarding complex economic arguments is rather poor. Considering also the "incommensurability of the stakes,"[3] Easterbrook noted, the task is even more difficult. In this chapter we observe that Easterbrook's insights on the "judicial" limits of antitrust crucially depend on the specific institutional design and the incentives it creates.

Institutional design delineates the allocation of power between the body with primary jurisdiction over antitrust matters, on the one hand, and the reviewing courts or tribunals, on the other.[4] In doing so, it defines the "proper relation"[5] between the primary decision maker (the enforcement agency) and the courts that scrutinize the actions of the enforcement agency. As we explain below, any institutional designer interested in pursuing this task within a particular regime needs to take into account two sets of fundamental variables related to both the "nature" of the administrative system and the substance of the law.

We analyze these variables and their trade-offs in the first section of the chapter. After that, we identify four models of judicial scrutiny that fit well in comparative practice. The remaining two sections focus on two of those models in more detail. We conclude by stressing that despite our still limited knowledge on institutional design, judicial review would benefit from a deferential standard of review applied by courts in relation to a competition authority's expert decisions.

Institutional Variables

When considering the institutional design of the competition regime, there are two important sets of questions to consider. First, is there a need for a unified administrative decision maker, or should the matter be left to a body separated from the one in charge of investigating and prosecuting anticompetitive conduct? As a follow-up question, if there is a separate body in charge of deciding antitrust violations, should it be a specialized tribunal, or should it be the courts of general jurisdiction? Second, what are the characteristics the reviewing court should have? Among the follow-up questions are what is the scope of the review under which it makes its decisions and how much deference should the judiciary show when scrutinizing the decision made by the primary decision maker?

The "Competition Authority"

From the institutional perspective, there are three fundamental powers that need to be allocated: investigation, enforcement, and decision making. These powers can be either accumulated in a single body or distributed among two or more bodies.

In case of accumulation, a single agency specialized in competition matters undertakes all the investigative, enforcement, and adjudicative functions. That is, it plays simultaneously the part of "law-maker, policeman, investigator, prosecutor, judge, and jury."[6] The competition authority exclusively comprises this body.

In case of distribution of powers, there are two bodies. The first body (the agency) fulfills mainly a prosecutorial role, including investigative and enforcement functions.[7] Formal complaints must be brought to a second, separated court or tribunal that holds decision-making power. In this case, there is an option for a specialized or mixed (quasi-judicial) court, on the one hand, or a court of general jurisdiction, on the other.[8]

The Reviewing Court

The second institutional variable is related to the reviewing court. Attending to its composition, the reviewing court can be either specialized or generalist; attending to its jurisdiction, it can be a special tribunal or a court of general jurisdiction. The reviewing court scrutinizes an antitrust decision within the scope allowed by the law (i.e., appellate review or judicial review), applying either a deferential or a nondeferential standard of review.

There are two possible institutional designs for the reviewing court: special tribunals and courts of general jurisdiction. The level of specialization affects the standards of judicial review and the extent of the bodies' discretion.

We consider specialization as a comprehensive concept composed of three parts; "generalist" courts lack one or more of them. The first one is expertise: a greater level of knowledge in the specific substantive area to be subject to judgments—in this case, competition law. Note that it is not necessary for the court to be more expert than the primary decision maker.[9] It suffices that it possesses an important knowledge in the area so as to decide on the details of the question at issue. As long as judges' knowledge (and/or that of their supporting teams) improves, they may claim proficiency akin to that of the competition authority.

The second part is experience, the accumulation of knowledge or skills. A court also specializes when it must revise a large number of decisions coming from the same agency, particularly if those decisions are of similar kind or nature. This means that, contrary to the common belief, expertise is not the defining feature of specialization.[10]

Finally, specialization also comprises object-specificity—the specific aim of introducing logical coherence to and protecting (at least one or some of) the objectives of one part of the legal system. The legislature considers that there are valuable public policy reasons to establish a specialized jurisdiction entrusted with a task that existing jurisdictions, it deems, are unable to accomplish. We deem the three components of specialization as equally relevant and arguably inseparable.[11]

Because of their lack of expert knowledge or their lack of experience, generalist courts do not revise all the aspects of the primary decision. Commonly, assessment will be directed to procedural questions and to review whether there are noticeable departures from the law. But questions of law and policy will normally be left to the competition authority, i.e., the competition policy makers. That is, courts will tend to maintain themselves bounded to discrete choices, with the expected result that they defer more to the competition authority's interpretation. Generally, policy makers stress arguments of economic complexity and technicalities to justify this sort of "light touch" approach.

Such arguments, however, are not particularly sound in the presence of specialized reviewing tribunals. Specialization creates incentives to increase judicial discretion, because the tribunal has incentives to revise all aspects of the decision—that is, a specialized tribunal makes continuous choices. Greater specialization allows tribunals to feel more confident of their own capabilities when dealing with topics that in principle would appear to fall almost exclusively under the remit of competition authorities—and hence they judge even on technically complex matters.

Specialized tribunals have a deeper understanding of relevant policy objectives, reduce the probability of simple inadvertence, pursue coherence (ideally), and minimize dependence on the views and adversarial skills of opposing counsel.[12] Indeed, all of these points do not imply an argument in favor or disfavor of specialization. Our argument, at least at this stage, remains merely positive: if a tribunal is specialized, it will arguably be more inclined to widen the review, no matter how expert the primary decision maker is.

The two systems of judicial scrutiny are appellate review and judicial review. Whereas the former is the general term for the process by which upper courts scrutinize matters decided by lower courts, the latter refers to the court's overriding power to determine if an administrative decision is legally defective. Each system has a different scope depending on the grounds for review, which may refer to questions of law, fact, and/or procedure. The scope of the review is legally set by statute or the rule of precedents.

Ideally, the scope of the judicial scrutiny should match the institutional characteristics of the reviewing body. If judges are nonexperts and therefore have an incentive to differ with the expert competition authority, at least in questions of policy but probably also in questions of fact and law, the legal framework should not compel judges to review these questions, because the outcome might be harmful for the objectives the system pursues. Conversely, if the body is specialist in the area and therefore will not tend to differ with the expert administration, the framework should not restrain that incentive. Otherwise, there is no reason to create such a specialized body in the first place.

Regardless of the scope, in practice judicial scrutiny can be deployed throughout a continuum that ranges from minimum scrutiny of the primary decision to total substitution of judgment. These two extremes represent the two administrative doctrines that set limits to the judicial control of decisions—the "deference" and "nondeference" approaches.[13] Both deference and nondeference are useful heuristic devices that can be used as a sort of shortcut to stress primary decision-maker discretion or judicial discretion, respectively.

For that reason, notwithstanding the fact that judicial control is a question of degree, the dichotomy is still useful as an analytical tool. The deference view indicates that whenever the meaning of a statute is ambiguous with respect to the specific question at issue, courts should refuse to consider the legal merit of the decisions. That is, the primary decision maker is given a wider margin of discretion in its pronouncements. On the other hand, nondeference can simply be defined negatively as the lack of deference. Only in its most extreme version does it mean the entire substitution of the judgment made by the primary decision maker by what a court believes to be the "right" interpretation of the issue in question.

The Relation Between the Reviewing Court and the Primary Decision Maker

The *ex post* type of review that a court adopts has an impact on the *ex ante* behavior of the competition authority. The reason is that, depending on the specific institutional characteristics, the authority can (and should) "anticipate" the possible outcome of the scrutiny.

Consider first the case of the nonspecialized court. Since a generalist, deferential court will only examine whether one part of the antitrust decision (i.e., the law) complies with the objective defined in the relevant statutes and case law, the outcome of the review is to a great extent clear for the competition authority. Either the court will affirm the decision maker's option if the chosen rule maximizes the objective, or it will reverse that option if the rule does not pursue the objective's maximization. The competition authority may know in advance that by following certain rules (generally, procedural rules) and/or using some mechanisms (including guidelines, agency adjudication, and rulemaking, among other tools), the probability of a court reversing a primary decision decreases.

In sharp contrast, the outcome of the judicial scrutiny is less clear when the court is specialized. Since a specialized, nondeferential court has incentives to focus on every aspect of the decision maker's judgment, the competition authority does not know whether the court will agree that certain facts in the decision lead to the maximization of the objective pursued (whatever that objective may be). The assessment of facts (or policies) comprises much more discretion, which leaves greater space for judicial revision of decisions. A specialized court can reach the conclusion that the facts, the law, or both of them do not maximize the objective.[14] As one commentator has accurately summarized, for competition authorities this reflects a "crude equation: review of experts by generalists—wide margin of appreciation; review of experts by other experts (potentially even 'more expert experts')—narrow margin."[15]

Institutional Models

The identified institutional variables give rise to four main institutional models. Table 10.1 summarizes their main characteristics.[16]

Indeed, the models represent only "pure" theoretical constructs. They often mingle or may vary in practice. However, notwithstanding that systems may not be reduced so easily, the comparative reality of most countries fits reasonably well with them.

Under the first model, which is indeed the traditional administrative law model, there is a single competition authority (usually a multimember commission) that is normally part of the executive. With or without institutional independence, policy making is located in one of the political branches of government. The most well-known example is the European Commission.[17] In turn, common courts (for example, the General Court in the EU[18]) review agencies' decisions, applying the traditional procedure for scrutiny of administrative agencies—judicial review. Reviewing courts tend to acknowledge the expertise of the agency and hence apply a deferential standard. This model is therefore no different than the paradigmatic administrative law institutional structure of governance.

The second model differs from the first one in both institutional variables. First, the competition authority comprises two bodies with different powers—a prosecutor and an adjudicator. Examples are the Canadian Competition Bureau (CB) and the Competition Tribunal (CT),[19] and the Chilean Fiscalía Nacional Económica (FNE) and the Tribunal de Defensa de la Libre

Table 10.1 Institutional variables and models

Institutional variables \ *Models*		*Model I: Generalist court reviews competition agency*	*Model II: Generalist court reviews specialized tribunal/court*	*Model III: Specialized court reviews competition agency*	*Model IV: Judicial governance (no judicial scrutiny)*
Number of bodies		*1*	*2*	*1*	*2*
Competition authority	*Allocation of powers*	Accumulated: single agency performs all functions	Distributed: special agency investigates and prosecutes cases; court/tribunal adjudicates	Accumulated: single agency performs all functions	Distributed: special agency investigates and prosecutes cases; court adjudicates
Competition authority	*Primary decision maker*	Competition agency	Specialized court/tribunal	Competition agency	Generalist court
Reviewing court	*Body*	Generalist Court	Generalist court	Specialized court/tribunal	—
Reviewing court	*Scope of review*	Judicial review	Appellate review/ judicial review	Appellate review	—
Reviewing court	*Standard of review*	Deference	Variable level of deference	Nondeference	—

Competencia (TDLC).[20] In turn, the antitrust decision by the specialized tribunal is normally subject to review by a generalist court.

Since the body subject to the revision is a tribunal, the reviewing court (in our example, a Federal Court of Appeal and the Chilean Supreme Court, respectively) applies either an appellate procedure (Canada) or a special procedure (Chile). In this sense, the task of the reviewing court may or may not differ from the one it fulfills in any other area of law. Finally, the standard of review accepts various degrees of deference depending on the regime. In Canada, for example, the standard is one of deference. In Chile it has not been formally defined, but the day-to-day practice shows low levels of deference.

The third model is a "hybrid." Its best example is the U.K. institutional design. In this model, the competition agency (the Office of Fair Trading, or OFT) makes the decision, which in then scrutinized by an expert tribunal (the Competition Appeal Tribunal or CAT).[21] However, it is not the nature of the reviewing court that makes this model rather "anomalous," but the standard of review. Unlike most traditional models, the CAT hears appeals on the merits against all sector regulators and the OFT for infringements and noninfringements of the Competition Act 1998.[22] Also, consistent with the nature of the CAT, the standard of review is one of nondeference.

Finally, the fourth model is one of judicial governance, and therefore, one of "no judicial scrutiny"—the investigative and enforcement agency must bring formal complaints before a generalist court, which is the body that actually adopts the decision. In this model, generalist courts do not scrutinize but perform as competition policy makers. This model is actually the original antecedent of the second model but, unlike its successor, it lacks a system of review specific for competition law. The main example of this model is antitrust enforcement in the United States by the Department of Justice (DOJ) before federal courts. Table 10.2 summarizes the examples of each model as described above.

In the next two sections we focus the assessment of the first two models, which are the most popular institutional design throughout the world. The third and fourth models are arguably idiosyncratic to the legal, institutional, and historical realities of the United Kingdom and United States, respectively.

Table 10.2 Examples of institutional models

Models / *Variables*		*Model I: Generalist court reviews competition agency*		*Model II: Generalist court reviews specialized tribunal/court*		*Model III: Specialized court reviews competition agency*	*Model IV: Judicial governance (no judicial scrutiny)*
Jurisdiction		*U.S.*	*EU*	*Chile*	*Canada*	*U.K.*	*U.S.*
Competition authority	*Bodies*	FTC	Commission	FNE/TDLC	CB/CT	OFT	DOJ/district court
	Primary decision-maker			TDLC	CT		Federal courts
Reviewing court	*Body*	Federal court of appeals	General court (CFI/ECJ)	Supreme court	Federal court of appeal	CAT	—
	Scope of review	Judicial review	Judicial review	*Reclamación*	Appeal	Appeal on the merits	—
	Standard of review	Deference	Deference	Nondeference	Deference	Nondeference	—

The Traditional Administrative Model

The Competition Agency

In the traditional administrative model (the first model) the agency must fulfill conflicting roles. Not only must it investigate, enforce, and punish. The agency also must perform broader policy maker functions. This is particularly clear in the EU. As the European Court of Justice (ECJ) states:

> The supervisory task conferred on the Commission by Articles [101(1)] and [102] of the [EU] Treaty . . . not only includes the duty to investigate and punish individual infringements but also encompasses the duty to pursue a general policy designed to apply, in competition matters, the principles laid down by the Treaty and to guide the conduct of undertakings in the light of those principles.[23]

From an administrative law perspective, these roles conflict because there is a trade-off between adjudication and implementation. This tension, an old and well-known problem in administrative law adjudication,[24] is due to the fact that these principles "promote different values in the sense that their rationale is to strike respectively different balances between social and individual interests."[25]

On the one hand, adjudicatory functions require the decision maker to protect the rights and interests of the affected person or firm. Under the demands of fairness, the decision maker must therefore be a neutral third-party. On the other hand, policy implementation forces the decision maker to promote and secure social and collective goals that go beyond the individual rights and interests of those immediately affected. The decision maker is not neutral, but a party interested in obtaining a certain policy outcome.[26]

As a consequence, in the administrative model the competition authority is a policy-motivated body not bound by the neutrality and independence imposed by other modes of governance, and then is capable of adopting aggressive policies that foster competition, actively pursuing efficiency and consumer protection in markets.

In addition, the agency normally has the power to adopt fines and cease and desist orders containing behavioral or structural remedies, including positive injunctions. For example, in the EU the Commission may impose upon firms "any behavioral or structural remedies which are proportionate to the infringement committed and necessary to bring the infringement effectively to an end."[27]

Yet the main challenge these bodies face is to accommodate their strong powers with the protection of individual rights and interests in investigations, adjudications, and the enforcement of decisions. For this reason, the use of the administrative model is normally accompanied by formal adjudicatory proceedings that pass muster under due process minimum standards.

In the EU there is no separation between investigation and adjudication, and the Commission can directly enforce injunctions, compliance, and orders.[28] Yet formal accusations are conducted through a highly regulated formal adjudicatory process that safeguards parties' rights and interests.[29] This process includes a pleading phase, an evidentiary phase, and the right to orally present arguments. A hearing officer, who does not belong to the Directorate General for Competition,[30] "plays an important role in guaranteeing fairness of procedure,"[31] but is limited to process issues.[32] The Commission issues its final decision after completion of a complex bureaucratic process.[33] In the end, the Commission decides on issues of conduct and remedies by majority vote without formally hearing arguments. However, the interested parties are able to visit individual commissioners to put forward their case.[34]

Judicial Scrutiny and Standards of Review

Given that the first model (the general administrative law one) supposes to a certain extent a preference for values connected to implementation over those of adjudication, an *ex post* process of judicial scrutiny is essential to fully restore fairness in those institutional designs that rely on full-powered agencies.

Article 263 of the TFEU allows parties to petition the courts to "review the legality" of the Commission's decisions on grounds of "lack of competence, infringement of an essential procedural requirement, infringement of the Treaties or of any rule of law relating to their application, or misuse of powers."[35] When performing judicial review "it is not the function of the Court to substitute its own judgment for that of the Commission but to ensure that the Commission keeps within the bounds of its powers and discretion and observes the law."[36] By exception, as provided by Article 261 of the TFEU, the General Court has "unlimited jurisdiction with regard to the penalties" imposed by the Commission under Regulation 1/2003. Even though the review is of legality, because of fairness requirements arising under the European Convention on Human Rights, the General Court examines "the factual basis for the Commission's decisions with particular rigor."[37] These findings on the standard of review are compatible with the generalist nature of the reviewing courts.

The Distributed Model with Application to the Chilean Case

As mentioned earlier, the Chilean institutional design is a classic example of the model where an administrative agency investigates and prosecutes cases, and a court adjudicates those cases that the agency brings before it. In Chile, a specialized and independent tribunal (the Tribunal de Defensa de la Libre Competencia, TDLC) is the decision-making authority, while the agency pursues mainly a prosecutorial role. The Supreme Court directly reviews decisions by the TDLC.

The TDLC

The TDLC is headed by a chair and has four other expert members (by law, two economists and three lawyers), the five members being appointed for six-year terms. The chair must be a "professionally prominent lawyer" with ten years of experience in competition matters, economic or commercial law. The president of the Republic appoints the chair from a list of five candidates proposed by the Supreme Court, selected through public examination of their qualifications. The president also appoints two of the members from two lists of three candidates each, proposed by the Central Bank Council and selected through public review of their qualifications. The Central Bank Council appoints the two remaining members, and their qualifications are also subject to public review.[38] Although these posts do not exclude other professional activity, in practice members of the TDLC serve nearly full time.[39] All five members attend hearings and vote on decisions.

An Ambiguous and Broad System of Judicial Scrutiny: "Reclamación"

Final decisions of the TDLC are subject to the judicial oversight of the Supreme Court of Justice (the highest court in Chile).[40] The Supreme Court reviews cases brought under a special recourse called "complaint recourse" (*recurso de reclamación*).[41] The scope of the review is not defined in the competition statute, and has been interpreted in the broadest possible terms. The Supreme Court has typically decided on questions of law, policy, or fact, and, on occasions, has substituted its judgment for that of the TDLC. That means the *reclamación* has functioned in practice as an appellate review.

We are aware of only one case in which the Supreme Court explicitly commented on the nature of the *reclamación*. In the decision concerning a *Consulta*—an *ex ante* proceeding that allows parties and government agencies to consult on whether an act or conduct is consistent with the competition law—by the undersecretary of telecommunication, the Court held that it had jurisdiction to "fully" review all the grounds considered by the TDLC, "including the legal and economic analysis that allowed it to reach the decision it took."[42]

Nondeference turns the *reclamación* into an extremely open procedural device. Arguably for this reason (which incentivizes parties to use this recourse), but also because the TDLC has issued more decisions than its predecessors, the Supreme Court's involvement in competition law matters has increased since 2003 (the year of the TDLC's creation).

Of the fifty-seven of TDLC's judgments that have been subject to the *reclamación* recourse between the TDLC creation in 2003 and the end of 2010 (we consider here cases that were full controversies, i.e., we exclude *consultas* and other noncontroversial matters), the Supreme Court upheld thirty-nine decisions, partially upheld twelve, and set aside six. One view of this would be that the TDLC's decisions are based on solid foundations. Below the surface, however, the Court has not been particularly deferential toward the TDLC in any of the subjects it has had the opportunity to scrutinize—including, among others, the standing of parties to request review, the scope of the TDLC's powers, the merits of the TDLC's fact analysis and the evidence submitted by the parties, the interpretation of substantive law, and the sufficiency of sanctions and other remedies. As we will show in the next section, in all of these subjects the Court has yet to define with precision the extent to which the *reclamación* entitles it to review TDLC's decisions.

However, before analyzing the scope of the *reclamación*, we note that the Supreme Court's approach to antitrust jurisprudence has not been dominated by efficiency considerations. Retributive justice concerns are usually the basis for review. In fact, the Supreme Court has held that antitrust punishment must be inspired by the "culpability" principle.[43] The conduct must be "reproachable," meaning a "voluntary act of illegal nature because of its disagreement with the norms that the law establishes in protection of the freedom that must exist to compete in markets."[44] Likewise, the proportionality principle also has played a relevant role in Supreme Court reviews of competition proceedings.[45]

There is one recent sign of an incipient turn to a more "economic approach." In a 2010 decision, the Supreme Court indicated that it may start to accept a more consequentialist approach to antitrust enforcement. Indeed, it endorsed an enforcement approach based on deterrence and efficiency:

> With respect to the determination of fines – which was a matter that petitioners objected in their three recourses of reclamation – this Court, in accordance with what was stated in the decision by the Competition Court, considers that *the fine must impose on [the defendant] costs greater than the expected benefit of having established artificial barriers to the market* as proved in the decision.[46]

The Nondeferential Approach to Judicial Review

The Chilean Supreme Court has not acknowledged the specialized nature of the TDLC as a ground for adopting a more deferential stance when hearing *reclamación* cases. An analysis of the fifty-seven decisions adopted by the Supreme Court between 2003 and 2010, summarized in Table 10.3, does not in itself say much. As noted, it certainly suggests a deferential stance, but it may be an instance of a "happy accident," that is, a situation where the Supreme Court's nondeferential decision coincides with the decisions adopted by the TDLC (empirically it is impossible to distinguish these two situations).[47]

With respect to the scope of the *reclamación* on issues of fact, the Supreme Court has been particularly nondeferential in cases dealing with proof of collusion by indirect evidence. Based on a criminal law understanding of antitrust sanctions, in both the *Oxigeno* and *Agencias Navieras* cases, the Supreme Court has required an extremely demanding standard of proof, invalidating the TDLC's findings that defendant firms had colluded.[48]

In the *Isapres* case, although the Supreme Court confirmed the TDLC's finding in rejecting the existence of a cartel, it criticized the way in which the TDLC examined and assessed the indirect evidence in the record.[49] More importantly, it rejected the economic reasoning followed by the TDLC, which had looked at each piece of evidence and analyzed whether it was more consistent with collusion or competition. The Supreme Court did not accept

Table 10.3 Chilean Supreme Court standard of review (2003–2010)

Facts		*Law*	
Deference	*Nondeference*	*Deference*	*Nondeference*
50	7	45	12

the probabilistic economic assessments of the TDLC, showing a manifest lack of deference toward the factual findings of the latter:

> The dispositions cited in the four preceding grounds are encased by imprecision and a lack of certainty unsuitable to the reasoning that gives basis to the resolutions adopted by the Republic's judges. In effect, said declarations are vague, equivocal, contradictory and unenlightening on defining if, effectively, there is a collusive agreement denounced in this case. It is not enough to mention the concurrence of elements that, eventually, could serve to establish that fact, but it is required to accurately determine if they accredit or not said circumstance.
>
> That said conviction is absent from the decision under examination, which, on the contrary, ponders on uncertain potentialities that could lead one way or another, forces to reject its grounds and leads this Court to establish, with clarity and certainty, that the means of proof included in the process are insufficient to prove the existence of collusion claimed by the Fiscalía Nacional Económica against the accused Isapres.[50]

Moreover, the Supreme Court has not been deferential to the TDLC on issues of legal interpretation. It seems that the Supreme Court simply will impose its statutory interpretations over the more policy-oriented interpretations of the TDLC. For instance, in the *James Hardie* predation case, the Court overturned a TDLC decision that held that predatory prices always require market power. Following a textualist interpretation of article 3(c) of DL 211, the Supreme Court held, showing no deference to the expert position of the TDLC, that the word "reach" used in the statute meant that firms that did not hold a dominant position but might acquire it at some future time should be punished:

> It is inferred from this disposition that it is not necessary for whoever is leading a predatory practice to have a dominant position in the market, as one of their objectives is explicitly to reach this position precisely because they do not have it.[51]

Finally, the Supreme Court has not shown signs of deference toward the TDLC on issues of the size of fines. In the *AM Patagonia* case, a case of a medical services cartel in the city of Punta Arenas, the Supreme Court indicated that it was "prudentially reducing" the fine imposed by the TDLC, giving the impression that it will simply apply its own discretion on fines (in this case, the Supreme Court applied a fine at a ridiculously low level—less than $100).

Finally, the Supreme Court has reduced the penalty amount established by the TDLC in six cases (in only three cases it has increased the fine). The Court characteristically starts its analysis by noting that the TDLC has not adequately indicated all the relevant facts and considerations necessary to correctly determine the fine size. This lack of reasoning on the part of the TDLC regarding financial sanctions affects the rights and interests of the parties, particularly regarding due process and proportionality. This process allows the Supreme Court to redetermine the size of the fine.[52]

Contradictory Behavior

The question is why the Supreme Court behaves nondeferentially even considering its nonspecialized institutional nature. The Supreme Court is a "generalist" because it lacks object specificity (for obvious reasons), accumulation of knowledge or skills (i.e., experience),[53] and expertise (for its members are not competition experts). It also lacks technical supportive capacity (unlike the TDLC, which has a staff of competition lawyers and economists) and it does not even have the power to request the opinion of experts. These features limit its ability to undertake a full review of the substantive merits of a case, particularly when the TDLC applies sophisticated economic analysis to its cases. These features also should provide fewer incentives for the Supreme Court to revise decisions of the specialized TDLC. Somewhat oddly, the outcome has so far been the reverse.

The reason seems to lie in distrust of the TDLC and its "excess" of economic analysis (instead of classic juridical syllogisms). The Supreme Court seems to confound the need for some form of hierarchical control over the TDLC with a demand for a strict standard of review. However, being less deferential does not equate to being less vigilant and readily available to control open, unrestrained behavior on the part of the TDLC.

A number of features of the Chilean institutional design already ensure the TDLC remains adequately restrained, even if the Supreme Court acts less deferentially. For example, there are principled substantive demands (such as proportionality) that cannot be overlooked. Beyond these features embedded in Chilean institutional design, however, one form to overcome the Supreme Court's incentives to be nondeferential would be to adopt a rather simple institutional solution similar to that applied, for example, in the U.K. CAT (on a de facto basis) or in the Canadian Competition Tribunal (by law). That is, Chile could establish a mix of "generalist" court judges and lay experts. Theoretically, this should both act as deterrent to avoid significant departures on the part of the TDLC from the common practice of the generalist courts, and discourage Supreme Court justices (at least to some extent) from overturning decisions made by one of their peers.

However, the Chilean practice in other areas of law suggests that this mixed approach would not be a suitable solution. Members of the Supreme Court do not tend to be particularly deferential toward their judicial colleagues; different chambers of the Court are well known in Chile for adopting conflicting decisions. Given these cultural practices, bringing down a Supreme Court member to the composition of the TDLC will not guarantee improving the rate of institutional deference.

A better solution would be to define more specifically the nature and characteristics of the *reclamación* recourse. During the most recent legal reform of the competition law in 2009 there were attempts at Congress to transform the *reclamación* into an appeal and, subsequently, into a nullity petition. Yet, in the absence of agreement, the drafters of the statute preferred to return to the status quo of an undefined *reclamación*.

Even though, in our opinion, the best interpretation of the current *reclamación* would be that of a petition that implies a considerable level of deference by the Supreme Court toward the TDLC, we believe it would be better to clearly state this in a reform of the competition statute. The statute should define the *reclamación* in reference to other judicial recourses that imply higher levels of deference toward facts (as *casación*) or even toward law (*queja*).

. . .

We have analyzed different institutional models used throughout the world to establish competition authorities and reviewing courts. Our knowledge of these and other models is still relatively limited to indicate which ones are superior. Political, legal and economic, and cultural idiosyncratic factors are too relevant to provide general answers.

Nonetheless, it is clear that, regarding judicial review, if a court is generalist it should act with deference with the competition authority's expert decisions. The examples of the European Commission on administrative models and Canada on "distributed" models are eloquent. Countries like Chile, which have similar institutional structures, should follow their path: the Supreme Court should adopt a deferential standard of review. That would be an enormous, positive improvement.

11

Competition Authorities

Independence and Advocacy

Frédéric Jenny

In January 2010, Korea's president Lee replaced Chairman Chung Ho-Yul of the Korean Fair Trade Commission (KFTC) before the end of his term. Press reports indicate that the appointment of a new chairman of the KFTC was made as part of a larger shake-up in the Lee government. This event was commented on rather unfavorably by members of the competition community. For example, Joseph Seon Hur, a former Korean competition official, remarked that the appointment of Chairman Kim Dong-Su has shocked the Korean competition community in government, business, and the private bar. He added that this event showed that the KFTC may be vulnerable to political interruption.

Two characteristics of the Korean competition system are of particular interest in the context of this chapter: the fact that the KFTC has played a pivotal role in reforming a wide range of anticompetitive regulations in Korea and the fact that the chairman of the KFTC is a cabinet member. The Korean situation, where the competition authority is not an independent body but has very large powers of advocacy, is an interesting starting point to revisit the issue of the relationship between the independence of competition authorities and their ability to advocate for competition.

The Case for the Independence of Competition Authorities

There is wide agreement that competition authorities should be independent both from the executive branch of government and from the business community. In a recent paper, John Vickers suggests that the rationale for independence of competition authorities from government, like the rationale for independence of central banks, has two strands: comparative advantage and commitment.[1]

If competition policy is the most effective way to achieve free and competitive markets but is not necessarily considered to be an effective way to achieve some other public policy goals, such as full employment, it is preferable to assign only one goal to the competition authority, that of protecting competition, rather than trying to use the competition authority to achieve other public policy goals that might be better achieved through other means. Thus, if competition authorities have a comparative advantage in promoting free competition but no comparative advantage in promoting other public policy goals, they should focus narrowly on the promotion of competitive markets, and public policy makers should not interfere with them and burden them with other goals.

The commitment argument states that if an independent agency is in charge of competition policy of a country, the commitment of the government of that country to pursue competition policy is more credible than if the competition policy is administered by an nonindependent part of the executive branch. Demonstrating a commitment to a continued and stable competition policy also may be important in the context of international trade relations. Indeed, it is frequently the case that countries negotiating trade liberalization agreements are willing to open their borders only on the condition that private restrictions on the access to the markets in the other countries involved do not replace the public barriers that have been eliminated through the negotiation of the trade agreement. This requires that these other countries be committed to enforce competition law that prohibits single firm exclusionary practices or collective behaviors with that effect.

Even if there is no direct attempt by the executive branch to influence the outcome of competition law enforcement cases in ways that either force the competition authority to take on board other social policy goals or show a lack of commitment to free competition principles, there is a risk that the lack of independence of a competition authority may lead it to different conclusions than the ones it would have reached had it been independent. For example, Professor George Yarrow explained:

> My strong view is that the big regulatory issues are best addressed via organisational cultures that are deliberative/adjudicative in nature. In relation to economic issues, for example, courts generally make better assessments than administrative agencies, because (a) they are usually much more interested in discovering what is the case/truth, and (b) they make use of a sort of competitive process (there will be alternative cases/narratives put before the court). In contrast, the attentions of executive/administrative agencies are easily distracted by bureaucratic and short-term media/political issues, and one of their central objectives (in practice possibly their central objective) is usually to convey a good impression of themselves, irrespective of that which is the case. (One of the lessons I have learnt from a lifetime of study in these areas is that it is difficult to overestimate the potential dysfunctionality of large bureaucracies which, for one reason or another, are in contact with the political system).[2]

Direct interference by the executive branch in the decision-making process of competition authorities or attempts by such authorities to "please" the executive have consequences that may go beyond the social costs involved when erroneous decisions occur in specific cases. Indeed, the mere possibility of such interference may discourage investment by making investors fear that the playing field will not be level, or even worse, that they may be partly or wholly expropriated by decisions masquerading as competition law decisions.

There is also a large consensus that the competition authorities should be independent from business interests. One of the fears frequently expressed is that the competition authority could be "captured" by private interests, particularly the interests of the most powerful (domestic or international) firms that have vast resources and may exert political influence, making the authority unable to discharge its law enforcement responsibilities in a fair and equitable manner. In such instances, not only would the faith in free markets of the population at large and of political elites be shaken, but the competition authority could end up undermining competition by turning a blind eye on some of the most glaring anticompetitive practices or transactions or by being used strategically to prevent the emergence of potential competition, to the benefit of incumbent cartelists or dominant firms.

The importance of an independent competition law enforcement agency making decisions on an objective basis is now well understood in many countries. For example, an International Competition Network (ICN) report on competition agency effectiveness stated, "It is generally agreed that competition agencies should be 'independent'—i.e., that their actions should be based on the facts and the law and not political considerations."[3]

Ministers often resist the idea that competition authorities or sectoral regulators should be independent of the executive branch. For example, in January 2010 the French minister for industry attracted a storm of criticism when he announced his intention to amend the telecommunication law in order to change the composition of the board of the French telecom regulator. He intended to create a position for a special government representative who would be entrusted with the task of informing the board of the government's views and would have some power over the agenda of the telecom regulator (since he could request the board to study questions of interest to the government without possibility for the board to refuse such a request). The European Commission immediately made it known that it would examine the compatibility of the draft amendment with the European regulation with a view to ensure that the French telecom regulator could discharge its functions in an impartial and independent way. Yet some ministers are also aware of the benefits of independence for the competition agency (or agencies), as Vince Cable, the United Kingdom minister for industry referred to the fact "that the UK competition regime is regarded as one of the best in the world, particularly because of its independence."[4]

Because of skepticism about the possibility that competition authorities in developing countries may be truly independent of the executive branch or of the business community, some commentators, fearing that competition decisions might be tainted by political expediency and discourage foreign direct investment, have suggested that those countries should not adopt a competition law at all. However, this extreme view never has been dominant. Indeed, in the 1990s and the first decade of the twenty-first century a large number of developing countries have enacted a competition law and created a competition commission independent of the executive branch.

The Characteristics of an Independent Competition Authority

There are numerous discussions about the meaning of independence for competition (and more generally for regulatory) agencies and about the ways to guarantee independence, both from the executive branch and from undue influence by the business community.

When discussing the independence of a competition authority from the government, it may be useful to explore the respective importance of structural and operational independence. When considering the issue of the independence of a competition authority from undue influence by some elements of the business community, it is useful to consider the transparency of the authority's decision-making process and the review mechanism of the authority's decision.

Structural independence means that the agency will be an entity separate from ministries. For example, the U.S. Federal Trade Commission (FTC), which reports to the U.S. Congress, is entirely separate from the executive branch of the U.S. government and is a structurally independent agency. The French Autorité de la Concurrence is another example of a structurally independent agency, not part of the Ministry for Economic Affairs or any other ministry. The Australian Competition and Consumer Commission is also an independent statutory agency. The BundesKartellamt in Germany is also independent of the executive. At the other end of the spectrum, some competition agencies are not structurally independent from the executive branch of government. Among them are the Antitrust Division, which is part of the U.S. Justice Department, or the Competition General Directorate of the European Commission (DG Comp).

Even though there is a widespread opinion that lack of structural independence may expose a competition authority to undue influence, this need not be so in all cases. For example, it is well known that despite the fact that it is not structurally independent from the Justice Department, the U.S. Antitrust Division is de facto independent in the sense that the executive (other parts of the administration of the president of the United States) consider intervening in the way the Antitrust Division conducts investigations or makes conclusions. At a more general level and as an Organisation for Economic Cooperation and Development (OECD) document recently noted, "there are many countries in which the competition agency is not structurally independent, but experience has shown that an aggressive, competent agency can acquire a significant degree of independence regardless of its place within the structure of government."[5]

Operational independence refers to the freedom that an agency has to investigate the cases it decides to pursue in its enforcement activity and to impose the solutions it deems appropriate. It also refers to the freedom of the competition agency to make comments and to otherwise participate in government and regulatory matters and, in the course of such advocacy activities, to take positions that are independent of those held by others in the public and private sectors.

Many organizational features contribute to the functional independence or the lack of independence of competition authorities. Some of the features that come to mind when assessing the functional independence of a competition authority are the conditions of appointment of the agency's head and of the board members. Issues include whether they have fixed term appointments, whether those fixed terms are renewable, what is the duration of appointments, who appoints the members of the board, whether they can be dismissed during their term (cf. the Korean case previously mentioned) and whether such dismissals can occur for policy-related reasons, what is the status of the head of the agency and the status of the commissioners, and whether they can hold other offices in government or in the private sector.

The issue of the selection of board members of competition authorities and the status of such board members is important to ensure the independence of a competition authority both from government influence and from private business interests. This is a particularly difficult issue in small countries, where economic experts are not numerous and where they tend to have important roles in business and be well connected with influential local politicians. Thus, ensuring that board members will not all be appointed by ministers or the president and that some board members will be sensitive to consumer issues appears to be crucial to both the credibility and the effectiveness of a competition authority. Such concerns include conditions related to the formal relationship between a competition authority and the legislative or parliamentary branch: for example, whether the independence of the authority is explicitly stated in the law, what kind of autonomy (decisional, organizational, and financial) the authority is granted, what body other than a court can overturn an authority's decision, how the authority is funded, who controls the authority's budget, who decides the internal organization of the authority, and who is in charge of the authority's personnel policy.

Additional issues include conditions related to the powers of the authority to remedy anticompetitive practices or transactions. For example, does the authority have the power to set up its own rules of procedure for its activities, use its own means of investigation, and adopt precautionary measures during investigations, and what kind of sanctions can it impose?

Related to the issue of the powers of the competition authority to remedy anticompetitive practices or transactions is the issue of the transparency of the authority's investigative and decision-making processes. It is much more difficult for an authority to be captured when its decisions are public and open to scrutiny by academics or the press. Finally, there is the issue related to the scope of intervention of the competition authority. In particular, the question of scope goes to the antitrust agency's powers vis-à-vis sectoral agencies in cases of overlapping competence.

Across countries there is a broad scope of different models and solutions for institutional arrangements. The status of competition authorities may range from structural independence from the executive to integration within an executive ministerial structure, with no evident predominance of any particular approach. Involvement in the working of government also varies widely, from a head of the competition authority having a seat in the government cabinet to authorities having no representation whatsoever at the political level. When it comes to the financial resources of competition authorities, there is also a very wide diversity of situations, in terms of both the magnitude of the budgets allocated to different competition authorities and their sources of financing. Some competition authorities benefit from filing fees paid by parties to a potential concentration when they notify of their intent to mergers. Other authorities are dependent on budgets allocated either by parliament or in some cases by government. Still others, like the Turkish Competition Authority, are financed by a tax paid by firms listed on the stock exchange. Finally, in a few cases, competition authorities benefit directly or indirectly from the sanctions they impose (thus creating the risk of a moral hazard).

This extreme diversity of the design of competition authorities makes comparisons difficult and means that most can claim (at least in some aspects) that they are "independent." Indeed one of the striking findings of a questionnaire sent to thirty-seven competition authorities by the OECD Secretariat was "the extent to which virtually all respondents, regardless of the institutional design of the competition agency in their jurisdiction, considered themselves to be totally or highly independent from political influence in the enforcement of competition law."[6] More specifically, "50% of the competition authorities considered themselves totally free from political influence in their competition law enforcement activity and another nearly 45% reported a high degree of independence. Only two competition authorities indicated that they had a medium degree of independence in competition law enforcement."[7]

Independence and Accountability

In a democratic system institutional independence must be counterbalanced by accountability. The close relationship between independence and accountability was underlined in a recent ICN seminar on competition agency effectiveness.[8] The report of this seminar stated, "Accountability is linked to the issue of independence, in that the two interact and are complementary, not antithetical (independence does not mean unaccountability). Accountability is in fact necessary to maintain independence in the longer term."[9]

In most countries, independent competition authorities must report on their activities either to parliament or to the executive through regular public reports and/or periodic hearings. Such reports and hearings are particularly useful to inform the public or members of parliament about how and for what purposes the competition authority has used its resources and its powers of investigation. They can provide a sense of the level of activity of the institution, given its resources, as well as of its general effectiveness.

However, such reports and public hearings cannot easily monitor the quality of the performance of the law enforcement activity of the competition authorities. On the one hand, such qualitative monitoring requires a profound understanding of competition law and of economic analysis, which members of parliament or the general public do not usually have. On the other hand, the monitoring of the substance of the decisions of an independent competition authority cannot rest with the executive branch of government since it would jeopardize the independence of the competition authorities.

In some countries, the competition agency is an independent prosecutor and the adjudicative function rests with the courts. But in many other countries, the independent competition authority has both prosecutorial and adjudicative functions. One of the reasons frequently invoked for granting adjudicative powers to an independent competition authority is that the foundation of antitrust law is to be found in economic analysis and that competition authorities, which frequently include board members with an economic background, are better equipped to deal with complex economic questions than courts. But when competition authorities have adjudicative powers, the control of their law enforcement activity usually rests with the judicial system. The extent of this control may vary. In some countries the review is merely a review of the legality of the decision. In other countries the appellate court may undertake a full review both of the legality and of the substance of decisions made by the competition authority. However, the difference between these two types of control may not be as important as it seems at first glance because in antitrust matters the distinction between issues of facts and issues of law is not as sharp as it is in some other areas of business law.

The considerable powers entrusted to competition authorities in their law enforcement activities, together with the necessity to control their independence both from government and from specific business interests, call for a detailed judicial review of their decisions. John Vickers, reflecting on why competition authorities' decisions need to be reviewed by courts, offers a number of reasons, such as the complexity of competition law, the fact that the accumulated case law may leave it unclear if a type of practice is unlawful, the necessity to oversee procedural fairness and say what the law is (in view of the fact that competition authorities do not have a monopoly on law enforcement, since private parties can bring cases too, as well as appeal against the acts and omissions of the authorities), and the fact that competition law decisions are not readily reversible.[10]

In some countries such as the United Kingdom, a specialist competition court (the Competition Appeals Tribunal) reviews the decisions of independent competition authorities. In this case the depth of the review can be greater than in countries, such as France, where nonspecialized courts of appeals are in charge of reviewing the decisions of competition authorities.

The ability or the willingness of general courts to effectively review the decisions of competition authorities (and therefore whether their review provides a sufficient degree of substantive accountability for independent competition authorities' decisions) raises many questions. The extent to which general courts will defer to the substantive analysis of independent competition authorities varies across countries and sometimes within a country over a period of time. For example, when reviewing the European Commission's *Microsoft* decision, the Court of First Instance stated that when cases raise complex economic and technical issues, the Court largely will defer to the European Commission on these matters and will limit itself to assessing whether the decision is flawed by a "manifest error of appreciation."[11] This very weak standard of review has been denounced as insufficient, particularly in view of the fact that investigation and adjudication powers in the EU system are in the hands of the Commission, which is part of the EU executive.

Having described some of the main structural or operational features related to independence, one must add that ultimately the independence of a competition authority is also due to factors that cannot easily be identified (for example, the personality of the head of the authority).

Advocacy

There is thus little controversy about the necessity to ensure the independence of competition authorities' law enforcement activities both from government and from private business interests and about the methods (and their limits) that can be used to further this goal. But competition authorities are also expected to play an important role as advocates for competition in a variety of contexts and in particular with government.[12] The reasons for which such a role is important are easy to understand.

First and foremost, if private restraints can reduce or distort competition, in many markets public restraints (laws, regulations, policies) can also have anticompetitive effects and in some cases allow private restraints to have lasting effects. Thus, the fight against private anticompetitive practices requires, as a necessary complement, an attempt to promote the elimination of restrictive public restraints.

Second, this function of competition advocacy with respect to public interventions in market mechanisms is all the more important because economists have long suggested that the benefit of restrictive laws and regulation is concentrated on a small number of (often very vocal) economic actors. However, the costs of such public restrictions to competition are spread among many consumers and are often nearly invisible. Thus, there is an inherent tendency of ministers and governmental departments to give in to lobbies advocating public restrictions to competition. Competition authorities are seen as among the few public bodies (or sometimes the only one) that are not "captured" and can counteract economic lobbies.

The amount of time and resources that competition authorities should devote to advocacy with the government or public policy makers is often discussed in competition circles, together with the most effective advocacy techniques. Although they are no magic figures, it is not uncommon, particularly for young competition agencies, to spend up to 50 percent of their resources trying to convince public policy makers to relax some of the restraints (such as price controls, licensing of market participants, and limits on the freedom of economic actors) that limit competition.

The effectiveness of competition authorities' advocacy with public authorities is difficult to measure. Competition authority officials often report on the number of times they have appeared in front of a parliamentary committee, the media exposure from their intervention in public policy debates, the number of advocacy documents they have published or seminars they have organized for public officials. Unfortunately, while useful to give some sense of the resources spent on the advocacy function by the competition authorities, this kind of information does not say much about the effectiveness of such efforts. Competition authority officials are quick to report on successes, such as when a government decides to relax some restrictive rules in certain sectors. Yet this may not necessarily reflect accurately the effectiveness of advocacy efforts by competition authorities, if for no other reason than because they rarely publicize the failures of their advocacy efforts.

The ability of competition authorities to advocate for competition with public authorities depends greatly from one country to the next on structural and operational issues. First, it depends on the scope of the competition law and its design. In the European Union, state aid control is an integral part of competition law, which allows the DG Comp to intervene in many areas of public policy. Furthermore, as part of the executive DG Comp is informed and can make its opinion known on a large variety of proposed pieces of legislation or regulations at the time when they are being considered rather than after they have been adopted.

In a number of countries, more than one public body is charged with competition-related oversight. Some countries have an independent authority with adjudicative powers and a ministerial department (often in the ministry of economic affairs or in the ministry overseeing domestic trade) that has prosecutorial and investigatory powers and a general mandate to promote market competition. (Examples are found in a number of Latin American countries.) When this is the case, the ministerial department may be in a better position than the independent body to influence the debate in intergovernmental discussions by promoting competition-friendly solutions or arguing against regulatory proposals that unnecessarily restrict competition.

Finally, in some countries (such as Korea) the head of the competition authority is a cabinet minister. The authority is then in the fortunate position of being informed of the legislative and regulatory projects of other ministers and being able to intervene *ab initio* when it is thought that they may create a competition problem. For example, the KFTC has been active on this front.[13]

When competition authorities are not part of the executive, they may still have the power to circulate opinions on policy issues that have a competition dimension. In some countries (for example, Italy), the competition authority has the power to give an opinion on any topic that it chooses and to publicize this opinion freely and therefore to catch the attention of the media, politicians, academics, and others. In some other countries (as for example France until 2008), the competition authority can only give an opinion if asked to do so by certain designated bodies (such as a professional organization, the government, or a parliamentary committee), and its opinions could not be made public unless the body that had requested the opinion agreed to make it public. In other countries (such as Korea in the recent past), the competition authority is given a decisive role in a comprehensive program of regulatory reform, allowing it to review masses of past regulations and to call for the elimination of unnecessary restrictions to competition or the redesign of regulations.

A final dimension of the problem of competition advocacy with respect to public interventions rests with the institutional relations between the competition authority and sectoral regulators. Sectoral regulators use *ex ante* tools (rather than the *ex post* tools favored by competition authorities in their enforcement activity) and may while using those tools, which are often geared toward the attainment of economic and technical targets, disregard or at least not give due consideration to the preservation of a competitive environment as a way to reach the goals assigned to the regulation.

There is no unique institutional model of the relationship between competition authorities and sectoral regulators. In some countries (such as Australia in the telecommunication sector), the competition authority has taken over regulatory responsibilities. In other countries (the United Kingdom and to a certain extent the United States), sectoral regulators are in charge of applying competition law to their sector (which they do not seem to be very keen to do). Many other countries, particularly in Europe, follow what has been characterized as a "mandate driven division of labor" where both the competition authority and the sectoral regulator intervene, hopefully on different issues. However, in the latter case, avoiding overlaps and facilitating cross-fertilization between the two agencies will be important goals. Success will crucially depend on the design of the competition law and the sectoral law and on the extent to which competition authorities and the sectoral regulators are allowed to or required to cooperate or exchange information.

Trade-off Between Relevance of Advocacy and Independence

For competition authorities, there may be a trade-off between their independence and their ability to advocate effectively for competition with public bodies (at least with those public bodies part of the executive branch). The existence of this trade-off, although not frequently discussed, is acknowledged by the competition community. For example, the existence of such a trade-off was explicitly discussed in a recent OECD publication[14] that stated:

> An agency that is created as a separate entity, not part of a ministry and responsible directly to the parliament or legislature for its budget, is structurally

> independent. All else being equal, it will enjoy relative freedom in carrying out its enforcement and advocacy functions. At the same time, however, structural independence can have ambiguous effects on competition advocacy. An agency that is entirely separate from other parts of government may lack good access to the decision-makers in the executive and legislative branches. It might not have the influence in government circles that it would have if it were part of a powerful ministry. It might even suffer from lack of information about activities in other parts of government that would benefit from its input.[15]

The existence of a trade-off between the independence of the competition authority and its ability to advocate with the executive branch was also discussed in a recent ICN seminar on competition agency effectiveness.[16]

This trade-off has long been recognized by heads of competition authorities.[17] The existence of a trade-off between the independence of competition authorities from the executive and their ability to effectively advocate for competition was vividly illustrated during the recent financial and economic crisis.

The level of government intervention dramatically increased starting in 2008 as a response to the crisis. Government interventions came in different forms and had different goals, but many of them had the potential to distort competition on financial or even real markets. First, governments adopted measures aimed at restoring confidence in financial markets and ensuring the stability of financial markets. For example, governments guaranteed the liabilities of some banks or financial institutions, recapitalized banks or insurance companies that were on the verge of collapse, or undertook to restructure the banking and financial sectors in order to increase their stability. Examples of such actions would be the Irish bank guarantee scheme announced in October 2008, or the recapitalization of Northern Rock followed by the fact that it was taken into partial temporary public ownership in February 2008, or the merger of Lloyds TSB and HBOS in the United Kingdom in September 2008.

Next, governments undertook measures to extend the reach of regulation in the financial sector by strengthening and extending prudential regulation for financial institutions, considering limiting the growth or the diversification of banks, regulating the incentives for executives in the financial sector, or regulating credit rating agencies. Then, governments adopted measures aimed at preventing the extension or the deepening of the economic crisis in the real sector. Stimulus packages included direct aid to ailing business firms or small and medium-size firms, firms that are collateral victims of the credit crisis; subsidized interest rates for certain types of firms; or sectoral aid designed to boost demand in specific sectors. For example, the United States adopted the American Recovery and Reinvestment Act (ARRA) in February 2009. Many other countries adopted similar programs.

Last, some governments were tempted to implement protectionist measures such as the imposition of antidumping duties or custom tariff increases or nontariff barriers, at least on a temporary basis, even though it must be acknowledged that overall the international community showed restraint in the use of such measures. Part of the reason such protectionist measures seemed attractive was the fact that governments that had adopted stimulus packages were concerned that such packages might lead to an increase in imports rather than boosting demand for local products. For example, in the United States a provision required the use of U.S.-produced steel, iron, and manufactured goods in public works funded by ARRA, subject to certain exceptions (public interest, nonavailability, or unreasonable cost). A second provision required the Department of Homeland Security to procure U.S.-manufactured textile and apparel goods.

Government interventions undertaken as a response to the crisis created a major challenge for independent competition authorities. On the one hand, it was clear that quite a number of these government interventions had the potential to impair competition directly or indirectly in a number of sectors. On the other hand, these measures were adopted by government departments that rarely if ever consulted with the competition authorities.

A telling example was provided in an OECD Competition Committee discussion of the responses to the crisis in 2009 when the chairman of the FTC stated that he had hoped that the FTC would be consulted on the competition implications of the bailout of General Motors on the automobile market. Neither the Treasury nor the White House had considered it necessary to consult the FTC. The terms of the bailout had been adopted without any input from his agency. Similarly, it seems that most of the changes in financial regulations were adopted without significant input from the FTC. There is some controversy about the extent to which the Antitrust Division of the Justice Department was consulted on those issues. The head of the Antitrust Division has informally suggested that the division was consulted but was not at liberty to discuss the extent or the nature of the consultations.[18]

This example is in sharp contrast with the deep involvement of the DG Comp. DG Comp not only has the power to control most interventions of member states governments, thanks to the state aid provisions of the European Treaty, but the Competition Commissioner is also one of the twenty-seven European Commissioners who have to unanimously agree on EC proposals on regulatory reforms for the financial sector.[19]

Reinforcement of the Powers of Independent Competition Authorities

In the 1990s and the early 2000s, government interventions in the market tended to decrease quickly. The deregulation and opening up to competition of a large number of sectors (such as telecommunications, electricity generation, and railway transportation) were popular policies in many developed countries. Eastern European countries were moving away from command economies toward the establishment of a free market that would bring, it was hoped, both static and dynamic efficiency through the development of free and fair competition. In numerous developing countries, partly under the influence of international economic organizations, politicians pursued the liberalization of trade, the abolition of price controls and compulsory licensing schemes, the privatization of public utilities and state-owned enterprises in industrial sectors, and the opening to competition of sectors formerly monopolized by state-owned firms.

Those developments mean that during the 1990s and most of the early 2000s, throughout the world, the importance of competitive market mechanisms became better understood and competition law enforcement gradually replaced administrative controls as a way to ensure good economic performances. In this atmosphere it is understandable that, during the 1990s and the early 2000s, an important concern of policy makers was the establishment of competition authorities that could act as credible law enforcers and therefore were as independent as possible from government. Toward the end of that period, in several European countries where ministers retained some decision-making power in the area of merger controls, reforms were introduced to shift those powers to independent competition authorities and/or to reinforce the independence of the previously existing competition authorities.

For example, in the United Kingdom the secretary of state was involved in merger control at several levels (referrals, ultimate decisions, and remedies). Furthermore, the Office of Fair Trading (OFT) did not exist as a legal entity but was merely the administrative support for the Director General of Fair Trading. The U.K. competition system was changed by the 2002 Enterprise Act and merger control powers were passed on for the most part to the OFT, which became a nonministerial government department that could decide to make a referral to the Competition Commission (also an independent public body). The merger decisions of the OFT or of the Competition Commission can be reviewed by the Competition Appeal Tribunal (a specialist judicial body).

In 2007 Spain adopted a new Competition Act that created a new competition authority (Comisión Nacional de la Competencia) with reinforced merger control and investigatory powers to replace the Servicio de Defensa de la Competencia and the Tribunal de Defensa de la Competencia. Commenting on Spain's new Competition Act, Paloma Martinez-Lage emphasizes that "with the entry into force of the New Competition Act, the Comisión Nacional de la Competencia will be the only public organism charged with the preservation and promotion of effective competition at the national level."[20]

In 2008, France replaced the Conseil de la Concurrence by a new independent authority, l'Autorité de la Concurrence. The government transferred to this new independent authority the decision-making powers previously held by the minister for economic affairs in the area of merger control as well as the investigatory powers and resources previously held by the Competition division of that ministry. Similar reforms are being considered in other countries (e.g., Brazil). These reforms have clearly made competition law enforcement more effective and more credible and they show that the importance of the role of competition to promote efficiency and growth is more widely recognized than a decade ago in many countries.

The Limits of the Advocacy Effectiveness of Independent Authorities

The impact of the movement to reinforce the powers and the independence of competition authorities on competition advocacy within the government is more difficult to assess. On the one hand, most independent competition authorities have a mandate and some means to advocate for competition. On the other hand, three considerations must be kept in mind.

First, unless the opinion of the independent competition authority is required by law at an early stage, it is not obvious that it will be able to advocate for competition in a timely way, particularly with regard to the regulatory process, which is often much more diffuse or less transparent than the legislative process.

Many competition authorities advocate either upon request or in a proactive fashion for pro-competitive legislation in other policy areas when such laws may have an impact on competition, although few seem to have an automatic right to be consulted on proposed legislative changes. With respect to regulations, a number of countries (but far from all) have established a system of compulsory consultation between the competition authority and regulatory authorities or some other governmental bodies (for example, sector regulators in telecommunications often have to consult with the competition authority before making an individual decision or adopting new rules). Other examples of decisions that are subject to compulsory consultation with the competition authority include the introduction of price and market controls. But there are vast areas of public policy such as industrial policy, trade policy, policy related to the financial sector, environmental policy, and health policy where regulatory decisions may distort competition without the competition authority ever being consulted or having the opportunity to make its opinion known.

Not being part of the executive means that independent competition authorities do not have access to a complete set of information about what competitive problems resulting from regulatory initiatives they should focus on and they do not participate in many administrative meetings where regulations are shaped.

Second, the opinions that independent competition authorities voice may, in certain circumstances, have less weight with the executive than they would carry if the same opinion were voiced by a minister with important economic responsibilities and the ability to block the adoption of the questionable regulation (for example by refusing to cosign it). What competition authorities gain in terms of intellectual consideration because of their independence, they may lose in terms of the necessity for government departments to adopt their opinions. This perception of a distance between "them" (the competition authorities) and "us" (the government) may be increased because competition authorities have taken the stand that their goal is to defend consumer welfare (rather than total welfare), when government officials may perceive their function as a wider mandate to advance the "public interest." In a survey of countries participating in the OECD Global Forum on Competition, more than half of the thirty-seven respondent competition authorities expressed the view that they had only medium influence on the government, parliament, and other public bodies through advocacy initiatives. Slightly more than 20 percent see their influence as low, and one respondent indicated that it had no influence.[21]

Independent competition authorities can point to a number of cases where their opinion was made public and did influence the course of action of the executive branch (particularly in the legislative area). But they also admit that some of their opinions were not followed or acted upon by the executive. In those cases, it is worth asking if their opinion would have had a better chance to influence government decisions if it had been voiced by a minister rather than by an independent authority.

Third, the movement toward increasing both the independence and the scope of activities of independent competition authorities has in some cases resulted in a transfer of most of the responsibilities and expertise in competition matters from the government departments that were previously in charge of competition (for example, the Secretariat of State for Business Enterprise and Regulatory Reform in the United Kingdom or the Ministry for Economic Affairs' directorate for Competition, Consumers and Frauds in France) to the independent competition authorities. These transfers have ocurred without any consideration of the importance of the advocacy role that those governmental departments could play (as a complement to the advocacy and enforcement activities of the competition authorities). As a result, the technical capacity of these governmental departments to advocate for competition has significantly decreased because most of the dedicated and able competition experts have chosen to leave them and join the independent authorities. As a result, some of these government departments seem to be less technically able than previously to advocate for competition and/or to promote within the administrative structure the ideas put forth by the independent competition agencies.

. . .

In a 2003 speech, Chairman Takeshima of the Japan Fair Trade Commission offered some thoughts about institutional designs of competition authorities to ensure the effectiveness of both competition enforcement and competition advocacy. He underlined the complexity of the problem:

> [T]he preferred position of competition authorities may differ according to the respective functions. For this reason, it may be an idea to have several authorities share responsibility for the respective functions. To promote fair and free competition in the marketplace, however, these dual functions constitute the two sets of wheels on an automobile. By combining both functions together, it becomes possible to make full use of the specialized knowledge and

> accumulated experience within the competition authority, making it possible to display even more effective capabilities based upon synergistic results. Accordingly, I believe many competition authorities seek to position themselves on the assumption that they will be responsible for both functions.[22]

Building on these remarks, while there are important synergies to be realized from entrusting independent enforcement agencies with an advocacy function, there may be costs associated with giving them (or letting them have) exclusivity on competition advocacy. An advocate for competition within the governmental structure can both complement the advocacy of the independent competition authority and reinforce it.

The importance of providing a sound and stable basis for this competition policy function has been largely overlooked in the 1990s and the early 2000s, a period of rapid economic expansion and retreat of state intervention. However, one of the lessons from the economic and financial crisis is that in times of economic difficulties, the existence of a strong competition advocacy function within government becomes a crucial part of a sound economic policy. A second lesson of the economic and financial crisis is that unless the "competition advocacy within government" function has been established as the permanent responsibility of a ministerial department and adequately promoted and funded, there is a serious risk that this department will lack the resources and the credibility to live up to its mission of protecting competition in times of economic distress.

12

Competition Law Remedies

In Search of a Theory

Ioannis Lianos

In his seminal work *The Limits of Antitrust*, Frank Easterbrook examined how judges have imperfect information on the effects of the business practices at stake and how the important costs of action and information established the limits of antitrust.[1] Easterbrook did not extend his analysis to competition law remedies, but a similar argument based on the lack of knowledge of judges and competition authorities over the effects of their remedial action in the marketplace, once antitrust liability has been identified, may lead to the imposition of some new limits to antitrust intervention. After all, in the complex world of business, any remedial measure might have unintended consequences, impose disproportional costs, and lead to welfare losses.

The importance of prospective economic analysis and likely anticompetitive effects in some areas of competition law highlight the difficulties of tailoring an appropriate remedy to the scope of the antitrust liability identified. In the absence of clear indications as to the exact scope of the liability, as this is based on likely anticompetitive effects, the decision maker might be tempted to engineer a market outcome that economic theory would recognize as efficient, notwithstanding the absence of a direct link with the ascertained violation of competition law. In other circumstances, the lack of a clearly identified remedy might undermine the strength of the antitrust case, if one follows Easterbrook's admonition to judges for self-restraint in situations of relative ignorance of the consequences of their actions. It follows that the existence, or not, of appropriate competition law remedies might set limits to competition law intervention. This is the core research question examined in this chapter.

The *Microsoft* decision in the United States and in the EU has been the catalyst of this increasing interest on the topic of remedies. There was little suspense over the existence of a dominant position or of an abuse. The main concern expressed related to the remedies that were adopted in this case.[2] Some authors argued that these remedies failed to achieve their objectives.[3] Other authors were more measured in their judgment.[4] The *Microsoft* case did indeed put competition authorities and the courts in the difficult position of engineering a remedy that would achieve a specific market outcome. In the U.S. case, Judge Jackson, of the D.C. District Court, had ordered the breakup of Microsoft into several different companies.[5] Microsoft's terms (royalties) for the licenses to its communication protocols also had to be made attractive so as to increase the number of licensees, relatively few at the beginning of the remedial process.[6] Microsoft also was asked to perform a number of promotional activities in order to attract new licensees. In the EU case, Microsoft was required to offer an unbundled version of the Windows operating system without Windows Media Player. The explicit aim of the remedy was to challenge Microsoft's distributional advantage and the implicit aim to lower Microsoft's market share in the operating system market.[7]

These relatively complex and far-reaching remedies, in terms of state intervention into the market, raise the issue of the European Commission's (hereinafter "Commission") discretion and the relation between the remedy and the antitrust liability phase in a competition law case. One position is to consider that "[t]he nature of the remedy sought in an antitrust case is often . . . an important clue to the soundness of the antitrust claim"[8] (the "if you cannot fix it, it isn't broken" argument). The effectiveness of the remedy would thus be a limit to the extension of the antitrust liability and the scope of Article 102 TFEU, prohibiting abuses of dominant position in the European Union.

Article 102 TFEU provides an excellent illustration of the difficulties raised by the issue of remedies and, in particular, of their interaction with the liability phase of a case, in view of the fact that in the EU, competition law liability can be established with only evidence of likely (not actual) anticompetitive effects.[9] Furthermore, the Commission often relies on a mixture of economic theory and factual inferences supporting the finding of likely consumer harm.[10] However, in contrast to merger control, there are no detailed guidelines on remedies for Article 102 TFEU with the aim to restrict the discretion of competition authorities and to provide transparency to undertakings.[11] The coming of age of EU competition law on Article 102 TFEU with a number of decisions on high-profile abuse of dominance cases involving important international undertakings and the adoption of complex remedial schemes has also brought the issue of remedies for the abuse of a dominant position to the center of the attention of competition law policy makers, enforcers, and academics.[12]

Although it is clear that, in principle, the costs of remedies should not outweigh the consumer benefit they achieve, some contend that plaintiffs employ a sequential information model that addresses one issue at a time. It would be therefore inappropriate to dismiss a case simply because the plaintiff did not identify an adequate remedy. Harry First rightly observes, "it seems inevitable that plaintiffs will refine their case as they learn more in the course of the litigation process," in particular in high-tech industries where technological change is so complex and so rapid that there is a need for quick action.[13]

However, I will argue that it would be risky, at the same time, to provide full discretion to the Commission, or more generally to a competition authority, to adopt remedies that have a remote link to the scope of the antitrust liability identified. As I will explain in the next section, one should not separate questions of remedy from questions of liability as proponents of "discretionary remedialism" often do. "Discretionary remedialism"[14] is the "view that courts [in this case we will add competition authorities] have discretion to award the 'appropriate' remedy in the circumstances of each individual case rather than being limited to specific (perhaps historically determined) remedies for each category of causative events."[15] The third section will attempt to integrate the issue of discretionary remedialism and the distinction between the liability and remedial phase to the broader question of the relation between efficiency, distributive justice on the one hand and corrective justice on the other. The thoughts included in this section are preliminary and are part of some ongoing work by the author. The fourth section will examine the importance of "discretionary remedialism," in particular in the context of antitrust, but also will analyze why it is important to limit its effects. The fifth section will explore the objectives pursued by competition law remedies, in order to show that a coherent theory of competition law remedies is incompatible with a sharp dichotomy between liability and remedy questions. The sixth section will provide illustrations of the link between the two issues by looking to the past jurisprudence on remedies of the European

Commission and the European courts. The emergence of a remedial proportionality test in EU competition law demonstrates the necessary logical connection between the remedy and the liability phase. The seventh section will explore if, and how, the remedial proportionality test will operate in the context of an "effects-based approach" under Article 102 TFEU.

Discretionary Remedialism and Its Necessary Limits

The legal nature of "remedies" in legal taxonomy has been a matter of controversy and doctrinal speculation. Is it important to distinguish what constitutes a substantive issue from what can be characterized as a remedial issue? Are remedies related to procedural issues, or should they be distinguished from both substance and procedure? Views of course diverge. Some authors have proclaimed that "there is no law of remedies."[16] At the same time they acknowledged that remedies "have always been the means by which the abstractions of the substantive law are translated into concrete terms," thus advancing the view that remedies are more a sort of social institution than a proper legal one.[17] Others defend the thesis that remedies "should be eliminated from our analytical vocabulary—that is from the vocabulary which we use when we mean to be taken seriously and to be understood."[18] The term "remedy" is found "chameleonic, for as the context shifts its meaning takes on different colours," for example, "in the medical world, a remedy may be either curative, therapeutic or both."[19] Undeniably, any attempt to provide a more precise legal definition of the term has faced important conceptual difficulties. One could consider that the term "remedy" refers to prevention as well as cure for the violation of a right. It is "the action or suit by means of which a right is protected" or "the protection which the action or suit affords."[20]

The linkage of remedies to rights was exemplified by the maxim *ubi jus, ibi remedium*, which assumes that rights are legal prerequisites for remedies while, at the same time, a right defines a remedy. We know of course that this thesis is not accurate, as there are rights for which there is no remedy. A different view is that remedies are secondary rights "of instrumental character"; they imply the existence of primary rights that are conferred "for the better protection and enforcement of those other rights and duties whose existence they so suppose."[21] This approach relies on the existence of a close connection between the substantive right and the remedy. The latter is conceived as a secondary right, superposed on the superstructure of the primary right that has been violated (wrong). Wrongs are violations of primary rights that give rise to secondary rights, whose nature may be sanctioning (preventive) or remedial (reparative). Before a wrong gives rise to a secondary (remedial) right, it is essential to examine if there is a legal cause of action. The concept of legal cause of action breaks the direct causality chain between primary rights and remedies implied by the maxim *ubi jus, ibi remedium*. A specific remedy does not necessarily follow the violation of the primary right.[22]

The reference to "causes of action" provides an intermediary step between primary rights and remedies, thus making clear that the two concepts should be distinguished from each other. The criteria used to define the violation of the primary right are not similar to those giving birth to the secondary right. The two can indeed operate independently of one another. The violation of a primary right may yield a whole range of responses: different types of secondary rights, which do not necessarily have any logical connection to the specific wrong, or violation of the primary right. For example, they might give rise to substitutionary remedies, such as damages or fines, even if these do not correspond to a specific type of wrong committed and might indeed be employed for various forms of violation of the primary right.[23]

Alternatively, it is possible to consider that a remedy is "an action, or the law's configuration of the actionability of a claimant's story" and thus to establish a strict separation between the concept of remedy and that of the violation of the primary right or wrong committed.[24] The term "remedial" will be used in this case essentially as a synonym of discretionary.[25] This position will conceptualize remedies as a specific form of judicial decision making. I will use the terminology of service judicial acts ("*actes juridictionnels de service*"), as opposed to declaratory judicial acts, whose main function is to acknowledge the violation of the primary right. The remedies will be in the decision maker's discretion according to the criteria of appropriateness. Liability and remedy thus would be separate concepts where "liability triggers the court's discretion in the matter of the remedy."[26] Rejecting the existence of a connection between primary rights and remedies, the theory of discretionary remedialism tolerates only procedural limits on remedial discretion. This could increase uncertainty and unpredictability as to the nature and form of the remedy.

Uncertainty and unpredictability are certainly to be avoided with regard to the areas of law that rely on private governance (i.e., contracts and torts), where the aim is to facilitate the exercise of private choice in the most efficient way.[27] But is predictability and certainty necessary to the same extent in competition law? For example, it is possible to argue that greater predictability of the competition law remedy might facilitate the breach of the primary right, as it would be possible for the undertaking to calculate precisely the costs and benefits of the violation and therefore to make sure that the breach of the primary right is profitable. However, contrary to what might happen in regimes of private governance,[28] a breach of the primary right can never be efficient in competition law, as efficiency is one of the criteria for defining the existence of a breach. Remedial discretion and the consequent unpredictability of the remedy are therefore tolerated, as long as it is within acceptable limits from the point of view of the rule of law. Discretion will be constrained by rules, but these rules do not provide a stable basis for predicting legal outcomes, and the way these rules apply owe much to variable and discretionary factors.

There are inherent risks in adopting a strict separation of primary rights and remedies and the strong discretionary remedialism that ensues. First, remedies have a purpose and this purpose is inevitably defined, at least, with regard to the primary right that has been violated or the wrong that has been committed. It is impossible to totally disconnect the two, even if they are subject to different criteria. Second, the requirements of the "rule of law" are not only procedural but also substantive. For example, the concept of proportionality, a justiciable expression of the rule of law, has both a procedural and a substantive nature. The latter is intrinsically linked to the scope of the primary right. It follows that there must be some degree of logical connection between primary rights or wrongs and remedies, without that, however, leading to questioning the existence of two separate legal categories. As Kit Barker rightly observes:

> [T]he way in which the primary right is described tends to suggest a certain logical range of responses to its violation: to adumbrate a range of viable secondary rights. . . . The criteria which set up the primary right none the less remain distinct from those which weigh upon a court's decision how to respond, when it is violated.[29]

In conclusion, the theoretical distinction between rights (or wrongs) and remedies should not lead one to conceptualize one category in isolation from the other. This chapter advocates a reflexive relationship between primary and secondary rights (rights and remedies).[30] Such an approach will facilitate the understanding of the meaning and the purpose of the right that has been violated:

> Just as the way the primary right is defined has an effect upon the range of responses which can logically attend its violation, so too, the selection of a

> particular response contributes to our impression of the meaning and the purpose of the right violated. . . . [W]e judge the nature and power of a primary right by observing the way courts react to its violation in their selection of remedy or—which is the same thing—in their allocation of secondary rights.[31]

Furthermore, this approach implies that the limits to discretionary remedialism should not only be of procedural nature but should also relate to the substance of the primary right.

The Liability/Remedy Distinction as an Expression of the Relationship Between Economic Efficiency/Distributive Justice and Corrective Justice

The question about discretionary remedialism also can be integrated into the broader framework of the relationship between economic efficiency and corrective justice or the relation between distributive justice and corrective justice. We will start with a definition of what each concept entails. The debate has been virulent in the area of torts. Competition law can be perceived as a special case of economic tort, and therefore the different positions in this debate could be relevant to our analysis.

For the proponents of economic efficiency as wealth maximization, the concepts of economic efficiency and corrective justice are collapsed. If the aim of the legal system is to promote wealth maximization, this objective will transcend the remedies phase as well.[32] This duty to act in conformity with the principle of wealth maximization could potentially confer an important remedial discretion, as it would be possible to promote through the adoption of remedies any measure that would achieve maximization of wealth, without any specific limit imposed by corrective justice.[33] For example, it is possible to adopt remedies that impose a better, from a wealth maximization perspective, competitive equilibrium than the one existing prior to the occurrence of the specific illegal practice. For example, the counterfactual to compute damages in case of an exclusionary abuse of dominant position may be that of perfect competition or an oligopoly equilibrium in which the competitors of the liable firm obtain profits and set up the investments to properly serve the market, whereas the situation prior to the violation was that of a dominant firm with a competitive fringe equilibrium. It is only if there is a presumption that the pretransactional situation is the most efficient one, from a wealth maximization perspective, that the principle of corrective justice could be constrained in modifying the pretransactional competitive equilibrium. In a legal framework inspired by economic efficiency, it would be theoretically possible to refuse to adopt a remedy. Thus, the remedy would ignore corrective justice, if the result of such implementation of corrective justice would be to reduce the aggregate total welfare.

Deterrence (as a facet of wealth maximization) also should be added. Economic analysts of law view tort law's function as mainly a deterrent device directed at potential tortfeasors with the view to ensure that the individuals responsible for the tort (specific deterrence), but also any other potential tortfeasor (general deterrence), would be given sufficient disincentive to be discouraged to engage in the activity in the future.[34] Penalties should thus be sufficient to induce offenders to internalize the full social costs of their behavior (the internalization thesis),[35] which supposes that if there is perfect detection and no social cost of imposing punishment, the optimal sanction will be equal to the net social (efficiency) loss post violation (compared to the situation prior the violation).[36]

The penalty should be equal to the net harm to everyone but the offender.[37] For cartels, the optimal penalty would be equal to the deadweight welfare loss plus the wealth transfer to the cartel from purchasers. This penalty would deter only those instances of the offense in which the deadweight welfare loss exceeds any savings in production costs to the cartel. Accordingly, if the enforcement costs are positive and the probabilities of detection and punishment are less than perfect, optimal penalties should exceed the social (efficiency) cost of the violation so that they correspond to the efficiency loss caused. The minimum punishment for deterrence to work will be equal to the expected gain from the violation (including interest) multiplied by the inverse of the probability of the punishment being effectively imposed.[38] The idea behind this is that the penalty must be sufficient to render the expected value of the violation equal to zero. By imposing this cost, the offense will be deterred. The internalization approach limits theoretically the discretion of the authorities to impose penalties, if it will lead to a less satisfactory, from an efficiency perspective, equilibrium than that existing prior to the violation.

At the same time, if the aim is to ensure that the tortfeasor will be given sufficient disincentive to be discouraged from engaging in the activity in the future, the expected value of the violation should be negative (pure deterrence model). As Gardner rightly explains:

> Its success in securing that actual tortfeasors bear the losses they have already wrongfully occasioned—its corrective success—is important mainly as a means of securing that, in future, fewer torts are committed, with the result that there will be fewer occasions, in future, for actual tortfeasors to bear the losses they wrongfully occasioned.[39]

In this case, it would make sense to include all possible losses, including those of the competitors of the offender that were, for example, foreclosed from the market (for the long-term effects persisting after the practice has been terminated), or those of upstream suppliers (for lost sales, which, as Hovenkamp notes, are "potentially unlimited" losses).[40] Of course, increased sanctions and excessive penalties also may deter efficient conduct and generate overinvestment in compliance, which might be inefficient. However, for the advocates of the pure deterrence model, that should not be a major issue, because of the future consequence of deterring harmful conduct (and therefore its future positive wealth maximization effects).[41] The boundaries between efficiency and distributive justice are blurred if the welfare of the victims is given more weight than that of the antitrust violators.

Deterrence also might be an objective of corrective justice. One could thus distinguish between two forms of deterrence: deterrence as wealth maximization and deterrence as a moral requirement for corrective justice to work effectively (thus a form of efficiency independent from wealth maximization). As Gardner forcefully explains, there is a distinction to be made between the moral content of corrective justice and the legal principle of corrective justice:

> [The legal principle of corrective justice] is supposed to be efficient at securing that people conform to certain . . . moral norm of corrective justice. . . . As well as correcting torts that have already been committed, this legal principle is apt systematically to deter the commission of torts that have not yet been committed.[42]

Thus, deterrence has a role to play even for societies valuing only the moral principle of corrective justice and rejecting efficiency as a normative value (deterrence-based corrective justice approach). As with the pure deterrence wealth maximization model, there seem to be few limits to the discretion of authorities to impose far-reaching remedies.

The distinction between distributive justice and corrective justice can be explained by the different emphasis given in each theory of justice. Distributive justice describes a morally required distribution of shares of resources among members of a given group, either because of their membership to that group or in accordance with some measure of entitlement that applies to them in virtue of their membership. This is understood dynamically, that is, across various situations in the specific jurisdiction. Corrective justice describes a moral obligation of repairing the harm caused to another person: it is thus more static as it concerns the specific transaction. Rights and duties in distributive justice are "agent-general," while in corrective justice "they are agent-specific."[43]

Corrective justice may be perceived as both an action triggered by and limited in scope to a specific transaction. The remedy is measured in terms only of the transaction, without regard to the extratransactional material holdings of the parties and as a "substantive principle of liability and remedy," which "requires those who impose wrongful losses on others to repair those losses."[44] What counts as a wrongful loss is not, however, something that is decided by corrective justice. On certain accounts, it is distributive justice that "sets the baseline against which wrongful costs are measured," distributive justice providing information on the set of material holdings that serve as the status quo against which the wrongful costs are measured.[45] It follows that corrective justice is the "remedial arm" of distributive justice.[46] If this is true, one could wonder on the exact role of corrective justice and the reasons it merits being held apart from distributive justice.

The relationship between the two concepts has been put in terms of either normative priority or independence.[47] The priority view conceives that distributive justice is normatively prior to corrective justice. The consequence is that corrective justice will be instrumental to distributive justice and its normative character will derive entirely from it. The duty to repair, therefore, would be granted exclusively on distributive justice claims. If distributive justice and corrective justice have completely coextensive domains, then one should reject corrective justice for the reason that distributive justice is logically prior, insofar as "there must be a distribution relative to which loss and compensation are measured."[48] As Benson notes, unless claims of corrective justice are grounded on independent, nondistributive measures of entitlement, corrective justice will inevitably collapse to distributive justice.[49] However, as the same author notes:

> [W]hat is to preclude the injury party from claiming that the infringement should be viewed simply as a redistribution of holdings in accordance with the same or a competing criterion of distribution? If the injury party can co-

> herently frame the dispute in this way, the correction of the infringement should also properly be characterized as an act of distributive justice, seeing that it can be viewed as a decision made between two competing distributive claims.[50]

The wrongdoer thus could claim a different distributive claim, based, for example, on an alternative distributive measure (the so-called Robin Hood defense). The only possibility, according to the same author, to avoid a counterclaim based on another distributive justice criterion is to presume that the distribution prior the commitment of the wrong was just and thus to bar the injuring party from framing the violation "in terms of a competing distributive claim."[51] However, it might be profoundly unjust and arbitrary to confer this presumption of validity to the pretransactional allocation rather than to the new arrangement.[52] In conclusion, corrective justice is independent from distributive justice only if one assumes that the pretransactional distribution is just. A similar conclusion is reached by Jules Coleman when he notes that "if corrective justice provides moral reasons for repairing a loss, then the underlying claims sustained by corrective justice must themselves express requirements of distributive justice. . . . This relationship appears to rob corrective justice of its moral independence."[53]

This debate is of particular interest for our discussion of discretionary remedialism. If corrective justice (the remedy) is derivative of distributive justice (liability for inflicting consumer harm), the assumption being that the pretransactional allocation of entitlements is just, then the remedy cannot go further than restoring the pretransactional situation. It cannot modify it to an allegedly superior distributive justice measure. In other words, the pretransactional distributive justice entitlement (the situation of consumers prior to the violation) is the only measure of the remedy.

On the contrary, proponents of the independence view advocate that corrective justice and distributive justice are normatively independent, in particular if an obligation of repair could apply without regard to the satisfaction of the demands of distributive justice. Steven Perry explains:

> Corrective justice is a general moral principle that is concerned, not with maintaining a just distribution, but rather with repairing harm. Individuals can be harmed in a number of different ways, and corrective justice accordingly protects a number of different kinds of interest and entitlement. Distributive justice often contributes to the legitimacy of an entitlement that corrective justice protects, and in that sense there is a normative connection between

> the two. But corrective justice does not protect the entitlement *qua* distributive share, and its purpose is not to maintain or preserve a distributive scheme as such. Rather it protects a legitimate entitlement because interference with the entitlement harms the entitlement-holder. In that sense, corrective and distributive justice are conceptually independent.[54]

This dissociation of corrective justice and distributive justice does not mean that corrective justice does not have distributive consequences but only that the preservation of distributive claims is not part of its purpose. The idea is that while corrective justice protects legitimate entitlements, this is not done because of a distributive justice consideration but because of the duty to repair harm imposed by corrective justice. The concept of harm thus dissociates the concept of corrective justice from that of distributive justice. Perry observes:

> The moral focus of the victim's claim is the harm she has suffered. She is saying: you harmed me, and therefore you have a moral obligation to compensate me. The injurer responds with the argument that, distributively speaking, it would be better if he did not have to pay compensation. At most we have two distinct kinds of moral claims which must be balanced against one another.[55]

The concept of harm responds to the inadequacy, according to this view, of applying the concept of distributive justice to momentary states, for the reason that distributive justice theories give rise to a "great deal of indeterminacy," as they operate through institutions and over time, that is, according to abstract and long-term patterns.[56] In contrast, corrective justice creates duties to repair that apply at particular *moments* and thus is normatively independent of distributive justice. Nevertheless, even if the concept of corrective justice is perceived as independent from that of distributive justice, the duty to repair is limited by the "harm" incurred by the injured party. It would not be thus possible to completely dissociate the remedy from the liability phase, as it is in the latter one that harm is effectively defined and occasionally measured.

In conclusion, it is only if one adopts a pure deterrence wealth maximization view or a deterrence-based corrective justice view that discretionary remedialism would be more pronounced. Having discussed the relation between the liability and the remedy phases and the interaction between the principles of efficiency as wealth maximization, corrective justice, and distributive justice, I will now turn to the aims pursued by competition law remedies.

The Aim of Competition Law Remedies

Competition law remedies are adopted with the principal aim to restore competition in the market.[57] This includes first the "micro" goals of putting the infringement to an end, compensating the victims,[58] and curing the particular problem to competition, but also the "macro" goal of putting incentives in place "so as to minimize the recurrence of just such anticompetitive conduct."[59] This study adopts a broader view of the concept of remedies than Council Regulation 1/2003 on the implementation of the rules on competition laid down in Articles 101 and 102 TFEU.[60] According to Article 7 of Regulation 1/2003, the aim of competition law remedies is "to bring the infringement effectively to an end." Remedies should therefore be distinguished from sanctions against undertakings, as the latter aim to punish the infringer and to provide compensation to victims or society in general.[61] This distinction does not adequately take into account that both sanctions and remedies affect the incentives of the wrongdoers' in their future behavior on the market and thus may lead to restored competition. Remedies have different objectives, such as stopping the illegal conduct and preventing its recurrence, restoring competition, deterring anticompetitive practices, providing just compensation, or disgorging of illicit profits. This overall approach may provide a more useful analytical framework for analyzing the effect of competition law on the specific market. Furthermore, the restrictive position adopted by Regulation 1/2003 concerns public enforcement and does not take into account the emerging role of private enforcement in EU competition law. One could thus better distinguish between substitutionary remedies, such as fines or damages, which proceed to money transfers as a substitute for the right that has been violated (to the victims of the anticompetitive practices for damages or the public at large valuing the principle of free competition for fines), and specific remedies, which operate to restore the victim of the anticompetitive practice to the "but for" situation. There are also declaratory remedies, which are neither substitutionary nor specific and whose goal is simply to provide an authoritative statement regarding the rights, obligations, or legal relationship of the parties.

Remedies seek generally to restore "the plaintiff's rightful position, that is, to the position that the plaintiff would have occupied if the defendant had never violated the law" or "to restore the defendants to the defendant's rightful position, that is, the position that the defendant would have occupied absent the violation."[62] In other words, remedies are a cure to a "wrong" the defendant committed, "in contravention of some legally-recognized right of the plaintiff's"[63] or of the category of right-recipients that the legislator intended to protect. The wrong of the defendant gives rise to the enforceable right of the plaintiff (or the protected category) to impose on the defendant a correlative duty to stop the illegal behavior, pay damages, make restitution, or adopt a specific behavior. Article 7 of Regulation 1/2003 does not oppose this conceptualization of remedies, as it links the adoption of a remedy to the end of the infringement, a concept that might be understood narrowly, the termination of the illegal conduct, but also more broadly, as outcome-oriented, thus requiring the reversal of the effects of the illegal conduct.

An important aspect in the definition of remedies is therefore to determine who would be the beneficiary of this right, in other words, the protected category who retain the right to impose a correlative duty on the defendant. We will assume that the protected category for competition law remedies is the consumers harmed by the "wrong" committed by the defendant.[64] A wider perspective would be to consider that the protected category consists of the "broader public" deriving benefits from the principle of free competition, allegedly jeopardized by the practices of the dominant firm.[65]

Whichever perspective is chosen, "restoring competition" should not be interpreted as reaching perfect competition (or free competition if one takes a deontological perspective), which is practically unattainable and in some cases a normatively undesirable objective from a public policy perspective.[66] The remedy aims to restore the market that would have existed in the absence of the conduct found illegal, that is, what is commonly called the "but for" market conditions.

Competition law remedies also serve a prophylactic objective. They are to "ensure that there remain no practices likely to result in monopolization in the future."[67] This is certainly a difficult enterprise that requires from the courts a guessing exercise linked to a counterfactual analysis of the situation in the market with and without the specific competition law violations. This is particularly true in complex and dynamically evolving markets, where static models cannot easily predict the situation that would have existed absent the restraint. It also requires a difficult decision on the appropriate remedy enforcement mechanism, as the judge or the authority should decide on the degree of her involvement (as opposed to market forces or regulatory institutions) in the operation. One could indeed perceive the operation of designing appropriate remedies as being, first of all, a decision over the need for regulatory interference in order to bring the self-correcting forces of the market back to their usual operation as the default mechanism that would adjust the incentives of market actors and therefore the interaction between supply and demand in the specific sector of the economy. Thus, remedies could be (1) setting up conditions for the market to work or (2) directly influencing or guiding the market.

There are of course different choices that can be made and combined in order to affect the incentives of market actors and restore "competition," defined as the best possible outcome for the consumers of the specific relevant market in terms of price, quality, variety, innovation, and so forth, if one assumes, as does this study, a consumer-driven competition law. First, it is possible to contract out the remedy to other affected market participants by enabling them to sue for the recoupment of the damages suffered because of the conduct found illegal or for more than the damages incurred in order to deter market participants from adopting a similar anticompetitive conduct in the future. Second, it is possible to develop remedies that would affect the discretion of market participants to run their business, in other words, affect their autonomy as market participants and consequently their incentives. The latter could be conceived as a *continuum* ranging from preserving some degree of discretion for market participants (in the case of contractual remedies, such as commitments) to purely nonvoluntary schemes, unilaterally imposed by the public authorities. In any case, the remedy is, however, adopted under the shadow of the potential action of the competition authority. One could also distinguish remedies that relate to the conduct of the market participants and attempt to affect their incentives to adopt a specific form of conduct (by creating disincentives such as fines, or, more brutally, by imposing injunctions, interdictions, or conduct remedies) from more intrusive remedies that affect the infringing company's assets (structural remedies) or the management's status (criminal sanctions) and thus produce direct effects within the boundaries of the corporation (hierarchy).[68]

Competition Law Remedies for Violations of Article 102 TFEU

An empirical analysis of the remedies adopted by the European Commission and the European courts in the enforcement of Article 102 shows that fines constitute the measure that is most frequently used, with conduct remedies being adopted in a small number of cases and structural remedies to even fewer cases (see Figure 12.1). Substitutionary remedies, such as fines, are obviously easier to impose and to administer than the generally more complex conduct remedies. Nonetheless, the novelty of the competition law issues that arose in the liability phase of the decisions have often led the Commission to decide not to impose any fine or a remedy. This demonstrates the interaction between remedies and the nature of competition law violations.

Conduct remedies may take different forms. A constant feature is that, in most cases, they respond directly to the nature of the competition law violation. A refusal to deal/license case often involves as a remedy an obligation to supply or to license. Price discrimination, selective price cutting, or predatory pricing claims are often dealt with by an obligation to ensure that prices are justified by objective considerations and by an injunction to stop imposing discriminatory, selective, or predatory prices. Exclusive dealing and tying claims might lead to conduct remedies that are more intrusive, in the sense that they affect the product or the contractual design. In some cases the Commission has also imposed divestiture remedies. In cases involving loyalty rebates the Commission and the courts have essentially imposed fines. Presumably the companies would not be able to use the exact rebate scheme that was found illegal. The choice of fines over other conduct remedies might be influenced by deterrence reasons and the difficulty to decide remedial schemes that might affect the commercial freedom of the undertakings in their pricing

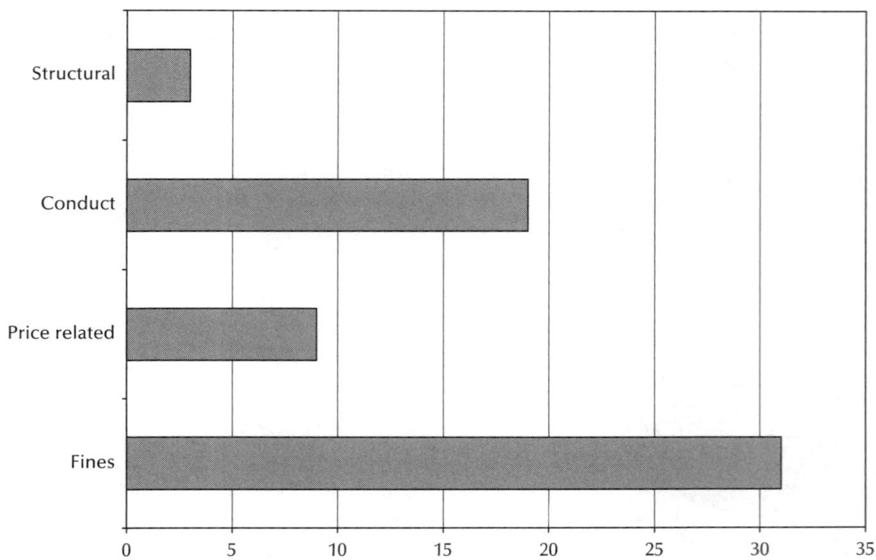

Figure 12.1 Remedies in Article 102 TFEU

decisions, in particular as the criteria for defining what constitutes a loyalty rebate have been unclear, at least before the publication by the Commission of its guidance on its enforcement priorities under Article 102 TFEU.[69]

However in a number of cases, the Commission has moved further than just adopting conduct remedies mirroring the abuse. The remedies attempt to engineer some form of market or product design. Prophylactic measures imposed on dominant undertakings include the implementation of broad competition law compliance programs, the duty to refrain not only from practices that were found abusive but also from any measure that would adversely affect the competitive position of their competitors, and the imposition of a duty to release capacity on the market.

This trend is particularly clear in the second EU *Microsoft* case.[70] Following complaints in December 2007 by Opera, the Norwegian Internet browser maker, the Commission alleged a violation by Microsoft of Article 102 TFEU for tying its web browser Internet Explorer to its dominant client PC operating system, Windows. On December 16, 2009, the Commission accepted Microsoft's commitments.[71] Microsoft committed to (1) distribute a "choices screen" through software update[72] to European users of Windows XP, Windows Vista, Windows 7, and Windows client PC operating systems and (2) allow both original equipment manufacturers and users to turn Internet Explorer on or off.[73] The choices screen will give those users who have set Internet Explorer as their default web browser an opportunity to choose whether to install (and which) competing web browser(s) in addition to the one(s) they already have.[74] Users will be able to select one or more of the web browsers offered through the choices screen. Microsoft has committed to distribute and install the choices screen software update "in a manner that is designed to bring about installation of this update at a rate that is as least as high as that for the most recent version of Internet Explorer offered via Windows Update."[75]

This remedy does not correspond to the consumer harm story that the Commission advanced in this case. The Commission relied on the relatively favorable case law on tying, which establishes a form of quasi per se illegality treatment under Article 102 TFEU if a company has a dominant position. However, the "must carry" commitment accepted by the Commission as an adequate remedy for the competition problem does not address directly this particular risk of abuse. Unbundling would seem to be the most appropriate remedy for a tying concern based on leveraging. However, the Commission reacted negatively when Microsoft decided to unbundle IE from Windows

7-E.[76] The "must carry" remedy that was ultimately adopted fits better with an essential facilities case, where Windows would have been considered indispensable for the distribution of an Internet browser.

This apparent lack of logical coherence between the remedy adopted and the theory of harm might be justified if one takes a position close to that of discretionary remedialism. But this is not without affecting the nature of the primary right and consequently the scope of the antitrust liability of the dominant firm that is delimited by the theory of harm. The risk of strategic litigation is also present if plaintiffs could employ theories of harm that are easy to prove (because of particular presumptions) in order to achieve the most far-reaching remedies, in terms of commitments from a dominant firm. Discretionary remedialism should thus give way to some form of logical (causal) connection between the remedy and liability without, however, that leading to collapse of the two legal categories to one. The principle of remedial proportionality provides a useful compromise between these two positions.

The Need for a Principle of Remedial Proportionality

The principle of proportionality constitutes an important limit to the European Commission's discretion in imposing remedies.[77] The principle is included in Article 49(3) of the Charter of Fundamental Rights of the EU, providing that "the severity of penalties must not be disproportionate to the criminal offence." It is explicitly provided in Article 7 of Regulation 1/2003 that the Commission may impose on undertakings any behavioral or structural remedies that are proportionate to the infringement committed and necessary to bring the infringement effectively to an end. This provision mainly codifies previous case law of the Court relying on Article 3(1) of Regulation 17/62 that the remedies imposed should "not exceed what is appropriate" and should be "necessary to attain the objective sought, namely [to restore] compliance with the rules infringed."[78] Structural remedies are generally not favored, unless there is no equally effective behavioral remedy or where any equally effective behavioral remedy would be more burdensome for the undertaking concerned, as otherwise the remedy might be disproportional. The principle of proportionality takes an arithmetic form in Article 23(2) of the Regulation, providing that the Commission may impose fines on undertakings that may not exceed 10 percent of its total turnover in the preceding business year (an attempt by the legislator to draw a rough balance between the anticompetitive harm and the harm to the undertaking's financial position). In addition, in fixing the amount of the fine, regard shall be had both to the gravity and to the duration of the infringement as well as to the effect of the competition law infringement on the market.[79]

The General Court (previously Court of First Instance) has also recently applied the principle of proportionality to commitment decisions adopted under Article 9 of Regulation 1/2003. In *Alrosa*, the Court held that "the voluntary nature of the commitments . . . does not relieve the Commission of the need to comply with the principle of proportionality, because it is the Commission's decision which makes those commitments binding" and that "giving that commitment, the undertakings concerned merely assented, for their own reasons, to a decision which the Commission was empowered to adopt unilaterally."[80] The Commission is subject to the same duty of applying the principle of proportionality in adopting Article 7 or 9 decisions, which would require, in the case of Article 9 "an appraisal *in concreto* of the viability of those intermediate solutions," that were not finally chosen by the Commission.[81] However, in a recent judgment, the Court of Justice of the EU (Court of Justice) struck down the judgment of the General Court for having applied the same level of proportionality control to Article 9 and to Article 7 decisions.[82] The Court of Justice noted that "the obligation on the Commission to ensure that the principle of proportionality is observed has a different extent and content, depending on whether it is considered in relation to the former or the latter article."[83]

The principle of proportionality is given a specific content in Article 7 of Regulation 1/2003 and in the competition law case law of the European courts.[84] It requires the following:

> [M]easures adopted by Community institutions do not exceed the limits of what is appropriate and necessary in order to attain the legitimate objectives pursued by the legislation in question; when there is a choice between several appropriate measures, recourse must be had to the least onerous, and the disadvantages caused must not be disproportionate to the aims pursued.[85]

Proportionality is also a general principle of Community law, applying as such to all measures adopted by Community institutions. According to settled case law:

> [B]y virtue of that principle, the lawfulness of the prohibition of an economic activity is subject to the condition that the prohibitory measures are

> appropriate and necessary in order to achieve the objectives legitimately pursued by the legislation in question; when there is a choice between several appropriate measures recourse must be had to the least onerous, and the disadvantages caused must not be disproportionate to the aims pursued.[86]

This three-part test has, of course, to take into account the margin of discretion of the European Commission in adopting appropriate remedies. In that sense, proportionality differs from a cost-benefit analysis, which would focus only on the gravity of harm and the alternative remedies that might have been imposed. That is, the remedy will be disproportionate when its costs and burdens outweigh its likely benefit of restoring competition or when its costs would be more important than an alternative remedy that would have also been equally effective. Proportionality may take into account other issues, such as the degree of judicial deference to the Commission's decision, as "the appropriateness of and the need for the contested decision must be assessed in relation to the aim pursued by the institution."[87] Although the principle of remedial proportionality does not exist as such in U.S. antitrust law, a constitutional proportionality requirement applies to most punitive damages cases as well as to other types of remedies.[88]

The first step of the proportionality principle is of particular interest for our purposes. It may indeed be advanced that the appropriate and necessary character of the remedies to be imposed would require a precise remedial measurement, not only with regard to the magnitude and scope (amount) of the harm to consumers/competition or the nature of the infringement, but also in relation to the type of violation that was identified. This might cover a specific competition law category (i.e., a refusal to deal, a tying case, an exclusive dealing case),[89] but also the theory of harm advanced in the specific case (i.e., maintenance of monopoly, leveraging, essential facilities). The importance of remedial fit is often stressed by antitrust law literature.[90] It is also indirectly linked with the existence of a causal relation between the undertaking's conduct and the theory of harm advanced, which has, as the D.C. Circuit held in the U.S. Microsoft case, "more purchase in connection with the appropriate remedy issue."[91]

Remedies should of course be effective. Their aim would be "to reestablish the competitive situation, i.e., the competitive process that would have prevailed *but for* the infringement."[92] However, it is also clear that the principle of proportionality requires a close fit between the harm and the remedy. Suggestions that remedies may go beyond "mirroring the abuse" profoundly misunderstand the relation between the remedy and the right it is attempting to protect.[93]

A strong approach of discretionary remedialism conceives the primary right as being distinct from the provision of the remedies for violation of that right. There is a dichotomy between rights and remedies, each concept being conceptually isolated from the other. This formalistic position might lead to imposing no remedies for the infringement of a right or to imposing stricter remedies than the nature and effect of the violation of the right would have required. For example, a remedy that would go beyond simply "mirroring the abuse" and would "give the infringer's competitors an advantage over the infringer in order to restore the competitive process"[94] fixes a high remedial target that might go beyond the violation of the right, the alleged abuse. It could eventually jeopardize the dominant position of the firm, as this is an anomaly to the competitive process, the dominant firm having the ability to behave independently from its competitors. However, Article 102 TFEU does not condemn a dominant position as such, nor does it restrict a dominant firm's ability to compete on the merits. That is a situation that has not been qualified as an abuse.[95] Remedies that go beyond mirroring the specific abuse could certainly be adopted in theory but that should be done either by advancing an additional theory of harm/liability under Article 102 that is more directly linked to the remedy sought or by employing a competition law instrument other than Article 102.[96]

An alternative view would be to consider that rights and remedies are profoundly interlinked with each other, so that the remedy is the measure of the right. This profoundly legal-realist view would consider that "the nature of the remedy sought in an antitrust case is often an important clue to the soundness of the antitrust claim"[97] (the "if you cannot fix it, it isn't broken" argument). Between these two poles, there is the principle of remedial proportionality. Without adopting a strict dichotomy between the identification of the right (or the liability step) and the remedy, the principle of proportionality requires a close link between the two. In an economically informed Article 102 this would require a fit between the theory of harm or the type of abuse and the remedy imposed.

This is certainly the position adopted by the General Court in its *Alrosa* decision. The Court held:

> [C]ompliance with the principle of proportionality requires that, when measures that are less onerous than those it proposes to make binding exist, and

> are known by it, the Commission should examine whether those measures are capable of addressing the concerns which justify its action before it adopts, in the event of their proving unsuitable, the more onerous approach.[98]

The Commission cannot prohibit "absolutely any future trading relations between two undertakings unless such a decision is necessary to re-establish the situation which existed prior to the infringement."[99] It is only in "exceptional circumstances" such as "where the undertakings concerned have a collective dominant position," that the Commission may prohibit undertakings completely and indefinitely from contracting among each other.[100]

The Court thus found that, in the absence of these exceptional circumstances, the Commission's decision—to require that undertakings refrain for an indefinite period from all direct or indirect trading relations between them—infringes the principle of proportionality. In this case, the Commission imposed a complete and indefinite cessation of trading relations between Alrosa, a Russian diamond supplier, and De Beers, a dominant undertaking on the markets downstream from the market for the supply of rough diamonds. The Commission feared that the exclusive supply commitment laid down in the agreement signed between Alrosa and De Beers would result in strengthening De Beers's market power by excluding Alrosa from the market for the supply of rough diamonds and, consequently, depriving other purchasers of access to the significant source of supply that it represented. The Commission found that imposing this termination to the contractual relation between the two parties was clearly necessary in order to allow third parties to have access to Alrosa's output and to allow Alrosa to compete fully with De Beers. The main concern was that De Beers benefited from an advantage over its competitors, not only because of its size but also because it was able to guarantee the best consistency in the supply of rough diamonds to its customers. This was based on De Beers having access to the output of a larger number of different mines producing a larger variety of rough diamonds and being the only producer keeping large stocks.[101] It was not, however, clear how the imposed remedy responded to the competition concern raised. First, the Commission had not explained how continuing supply to De Beers would affect Alrosa's ability to guarantee a regular supply of significant quantities of rough diamonds. Second, even if this had been the case, and the continuation of the supply would have increased the competitive advantage of De Beers, thus contributing to maintain or reinforce its dominant position on the market, this does not constitute an abuse of a dominant position. As the Court puts clearly:

> [S]ince the object of Article [102 TFEU] is not to prohibit the holding of dominant positions but solely to put an end to their abuse, the Commission cannot require an undertaking in a dominant position to refrain from making purchases which allow it to maintain or to strengthen its position on the market, if that undertaking does not, in so doing, resort to methods which are incompatible with the competition rules. While special responsibilities are incumbent on an undertaking which occupies such a position, they cannot amount to a requirement that the very existence of the dominant position be called into question.[102]

The judgment of the General Court in *Alrosa* was set aside by the Court of Justice, mainly for applying the same standard of proportionality to Article 7 and 9 decisions. Interpreted as such, the judgment of the Court of Justice may be limited to Article 9 decisions, thus not denying to the General Court the possibility to subject Article 7 decisions to a strict proportionality test. However, there is also some language in the Court of Justice's judgment that might constrain the ability of the General Court to perform a thorough analysis of the substantive proportionality of the remedy and its fit to the liability theory advanced: the General Court should in no case put forward its own assessment of complex economic circumstances and should not substitute its own assessment for that of the Commission.[103] The Commission may therefore enjoy a wide remedial discretion by being able to find cover behind the nebulous and still undetermined concept of complex economic assessment and thus avoid a strict proportionality control of its remedial action. Although one could accept that commitment decisions are subject to less intensive review standards, simply because of their voluntary, almost contractual, nature, such an approach will not be optimal with regard to final decisions reached by the competition authorities. It remains to be seen if the Court of Justice's approach will extend to Article 7 decisions.[104]

. . .

The topic of competition law remedies has not attracted sufficient attention from competition law scholarship worldwide.[105] There is an important difficulty in devising a coherent theory of competition law remedies that would accommodate the discretion that competition authorities traditionally enjoy in this field, while preserving some logical connection between the measure adopted and the competition law issue identified in the liability phase of their decisions. The problem is more acute in the new era of the effects-based approach, as this can be illustrated by the enforcement of Article 102 TFEU in Europe. An important ingredient of this approach is the identification of a coherent theory of harm that will be subject to the assessment of the decision maker through different analytical steps.[106] The implications of this move toward an effects-based approach for the selection of remedies and the operation of the proportionality principle have not, however, been adequately examined yet.

An effects-based approach certainly provides fuel to competition authorities' discretion, even if a considerable effort is made to create some formalistic safe harbors, such as the price/cost test for loyalty and bundled discounts and predatory pricing abuses in Europe and the United States that attempt to structure, if not to restrict, the competition authorities' discretion by bringing within the scope of the antitrust prohibitions only practices that exclude "efficient competitors."[107] This chapter advances the argument, however, that even if competition authorities should be recognized as having an important discretion in adopting the most effective remedies, it would be particularly damaging for competition law to lean toward discretionary remedialism. The effect will be even more devastating for the coherence and legitimacy of competition law, in view of the increasing role of private enforcement, in particular if plaintiffs could employ the less demanding, in terms of standard of proof, theory of consumer harm in order to achieve the most far-reaching remedies, in terms of commitments from a dominant firm. As is shown by the operation of the proportionality test in Europe, logical coherence between the remedy and the wrong is required in EU competition law.

The question that this chapter has explored is the transformation of the proportionality test in an effects-based approach. Should the proportionality test be limited to the examination of the reasonableness of the measure or the existence of less restrictive (to the undertaking's freedom of action) ways of achieving the same purposes? Should the proportionality test include a cost-benefit analysis of the remedy with regard to its purpose, thus integrating with the assessment of the remedy the consideration of the adverse effect on competition? How could this ends-benefits proportionality test operate in the absence of a quantifiable adverse anticompetitive effect? This is particularly problematic in the context of Article 102 TFEU, where the simple likelihood of an anticompetitive effect provides sufficient evidence of an abuse of a dominant position. Would the proportionality test in this case require an analysis of the theory of harm that has been advanced and a correspondence between the theory of harm and the type of remedy imposed? All these are important questions that need further elucidation. The topic of competition law remedies is the next challenge of antitrust law scholarship.

Part V

Competition Law and Culture

13

How Culture May Change Assumptions in Antitrust Policy

Thomas K. Cheng

This chapter tackles a topic that has received scant attention in antitrust circles—culture and antitrust. The conventional belief is that antitrust is concerned with economics. Antitrust enforcement entails an understanding of the market behavior of firms and consumers. Economics explains and predicts how firms compete with one another and how consumers make their consumption decisions in different market conditions. Neoclassical economics postulates that firms are profit maximizing; consumers are economic actors and in general are rational. These two beliefs have been the fundamental behavioral assumptions that underpin modern antitrust analysis. Some commentators, however, have begun to challenge them and have suggested that individual and firm behavior may sometimes deviate from profit maximization and rationality.[1] The implication is that antitrust may need to embrace a wider range of behavioral economics assumptions about firm and consumer behavior than its existing ones.

One source of variance of firm and consumer behavior from the conventional set of assumptions is culture. The thesis of this chapter is that the analytical framework and enforcement priorities of antitrust may need to be adjusted to take into account cultural differences. Divergent cultural norms mean that firms and consumers may behave differently across countries. Take cartels as an example. The formation of cartels exhibits the characteristics of a classic prisoner's dilemma.[2] There are strong incentives for a cartel member to defect in light of the substantial fines and criminal sanctions that are imposed for cartel infringement. Trust alleviates this dilemma and stabilizes cartels by reducing the probability of defection.[3] Cross-cultural differences in the ways trust is formed and functions is a well-documented fact within the social science disciplines.[4] Cartels in countries with a more trusting culture will tend to be more stable. Traditional mechanisms that have proved to be effective in breaking down the trust among cartel members may be less useful in these countries.

Cultural considerations also may affect the analysis of vertical restraints. Social scientists have learned that stability and long-term relationships are more valued in some cultures than in others.[5] For example, Japanese manufacturers often forge long-term relationships with their suppliers, known as relational contracting, that last for decades. A network of such long-term supply relationships is sometimes known as a *keiretsu*.[6] The prevalence of relational contracting in Japan has been attributed to a cultural preference for stability and long-term relationships.[7] How antitrust should incorporate such cultural considerations into its analysis will be further discussed. It is sufficient to note for now that the incentives to enter into vertical agreements may vary across cultures. These variations may not be fully captured and explained by economic theories.

The foregoing discussion, however, is not intended to propose a wholesale revision of economic analysis and antitrust doctrines. Nor is it intended to imply that there are fundamental differences in the way the competitive process operates across countries. The differences are in degree rather than in kind. There is no denying the general applicability of economic learning about markets and the behavior of economic actors.[8] What this discussion intends to suggest is that cultural considerations may require fine-tuning of antitrust analysis and enforcement under some limited circumstances. There are limits to the universality and absolutism of economic learning as the basis of antitrust. Cultural variations undermine the feasibility of a one-size-fits-all approach to antitrust.

An Overview of Social Scientific Studies of Culture Pertaining to Economic Behavior

One reason that the antitrust community has largely overlooked cultural considerations is perhaps the general lack of precision in the articulation and discussion of culture. Economists tend to view culture as vague, subjective, and open ended. It often seems, like beauty, to be in the eye of the beholder. This means that characterizations of culture are often open to challenges. Unlike most economic concepts, culture is not susceptible to precise measurement. This presents considerable difficulty for meaningful comparison and analysis. For instance, while the general belief is that Chinese are collectivist and collaborative, as opposed to individualistic and competitive, there are studies that reach the contrary conclusion. Green, Deschamps, and Paez found that Chinese are generally self-reliant and are more competitive than is generally assumed.[9] In fact, their study found Chinese to be more self-reliant and competitive than Americans, which will no doubt surprise many.[10]

Furthermore, even if cultures could be precisely articulated and compared, there are few theoretical frameworks that allow these conclusions to be incorporated into economic and antitrust analysis. In recent decades, neoclassical economists largely ignored cultural considerations in their analysis.[11] This was not always the case; economists used to be more receptive to culture-based arguments. Adam Smith himself considered culture to be integral to understanding and explaining economic phenomena, a belief that was shared by many other classical economists.[12] After the Second World War, Guiso, Sapienza, and Zingales observed, "[n]ot only did economics lose interest in its relation with culture, but as economics became more self-confident in its own capabilities, it often sought to explain culture as a mere outcome of economic forces."[13] This dismissive attitude toward culture was largely inspired by the Chicago School.[14] Not only are Chicago School scholars unwilling to pay heed to cultural considerations, they even proposed "to interpret religious and social norms as the result of a group-level optimization."[15] The development of a theoretical framework that permits the incorporation of cultural considerations into economic analysis is beyond the scope of this short chapter. Its more modest scope is to highlight circumstances in which cultural considerations may require adjustments to standard antitrust analysis.

Methodologies for Studying Culture

Given its intangible nature, the reliability of cultural research crucially depends on its methodology. Specifically, it depends on the accuracy of the methodologies in gauging cultures. Social scientists have used a variety of methodologies for this purpose. One methodology consists of multinational surveys of individuals. The most famous such survey is probably that performed by cross-cultural psychologist Geert Hofstede in the late 1960s and early 1970s.[16] The survey covered employees of IBM subsidiaries in sixty-four countries and focused on five dimensions of cultural differences. His survey has been highly influential and its results have been utilized by other researchers since. His conceptualization of cultural value dimensions has also become the standard reference framework for researchers on culture.[17] Shalom Schwartz conducted a more recent transnational survey. The participants in his survey were teachers and college students from more than seventy countries and eighty-one cultural groups.[18] Data were collected on seven cultural value orientations that are slight variations of the five dimensions identified by Hofstede.

Another methodological approach focuses on secondary materials and social institutions that encapsulate and reflect cultural values. Schwartz identifies the following as possible sources of information on the cultural orientations of a society: popular children's stories, proverbs, movies, literature, socialization practices, legal systems, and modes of economic exchange.[19] For example, David Ho and Chi-Yue Chiu ascertained the individualistic and collectivist tendencies in Chinese culture by examining more than 2,000 popular sayings.[20] Part of Jae-Ho Cha's study of the same topic in Korean culture consists of an examination of travelogues written by foreign visitors from 1870 to 1970.[21] In his comparison of the prevailing types of business organization in China, Korea, and Japan, Richard Whitley focuses on how social and economic institutions reflect the cultural values and historical development of the three respective countries.[22] When empirical studies are not available or feasible, as in the case of Cha's study, which covers changes in Korean culture over more than a century, secondary sources become an important substitute source of information.

Definitions of Culture

For something as open ended as culture, it should hardly be surprising that social scientists have failed to agree on a common definition. In fact, two commentators managed to identify more than 160 definitions of culture fifty years ago.[23] Culture has been defined by Namenwirth and Weber, Clark, and Hall and Hall respectively as a "system of ideas that provide a design for living"; "a distinctive, enduring pattern of behavior and/or personality characteristics"; and "a system for creating, sending, storing, and processing information."[24] Charles Hill integrates various definitions and proposes that culture is "a system of values and norms that are shared among a group of people and that when taken together constitute a design for living."[25] Geert Hofstede, one of the leading cross-cultural psychologists in the study of cultures, understands culture as "the collective programming of the mind which distinguishes the members of one group from another."[26]

Shalom Schwartz has propounded one of the most sophisticated and complete conceptions of culture. He views culture "as a latent, hypothetical variable that we can measure only through its manifestations."[27] He believes that "culture is not located in the minds and actions of individual people. Rather, it is outside the individual. It refers to the press to which individuals are exposed by virtue of living in particular social systems."[28] He in turn defines cultural press as "stimuli ('primes') that individuals encounter more or less frequently in their daily life, stimuli that focus conscious and unconscious attention."[29] Schwartz contrasts his conception of culture with the view that culture is a psychological variable, which regards "culture as beliefs, values, behaviors and/or styles of thinking distributed in a distinctive pattern among the individuals in a society or other cultural group. Culture, as [Schwartz] conceptualizes it, influences the distribution of individual beliefs, actions, goals and styles of thinking through the press and expectations to which people are exposed."[30]

The fundamental difference between these two conceptions of culture is its locus. As a psychological variable, culture is believed to be internal to the individuals. Meanwhile, according to Schwartz, culture permeates the social environment and conditions an individual's behavior from outside. The divergence between these two conceptions, however, may be smaller than it initially seems. After all, the kind of cultural presses referred to by Schwartz are tangible manifestations of individuals' values and beliefs. Whatever cultural values are carried by language patterns, social institutions, or other cultural presses must ultimately emanate from individuals. In any case, the reconciliation of these two views need not detain us further, as this debate is about the locus of culture. Meanwhile, this chapter is concerned with the different issue of the impact of cultural differences on competitive conduct and antitrust enforcement. So long as the locus of culture does not affect the articulation and comparison of cultural values, the resolution of the debate has little implication for us. Fortunately, there seems to be a consensus on the metric that is used to describe and compare cultures—cultural value dimensions (the term preferred by Hofstede) or value emphases or orientations (the terms used by Schwartz).

Specific Cultural Values

Hofstede identifies five dimensions of cultural values: power distance, uncertainty avoidance, individualism vs. collectivism, masculinity vs. femininity, and short-term vs. long-term orientation. These dimensions do not encompass every important aspect of culture and cultural differences. For instance, a cultural value dimension directly related to familial relationships is conspicuously absent. This absence is explained by the fact that the object of Hofstede's research was work culture. The five value dimensions were conceived to ascertain cultural differences in the workplace. There was no attempt to examine familial or other interpersonal relationships. Similarly, Schwartz identifies seven cultural value orientations, which can be aligned into three dimensions: mastery vs. harmony, autonomy vs. embeddedness, and hierarchy vs. egalitarianism. Autonomy is further divided into intellectual and affective, making up seven cultural value orientations altogether.

Hofstede defines power distance as "[t]he extent to which the less powerful members of institutions and organizations within a country expect and accept that power is distributed unequally."[31] Schwartz uses slightly different terminologies to encapsulate this concept—hierarchy and egalitarianism. A hierarchical organization or society sees substantial power distances between its members. Within such an organization or society, "unequal distribution of power, roles, and resources [are regarded] as legitimate and even desirable."[32] Meanwhile, cultural egalitarianism recognizes members of an organization or society "as moral equals who share basic interests as human beings."[33] Values that are treasured by hierarchical cultures include "social power, authority, humility, and wealth,"[34] while those deemed important by egalitarian cultures are "equality, social justice, responsibility, help, and honesty."[35] Examples of hierarchical cultures include China and Russia, while most Western cultures are egalitarian.[36]

The second cultural value dimension identified by Hofstede is uncertainty avoidance, which he defines as "[t]he extent to which the members of a culture feel threatened by uncertain or unknown situations."[37] Rui Baptista explains uncertainty avoidance as "feeling uncomfortable . . . in risky, unstructured, uncertain or ambiguous situations, particularly regarding the future, and hence valuing . . . beliefs (religion) and institutions (government) that provide certainty and conformity."[38] Uncertainty avoidance as a society's cultural trait is strongly associated with and dependent on, the risk preferences of its citizens.[39] Despite intrasociety variations in the risk preferences of its members, there are systemic differences between cultures in their tolerance of uncertainty. Western cultures, especially the Anglo-Saxon ones, exhibit greater tolerance for uncertainty than most other cultures.[40] One consequence of uncertainty avoidance is a penchant for government regulation that reduces uncertainty. Baptista observes that "[i]ndividuals in societies displaying greater uncertainty avoidance look for structure in their institutions in order to make events clearly interpretable and predictable. This structure is often provided by greater regulation."[41] Although Baptista's research is concerned with government regulation of new firm entry, his conclusion seems equally applicable to antitrust enforcement. In the face of uncertainty created by market competition, firms in countries characterized by high uncertainty avoidance may prefer (excessive) antitrust intervention to reduce competition.

The third cultural value dimension identified by Hofstede is the dichotomy of individualism vs. collectivism. This dimension is probably one of the most familiar distinctions between cultures. Western cultures are generally supposed to be individualistic, while Asian and Muslim cultures are considered collectivist. Hofstede understands these two terms as: "Individualism stands for a society in which the ties between individuals are loose. . . . Collectivism stands for a society in which people from birth onwards are integrated into strong, cohesive in-groups, which throughout people's lifetime continue to protect them in exchange for unquestioning loyalty."[42] Again, Schwartz uses slightly different terminologies—autonomy and embeddedness. In autonomous cultures, "people are viewed as autonomous, bounded entities. They are encouraged to cultivate and express their own preferences, feelings, ideas, and abilities."[43] Cultures characterized by embeddedness "emphasize maintaining the status quo and restraining actions that might disrupt in-group solidarity or the traditional order."[44] While Hofstede may have overstated the cohesiveness of in-groups and the loyalty demanded of group members, the point remains valid that in a collectivist society, collective concerns trump individual interests. Members of an in-group may impose severe social sanctions for exceedingly self-interested conduct.[45]

The fourth cultural dimension identified by Hofstede is the dichotomy of masculinity and femininity. According to Hofstede, a masculine society is one in which social gender roles are clearly distinct.[46] There is greater emphasis on assertiveness, toughness, and material success, at least if they are exhibited and pursued by men.[47] A feminine society is one in which social gender roles overlap, where "[b]oth men and women are supposed to be modest, tender, and concerned with the quality of life."[48] The corresponding cultural value dimension posited by Schwartz is the dichotomy of mastery vs. harmony. Although both Hofstede and Schwartz are concerned with similar outward conduct manifestation, Schwartz's dimension has a slightly different focus. Instead of gender, it focuses on an individual's treatment and use of human and natural resources. Mastery "encourages active self-assertion in order to master, direct, and change the natural and social environment to attain group or personal goals."[49] It emphasizes ambition, success, self-sufficiency, and competence.[50] In contrast, harmony attaches less importance to ambition and success. It encourages peace and coexistence with the environment. Cultures that are masculine or that emphasize mastery are generally more competitive. Feminine or harmony-oriented cultures may prefer peaceful coexistence of competitors and downplay competition.

The last cultural value dimension identified by Hofstede is short-term/long-term orientation. According to Hofstede:

> Long Term Orientation stands for the fostering of virtues oriented towards future rewards, in particular, perseverance and thrift. Its opposite pole, Short Term Orientation, stands for the fostering of values related to the past and present, in particular, respect for tradition, preservation of "face" and fulfilling social obligations.[51]

While this dimension may not seem to be directly related to competition as such, it may still have bearing on antitrust enforcement, especially vertical agreements. To the extent that firms in a particular country prefer long-term vertical supply or distribution relationships, antitrust analysis should take that into account. Firms that display such a preference may be more willing to make relation-specific investment into such relationships, creating greater efficiency gains and procompetitive benefits from these relationships.

Trust as a Cultural Phenomenon

Apart from these cultural value dimensions, one aspect of culture that may have particular salience to antitrust enforcement, especially cartel enforcement, is the formation of trust. As noted in the introduction, trust can alleviate the prisoner's dilemma facing every cartel. Social scientists have identified a number of cognitive processes through which trust is built: calculative, prediction, intentionality, capability and transference.[52] Under a calculative process, the trust-building process is based on a cost-benefit analysis. One individual, the trustor, decides whether to trust another individual, the target, by estimating the target's costs and benefits from cheating.[53] If the estimated benefits outweigh the costs, the trustor will deem the target to be trustworthy. Under a prediction process, the trustor predicts the target's likely conduct based on the latter's past action. The greater the trustor's ability to make accurate predictions, the more likely that he will trust the target.[54] The intentionality process is still a predictive process, but the focus is not the course of future conduct itself, but the intentions or motives of the target. The trustor deciphers the target's motives and intentions through his actions and words.[55]

If the target is deemed to have selfish intentions, the trustor is unlikely to trust him.[56] A target will be deemed to be trustworthy if he is thought to harbor altruistic intentions.[57] Under a capability process, the trustor estimates the target's ability to fulfill his obligations. Last, under a transference process, "the trustor transfers trust from a known entity to an unknown entity."[58]

Culture plays a role in all these trust-building processes. For example, Doney, Cannon, and Mullen argue that, under a calculative process, trust is less likely to form in an individualistic and masculine society due to higher incidence of self-serving and opportunistic behavior.[59] Such behavior is deemed more acceptable and is likely to be more prevalent in an individualistic and masculine society than in a collectivist and feminine society. Moreover, the social sanction for such behavior is likely to be more severe in a collectivist society than in an individualistic society. They also argue that trust can be built more easily through a prediction process in a collectivist and feminine society because individuals are less prone to idiosyncratic behavior, which lowers the accuracy of prediction.[60] Social conformity that is encouraged in a collectivist and feminine culture will inevitably limit the range of possible behavior. Individuals are more likely to hold benevolent intentions in a collectivist and feminine society, rendering them generally more trustworthy.[61] Last, given the emphasis on group identity and conformity in a collectivist and feminine society, transference of trust from one member of an in-group to another is likely to be easier.[62]

In short, cultural norms may facilitate or retard trust formation, and the ease of trust building varies across countries. This variation has been confirmed by empirical studies. Guiso, Sapienza, and Zingales found that the level of trust among different ethnic groups in the United States shows significant divergences, with Japanese Americans being most trusting and African Americans being least so.[63] The pattern of divergence is consistent with the variations in the level of trust in their countries of origin. They also found that religious beliefs affect the level of trust of individuals.[64] For example, Protestants and Catholics in the United States were found to be generally more trusting than adherents to other beliefs.[65] The implications of these cross-cultural variations for antitrust enforcement, especially anticartel policy, will be further explored below.

The Impact of Culture on Antitrust Enforcement

What is the relevance of the above discussion about culture to antitrust enforcement? After all, none of the cultural value dimensions identified in the previous section is directly related to competition. Hofstede's survey was conducted to gauge the work-related attitude of individuals in different cultures. While such attitude may overlap with the cultural values related to competition, there are also likely to be discrepancies. Nonetheless, as will be obvious from the ensuing discussion, many of the cultural traits identified previously have relevant implications for antitrust enforcement.

Cartel Enforcement

The cultural characteristic identified in the previous section that may have the most immediate application to antitrust enforcement is trust. To the extent that trust is more easily built and maintained in a culture, cartel enforcement may need to be more vigilant. Cartel members are less likely to defect if they have greater trust in each other. Moreover, in collectivist, feminine, and harmony-oriented societies, cartel members are less likely to defect. Being involved in the same industry means that executives of cartel member companies may belong to the same in-group. Given their common in-group membership and the high value attached to it in a collectivist society, the deterrence from defection will be particularly strong. The social sanction that will be inflicted for defection may also be particularly severe. Likewise, in a harmony-oriented society, individuals are less likely to defect; defection results in confrontation that violates the harmony within the in-group and in society generally.

Andreas Stephan has noted that connections, or *guanxi*, are particularly important to businesspeople in China.[66] The in-group identity of Chinese businesspeople operating in the same industry is often reinforced by trade association membership, repeated transactions, familial and geographical ties,[67] social visits, dinner invitations, gift giving, and so forth.[68] Defection may have grave consequences for Chinese businesspeople, including social isolation, loss of business connections, or even difficulty in obtaining credit and hostile treatment by public authorities.[69] Given such a collectivist cultural environment, trust among cartel members is easily built, or perhaps even preexisting. It is also easily maintained. Cartels hence can be more easily formed. Antitrust authorities in countries with a collectivist, feminine, and harmony-oriented culture should pay particular attention to cartel enforcement.

Ki Jong Lee has shown that a culture's attitude toward uncertainty avoidance is also correlated with cartel enforcement. By combining Hofstede's indices on individualism and uncertainty avoidance, Lee demonstrated an "undeniable correlation" between these two cultural value dimensions and a jurisdiction's anticartel policy, as indicated by its imposition of fines and prison sentences for individuals involved in cartels.[70] He found that a culture that is characterized by individualism and high tolerance for uncertainty is likely to impose harsher penalties for cartel infringement.[71] Lee did not proffer an explanation for this correlation. At first glance, there seems to be no obvious reason why the rigor of cartel enforcement should be related to cultural attitude toward uncertainty. Meanwhile, uncertainty avoidance may be correlated with the incidence of cartel conduct. In a culture with a lower tolerance for uncertainty, businesspeople may try to substitute the peace and quiet of cartelization for the tumult created by competition. After all, competition breeds uncertainty. Introduction of new products and constant changes in marketing strategies by rivals are but some of the regular occurrences in a competitive market that create uncertainty for a firm's business. This suggests that cultures with a lower tolerance for uncertainty are likely to have a greater incidence of cartels and hence a more urgent need for rigorous cartel enforcement. This is the opposite of what Lee found in his study. Cultures with low tolerance for uncertainty are plagued by a higher incidence of cartels and more lax cartel enforcement.

Leniency programs are a crucial component in cartel enforcement. Just as cultural traits influence the ease of trust information, which in turn may facilitate cartelization, culture also needs to be taken into account when formulating and implementing leniency programs. There is reason to believe that leniency programs may work less well in cultures that are collectivist, feminine, and harmony oriented. Given the social ties among business executives in the same industry and the general aversion to confrontations and disputes, defection, which will result in hefty fines or perhaps even incarceration for fellow cartel members, is likely to be frowned upon. Not only will the defector firm likely be expelled from the trade association, the business executives involved will also likely be ostracized and lose business connections. As Lee noted, "[i]n a culture . . . which regards cartel as a form of cooperation rather than a conspiracy for crime, an informer [*sic*] is nothing but a betrayer."[72] In order to increase the attractiveness of leniency programs and induce defection, criminal sanctions may be necessary. Only when the cost of belated defection is prohibitively high, as in the case of imprisonment of executives, will firms break away from their cartels and take advantage of leniency programs. Noncriminal sanctions are unlikely to serve as a sufficient incentive for defection in a collectivist and harmony-oriented culture.[73]

Unfortunately for cartel enforcement, cultures that discourage defection are usually also tolerant of cartels and unsupportive of criminal sanctions.

Andreas Stephan has documented the prevalence in many cultures of a cavalier attitude toward cartels.[74] These are often the same ones that have not had active criminal enforcement against cartels, or have eschewed criminal sanctions altogether. Given the country's collectivist culture and lack of history of cartel enforcement, Chinese businesses have not regarded cartels as particularly morally reprehensible. The People's Republic of China's Anti-Monopoly Law does not impose criminal sanctions for cartel infringement, even though the law was enacted in 2007, when there was already a clear global trend toward criminalization of cartels. Despite the fact that criminal sanctions for cartels have been on the books in Japan for decades, cartels were commonplace during the 1960s and 1970s, when the country underwent rapid economic development.[75] Until recently, the only criminal prosecution of cartel activity was during the oil crisis in the 1970s. In fact, until the 1980s, the Japanese government actively encouraged cartelization as a tool of industrial policy and regularly authorized crisis cartels.[76] When sales tax was first introduced in Japan in 1989, the government allowed small and medium-sized businesses to fix prices so that they could pass on the tax burden to consumers.[77] The statutory provision authorizing crisis cartels was finally repealed in 1999.[78]

Not only is the Japanese culture permissive of cartels, it also poses obstacles to the implementation of leniency programs. Leniency has been often compared to plea bargaining, which is regarded as "evil" in Japan.[79] During the debate over the introduction of a leniency program in Japan, opponents attempted to derail the reform by comparing leniency to plea bargain.[80] Given its short history, the effectiveness of the leniency program in Japan remains to be seen. What is clear is that cartel enforcement is doubly difficult in countries where the culture is both permissive of cartels and unfavorable to the functioning of leniency programs.

Other Horizontal Restraints

Culture may have relevance to antitrust enforcement beyond cartels. It may need to be considered in other areas of horizontal restraints as well. One obvious area, which in a way is a natural extension of cartels, is the inference of a horizontal agreement from parallel conduct. When faced with this issue, courts in the United States and EU have looked for additional indicators, known as plus factors in the United States, to distinguish between permissible oligopolistic interdependent conduct and collusion. Some U.S. courts have suggested that evidence of a motive for common action among competitors tips the inference in favor of collusion.[81] In order for tacit collusion to work, there must be trust among the coconspirators. Each must believe that the others will abide by the tacit understanding reached by them. Trust is arguably even more important for tacit collusion than for cartels because of the lack of direct communication among the coconspirators. In cultures that are more conducive to trust formation, tacit collusion will be easier to maintain.

In fact, culture may play a role beyond the maintenance of the tacit agreement. It may help the tacit understanding to be reached in the first place. One crucial difference between cartels and tacit collusion is that the coconspirators in the latter do not explicitly negotiate with one another. They must be able to reach terms of understanding among themselves tacitly. In cultures that are collectivist, feminine, and harmony oriented, tacit understanding can be more easily attained. Coconspirators can decipher and predict each other's conduct with less uncertainty as the range of possible conduct and motives will be narrower. Power distance may also be relevant here. In a culture marked by considerable power distance, small firms in the industry may be more likely to follow the industry leader or the trade association's direction. Such behavior will obviously make it easier for the industry leader to facilitate tacit collusion. All these factors suggest that tacit collusion will be more easily attained in certain cultures than in others.

To maintain the effectiveness of antitrust enforcement against tacit collusion in these cultures, adjustments in the doctrinal treatment of tacit collusion are needed. One possible adjustment is to shift the burden of proof from the plaintiff to the defendant. Once the plaintiff has provided evidence of parallel conduct, the burden would shift to the defendant to disprove the existence of tacit collusion, perhaps by furnishing evidence of independent rational economic motive for their conduct. Evidence of parallel conduct creates a presumption of tacit collusion. Moreover, the list of plus factors may need to be revised to incorporate cultural considerations. In collectivist, feminine, and harmony-oriented cultures, the fact that the composition of the industry has remained stable over time or that the trade association is powerful will render tacit collusion easier to achieve. Industry structural or behavioral characteristics that indicate strong in-group identity or cohesion should be considered as plus factors in these cultures.

Culture may have relevance to yet another category of horizontal restraints: facilitating practices such as information exchange arrangements. The general concern about these practices is that they may facilitate collusion. It follows from the above discussion that in cultures where collusion is already easier to achieve, facilitating practices should be viewed suspiciously. Price information circulated and recommended prices issued by trade associations are more likely to lead to price convergence in cultures that are collectivist, feminine, and harmony oriented. For countries with such a culture, the antitrust authority may want to adopt a stricter standard for facilitating practices to restrict the flow of sensitive information among competitors.

Vertical Restraints

Given the variety of vertical restraints, it is difficult to explore thoroughly the implications of cultural considerations to their treatment under antitrust law within the space of this short chapter. The cultural values implicated by vertical restraints are likely to be somewhat different from those pertinent to horizontal restraints. For horizontal restraints, the cultural values with the greatest salience are collectivism, harmony, and trust. These values affect how easily competitors collaborate and collude with each other. For vertical restraints, the most relevant cultural values are likely to be stability, uncertainty avoidance, and short-term/long-term orientation. In cultures that value stability and are long-term oriented, firms are more likely to enter into long-term supply and distribution arrangements. Trust may also play a role here. To the extent that trust is particularly important to business transactions in these cultures, firms may prefer supply and distribution relationships with fewer firms, or perhaps even on an exclusive basis.

It is well documented that Japanese firms prefer to form long-standing relationships with suppliers and distributors, in no small part due to the cultural preference for stability and their willingness to make long-term, relation-specific investment.[82] According to Richard Whitley, the Japanese mode of industrial and business organization can be traced to a variety of sociopolitical institutions in the past.[83] A cultural preference for long-term business relationships, coupled with a willingness to make relation-specific investment, may suggest that vertical restraints are more likely to be motivated by procompetitive reasons. The antitrust authority in such a country should still apply standard economic analysis to assess the efficiency gains from such restraints. Cultural considerations do not replace economic analysis. The authority, however, may want to adopt a more permissive attitude toward claims of efficiency gains.

Abuse of Dominance

The cultural value that is most directly implicated by abuse of dominance claims is competitiveness. Firms in every culture compete rigorously. However, there seem to be marginal differences in competitiveness across different cultures that may affect the likelihood of abusive conduct by dominant firms. Hofstede's and Schwartz's studies suggest that cultures differ substantially along the dimensions of uncertainty avoidance, individualism vs. collectivism, masculinity vs. femininity, and mastery vs. harmony, which bear on competitiveness. Other studies have attempted directly to measure competitiveness and have found substantial differences across cultures.[84] For example, Green, Deschamps, and Paez found that Russians, Turks, Peruvians, and Venezuelans tend to be particularly competitive.[85]

One can surmise that in less competitive, more feminine, and more harmony-oriented cultures, firms are less likely to engage in exclusionary conduct that will drive their competitors out of business. What this means is that in countries that exhibit these cultural traits, abusive conduct such as predatory pricing, which is easily confused with procompetitive price-cutting, presents particular analytical difficulty. The antitrust authority in these countries should use extra caution before finding an infringement. Perhaps the authority can insist on proof that the price-cutting has a reasonable likelihood of eliminating the competitor and allowing the dominant firm to recoup its losses, which means that the authority should favor the U.S. analytical approach over the EU one to predatory pricing.

. . .

The adjustments that have been suggested in this chapter may seem daunting to formulate. Given the intangible nature of culture and the difficulty in articulation and measurement of cultural differences, a systematic effort, especially by a cultural outsider, to come up with adjustments that need to be made to the antitrust enforcement of a particular jurisdiction may seem elusive. Thankfully, domestic enforcers should have a nuanced appreciation of their own culture and probably already make informal adjustments to their analysis in their minds. One must remember that these adjustments are likely to be minor. They are generally more a matter of emphasis than wholesale changes. This chapter in no way intends to suggest that cultural considerations should displace or revamp economic analysis. Antitrust law and enforcement ultimately is, and should be, based on sound economics. Given the fact that cultural differences do affect economic and competitive behavior, however, economic analysis does face certain limits as the basis for antitrust enforcement. Other considerations need to be taken into account.

Once one is willing to acknowledge that there are limits to the analytical scope and applicability of economics, which is the presumed universal basis for antitrust analysis, one must be ready to question the extent to which complete convergence of antitrust laws across the globe is desirable or even feasible. There is no doubt that the convergence movement has improved the quality of antitrust enforcement in emerging jurisdictions. However, one should not lose sight of the fact that competition does not take place in a vacuum. It proceeds in a complex socioeconomic environment. A drive for complete convergence is likely to be counterproductive and may even compromise the effectiveness of enforcement in jurisdictions with a significantly different cultural milieu from the mainstream antitrust jurisdictions in the West.

14

Promoting Convergence of Competition Policies in Northeast Asia

Culture-Competition Correlation and Its Implications

Ki Jong Lee

The development toward regional economic integration in Northeast Asia had been seriously hindered by the political and economic conflict of interests among the regional powers, of which the recent territorial dispute between China and Japan is just one illustration. However, since the summit meeting between Korea, Japan, and China in May 2010, which drew the integration within visibility, these obstacles began to seem quite surmountable. After the summit the regional powers expressly proclaimed in their "Trilateral Cooperation Vision 2020"[1] that they "will continue to work towards further economic integration of the three countries in the long-term, including the establishment of a common market in the region."[2] They also agreed to set up a permanent secretariat in Korea for closer trilateral cooperation, which is expected to contribute toward the institutionalization of trilateral cooperation.

To sustain the momentum for the integration, various obstacles to it have to be dealt with in a proper and timely manner. Among others, the issue of competition policy should be included as one of the top priorities in the agenda for the trilateral cooperation. As we observed in the process of regional integration in Europe, competition policy could play a leading role in Northeast Asian economic integration.[3] Of course, the EU has been regarded as an exception rather than a rule in that it accomplished hard convergence of its national competition policies and established a regional competition regime. However, an increasing number of regions have succeeded in establishing their own version of regional competition regimes (e.g., the Caribbean Community, CARICOM) and some mitigated models of regional competition regime that aim at promoting harmonization of competition laws have been suggested for regions where unified regional competition law is too ambitious a goal at the current stage of development.[4] Thus Northeast Asian countries need at least to strive for promoting convergence of competition policies in the short term to sustain the momentum for regional economic integration. In the long run, the convergence of competition policies could facilitate the overall economic integration in the region, with or without establishing a regional competition regime.

This chapter examines the correlation between national cultures and competition policies in searching for measures to promote convergence of competition policies in Northeast Asia, as the cultural similarity between the regional powers could help them cope with the obstacles to the convergence of their competition policies. This chapter presents evidence on culture-competition correlation, discusses the implications of the correlation for the convergence of competition policies, and suggests some measures to promote the convergence in Northeast Asia.

The Correlation Between National Culture and Competition Policy

Previous Findings

This chapter attempts to establish the correlation between competition policies and national cultures by enlisting the research of cross-cultural psychologists. Among others, Geert Hofstede identified five independent dimensions of national culture differences: Power Distance (PDI), Uncertainty Avoidance (UAI), Individualism/Collectivism (IDV), Masculinity/Femininity (MAS), and Long-term/Short-term Orientation (LTO).[5] Based upon the data collected between 1967 and 1973, his research shows the index scores for fifty countries and three regions (Arab countries, East Africa, and West Africa) concerning each dimension (Table 14.1)[6] and clusters the countries and regions into twelve branches.[7] He also estimated index scores for sixteen additional countries from data collected later (Table 14.2).[8]

Even without the help of econometrics, this chapter demonstrates some correlation between Hofstede's cultural value dimensions, especially UAI and IDV, and competition policies. On a national level the findings are as follows: Countries with individualistic values are likely to have a more rigorous anticartel policy than those with collectivist ones; countries with high tendency to avoid uncertainty are inclined to have a relatively lax anticartel policy and countries with a similar combination of cultural values to that of the United States tend to have a more rigorous anticartel policy; Anglo cluster countries (United States, Canada, United Kingdom, Ireland, Australia, and New Zealand) tend to have a relatively rigorous anticartel policy.[9]

Major findings on a regional level are as follows: Regional trade agreements (RTAs) within the same branch of countries are inclined to have relatively strong competition-related provisions (CRPs); RTAs between Anglo cluster countries and those outside the cluster are likely to have weaker CRPs, while RTAs outside the cluster tend to have stronger ones; and RTAs between countries that are similar in their Individualism/Collectivism index and/or Uncertainty Avoidance index are apt to have relatively strong CRPs.[10]

When quantifiable data on competition policies are available, econometrics assists in describing the correlation between national cultures and competition policies in numerals. An increasing number of researchers have developed numerical indexes on competition policies. The World Economic Forum (WEF) published the ratings of the effectiveness of antitrust policy on a comprehensive set of countries in 2002.[11] Michael Nicholson provided the index scores on the resources available to the competition law enforcement authorities, based on the data published by the *Global Competition Review* (GCR) in 2003.[12] Nicholson also presented the Antitrust Law Index (ALI) for laws in effect in 2003, which quantifies the presence of antitrust laws in different countries.[13] This article tries to find the correlation between these indexes on competition policies and Hofstede's cultural indexes.

Competition Agency Effectiveness and National Culture

The WEF asked local business leaders to rate the effectiveness of the antimonopoly policy of their countries in promoting competition, from 1 (lax) to 7 (effective). The results[14] are shown in Table 14.3 and have been quoted as a proxy for agency effectiveness in various research papers.[15] Regression analysis tells us that the WEF antitrust index is highly correlated with Hofstede's cultural indexes: the WEF measure has a strong positive correlation with Individualism/Collectivism (IDV) index scores (correlation = 0.72823) and strong negative correlations with Power Distance (PDI) (correlation = −0.66696) and Uncertainty Avoidance (UAI) index scores (correlation = −0.29382) (Table 14.4). The WEF measure's positive correlation with the IDV index and negative correlation with the UAI index seem to be in line

Table 14.1 Index scores and ranks for countries and regions from the IBM set

	Power Distance		Uncertainty Avoidance		Individualism/ Collectivism		Masculinity/Femininity		Long-term/ Short-term Orientation	
Country	*Index*	*Rank*	*Index*	*Rank*	*Index*	*Rank*	*Index*	*Rank*	*Index*	*Rank*
Argentina	49	35–36	86	10–15	46	22–23	56	20–21		
Australia	36	41	51	37	90	2	61	16	31	22–24
Austria	11	53	70	24–25	55	18	79	2	31	22–24
Belgium	65	20	94	5–6	75	8	54	22	38	18
Brazil	69	14	76	21–22	38	26–27	49	27	65	6
Canada	39	39	48	41–42	80	4–5	52	24	23	30
Chile	63	24–25	86	10–15	23	38	28	46		
Colombia	67	17	80	20	13	49	64	11–12		
Costa Rica	35	42–44	86	10–15	15	46	21	48–49		
Denmark	18	51	23	51	74	9	16	50	46	10
Ecuador	78	8–9	67	28	8	52	63	13–14		
Finland	33	46	59	31–32	63	17	26	47	41	14
France	68	15–16	86	10–15	71	10–11	43	35–36	39	17
Germany	35	42–44	65	29	67	15	66	9–10	31	22–24
Great Britain	35	42–44	35	47–48	89	3	66	9–10	25	28–29
Greece	60	27–28	112	1	35	30	57	18–19		
Guatemala	95	2–3	101	3	6	83	37	43		
Hong Kong	68	15–16	29	49–50	25	37	57	18–19	96	2
Indonesia	78	8–9	48	41–42	14	47–48	46	30–31		
India	77	10–11	40	45	48	21	56	20–21	61	7
Iran	58	29–30	59	31–32	41	24	43	35–36		
Ireland	28	49	35	47–48	70	12	68	7–8	43	13
Israel	13	52	81	19	54	19	47	29		
Italy	50	34	75	23	76	7	70	4–5	34	19
Jamaica	45	37	13	52	39	25	68	7–8		
Japan	54	33	92	7	46	22–23	95	1	80	4
Korea(South)	60	27–28	85	16–17	18	43	39	41	75	5

Malaysia	104	1	36	46	26	36	50	25–26		
Mexico	81	5–6	82	18	30	32	69	6		
Netherlands	38	40	53	35	80	4–5	14	51	44	11–12
Norway	31	47–48	50	38	69	13	2	52	44	11–12
New Zealand	22	50	49	39–40	79	6	52	17	30	25–26
Pakistan	55	32	70	24–25	14	47–48	50	25–26	0	34
Panama	95	2–3	86	10–15	11	51	44	34		
Peru	64	21–23	87	9	16	45	42	37–38		
Philippines	94	4	44	44	32	31	64	11–12	19	31–32
Portugal	63	24–25	104	2	27	33–35	31	45	30	25–26
South Africa	49	35–36	49	39–40	65	16	63	13–14		
Salvador	66	18–19	94	5–6	19	42	40	40		
Singapore	74	13	8	53	20	39–41	48	28	48	9
Spain	57	31	86	10–15	51	20	42	37–38	19	31–32
Sweden	31	47–48	29	49–50	71	10–11	5	53	30	20
Switzerland	34	45	58	33	68	14	70	4–5	40	15–16
Taiwan	58	29–30	69	26	17	44	45	32–33	87	3
Thailand	64	21–23	64	30	20	39–41	34	44	56	8
Turkey	66	18–19	85	16–17	37	28	45	32–33		
Uruguay	61	26	100	4	36	29	38	42		
United States	40	38	46	43	91	1	62	15	29	27
Venezuela	81	5–6	76	21–22	12	50	73	3		
Yugoslavia	76	12	88	8	27	33–35	21	48–49		
Regions										
Arab Countries	80	7	68	27	38	26–27	53	23		
East Africa	64	21–23	52	36	27	33–35	41	39	25	28–29
West Africa	77	10–11	54	34	20	39–41	46	30–31	16	33

NOTE: As the Long-term/Short-term Orientation Index (LTO) was added later than the other four indexes after the survey of Chinese culture around 1985, this table shows LTO for only 34 countries. *Id.* at 351.

SOURCE: Geert Hofstede, *Culture's Consequences: Comparing Values, Behaviors, Institutions and Organizations Across Nations*, 2nd ed. (Sage, 2001) 500, Exhibit A5.1. Included with permission.

Table 14.2 Index score estimates for countries not in the IBM set

Country	*Power Distance index*	*Uncertainty Avoidance index*	*Individualism index*	*Masculinity index*	*Long-term Orientation index*
Bangladesh	80	60	20	55	40
Bulgaria	70	85	30	40	
China	80	30	20	66	118
Czech Republic	57	74	58	57	13
Estonia	40	60	60	30	
Hungary	46	82	80	88	50
Luxembourg	40	70	60	50	
Malta	56	96	59	47	
Morocco	70	68	46	53	
Poland	68	93	60	64	32
Romania	90	90	30	42	
Russia	93	95	39	36	
Slovakia	104	51	52	110	38
Surinam	85	92	47	37	
Trinidad	47	55	16	58	
Vietnam	70	30	20	40	80

SOURCES: Based on Geert Hofstede, *Culture's Consequences: Comparing Values, Behaviors, Institutions and Organizations Across Nations*, 2nd ed. (Sage, 2001), and Geert Hofstede, Gert Jan Hofstede, and Michael Minkov, *Cultures and Organizations, Software of the Mind*, 3rd rev. ed. (McGraw-Hill, 2010). Included with permission.

with the author's earlier findings that individualistic values have a positive correlation and the tendency to avoid uncertainty has a negative correlation with the rigor of anticartel policy. Moreover, the negative correlation between the WEF measure and the PDI index, which stands for citizens' willingness to accept the unequal distribution of power,[16] indicates that authoritarian governments might be an obstacle to the enhancement of competition agency effectiveness.

Resource Inputs into Competition Policy and National Culture

The resources available for the institutions responsible for competition policy enforcement could affect the performance of a competition regime and, to a certain degree, indicate how strongly competition policy is supported in that jurisdiction. The GCR publishes annual surveys on rating enforcement of competition policies in several countries, including the data on budget and staffing. Based on the GCR dataset published in 2003,[17] Nicholson fleshes out values for budget per staff and budget as a percentage of national income, indexed to the value of the United States (Table 14.5).[18]

Regression analysis shows us that the budget/national income index has strong negative correlations with the Power Distance (PDI) index (correlation=

Table 14.3 Results of 2003 World Economic Forum survey on antimonopoly policy

Country	*Rating*	*Country*	*Rating*	*Country*	*Rating*
Argentina	3.8	Israel	5.7	Romania	3.7
Australia	5.7	Italy	5.7	Russia	3.1
Belgium	5.8	Jamaica	3.9	Slovakia	3.8
Brazil	4.7	Japan	5.0	Slovenia	4.2
Canada	5.6	Korea	4.7	South Africa	4.8
Chile	5.1	Latvia	3.8	Spain	5.2
Costa Rica	3.7	Lithuania	3.4	Sri Lanka	3.8
Czech Republic	3.7	Mexico	4.0	Sweden	5.5
Denmark	5.7	Netherlands	6.2	Switzerland	5.0
Estonia	4.2	New Zealand	5.5	Taiwan	5.2
Finland	6.6	Norway	5.3	Thailand	3.9
France	5.8	Panama	4.0	Turkey	4.1
Germany	6.2	Peru	3.8	Ukraine	3.3
Greece	4.1	Philippines	3.8	U.K	5.8
Hungary	4.8	Poland	4.6	United States	6.0
Indonesia	3.6	Portugal	4.5	Venezuela	3.8
Ireland	5.0				

SOURCES: Based on Geert Hofstede, *Culture's Consequences: Comparing Values, Behaviors, Institutions and Organizations Across Nations*, 2nd ed. (Sage, 2001), and Geert Hofstede, Gert Jan Hofstede, and Michael Minkov, *Cultures and Organizations, Software of the Mind*, 3rd rev. ed. (McGraw-Hill, 2010). Included with permission.

Table 14.4 Correlation between WEF's anti-monopoly index and national culture

Pearson Correlation Coefficients
Prob>|r| under HO: Rho=0
Number of observations

	Power Distance index	*Uncertainty Avoidance index*	*Individualism/ Collectivism index*	*Masculinity/ Femininity index*	*Long-term/ Short-term Orientation index*
Antimonopoly index	−0.66696	−0.29382	0.72823	−0.14923	−0.17023
	<.0001	0.0558	<.0001	0.3395	0.3959
	43	43	43	43	27

SOURCES: Based on data from Geert Hofstede, *Culture's Consequences: Comparing Values, Behaviors, Institutions, and Organizations Across Nations*, 2nd ed. (Sage, 2001), 500, Exhibit A5.1 and 502, Exhibit A5.3 (Tables 14.1 and 14.2 above); World Economic Forum, *The Global Competitiveness Report 2001–2002* (New York: Oxford University Press, 2002), 413, Table 8.07 (Table 14.3 above).

−0.43590) and the Uncertainty Avoidance (UAI) index (correlation = −0.47086) (Table 14.6). And the budget/staff index shows strong negative correlation with the PDI index (correlation = −0.30185). These results are also in line with the above findings that PDI and UAI have negative correlations with the rigor of anticartel policy and the agency effectiveness.

Table 14.5 Normalized input measures (United States=100)

Country	*Budget/staff*	*Budget/national income*	*Country*	*Budget/staff*	*Budget/national income*
Argentina	4	2	Kenya	7	34
Armenia	3	40	Korea	24	101
Australia	44	253	Latvia	62	616
Belgium	4	2	Lithuania	7	88
Brazil	15	15	Mexico	44	54
Canada	29	82	Netherlands	97	247
Chile	23	46	New Zealand	57	455
Czech Republic	8	45	Norway	50	217
Denmark	57	173	Panama	24	179
Estonia	8	174	Poland	10	47
Finland	9	21	Romania	2	41
France	124	178	Slovakia	8	56
Germany	40	20	Slovenia	17	40
Indonesia	14	15	South Africa	37	62
Ireland	52	131	Spain	13	11
Israel	24	114	Sweden	43	135

SOURCES: Based on Geert Hofstede, *Culture's Consequences: Comparing Values, Behaviors, Institutions and Organizations Across Nations*, 2nd ed. (Sage, 2001), and Geert Hofstede, Gert Jan Hofstede, and Michael Minkov, *Cultures and Organizations, Software of the Mind*, 3rd rev. ed. (McGraw-Hill, 2010). Included with permission.

Table 14.6 Correlation between resource inputs in competition policy and national culture

Pearson Correlation Coefficients
Prob>|r| under HO: Rho=0
Number of observations

	Power Distance index	*Uncertainty Avoidance index*	*Individualism/ Collectivism index*	*Masculinity/ Femininity index*	*Long-term/ Short-term Orientation index*
Budget/staff	−0.30185	−0.26809	0.51723	−0.02785	−0.13612
	0.0989	0.1448	0.0029	0.8818	0.5563
	31	31	31	31	21
Budget/national income	−0.43590	−0.47086	0.38962	−0.18348	−0.16737
	0.0142	0.0075	0.0303	0.3232	0.4684
	31	31	31	31	21

SOURCES: Based on data from Geert Hofstede, *Culture's Consequences: Comparing Values, Behaviors, Institutions, and Organizations Across Nations,* 2nd ed. (Sage, 2001), 500, Exhibit A5.1 and 502, Exhibit A5.3 (Tables 14.1 and 14.2 above); Michael W. Nicholson, "An Antitrust Law Index for Empirical Analysis of International Competition Policy," *J. Competition L. & Econ.* 4 (2008): 1018, Table 3 (Table 14.5 above). Included with permission.

Antitrust Law Index and National Culture

Nicholson created the Antitrust Law Index (ALI) to indicate an additive summary of the established laws for each country. He determined criteria for the ALI based on the guidelines for draft laws of the United Nations Conference on Trade and Development, the Organisation for Economic Co-operation

Table 14.7 Antitrust law index (for laws in effect in 2003)

Country	*Index*	*Country*	*Index*	*Country*	*Index*
United States	21	Italy	15	Denmark	12
Ukraine	20	Czech Republic	14	Brazil	11
Turkey	19	Israel	14	Costa Rica	11
Belgium	18	Korea	14	Finland	11
Latvia	18	Slovenia	14	Norway	11
Poland	18	Taiwan	14	Germany	10
Romania	18	Venezuela	14	Jamaica	10
Argentina	17	Zambia	14	New Zealand	10
Lithuania	17	Australia	13	Panama	10
South Africa	17	Canada	13	Sri Lanka	10
Uzbekistan	17	Indonesia	13	Tunisia	10
France	16	Macedonia	13	Japan	9
Ireland	16	Mexico	13	U.K.	9
Kenya	16	Peru	13	Yugoslavia	8
Slovakia	16	Spain	13	Netherlands	7
Sweden	16	Thailand	13	Chile	4
Croatia	15	Armenia	12	Malta	4
Estonia	15				

SOURCES: Based on Geert Hofstede, *Culture's Consequences: Comparing Values, Behaviors, Institutions and Organizations Across Nations*, 2nd ed. (Sage, 2001), and Geert Hofstede, Gert Jan Hofstede, and Michael Minkov, *Cultures and Organizations, Software of the Mind*, 3rd rev. ed. (McGraw-Hill, 2010). Included with permission.

and Development, and the World Bank and registered the presence of each criterion for each country. He summed up the individual components to yield a total score and lists the ALI for fifty-two countries for laws in effect in 2003 (Table 14.7).[19]

As the ALI used the model laws to select criteria, transition economies in Central and Eastern Europe, which adopted language of their competition laws from the Treaty of Rome, rank top in the list. Thus the ALI is not necessarily associated with effective policy and shows little significant correlation with the WEF measure for antitrust policy.[20] Likewise, regression analysis does not show any significant correlation between the ALI and Hofstede's cultural index scores either (Table 14.8). But, despite the inherent restriction, the ALI shows a strong positive correlation with the ranks of each country on the Long-term/Short-term (LTI) index (correlation = 0.58477) (Table 14.9). If we could develop an antitrust index that reflects not only de jure laws but also de facto laws, we might be able to discern more strong correlations between the antitrust index and the cultural indexes.

Table 14.8 Correlation between Antitrust Law Index and national culture (index scores)

Pearson Correlation Coefficients
Prob>|r| under HO: Rho=0
Number of observations

	Power Distance index	*Uncertainty Avoidance index*	*Individualism/ Collectivism index*	*Masculinity/ Femininity index*	*Long-term/ Short-term Orientation index*
Antitrust Law Index	0.12045	−0.01652	0.13844	0.22483	−0.17731
	0.4651	0.9205	0.4006	0.1688	0.4183
	39	39	39	39	23

SOURCES: Based on data from Geert Hofstede, *Culture's Consequences: Comparing Values, Behaviors, Institutions, and Organizations Across Nations*, 2nd ed. (Sage, 2001), 500, Exhibit A5.1 and 502, Exhibit A5.3 (Tables 14.1 and 14.2 above); Michael W. Nicholson, "An Antitrust Law Index for Empirical Analysis of International Competition Policy," *J. Competition L. & Econ.* 4 (2008): 1022, Table 5 (Table 14.7 above). Included with permission

Table 14.9 Correlation between Antitrust Law Index and national culture (ranks)

Pearson Correlation Coefficients
Prob>|r| under HO: Rho=0
Number of observations

	Power Distance index	*Uncertainty Avoidance index*	*Individualism/ Collectivism index*	*Masculinity/ Femininity index*	*Long-term/ Short-term Orientation index*
Antitrust Law Index	0.09223	0.05097	−0.22963	−0.26909	0.58477
	0.7341	0.7747	0.2804	0.2653	0.0281
	16	34	24	19	14

SOURCES: Based on data from Geert Hofstede, *Culture's Consequences: Comparing Values, Behaviors, Institutions, and Organizations Across Nations*, 2nd ed. (Sage, 2001), 500, Exhibit A5.1 and 502, Exhibit A5.3 (Tables 14.1 and 14.2 above); Michael W. Nicholson, "An Antitrust Law Index for Empirical Analysis of International Competition Policy," *J. Competition L. & Econ.* 4 (2008): 1022, Table 5 (Table 14.7 above). Included with permission.

The Implications of Culture-Competition Correlation for the Convergence of Competition Policies in Northeast Asia

The evidence on culture-competition correlation presented above is far from comprehensive, but we could discern fairly convincing correlations between antitrust policy and some of the cultural indexes: the Individualism/Collectivism (IDV) index has strong positive correlations with the rigor and effectiveness of antitrust policy, while the Power Distance (PDI) index and Uncertainty Avoidance (UAI) index have strong negative correlations.

We describe these findings as follows: (1) individualistic values have a strong positive correlation with the rigor and effectiveness of antitrust policy, while collectivist values have negative one; (2) willingness to accept the unequal distribution of power has a strong negative correlation with the rigor and effectiveness of antitrust policy; and (3) high tendency to avoid uncertainty has a strong negative correlation with the rigor and effectiveness of antitrust policy.

The implications of the Long-term/Short-term Orientation (LTO) index are somewhat obscure, as we only have a small piece of evidence on its correlation with antitrust policy. Thus this chapter focuses on IDV, PDI, and UAI in illuminating the implications of culture-competition correlation for the convergence of competition policies in Northeast Asia.

Earlier findings of the author indicate that cultural similarities could facilitate the regional cooperation on competition policies concerning RTAs. Chances of the convergence of competition policies could also be greater if the participants share similar cultural characteristics. For example, New Zealand and Australia substantially harmonized their national competition laws in the context of deep economic integration, even without the political integration found in the EU.[21] According to Hofstede, New Zealand and Australia belong to the same cultural cluster[22] (Anglo) and show very similar index scores in UAI and IDV indices and fairly similar index scores in the PDI index (Table 14.1).

Although Korea, China, and Japan do not share as much cultural similarity with each other as New Zealand and Australia, their overall cultural characteristics are quite similar (Tables 14.1 and 14.2). Korea and Japan show similar index scores in PDI and UAI, and Korea and China in IDV. The differences between the index scores of Korea/Japan and China in PDI seem to be within the boundary of compatibility, just like the difference between the index scores of Korea/China and Japan in IDV. But the difference between the index scores of Korea/Japan and China in the UAI index is quite huge.

We could describe these cultural characteristics of Korea, China, and Japan as follows: (1) the Northeast Asian countries, especially Korea and China, share relatively collectivist values; (2) the Northeast Asian countries, especially China, accept relatively easily the unequal distribution of power; and (3) Korea and Japan have a relatively high tendency to avoid uncertainty, while China has a relatively low tendency to avoid uncertainty.

China's willingness to accept the unequal distribution of power could impede the effectiveness of antitrust policy, according to our findings above. It is not clear whether China's low PDI index score is the result of decades of communist regime or has deeper roots in its history. But it is quite probable that the communist regime has reinforced Chinese citizens' willingness to accept the unequal distribution of power. It will take time to remove the traces of the centrally planned economy.[23]

On the other hand, China's low tendency to avoid uncertainty is quite surprising. Despite decades of rule by a communist regime, Chinese citizens show little hesitation in confronting the uncertainties inherent in their transitional economic system. The rapid pace of China's participation in the World Trade Organization and its aggressive pursuit of free trade agreements with various partners have been quite in accord with its cultural characteristics. China's low tendency to avoid uncertainty could help overcome its communist legacy and promote the rigor and effectiveness of its competition policy more easily than is usually expected.

The overall implications of the cultural characteristics of Northeast Asian countries for the convergence of competition policies are twofold. First, in the short term, Korea, China, and Japan could capitalize on their cultural similarities for the convergence of competition policies in Northeast Asia. Second, however, if they do not go further in convergence than their current cultural texture allows, it might, in the long term, impede their endeavor to promote the convergence of competition policies with the countries outside of the region, which do not share much cultural similarity with Northeast Asian countries. We should also recall that collectivist values, high tendency to avoid uncertainty, and willingness to accept the unequal distribution of power have strong negative correlations with the rigor and effectiveness of antitrust policy. This suggests the need for the promotion of competition culture by facilitating competition-friendly values and broadening cultural common ground between Northeast Asian countries, which this chapter elaborates in more detail below.

Measures to Promote the Convergence of Competition Policies in Northeast Asia

Promoting Competition Culture

Northeast Asian countries need to build a strong consensus on the value of competition and competition policy among their citizens to facilitate the convergence of their competition policies.[24] As national cultures in the region are not fully in accord with competition-friendly values, the regional powers might have to try to change their cultures into more competition-friendly ones. However, the possibility of culture change has been a subject of ongoing debate. Some regard national cultures as extremely stable,[25] while others present strategies for progressive culture change.[26] This chapter provides some prescriptions for enhancing competition-friendly values among citizens in Northeast Asia, building upon earlier suggestions by the author.[27]

In the short term, Northeast Asian countries could maximize the receptiveness of their competition policies by aligning them with their current national culture. For example, China's low tendency to avoid uncertainty suggests that its citizens might value innovation highly and seem to be totally in line with its reform campaigns focused on innovation. China could overcome the resistance from its socialist tradition more easily by focusing on innovation-friendly policy areas, such as R&D joint ventures, in the initial stage of the development of its competition policy.

In the long term, Northeast Asian countries could revive competition-friendly traditions in their history to facilitate competition-friendly values on the basis of historical continuity.[28] For instance, in Korea, Kaegjoo (commission agencies) of the Joseon Dynasty could be recast as innovative entrepreneurs, who fought against government-supported monopolies by Yookeuijeon (six regular markets) and provided the benefits of competition to consumers.[29] In Japan, we could find a rich tradition of competition-friendly values in the history of the Meiji Restoration.[30]

As the national cultures of Northeast Asian countries are similar in many respects, the regional powers could pursue strong CRPs in the RTA(s) among themselves, according to the author's earlier findings. But, as we could still discern some discrepancies between their cultural indexes, we need to promote competition-friendly values on a regional level, as well as on a national level, in order to promote the convergence of competition policies in the region. Special attention should be paid to the widely different UAI (Uncertainty Avoidance) index scores between the regional powers. As the convergence of competition policies in the context of regional economic integration provides enormous uncertainty to the participating countries, the high tendency to avoid uncertainty might work not only against the convergence, but also against the integration itself. Thus one could devise effective measures to mitigate the tendencies to avoid uncertainties on a regional level. For example, in the short term, one could nurture an uncertainty-welcoming attitude by enlisting innovation-friendly traditions and popular cultural codes that could be shared by the general public across the region. In the long run, however, measures more directly focused on citizens' uncertainty-avoiding tendency should be taken from various angles, so that citizens could accept more easily the uncertainties that the extended competition on a regional level might provide. But it is far beyond the ordinary scope of competition advocacy to devise and implement such measures for the general public. Thus, this chapter focuses more narrowly on the antitrust community in Northeast Asia.

Facilitating Cooperation Among Competition Experts

In early September 2010, hundreds of antitrust lawyers, academics, and bureaucrats participated in a series of conferences held back-to-back in Seoul: the 6th Seoul International Competition Forum (SICF), the East Asia Top Level Official's Meeting on Competition Policy, and the Asia Competition Association (ACA) 2010 Annual Conference. Two of the most distinct features of the group are its diversity and comprehensiveness—the ACA is a nongovernmental forum, while the other two are intergovernmental forums. The SICF is a global forum, while the other two are regional forums. Participants came from jurisdictions all around the world and had expertise in such a variety of areas concerning competition policy. More than two hundred competition experts from Northeast Asia exchanged ideas with counterparts from other regions. One could discern a Northeast Asian antitrust community already in the process of rapid growth. The converging vision and values of this community could warrant greater harmonization efforts in the future.[31] Thus, serious measures should be taken to enhance exchange and cooperation among the antitrust experts in Northeast Asia. For instance, the secretariat for trilateral cooperation among the regional powers, which will be established in Korea in 2011, could play a pivotal role in facilitating cooperation between antitrust experts in the region by integrating competition cooperation both at governmental and nongovernmental levels.

. . .

From a static point of view, the correlation between national culture and competition policy might simply represent the cultural limits on competition policy. But the correlation works both ways—culture affects competition policy and vice versa. Countries could maximize the receptiveness of their competition policies by aligning them with their national culture. They also could promote the convergence of competition policies by capitalizing on the cultural similarity between countries and facilitating competition-friendly values among citizens. That is, culture could be seen as a key to the convergence of competition policies from a more dynamic viewpoint.

Northeast Asian countries share much cultural similarity between them. However, it might not suffice to capitalize on their cultural common ground for the convergence of competition policies, as their cultural values are not entirely competition friendly. They need to facilitate competition-friendly values at a regional level to promote the convergence of competition policies. In the long run, measures directly focusing on citizens' values need to be taken beyond the traditional scope of competition advocacy programs. But, in the short term, the antitrust community in Northeast Asia could play a key role in promoting the convergence of competition policies in the region.

15

The Limits of Competition Law in Latin America

Julián Peña

Many Latin American countries have "discovered" or "rediscovered" competition law recently. Until the early 1990s, very few countries in the region had competition laws. Those that did had a very poor enforcement record. It was during the 1990s, through Washington Consensus–based policy reforms, that laws enacting or modernizing the competition law regimes through most Latin American countries emerged.

A decade and a half after this process began, the stage of development of competition policies in the region is different from what people expected. Competition law enforcement differs substantially in most Latin American countries from that of developed countries. Ironically, however, even in countries where governments have been critical of Washington Consensus policies, the governments consider competition law to be one of the pillars of their public policies.

Although Latin America is a broad regional designation that covers very different situations at the country level, it is possible to point to some common limits to the development of competition law in the region. These limits are mainly cultural, political, economic, and institutional. The purpose of this chapter is to analyze each of these limits in order to assess the challenges faced by implementing policies designed for a different context without making the necessary adjustments to the reality of each country (or region as a whole).

Cultural Limits

Lack of Competition Culture

Latin American countries do not have a competition culture. Centuries of Spanish and Portuguese (in the case of Brazil) colonialism forged the roots of an anti-market institutional system where the government is omnipresent. As Ignacio de León points out, "colonial mercantilism was a natural response to the increasing militarization propelled by the colonization of the Indies and the huge indigenous civilizations that needed to be Christianized. . . . The proliferation of legal monopolies was a natural outcome of this process."[1]

Although free market ideas inspired most nineteenth-century Latin American constitutions, from the 1920s to the 1980s, the vast majority of the region's governments followed a paradigm of strong state interventionism in the market.[2] The two pillars of development policies within Latin America were protecting local industries from foreign competition and regulating internal markets. The major policies in the region during this period included: (1) price and exchange controls, (2) large state-owned enterprises, (3) strong government incentives to promote production of certain goods or regions, (4) foreign investment limitations, and (5) high trade barriers to implement import substitution mechanisms.

Since the late 1980s (at least until the late 1990s), Latin American countries started implementing the promarket policies included in the so-called Washington Consensus. In particular the different countries, at their own pace and manner (1) deregulated their economies, (2) privatized the state owned enterprises, (3) eliminated some government subsidies, (4) received strong foreign investments inflows, (5) liberalized their foreign trade, and (6) implemented competition policies. This overnight pendulum shift of the economic paradigm was not a result of a drastic self-examination and recognition of the failure of the previous paradigm. Instead, it was a set of "recommendations" from the Washington-based international financial institutions, which needed to be followed by the different countries in order to attain debt relief.

The failure of the Washington Consensus policies to provide sustainable development with social welfare in the region resulted in a return to the greater state interventionism paradigm. Since the return of significant state intervention, there has not been a common paradigm but many different approaches. In December 1994, with the onset of the Mexican crisis, a turning point in the development of policies occurred in the region. In 1998, disenchantment with the Washington Consensus policies began to materialize.

Afterward, the regional economic situation started to deteriorate, as did the political support for the structural reform process. Since then, the people of Venezuela, Ecuador, Brazil, Argentina, Bolivia, and Uruguay have, among others, elected as their presidents the candidates who had, at least in their political discourse, an anti–Washington Consensus position.

Instead of having a new positive consensus, there is now an agreement merely of the failure of the Washington Consensus policies to solve the region's historical development problems. Most Latin American governments would agree that a fiscal-oriented model without equity and social awareness cannot be a legitimate path toward integrating the region in a globalized world.

However, there are currently at least as many alternative paths as there are countries in the region. The role of state intervention in the market is a crucial issue that has been interpreted differently throughout the region. A common response to the crisis of the Washington Consensus in the region is characterized by a greater presence of the state in the market. The difference is, however, the degree of this return to state interventionism.

Government Dirigisme, *Institutional Corporativism, and Protectionism*

The long-standing tradition of government *dirigisme* has resulted in a strong institutional corporatism. According to De León, "Latin American corporatism follows an organization format imposed 'from above' by governments, and was institutionalized prior to the consolidation of industrial capitalism or any autonomous social movement."[3] The strength of this corporatism is reflected in the various exemptions from antitrust enforcement introduced in the different antitrust legislations in Latin America. These exemptions that, as De León points out, in some countries cover over 60 percent of the GDP, evidence "that antitrust provisions in Latin America are deeply influenced by the institutional corporatism and fragmentation of property rights that have long influenced policy making in the region."[4] Examples of antitrust exemptions include labor unions (Dominican Republic), agricultural producers (Venezuela), public services (Costa Rica and Colombia), or nationalized industries (Brazil, Chile, and Mexico, among others).

Historically, Latin American countries utilized protectionist policies. The import substitution schemes imposed throughout the region are just one of the many mechanisms used by Latin American governments over time to protect local industries from foreign competition. The pendulum shift toward trade liberalization in the 1990s led to a severe injury to the local industries that overnight faced competition, without a sufficient transition period. Latin American countries launched regional trade agreements (e.g., Mercosur, Caribbean Community [CARICOM]) or revised existing agreements (Andean Community) in the 1990s. Moreover, negotiations for broader free trade agreements were launched (Free Trade Area of the Americas [FTAA], EU-Mercosur) and the Latin American countries agreed to the Uruguay Round agreements signed in Marrakesh that are the basis for the World Trade Organization.

These developments led to a fierce counterreaction by local businessmen who demanded that governments create protectionist measures to favor domestic industries. Consequently, during the first decade of the new century the regional trade agreements suffered severe setbacks, the broader free trade projects were frozen, and many nontrade barriers were enacted. These developments significantly reduced potential entry by foreign firms.

However, the new shift toward protectionism has not been the same across the region. Each Latin American country has adopted a different attitude toward the post–Washington Consensus paradigm, from mere declarations to strong protectionist measures. The degree of protectionism also has varied in intensity over time, in which the international financial crisis of 2008 has had a relevant impact on the adoption of these measures.

For many decades, businessmen were forced to negotiate with or to apply to government officials for permission to set prices or to increase them. This practice obliged competitors to meet among themselves to negotiate a common strategy. Some industries were regulated and had special government agencies that set prices and quantities (e.g., meat, sugar, and grains). In other industries, to fight inflation governments arranged price agreements with the businessmen and treated these agreements as necessary and beneficial for consumers. Although these agreements were difficult to enforce, they trained generations of businesses in the practice of arranging prices with their competitors with the government's consent.

The combination of deregulation and of competition law enforcement in the 1990s created difficulties for local businesses since they were not prepared for such an abrupt change in price-setting practices. In prior decades, it was more profitable for businesspeople to spend more time and resources lobbying government officials for prices and protectionist measures than investing in improving their competitiveness. Ironically, there have been cases in different countries where the competition agencies have opened investigations on price or quota agreements consented to by a previous government (e.g.,

Brazil, Argentina), though there are no known cases where fines were actually imposed for such practices.

For decades Latin American markets were protected from foreign competition. In many markets, there was no price competition. Consequently, Latin American businesses lacked incentives for innovation. This was reflected in low levels of investment and research and development. This situation was aggravated by insufficient protection of intellectual property rights and inefficient and sometimes nonexistent government policies to promote investment. Furthermore, restrictions on technology transfer and on imports of capital goods and new technologies together with limited access to financial markets created a situation that discouraged innovation.

The state presence in the market in Latin America has been very strong since colonial times. Manifesting this presence has been price controls, state-owned enterprises (particularly in utilities), government subsidies to promote production of certain goods or regions, and trade barriers, among other means of intervention. Governments also implemented foreign investment laws to restrict the entrance of new competitors.[5] The consequence of the policies implemented during various decades resulted in the development of obsolete industries and highly indebted governments ending up in what was called the "lost decade" of the 1980s.

Different Social Values and Market Behaviors

The existence of different social values has a significant influence in the success of the adoption of competition policies in Latin America. Since antitrust law originally developed in the United States, the system of values in which the antitrust law exists affects implementation. Given the Protestant roots of the American values, competition is a natural means to reach the success requested by Calvinism's predetermination beliefs.

On the contrary, Latin American countries have inherited Catholic values brought by their Spanish and Portuguese conquerors. Based on that system of values, individual success is relegated to social justice and to the prioritization of family and friendship. Also, individual success is not necessarily perceived by society as something positive and generally provokes distrust as to the means used to achieve such success.

The differences in the value systems helps to explain the difficulties encountered in introducing antitrust leniency programs. In Latin American societies, the snitch is seen as the worst social pariah. This different value system is seen even from early ages. For instance, classmates at school condemn the snitch who denounces a classmate to the teacher for cheating, while the cheater receives no social punishment from his peers.

Market participants in Latin America behave differently than in the developed countries. The existence of strong competition from informal markets and the existence of economic instability or inflation have a relevant influence in the way market participants behave, both from the supply and the demand side. The difficulty of access to the financial system, local consumption habits, and insufficient transportation infrastructure also impact market behavior. Supermarkets are an example of how the same product market should be analyzed differently between developed and developing country antitrust agencies. Consumption habits, distances, transportation infrastructure, and competitors are substantially different in the United States, Europe, or Latin America. Therefore, basing an antitrust market analysis on the case law of other jurisdictions could lead to conclusions that could even be negative for consumers. Also, the level of substitutability in the determination of the relevant market should also reflect the peculiarities of the local habits. With fewer economic resources, Latin American consumers may be more open to adopt an alternative product more easily than what a consumer in a developed country might do. The adoption by Latin American antitrust enforcement agencies of foreign relevant market definitions may also lead to improper conclusions as well.

Political Limits

Long-standing Tradition of Antimarket Beliefs

Latin American governments have long been used to mistrust of the market. As a result, in the name of social justice, they have subordinated the market to governmental control through various means. It could be argued that those beliefs never disappeared. The fact that, after the end of the Washington Consensus decade, promarket policies like competition law are strongly supported by populist governments suggests that although the economic terms may sound similar, the concepts have been substantially modified. As Ignacio De León implies, competition law may have become a politically correct and modern tool for Latin American governments to intervene in the markets.

A clear example that supports this thesis is the way over the past decade Latin American governments introduced many nonantitrust considerations in their antitrust analysis. Social considerations have been comingled within the technical analyses of both anticompetitive behavior and merger cases. The introduction of these social considerations has significantly increased the discretion of antitrust agencies. As Bullard suggests, social considerations introduce the idea of "social convenience" in solving the conflicts in a particular way, according to the *coyuntura*.[6] This has been reflected in a more flexible position toward certain anticompetitive conduct. Bullard argues that the problem for a populist politician who wants to take a hard line against cartels is that he will see his discretionary powers reduced, and this could be politically awkward.

An example of how nonantitrust concerns have been introduced in merger control is the acquisition of the joint control over the only energy transportation company in Argentina by a Brazilian company. The transaction, which included the acquisition of other companies as well, led the presidents of Argentina and Brazil to subject the approval of the transaction to the submission of an agreement by Petrobras to divest the company, since due to national security concerns a Brazilian company could not control such a strategic asset in Argentina.

In Peru, the per se rule has been interpreted in such a flexible manner that now a cartel may be legal if the National Institute for the Defense of Competition and Intellectual Property (INDECOPI) finds it "reasonable," applying a sui generis rule of reason system that does not contemplate, for instance, market power elements. In another case, the Peruvian agency has obliged an energy company to allow a cable TV operator to use its power supply network because the "exercise of the private interests of an individual . . . can damage neither the equality among the competitors nor the legitimate interests of the consumers."[7] In other words, it invoked the antitrust law in order to force a company to do something against its will, regardless of the nonexistence of an anticompetitive conduct. INDECOPI also has interpreted traditional antitrust concepts in unconventional ways. In another case, a Peruvian appellate court reversed a first-instance decision by defining that a bank branch was an "essential facility." Similarly, the Tribunal reversed another of INDECOPI's rulings by interpreting "excessive pricing" as behavior banned by the competition law,[8] something similar to what occurred in Mexico in the *Nestlé* case in 2001 and in Chile in at least two cases. In Brazil, the Administrative Council for Economic Defense (CADE) denied the *Nestlé-Garoto* merger, where the Secretariat of Economic Law (SDE) and the Secretariat of Economic Monitoring introduced the element of a social welfare increase in their analyses.[9]

Existence of Other Political Priorities

The protection of competition is an objective that can be assessed by different governments along with the other policy objectives and should determine the level of priority considering the needs of each particular jurisdiction in each particular time. Therefore, since competition policy is just one of the instruments that governments have to implement their economic policy, it is very common in developing countries (such as in Latin America) to find governments that relegate competition enforcement with respect to other priorities such as protecting labor, fighting inflation, combating poverty or attracting foreign investments.

Regarding merger cases in Argentina, the National Commission for the Defense of Competition (CNDC) approved, with certain conditions, the merger between the two most important local industrial bakeries (*Bimbo* and *Fargo*). It did so by taking into consideration the effects that a possible bankruptcy of the acquired company could have on unemployment levels while not applying the failing firm doctrine.

In countries with high inflation, there are examples of the subordination of competition policies to anti-inflationary measures. In Argentina, the government has promoted various maximum price agreements with different sectors (mainly consumer products) to avoid inflation and also has started selling bottled gas to establish "witness prices" to reduce costs for lower income groups. Moreover, Argentina provides an example of how competition enforcement could be misunderstood as an anti-inflationary instrument. In 2005, the minister of economy announced fines on oxygen and cement companies allegedly involved in cartel practices, amidst the announcement of other anti-inflation measures. Moreover, in 2010, the CNDC conditioned the approval of a merger on the establishment of a price monitoring system for a four year period.[10]

Long-Term "Benefits" vs. Short-Term Costs

Given significant capacity and resource constraints, Latin American governments have to prioritize goals. Fighting anticompetitive conduct is complex, costly, and time demanding. Given the long time horizon of an investigation from the moment it is opened until the time the judicial review is over, governments lack the incentive to initiate serious actions, since most likely it will be a future administration that benefits politically by the eventual penalties against offending firms. Even if a sanction is imposed, the impact to any individual consumer is diffuse and most likely would not be properly recognized by the general population. Furthermore, the short-term costs to active enforcement are very high, since the human and economic resources an antitrust investigation requires are significant. There is a political cost of an investigation against potential campaign contributors.

Economic Limits

Latin America is perhaps too broad a region to provide a unified economic perspective. The significant differences of sizes and levels of economic development of the different Latin American countries are major impediments to reaching conclusions that would be valid at a regional level. However, there are some common characteristics that, although not true for the whole region, are representative of the vast majority of the Latin American countries.

Some of these common characteristics also represent economic limits to the development of competition policies in Latin America, such as the existence of highly concentrated small markets, the strong presence of an informal economy, scarce governmental resources, significant inflation, and insufficient market data.

Highly Concentrated Small Markets

Most Latin American countries have small internal markets due to the high levels of poverty because of an inefficient wealth distribution. The existence of significant levels of poverty reduces the size of the market, since a vast part of the population is not able to participate in the formal economy. As a result, the market is not the whole population, but only a reduced part of it, even in countries with large populations. The small size of the markets creates a market dynamic of few players in order to be economically viable. Thus, Latin American markets are much more concentrated than in developed countries.

As a result, antitrust instruments designed for developed countries such as the Herfindahl-Hirschmann Index (HHI), used to measure when the level market concentration of a merger is understood to create antitrust concerns, if adopted without considering the local market dimensions, may create misleading conclusions. The same is true with regard to the standards to determine the existence of a dominant position. As Ibarra explains, efficiency considerations in imperfect economies and markets should be given greater weight than in developed economies, and other factors such as trade barriers and market contestability should be especially emphasized in antitrust analysis.[11] Moreover, mergers in small economies may be needed to compete more efficiently with imports.[12]

Strong Presence of Informal Economy

An economic characteristic common to all of Latin American economies is the strong presence of an informal economy. In a recent survey of Latin America, *The Economist* estimated that as much as half the population works in the informal economy.[13] These figures are significantly higher than the presence of the informal economy in industrialized countries, which is estimated to be 15 percent of the GDP.

The Organisation for Economic Co-operation and Development (OECD) states that the informal economy "refers to economic activity which is not fully compliant with laws and regulations"[14] and is most commonly represented by, though not limited to, tax evasion, counterfeited products, and smuggled goods. Given the nature of the informal economy, it is very difficult to calculate it accurately and only broad estimates are available. The estimates of the presence of the informal economy vary significantly in the different countries in general and in different product markets in particular.

A recent Inter-American Development Bank book on Latin American productivity[15] (based on a 2009 McKinsey report) indicates that in countries like Brazil and Panama, companies declare only 60 percent of their sales. The same study indicates that almost 70 percent of Mexico's small businesses are not registered (and therefore do not pay taxes), while in El Salvador that number reaches 99 percent for small business and 97 percent for larger firms. According to the OECD, the share of the workforce employed in the informal sector in Latin America ranges from nearly 40 percent in Chile to 70 percent in Bolivia.[16]

Ignoring these facts generates a significant distortion in the antitrust market analysis made by the region's competition authorities. Since the informal economy cannot be properly calculated, competition authorities tend to ignore its existence when assessing market shares. However, by ignoring the informal economy, the authorities are quantifying the informal economy as 0, which distorts the antitrust analysis in a greater way than by estimating a nonscientific number. In Argentina, for instance, 60 percent of the sports footwear and apparel market sales are considered to be related to the informal economy according to government officials.[17] However, when assessing the sports footwear market, the CNDC only calculated the formal economy's numbers.[18]

Significant Inflation Levels

The significant inflation level experienced in many Latin American countries is also a reality not contemplated in the design of competition laws in developed countries. The existence of inflation distorts not only prices but also the market data needed to analyze an anticompetitive behavior. Relatively high levels of annual inflation do not permit comparing price behaviors over time, since these prices (and their rises) constantly fluctuate in a way that distorts any kind of measurement.

This is relevant, for instance, in the application of tools such as the test of Small but Significant and Nontransitory Increase in Price (SSNIP) used to define relevant markets in antitrust analysis. The use of the SSNIP, which is crucial both for determining the existence of dominance as well as for analyzing mergers, in an economy with significant inflation levels is therefore distorted, since it bases the relevant market definition on whether a hypothetical monopolist could profit from a 5 percent price increase for at least one year.

Insufficient Market Data

As a result of the characteristics of most Latin American economies described above (mainly the strong presence of the informal economy), there is insufficient reliable market data. Many times Latin American antitrust agencies have to rely on market estimations made by the parties since there is no other way to measure market shares in order to adjust the analysis to the standards imported from developed countries such as the HHI. This limitation is also valid for the measurement of both prices and volumes.

Due to the inaccuracy of the economic information, antitrust agencies must base their analysis on an unrealistic diagnosis of how the market is structured, thus drastically diminishing the chances of arriving at the proper conclusions. Reaching the wrong conclusions on market structure not only hurts the effectiveness of the eventual remedy to overcome the antitrust concern, but it may well lead to a decision that could eventually reduce consumer welfare.[19]

Institutional Limits

Latin American countries face a weak institutional framework to properly support the implementation of competition policies. This weakness is reflected in agencies with irregular performances that are politically influenced, a judicial review mechanism marked by the lack of sufficient antitrust technical knowledge, and an overworked judicial system. Accordingly, the institutional framework of competition enforcement in Latin America is more dependent on the political will of specific leaders rather than on the strength of the system itself at both the country and agency levels.

Latin American countries, ever since their nineteenth-century independence, have historically given more importance to following strong leaders rather than building strong institutions. Weaker institutions impose fewer restrictions on strong leadership. This is also true for competition agencies. This dynamic explains why agencies initially received more human and economic resources but eventually less political and economic support when the agencies sought to undertake more enforcement. As De León states, "in certain institutional settings characterized by interventionism and corporatism, such as those found in Latin American countries, trade-offs between institutional credibility and government intervention are particularly crucial"[20] and therefore, as Castañeda concludes, "weak enforcement agencies typical of the Latin American region undermine policy and strengthen the power of prominent monopolists."[21]

Administrative Procedures

Most Latin American governments have created competition agencies within their administrative structures. As such, the agencies lack sufficient political and economic independence. There are some partial exceptions in some jurisdictions (e.g., Chile and Brazil), but there is no jurisdiction where the competition enforcement is completely independent. This is not an exclusive characteristic of Latin American jurisdictions. In fact, even the United States and Europe have institutional frameworks with different levels of political influence. The main difference perhaps is the level of such influence and the fact that in Latin American countries the influence is more politics related than policy related.

Although when most competition agencies were created or relaunched in the 1990s, the various Latin American governments tried to strengthen the independence of the antitrust authorities, over time these agencies have suffered some setbacks in their independence. The weakening of competition policy institutional frameworks was accomplished mainly by introducing structural changes either through budget reductions, institutional reforms, or politically driven appointments and by forsaking the technical expertise acquired in the past decade. Governments from different political parties have decided to reduce the competition agencies' budgets (e.g., Argentina and Peru). The reason behind these cuts may be general budget reductions due to economic crises, political decisions to give a higher priority to other policies, or the creation of a new hierarchy of political objectives.

Combining Prosecution and Adjudication Roles

The institutional framework of most Latin American countries has a potential problem in combining within a single agency both the prosecution and adjudication roles. This mix challenges due process since an antitrust enforcer will rarely admit that the investigation it opened (for either political or technical reasons) was improper. Sometimes, the opening of an investigation is followed by either dawn raids or the adoption of injunctions, which generally obtain press coverage. After such a public positioning, the competition authorities have scarce political room to back down and accept that there were insufficient reasons for taking action. Therefore, the investigation process turns into a formality until the agency provides a final administrative decision. The defendant is then forced to appeal to the courts in order to properly defend himself, since the agency may not always provide necessary impartiality in the decision-making process during the administrative investigation. Some jurisdictions, such as Chile, have separated the prosecution and adjudication roles.

Insufficient pay hurts the capacity of competition agencies. Although the gap between public and private salaries is a common problem in all jurisdictions, in Latin American agencies the disparity is larger than in developed countries. This difference is aggravated by the fact that the demand of antitrust-related private sector work is very limited in Latin American countries. Therefore trained antitrust professionals have to move to other fields for financial enhancement. This development means that antitrust knowledge is not maintained within the country as staff retool to other areas of practice.

At the decision making level, except in Mexico where the Federal Competition Commission's presidential mandate is for ten years, many antitrust authorities face much shorter terms (two years in Brazil for CADE commissioners) or their terms depend on government fiat (in Argentina the CNDC president's term depends entirely on the president of Argentina's will). This high turnover at both managerial and case handler levels reduces the effectiveness of international technical assistance programs for agencies. Most of the beneficiaries of the training programs will likely be out of the system within a few years.

Insufficient budgetary resources for the competition agencies are a major limit to the development of competition law in Latin America. This shortage of resources reduces the possibility of obtaining and maintaining top economists and lawyers to work in the agencies as well as having a number of experienced professionals necessary to staff complex cases. The introduction of merger control systems also impacts resource allocation. Merger control is resource intensive and takes away from case investigation for cartel or dominance conduct.

Having insufficient resources also reduces the possibility for agencies to maintain an intensive competition advocacy program and undertake market investigations. The complexity of certain investigations requires that the antitrust agencies possess certain technical tools that most of the Latin American competition agencies do not have due to budget restraints. Furthermore, the high level of staff rotation hampers the continuity of investigations since new professionals continuously have to catch up with what others have done. The lack of sufficient internal technical support in the agencies increases the possibility of increased external political influence, since competition law and policy becomes less technocratic due to agency capacity constraints. As a result, the introduction of nonantitrust elements such as social concerns into antitrust analysis has distorted the way competition law has been enforced in some jurisdictions.

Limited Judicial Review

In Latin America, judicial review of competition enforcement decisions historically has been very limited in quantity and scope. There are several reasons for this low level of development of judicial review. Most reasons are structural, such as a weak judicial system and the scarce technical knowledge of a legal framework that is very different than what the courts are used to analyzing in terms of cases. As a result, the decision process takes a very long time and most of the court decisions are limited to formal or procedural issues.

Due to a significant work load and insufficient economic and human resources, most Latin American countries have weak judicial systems. Although some reforms have been made since the 1980s and the introduction of technology has helped, much has yet to be done in most Latin American jurisdictions to improve the efficiency of the judiciary. The small number of courts and the increasingly high number of cases and their complexity undermine the efficiency of the judicial activity in general and of the judicial review of competition-related cases in particular.

Another limit to the development of competition law in Latin America is the lack of sufficient technical knowledge by the judiciary. This is based on a resistance by the courts to understand the economic reasoning behind antitrust enforcement and due to the positivistic legal approach characteristic of the Civil-Roman legal system. As a result, courts in Latin American countries primarily have limited their rulings on competition cases to formal or procedural issues. This is done to avoid reviewing the economic analysis supporting the enforcers' decisions. Most Latin American judges are not used to analyzing cases where economic concepts determine whether a conduct is to be considered illegal or not. Furthermore, judges in Latin American countries are used to the positivistic approach of the Civil-Roman legal system while antitrust law originated in a common law jurisdiction (the United States), where the case law is a relevant part of the legal framework. In other words, not only are judges in Latin America forced to adopt economic concepts in their analysis of antitrust cases but they are forced to refer to the case law in a way they are not used to in other kinds of cases.

There has been a change in recent years in some Latin American jurisdictions, mainly in Brazil and Argentina, where due to the greater importance of the cases dealt with by the respective competition agencies, both in merger and anticompetitive conduct cases, courts have gained some expertise over the enforcers' decisions. Consequently, a process of so-called "judicialisation" of competition laws has begun in the region. Franceschini argues that the "judicialisation" of antitrust in Brazil is an empirical evolutionary process and "the more attention is given to the Repression Regime, the more the adversely affected private parties will resort to the Courts to question the legality or the merits of CADE's opinion."[22] Franceschini foresees the judiciary taking over the exclusive role of adjudicator of Brazilian competition law, leaving CADE as an expert agency dedicated to assist in judicial enforcement.[23]

. . .

A combination of cultural, political, economic and institutional limits has undermined the development of competition law enforcement in Latin America. Most of these limits do not exist in developed countries and were not properly contemplated when competition laws were adopted in most Latin American countries. This is why competition laws in Latin America in theory look identical to those of developed countries but their enforcement differs substantially given different economic, political, institutional, and cultural environments.

In spite of these limits, the development of competition law enforcement in Latin America has been significant in the past couple of decades. In some jurisdictions, the level of enforcement has grown significantly both in size and in quality, though in others the development has been more erratic. However, the future outcome depends heavily on how the limits described above are dealt with. Implementing or enforcing competition law in Latin America without recognizing and considering the existence of these limits can produce effects contrary to those expected or desired.

Notes

Preface

1. Frank H. Easterbrook, *The Limits of Antitrust*, 63 Tex. L. Rev. 1 (1984).
2. Robert Pitofsky, How the Chicago School Overshot the Mark (2008).

Chapter 1

An earlier version of this chapter was published at 6J. Competition L. & Econ. 1 (2009). I am grateful to the editors of that journal and to the Oxford University Press for permission to publish this revised version.

1. Jack Hirshleifer, *Capitalist Ethics—Tough or Soft?*, 2J.L. & Econ. 114 (1959).
2. Jack Hirshleifer, *The Sumptuary Manifesto*, 2J.L. & Econ. 120 (1959).
3. James M. Buchanan, *Positive Economics, Welfare Economics, and Political Economy*, 2J.L. & Econ. 124 (1959). Buchanan became a member of Mont Pelerin somewhat later, in 1957; subsequently, a Life Member.
4. Jacob Viner, *The Intellectual History of Laissez Faire*, 3J.L. & Econ. 45 (1960).
5. George J. Stigler, *Private Vice and Public Virtue*, 4J.L. & Econ. 1 (1961).
6. Marshall R. Colberg, *Minimum Wage Effects on Florida's Economic Development*, 3J.L. & Econ. 106 (1960); Yale Brozen, *Minimum Wage Rates and Household Workers*, 5J.L. & Econ. 103 (1962).
7. Many articles in the early volumes addressed the effects of unions. *See, e.g.*, Albert Rees, *Do Unions Cause Inflation?*, 2J.L. & Econ. 84 (1959); Melvin Lurie, *Government Regulation and Union Power*, 3J.L. & Econ. 118 (1960). The entirety of volume 6 was devoted to studies of unionization.
8. Thomas G. Moore, *The Purpose of Licensing*, 4J.L. & Econ. 93 (1961).
9. D. S. Lees, *The Logic of the British National Health Service*, 5J.L. & Econ. 111 (1962) (Lees found the N.H.S. incompatible in important ways with the basic assumptions of a free society).
10. John S. McGee, *Predatory Price Cutting: The Standard Oil (N.J.) Case*, 1J.L. & Econ. 137 (1958).
11. McGee credits Director for the basic analysis of the economic superiority of acquisition to predatory price cutting as a means of creating a monopoly. *Id.* at 138 n.2.
12. Lester G. Telser, *Why Should Manufacturers Want Fair Trade?*, 3J.L. & Econ. 86 (1960).
13. Ward Bowman, *Tying Arrangements and the Leverage Problem*, 67 Yale L.J. 19 (1957).
14. Kenneth W. Dam, *Fortner Enterprises v. United States Steel: "Neither a Borrower, nor a Lender Be,"* 1969 Sup. Ct. Rev. 1.
15. George J. Stigler, *The Dominant Firm and the Inverted Umbrella*, 8J.L. & Econ. 167 (1965).
16. John L. Peterman, *The Brown Shoe Case*, 18J.L. & Econ. 81 (1975); John L. Peterman, *The Federal Trade Commission v. Brown Shoe Company*, 18J.L. & Econ. 361 (1975); John L. Peterman, *The International Salt Case*, 22J.L. & Econ. 351 (1979).
17. Ronald H. Coase, *The Problem of Social Cost*, 3J.L. & Econ. 1 (1960).
18. A.C. Pigou, The Economics of Welfare (1920).
19. Ronald H. Coase, *The British Post Office and the Messenger Companies*, 4J.L. & Econ. 12 (1961). Several years later, as a student, I was able to write a paper that Ronald had encouraged Richard

Posner to write but that Dick, less interested in Ronald's program to attack state intervention in the market, handed off to me, his research assistant on the project. George L. Priest, *The History of the Postal Monopoly in the United States*, 18J.L. & Econ. 33 (1975).

20. Ronald H. Coase, *The Nature of the Firm*, 4 Economica 386 (1937).

21. An interesting question is why Chicago School economists initially disbelieved the Coase analysis. I address this issue in George L. Priest, *The Rise of Law and Economics: A Memoir of the Early Years, in* Law and Economics: Essays by the Founding Fathers 350, 350 (Charles Rowley & Francesco Parisi eds., 2005). I attribute their skepticism as deriving from Coase's third example of his approach in which he shows that there are conditions under which courts making appropriate allocative assignments of liability will still reduce aggregate societal welfare because they are focusing on marginal, rather than total, welfare effects. This proposition conflicts with the general Chicago School assumption that the world is always very close to a position of allocative efficiency so that marginal changes are all that are necessary to achieve a wealth-maximizing outcome.

22. Aaron Director, *The Parity of the Economic Market Place*, 7J.L. & Econ. 1 (1964).

23. *Id.* at 2.

24. *Id.* at 10.

25. Guido Calabresi & Douglas Melamed, *Property Rules, Liability Rules and Inalienability: One View of the Cathedral*, 85 Harv. L. Rev. 1089 (1972).

26. In some contexts, firms can evade such rules subtly as the vertical restraint cases—*Copperweld*, *Monsanto*, and the like—demonstrate.

27. Christine A. Varney, Panel on Re-energizing Section 2 of the Sherman Act at the AAI Annual National Conference and 10th Anniversary Celebration (June 19, 2008).

Chapter 2

The author wishes to thank D. Daniel Sokol and Maurice E. Stucke for the feedback on an earlier draft of this chapter. This work has also benefited from helpful discussions with a number of colleagues at the fourteenth workshop of the Competition Law Scholars' Forum (ClaSF), held at the Inns of Court School of Law, City University of London, on September 10, 2009. The usual disclaimer applies.

1. Council Regulation 17/62, First Regulation Implementing Articles 85 and 86 of the Treaty, 1959–1962 O.J. Spec. Ed. 57, *repealed by* Council Regulation 1/2002, The Implementation of the Rules on Competition Laid Down in Articles 81 and 82 of the Treaty, 2003 O.J. (L 1) 1.

2. *See Commission White Paper on Modernisation of the Rules Implementing Articles 85 and 86* [now 81 and 82] *of the EC Treaty*, COM (99) 101 final (Apr. 28, 1999); Council Regulation 1/2003, recitals 2–4, 2003 O.J. (L 1) 1 (EC).

3. *See* Council Regulation 1/2003, recital 6, 2003 O.J. (L 1) 1 (EC).

4. Joint statement of the Council and the Commission made at the time when regulation No 1/2003 was adopted, Brussels 3.3.2003 (13.03), ¶¶ 2, 5, 7.

5. *Id.* ¶ 7; Arianna Andreangeli, *The Impact of the Modernisation Regulation on the Guarantees of Due Process in Competition Proceedings*, 31 Eur. L.J. 342, 343–44 (2006).

6. *See* Council Regulation 1/2003, *supra* note 3, at art. 22; Commission Notice on Cooperation within the Network of Competition Authorities, ¶¶ 2 and 27.

7. *See, e.g., id.* at paras. 27–28; *see also* Office of Fair Trading, Powers of Investigation, (2004) OFT 404a, ¶ 6.3.

8. Neelie Kroes, Commissioner, European Commission for Competition, Private and Public Enforcement of EU Competition Law—5 Years On, Brussels: Many Achievements, More to Do (Mar. 12, 2009).

9. *See* Case 11/70, Internationale Handelsgesellschaft v. Einfuhr und Vorrastelle fur Getreide und Futtermittel, 1970 E.C.R. 1125.

10. *See, e.g.*, Rein Wesseling, *The Draft Regulation Modernising the Competition Rules: The Commission Is Married to One Idea*, 26 Eur. Competition L. Rev. 357 (2001).

11. *See, e.g.*, Case 4/73, Nold v. Commission, 1974 E.C.R. 491; Case C-60/00, Carpenter v. Secretary of State for the Home Department, 2002 E.C.R. I-6297.

12. *See, e.g.*, Case 4/73, Nold v. Commission, 1974 E.C.R. 491, ¶ 13; Opinion 2/94, Re: Accession to the European Convention on Human Rights, 1996 E.C.R. I-1759; Case T-156/94,

Siderurgica Aristrain Madrid v. Commission, 1999 E.C.R. II-645, ¶¶ 26–27; for the ECHR, *see, inter alia*, C.F.D.T. v. Commission, App. No. 8030/77, (1979) 13 D. & R. 231; *see also* M. & Co. v. Germany, App. No. 13258/87, (1990) 64 D. & R. 138.

13. Charter of Fundamental Rights of the European Union art. 52(3), Dec. 14, 2007, 2007 O.J. (C303) 01; *see* Treaty of Lisbon Protocol 8, Dec. 13, 2007, 2008 O.J. (C115) 1; *see also id.* at Recital IV(Preamble to the Treaty on the European Union and the Treaty on the Functioning of the European Union).

14. *See* Marius Emberland, The Human Rights of Companies: Exploring the Structure of ECHR Protection 25, 33–34, 40–41, 47 (2006).

15. *See* Brian Tamanaha, *A Concise Guide to the Rule of Law* 3, St John's University School of Law, Legal Studies Research Paper Series, #07-0082.

16. Friedrich Hayek, The Road to Serfdom 75–76 (2008) (1944); *see also* Tamanaha, *supra* note 15, at 9.

17. Hayek, *supra* note 16, at 37–39.

18. *See* Groppera Radio v. Switzerland, App. No. 10890/94, 12 Eur. H.R. Rep. 321, ¶ 48 (1990); Markt Intern Verlag GmbH and Klaus Bermann v. Germany, Ser. A No. 165, 12 Eur. H.R. Rep. 161, ¶ 33. In EU law, *see, e.g.*, Case T-67/00, JFE and others v. Commission, 2004 E.C.R. II-2501, ¶¶ 173, 177–78; *see also* Case C-413/08, Lafarge SA v. Commission, Judgment of June 17, 2010, not yet reported, ¶¶ 29–30.

19. *See, e.g.*, Niemitz v. Germany, App. No. 13710/88, Ser. A No. 251-B, 16 Eur. H.R. Rep. 17, ¶¶ 29–31 (1993); *see also* Ste Colas Est and others v. France, App. No. 37971/97, 39 Eur. H.R. Rep. 17, ¶¶ 40–41, 43–49 (2004); Casado Coca v. Spain, App. No. 15450/89, Ser. A No. 285, 18 Eur. H.R. Rep. 1, ¶ 40 et seq. (1994).

20. Brian Z. Tamanaha, *The Dark Side of the Relationship Between the Rule of Law and Liberalism* 30, St. John's University School of Law, Legal Studies Research Papers Series, #08-0096.

21. *See, e.g.*, Markt Intern Verlag GmbH and Klaus Bermann v. Germany, Ser. A No. 165, Eur. H.R. Rep. 161, ¶ 33 (1990); *cf., e.g.*, Silver v. United Kingdom App. No. 5947/72, 5 Eur. H.R. Rep. 347, ¶ 97 (1983); Arianna Andreangeli, EU Competition Enforcement and Human Rights 22 et seq. (2008).

22. *See* Emberland, *supra* note 14, at 190–91; *see, e.g.*, Beyeler v. Italy, App. No. 33202/96, 33 Eur. H.R. Rep. 52, ¶ 109 (2001); Lithgow v. United Kingdom, App. No. 9006/80, 7 Eur. H.R. Rep. 56, ¶ 110 (1985).

23. *See* Groppera Radio v. Switzerland, *supra* note 18, ¶¶ 49–50 (1990); *cf.* Lingens v. Austria, App. No. 9815/82, 8 Eur. H.R. Rep. 407, ¶¶ 40–41 (1986).

24. *See, e.g.*, Emberland, *supra* note 14, at 193.

25. *See, inter alia*, Ozturk v. Germany, App. No. 8544/79, 6 Eur. H.R. Rep. 409, ¶¶ 55–56 (1984).

26. *See, inter alia*, Schmautzer v. Austria, App. No. 15523/89, 16 Eur. H.R. Rev. 511, ¶ 28 (1996); Stenuit v. France, App. No. 11598/85, E.C.C. 401, ¶¶ 56, 61–63 (1992); *see also* Case T-7/89, SA Hercules Chemicals v. Commission, E.C.R. II-1771, per AG Vesterdorf, ¶ I.3 (1991); *see also, inter alia*, Case C-185/95, Baustahlgewebe v. Commission, E.C.R. I-8417, per AG Leger, ¶ 31 (1998); Case C-105/04 P, NFVGEG v. Commission (Re: Dutch Electricians' cartel), E.C.R. I-8725, per AG Kokott, ¶ 107 (2006).

27. Funke v. France, App. No. 10828/94, 16 Eur. H.R. Rep. 297, ¶¶ 41–42 (1993).

28. Saunders v. United Kingdom, App. No. 43/1994/490/572, 23 Eur. H.R. Rep. 313, ¶ 68 (1997).

29. *Id.* ¶ 69.

30. O'Halloran and Francis v. United Kingdom, App. Nos. 15809/02 and 25624/02, 46 Eur. H.R. Rep. 21, ¶ 53 (2008).

31. Jalloh v. Germany, App. No. 54810/00, 44 Eur. H.R. Rep. 32, ¶ 117 (2007).

32. O'Halloran and Francis v. United Kingdom, *supra* note 30, ¶ 57; *see also, mutatis mutandis*, Brown v. Stott, Privy Council, December 5, 2000, 1 A.C. 681, per Lord Bingham, 703 (2003).

33. *See, e.g.*, Jalloh v. Germany, *supra* note 31, ¶¶ 95–97.

34. Case 27/88, Orkem v. Commission, E.C.R. 3355 (1989).

35. *Id.* ¶ 32.

36. *Id.* ¶ 34.

37. *Id.* ¶ 35.

38. *Id.* ¶ 44; *see also* ¶ 42; *see also* Case T-112/98, Mannesmannrohren—Werke v. Commission, 2001 E.C.R. II-729, ¶ 66.

39. Saunders v. United Kingdom, *supra* note 28, ¶ 57; *see also id.* ¶ 68; Jalloh v. Germany, *supra* note 31, ¶¶ 114–115, 117.

40. *See, e.g.*, Case C-238/99, LVM NV and Others v. Commission, 2002 E.C.R. I-8375, ¶ 275; *see also id.* at ¶¶ 279–282; Andreangeli, *supra* note 21, at 134–35.

41. *See also* Case T-112/98, Mannesmannrohren—Werke v. Commission, 2001 E.C.R. II-729, ¶ 66.

42. O'Halloran and Francis v. United Kingdom, App. Nos. 15809/02 and 25624/02, 46 Eur. H.R. Rep. 21, ¶ 53 (2008).

43. *See, e.g.*, Wouter P. J. Wils, *Self-Incrimination in EC Antitrust Enforcement: A Legal and Economic Analysis*, 26 W. Competition L. & Econ. Rev. 567, 577–78 (2003).

44. *See, e.g.*, Case C-238/99, LVM NV and Others v. Commission, 2002 E.C.R. I-8375, ¶ 275; *see also id.* ¶ 279–82.

45. *See, mutatis mutandis*, Jalloh v. Germany, *supra* note 31, ¶ 114–15; *see also* Ravon v. France, App. No. 18497/03, judgment of Feb. 21, 2008. unreported, ¶ 28.

46. Article 5, Council Regulation No 1/2003.

47. Recitals VI and VIII, Preamble to Council Regulation No 1/2003.

48. *Id.*, ¶ 5; *see, e.g.*, Alec Burnside & Helen Crossley, *Cooperative Mechanisms Within the EU: A Blueprint for Future Cooperation at the International Level*, 10 Int'l Trade L. & Reg. 25, 27 (2004).

49. European Commission, *Commission Notice on Cooperation Within the Network of Competition Authorities*, 2004 O.J. 101/43, ¶¶ 7–8 [hereinafter referred to as Network Notice].

50. *See id.*, ¶ 3,14.

51. Cases C-238/99, C-244/99, C-245/99, C-247/99, C-250/99 to 252/99, C-254/99, Lymburgse Vinyl Maatschappij and others v. Commission, E.C.R. I-8375, ¶ 59 (2002).

52. *See* Denis Waelbroeck, '*Twelve Feet All Dangling Down and Six Necks Exceeding Long': The EU Network of Competition Authorities and the European Convention on Fundamental Rights*, *in* European Competition Law Annual 2002: Constructing the EU Network of Competition Authorities 465, 470 (Claus-Dieter Ehlermann & Isabela Atanasiu eds., 2004).

53. *See, e.g.*, Case 14/68, Walt Wilhelm v. Bundeskartellamt, 1969 E.C.R. 1, ¶ 11.

54. Case 7/72, Boehringer Mannheim v. Commission, 1972 E.C.R. 1281, per AG Mayras, ¶¶ 3–5; *see also, mutatis mutandis*, Case C-308/94 P, SGL Carbon v. Commission, 2006 E.C.R. I-5977, ¶¶ 30–31.

55. Case 14/68, Walt Wilhelm v. Commission, *supra* note 54, ¶ 11.

56. Gradinger v. Austria, App. No. 15963/90, judgment of October 23, 1995, Ser A No. 328-C, ¶¶ 53–55.

57. Franz Fischer v. Austria, App. No. 37950/97, judgment of May 29, 2001, ¶¶ 22, 25, and 29; *see also* Oliveira v. Switzerland, App. No. 25711/94, 28 Eur. H.R. Rep. 289, ¶¶ 24–27 (1998).

58. *See, inter alia*, Denis Waelbroeck, *supra* note 52, at 470 .

59. Case C-308/94 P, SGL Carbon v. Commission, 2006 E.C.R. I-5977, ¶ 93.

60. Wouter P. J. Wils, *The Principle of ne bis in idem in EC Antitrust Enforcement: A Legal and Economic Analysis*, 26 W. Competition L. & Econ. Rev. 131, 146 (2003).

61. *See, inter alia*, Celine Gauer, *Due Process in the Face of Divergent National Procedures and Sanctions* (paper presented at the International Bar Association 2005 Conference: "Decentralisation of EC Competition Law: A Year in Practice"), at 9.

62. *See* Hayek, *supra* note 16, at 83–84.

63. *See, e.g.*, Denis Waelbroeck, *supra* note 52, 470.

64. Laurent Garzaniti, Jason Gudofsky & Jane Moffat, *Dawn of a New Era? Powers of Investigation and Enforcement Under Regulation 1/2003*, 72 Antitrust L.J. 159, 203–04 (2004).

65. *Network Notice*, *supra* note 49, ¶ 14.

66. *See, e.g.*, Andreangeli, *supra* note 21, at 210–11.

67. *See, e.g., mutatis mutandis*, Case C-150/05, Van Straaten v. Staat der nederlanden und Republiek Italie, E.C.R. I-9327, ¶¶ 53, 57 (2006); *cf.* Gradinger v. Austria, App. No. 15693/90,

judgment of October 23, 1995, Ser. A No. 328-C, ¶ 53; *see also* Oliveira v. Switzerland, App. No. 25711/94, 28 Eur. H.R. Rep. 289, ¶¶ 25–27 (1998).

68. *See* Andreangeli, *supra* note 21, at 223.

69. Hayek, *supra* note 16, at 108.

70. Ronald A. Cass, *Property Rights Systems and the Rule of Law*, at 2, 4, Boston University School of Law, Working Paper Series—Public Law and Legal Theory, #03-6.

71. *Id.* at 8.

72. Van Marle v. The Netherlands, App. 8543/79, 6 Eur. H.R. Rep. 483, ¶¶ 39–41 (1986); *see also* Anheuser Busch v. Portugal, App. No. 73049/01, 45 Eur. H.R. Rep. 36, ¶¶ 72, 75–79 (2007).

73. Melnychuk v. Ukraine, App. No. 28743/03, admissibility decision of July 5, 2005, unreported, ¶ 3.

74. Pressos Compania Naviera v. Belgium, App. No. 17849/91, 21 Eur. H.R. Rep. 301 (1996); *see also* Kopecky v. Slovakia, App. No. 44912/98, judgment of September 28, 2004, ¶ 52; *see also, mutatis mutandis*, Stran Greek Refineries and another v. Greece, App. No. 13427/87, 19 Eur. H.R. Rep. 293, ¶ 60 (1995); Schirmer v. Poland, App. No. 68880/01, 40 Eur. H.R. Rep. 47, ¶¶ 33–34 (2005); *cf., e.g.*, Prince Hans-Adam II of Liechtenstein v. Germany, App. No. 42527/98, 11 B. H.R. C. 526, ¶¶ 82–83 (2001).

75. *See, inter alia*, Sporrong & Lonroth v. Sweden, App. No. 7151/75–7152/75, 5 Eur. H.R. Rep. 35, ¶ 63 (1983); Ghigo v. Malta, App. No. 31122/05, judgment of Sept. 26, 2006, unreported, ¶ 50.

76. *See, e.g.*, Beyeler v. Italy, App. No. 33202/96, 33 Eur. H.R. Rep. 52, ¶ 109 (2001); *see also* Lithgow v. United Kingdom, App. No. 9006/80, 7 Eur. H.R. Rep. 56, ¶ 111 (1985); Pye (Oxford) Ltd. and another v. United Kingdom, App. No. 44302/02, judgment of Aug. 30, 2007, ¶ 55.

77. *See, e.g.*, Schirmer v. Poland, *supra* note 74, ¶¶ 34–35, 42–45; *see also* Balan v. Moldova, App. No. 19247/03, judgment of Jan. 29, 2008, not yet reported, ¶ 38–39, 45–46; Holy Monasteries v. Greece, App. No. 13092/87 and 13984/88, 20 Eur. H.R. Rep. 1, ¶¶ 80–83, 85 (1995); Lithgow v. United Kingdom, *supra* note 76, ¶ 205; more recently, B v. The Netherlands, App. No. 19589/92, Commission Report, May 19, 1994, ¶¶ 71–72; *see also id.* ¶¶ 60, 65–66; Beyeler v. Italy, *supra* note 76, ¶ 110; Scollo v. Italy, App. No. 24/1994, 22 Eur. H.R. Rep. 514, ¶¶ 26–27 (1996).

78. Balan v. Moldova, *supra* note 77, ¶¶ 38–39.

79. *Id.* ¶ 45–46.

80. Smith Kline and French Laboratories Ltd. v. The Netherlands, App. No. 12633/87, decision of Oct. 4, 1990 [hereinafter Smith Kline].

81. Report of the European Commission on Human Rights, July 10, 1991.

82. Smith Kline, *supra* note 81, at part III.

83. *Id.*

84. *Id.*

85. *Id.*

86. *Id.*

87. *Id.*

88. *Id.*

89. *Id.*

90. *See, e.g.*, A. Ohly et al., *Artistic Freedom Versus Privacy—A Delicate Balance*, 38 Int'l Rev. of Intell. Prop. & Competition L. 526, 551–552 (2008); *cf., e.g.*, Verlagsgruppe News GmbH v. Austria, App. 10520/02, judgment of Dec. 14, 2006, E.M.L.R. 13.

91. *See, mutatis mutandis*, Peter K. Yu, *Reconceptualising Intellectual Property Interests in a Human Rights Framework*, 40 U.C. Davis L. Rev. 1039, 1090–91.

92. *See* Article 7(1), Council Regulation 1/2003.

93. *See, e.g.*, Commission Decision 94/19/EEC, *Sea Link v. Stena Line*, 1994 O.J. L15/8.

94. Joined Cases 6/7/73, ICI and Commercial Solvents v. Commission, 1974 E.C.R. 223; most recently, Case T201/04, Microsoft v. Commission, 2007 E.C.R. II-3601.

95. Case T201/04, Microsoft v. Commission, 2007 E.C.R. II-3601.

96. Article 7, Council Regulation No 1/03; *see also* Article 3, Council Regulation No 17/62.

97. *See* Recital 13, Preamble to Council Regulation No 1/2003; *see also* Case T-170/06, Alrosa v. Commission, 2007 E.C.R. II-2601, especially ¶¶ 86–87, 99–100.

98. *See, e.g.*, Joined Cases 6/7/73, ICI and Commercial Solvents v. Commission, 1974 E.C.R. 223, ¶¶ 44–46.

99. Hubertus Von Rosenberg, *Unbundling Through the Back Door . . . The Case of Network Divestiture as a Remedy in the Energy Sector*, 30 ECLR 237, 241–42 (2009); *see also* Commission Notice on Remedies, 2008 O.J. C267/1, ¶ 7.

100. *See, e.g.*, Hutten-Czapska v. Poland, App. No. 35014/97, judgment of June 19, 2006, 45 Eur. H.R. Rep. 4, ¶ 195, 223–24 (2007).

101. *See, e.g.*, Volvo v. Veng, Case 238/87, 1988 E.C.R. 6211, ¶¶ 8–9. For commentary, see Robert O'Donaghue and Jorge Padilla, The Law and Economics of Article 82 EC Treaty 409–10, 424 (2006).

102. Case C-7/97, Bronner v. Mediaprint, 1998 E.C.R. I-7791, ¶ 28; *cf.* Case T-201/04, Microsoft, *supra* note 95, ¶ 331; *see also id.* ¶¶ 434–37.

103. Case C-418/01, IMS Health GmbH & Co v. NDC Health GmbH & Co, 2004 E.C.R. I-5039, ¶ 49.

104. Case C-241/91, RTE and ITP v. Commission, 1995 E.C.R. I-743, ¶¶ 50–52; *see also id.* ¶¶ 54 and 73.

105. *See, inter alia*, Vassilis Hatzopoulos, *Refusal to Deal: The EC Essential Facilities Doctrine*, *in* EC Competition Law: A Critical Assessment 354, 354 (Giuliano Amato & Claus-Dieter Ehlermann eds., 2006).

106. Case C-418/01, IMS Health, *supra* note 103, ¶ 49; *see also* Opinion of AG Tizzano, ¶ 62.

107. Ekaterina Rousseva, *Abuse of Dominant Position Defences: Objective Justification and Article 82 in the Era of Modernisation*, *in* EC Competition Law: A Critical Assessment 417–18, 430–31 (Giuliano Amato & Claus-Dieter Ehlermann eds., 2006).

108. App. No. 12633/87, decision of Oct. 4, 1990, part III.

109. *See* 2005 DG Competition Discussion Paper on the application of Article 82 to exclusionary abuses, available at: http://ec.europa.eu/competition/antitrust/art82/discpaper2005.pdf, ¶¶ 239–40; *see also* IMS Health, *supra* note 103, ¶ 49.

110. Case T-201/04, Microsoft, *supra* note 95, especially ¶ 621 et seq.; *see also* European Commission, Guidance on the Commission's Enforcement Priorities in Applying Article 82 of the EC Treaty to Abusive Exclusionary Conduct by Dominant Undertakings, ¶ 89, C(2009) 864C (final), Feb. 9, 2009 [hereinafter referred to as 2009 Guidance].

111. 2009 Guidance, *supra* note 110, ¶ 82; *cf.* Case C-7/97, Bronner GmbH v. Mediaprint, E.C.R. I-7791, ¶¶ 41, 43–44 (1998).

112. *See* 2009 Guidance ¶ 81; *see also* Case T-201/04, Microsoft, *supra* note 95, ¶¶ 389–90, 434–35; Arianna Andreangeli, *Interoperabilty as an "Essential Facility" in the Microsoft Case: Encouraging Competition or Stifling Innovation?*, 34 Eur. L. Rev. 584, 608–09 (2009).

113. 2009 Guidance, *supra* note 110, ¶ 87.

114. *Id.*

115. *Id.* ¶ 87; *see also* Case T-201/04, Microsoft, supra note 95, especially ¶¶ 646–47, 696, 702, 710–11.

116. *See*, *inter alia*, Andreangeli, *supra* note 112, at 610–11.

117. *See, e.g.*, 2005 Discussion Paper, *supra* note 109, ¶ 235; *see also* 2009 Guidance, *supra* note 111, ¶ 89; *see also* Case T-201/04, Microsoft, *supra* note 95, ¶ 705 et seq. ; *cf.* Case C-95/04, British Airways v. Commission, 2007 E.C.R. I-2331, ¶ 86.

118. 2009 Guidance, *supra* note 110, ¶¶ 28–29.

119. *See* Case T-201/04, Microsoft, *supra* note 95, ¶¶ 331, 434–53; *see also* Commission Decision of May 24, 2004, C (2004) 900, 2007 O.J. C32/23, ¶¶ 669, 684–85. For commentary, *see, inter alia,* Roberto Pardolesi and Andrea Renda, *The European Commission's Case Against Microsoft: Kill Bill?* 27 W. Comp. 513, 537–41 (2004).

120. Case C-418/01, IMS Health GmbH, *supra* note 103, ¶ 48.

121. 2009 Guidance, *supra* note 110, ¶ 87; *cf.*, *inter alia*, Hutten-Czapska v. Poland, *supra* note 100, ¶¶ 195, 223–24.

122. *See* Case C-418/01, IMS Health GmbH, *supra* note 103, ¶ 48; *cf.* 2007 Microsoft judgment, ¶ 647. For commentary, *see, inter alia*, Hatzopoulos, *supra* note 105, at 354.

123. *See, e.g.*, App. No. 8795/79, James v. United Kingdom, 8 Eur. H.R. Rep. 123, ¶ 67 (1986); Malone v. United Kingdom, App. No 8691/79, 7 Eur. H.R. Rep. 14, ¶¶ 67–68 (1985).

124. *See, e.g.*, Andreangeli, *supra* note 21, at 609–10.

125. *See* 2009 Guidance, *supra* note 110, at ¶¶ 86–89.

126. Andreangeli, *supra* note 112, at 608.

127. *See, e.g.*, Richard H. Fallon, *The Rule of Law as a Concept in Constitutional Discourse*, 97 Colum. L. Rev. 1, 7–8 (1997).

128. *See, e.g.*, Hatzopoulos, *supra* note 105, at 348–50.

129. *See, inter alia*, Andreangeli, *supra* note 112, at 609–10.

130. *See, e.g.*, Jussila v. Finland, App. No. 73053/01, judgment of Nov. 23, 2006, Eur. H.R. Rep. 45, ¶ 43 (2007).

131. *See, e.g.*, O'Halloran and Francis v. United Kingdom, *supra* note 30, ¶ 53.

132. *See, e.g.*, Denis Waelbroeck, *supra* note 52, 468.

133. *See, e.g.*, Balan v. Moldova, *supra* note 77, ¶ 39, 45–46.

Chapter 3

1. In the European Commission's language, a "more economic approach" is often associated with the term "modernization."

2. Market definition is an example of partial transplant—what has been borrowed by law (a method for defining markets) and the status market was given through the legal requirement that market be defined in (nearly) all cases miss the core economic message on why define markets.

3. I assume here that the fictional economist is addressing a European fictional judge and has been briefed by a lawyer to use the term "dominant position" rather than the more familiar "market power."

4. *See* Case 85/76, Hoffmann-La Roche v. Commission 1979 E.C.R. 461, ¶¶ 42–48.

5. *See, e.g.*, Case T-102/96, Gencor v. Commission, 1999 E.C.R. II-753.

6. This leitmotiv of economic discourse about EU law of abuse of dominance is inter alia expressed—in these exact words—in the report commissioned from the Economic Advisory Group on Competition Policy (EAGCP) by the European Commission, An Economic Approach to Article 82 (July 2005) at 7. As a leitmotiv, this idea has been adopted by the Commission. *See* Communication from the Commission—Guidance on the Commission's Enforcement Priorities in Applying Article 82 of the EC Treaty to Abusive Exclusionary Conduct by Dominant Undertakings, 2009 O.J. (C 45) 7, ¶¶ 5 and 19. The effect on consumers has long been considered legally relevant by EU courts. See Case C-6/72, Continental Can v. Commission, 1973 E.C.R. 215, ¶ 26. The reason for the prevailing feeling that courts *do not* reason in accordance with "sound economic principles" is that the case law does not require separate evidence of consumer harm and continues to infer such harm from a change in market structure. Liza Lovdahl Gormsen, A Principled Approach to Abuse of Dominance 115 (2010).

7. For an example of courts recognizing incentives as key elements in merger analysis, see Gencor, *supra* note 5.

8. This may of course be influenced by the style of judgments in a given legal culture. For example, French courts rarely give lengthy grounds for their judgments.

9. Cases T-68/89, T-77/89, and T-78/89, SIV e.a. v. Commission, 1992 E.C.R. II-1403, ¶ 159; Case T-17/93, Matra Hachette v. Commission, 1994 E.C.R. II-595, ¶ 85, ¶ 3.

10. Anne-Lisse Sibony, Le Juge et le Raisonnement Économique (2008). For a convergent, more recent and more radical proposition from a U.S. perspective, see Louis Kaplow, *Why (Ever) Define Markets?*, 124 Harv. L. Rev. 438 (2010).

11. David Evans, *How Economists Can Help Courts Design Competition Rules: An EU and US Perspective*, 29 World Competition 93 (2005).

12. European Commission, *supra* note 6, at 21.

13. *Id.* at 4 (in the text, this proposal to restructure the assessment of abuse, which is a matter of law, is erroneously presented as a matter of "procedure").

14. Other elements of this report laid the basis of the Commission's communication on exclusionary abuses.

15. Advocates general sometimes use the phrase "interim conclusion" to mark those steps. *See, e.g.*, Opinion of Advocate General Kokott in British Airways, 2007 E.C.R. I-2331, ¶¶ 62 and 133. In the context of this discussion, only economic categories are concerned, but in areas of law other than competition law, the same may be true of categories borrowed from, say, medicine or a particular trade. For a more extensive discussion see Sibony, *supra* note 10, at 446 et seq.

16. For example, EU courts refused to revise the *AKZO* test in light of economic argument that recoupment should be part of the legal test.

17. *See, e.g.*, C. Scott Hemphill, *The Role of Recoupment in Predatory Pricing Analyses*, 53 Stan. L. Rev. 1581, 1610 (2001), arguing that the holdings of the U.S. Supreme Court in *Matsuhita* became "ossified" in their application by lower courts.

18. Case T-342/99, Airtours v. Commission, 2002 E.C.R. II-2585, ¶ 62.

19. Case T-464/04, Impala, 2006 E.C.R. II-2289, ¶ 251.

20. Evans, *supra* note 11, argues that it is more reasonable to expect of economists that they identify sufficient *or* necessary conditions for a given conduct to be anticompetitive.

21. Richard Posner, Antitrust Law 214 (2nd ed. 2001). The same arguments apply to abuse of dominance under EU law. *See, e.g.*, A. Bavasso, *The Role of Intent Under Article 82 EC: From "Flushing the Turkeys" to "Spotting Lionesses in Regent's Park,"* 26 Euro. Common L. Rev. 616 (2005).

22. For an attempt at distinguishing them, see Thomas Eilmansberger, *How to Distinguish Good from Bad Competition Under Article 82 EC: In Search of Clearer and More Coherent Standards for Anti-Competitive Abuses*, 42 Common Market L. Rev. 129 (2005).

23. European Commission, *supra* note 6.

24. Case 27/76, United Brands Company v. Commission, 1978 E.C.R. 207, ¶ 189; Case T-203/01, Michelin v. Commission, 2003 E.C.R. II-4071, ¶ 241.

25. *See, e.g.*, Case T-340/03, France Télécom v. Commission, 2007 E.C.R. II-107, ¶ 195.

26. Case C-62/86, AKZO v. Commission, 1991 E.C.R. I-3359.

27. *Id.* ¶ 71.

28. *Id.* ¶ 72.

29. Case T-340/03, France Télécom v. Commission, 2007 E.C.R. II-107, ¶¶ 195, 197.

30. Philip Areeda & Donald Turner, *Predatory Pricing and Related Practices Under Section 2 of the Sherman Act*, 88 Harv. L. Rev. 697 (1975).

31. Case C-202/07 P, France Télécom v. Commission, 2009 E.C.R. I-2369.

32. Brooke Group Ltd. v. Brown & Williamson Tobacco Corp., 509 U.S. 209 (1992).

33. Case C-202/07, *supra* note 30, ¶ 110.

34. *Id.* ¶ 111.

35. *Id.* ¶ 112.

36. *Id.* For a different discussion on this point see Ekaterina Rousseva, Rethinking Exclusionary Abuses in EU Competition Law 410 (2010).

37. This recommendation, in line with economic thinking, was made inter alia in OECD, *Predatory Foreclosure*, DAF/COMP (2005), 14.

38. Rousseva, *supra* note 35, at 166.

39. Commission's Communication on Exclusionary Abuses, *supra* note 5, ¶ 19 et seq.

40. This presumption goes back to Case 322/81, Michelin I, 1983 E.C.R. 3461.

41. *See, e.g.*, Case C-95/04, British Airways v. Commission, 2007 E.C.R. I-2331, ¶¶ 106–107.

42. "[L]imiting production, markets or technical development to the prejudice of consumers" is the only example of abusive conduct given in Article 102 TFEU where consumer harm is explicitly mentioned.

43. Following its communication on exclusionary abuse, the Commission now devotes more effort to show consumer harm. *See, e.g.*, Commission's Decision in Intel, COMP/C-37.990 (May 13, 2009), ¶ 1604 et seq.

44. Case T-5/02, Tetra Laval v. Commission, 2002 E.C.R. II-4381, ¶ 155.

45. *Id.*

46. Case C-12/03 P, Commission v. Tetra Laval, 2005 E.C.R. I-987, ¶ 41.

47. *See, e.g.*, David Bailey, *Standard of Proof in EC Merger Proceedings: A Common Law Perspective*, 40 Common Market L. Rev. 845 (2003).

48. Lord Hoffmann in Secretary of State for Home Department v. Rehman, [2003] 1 AC 153. Lord Hoffman draws on Lord Steyn in In Re H. and Others (Minors) (Sexual Abuse: Standard of Proof) [1996] AC 563 at 585.

49. For another presumption based on a statement of economic normality, see Case T-342/99, Airtours v. Commission, 2002 E.C.R. II-2585, ¶¶ 134 and 139, where the CFI similarly relied on

economic literature to hold that price volatility normally makes it harder for members of an oligopoly to observe each others' behavior.

Chapter 4

1. Technically, a monopsonist would mean a single buyer. In this discussion, monopsony will also signify "collusive monopsony" and oligopsony. All the terms are used to indicate instances of buyer power. Buying power is the power to pay less than competitive prices and do so profitably over a significant period of time.

2. Weyerhaeuser Co. v. Ross-Simmons Hardwood Lumber Co., 549 U.S. 312 (2007).

3. *Id.*

4. This is explained more fully in the first section to follow but the logic is easy to understand. Paying a lower price will mean less of an input is offered for sale. If fewer units of inputs are purchased, fewer units of output will be produced. Lower quantities typically mean higher prices.

5. The shape of the supply curve may differ when the input is labor.

6. The comparison is the same as under perfect competition except that the buyer has an impact on the prices paid for inputs.

7. This will not be the case if the buyer is a perfectly discriminating monopsonist.

8. *See, e.g.*, Balmoral Cinema v. Allied Artists Pictures, 885 F.2d 313 (6th Cir. 1989).

9. *See* Roger D. Blair & Jeffrey L. Harrison, Monopsony in Law and Economics 45–48 (Cambridge University Press, 2010).

10. Richard G. Layard & A. A. Walters, Microeconomic Theory 224 (McGraw-Hill, 1978). An example of an all-or-none situation appears in All Care Nursing Services v. Bethesda Memorial Hospital Inc., 887 F.2d 1535 (11th Cir. 1989). It probably also characterizes some agricultural markets. *See* Blair & Harrison, *supra* note 9, at 172–79.

11. The problem is that ruling that pricing alone is a misuse of monopoly or monopsony power quickly leads a court into the realm of price regulation. *See, e.g.*, Kartell v. Blue Shield of Mass., 749 F.2d 922 (1st Cir. 1984), *cert. denied*, 471 U.S. 1029 (1985).

12. Prior cases did involve buying-side power but the Court did not address in a direct manner. *See* Blair & Harrison, *supra* note 9, at 76–78.

13. *See generally*, E. Thomas Sullivan & Jeffrey L. Harrison, Understanding Antitrust and Its Economic Implications 286–90 (5th ed. 2009).

14. Liggett v. Brown and Williamson Tobacco, 509 U.S. 209 (1993).

15. *Id.* at 222. The Court did not specify which measure of costs.

16. *Id.* In actuality, the idea is that it is irrational to charge less than cost applies most aptly to marginal cost.

17. *Id.*

18. Weyerhaeuser Co. v. Ross-Simmons Hardwood Lumber Co., 549 U.S. 312 (2007).

19. *Id.*

20. The indirect purchaser doctrine was devised by the Court before it addressed the issues of standing and injury. It seems almost certain that had the indirect purchaser issue come up after those questions, it would have been assessed as a standing issue. *See* Roger D. Blair & Jeffrey L. Harrison, *Rethinking Antitrust Injury*, 42 Vand. L. Rev. 1539 (1989).

21. The competing position would favor maximizing social welfare, which would be the sum of consumer and producer surplus.

22. It should be noted, however, that there are sound arguments that collective buying from a monopolist, creating bilateral monopoly, may be beneficial.

23. Northwest Wholesale Stationers, Inc v. Pacific Stationery and Printing Co., 472 U.S. 284 (1985).

24. *Id.* at 295.

25. A false negative occurs when a practice is permitted when it is actually anticompetitive.

26. Blair & Harrison, *supra* note 9, at 205–09.

27. *See* E. Thomas Sullivan & Herbert Hovenkamp, Antitrust Law, Policy and Procedure 510 (5th ed. 2007).

28. These are known as "classic boycotts." *See* Jeffrey L. Harrison, *The Law of Group Boycotts and Related Economic Considerations*, *in* Antitrust Law and Economics 46 (Keith N. Hylton ed., 2010).

29. Northwest Wholesale Stationers v. Pacific Stationery and Printing Co., 472 U.S. 284, 294 (1985).

30. United States v. Topco, 405 U.S. 596 (1972).

31. Palmer v. BRG of Georgia, Inc., 498 U.S. 46 (1990).

Chapter 5

1. *See* Herbert Hovenkamp, *The Neal Report and the Crisis in Antitrust*, 5 Competition Pol'y Int'l 217 (2009). On the S-C-P paradigm's development and dominance prior to its collapse, *see* Herbert Hovenkamp, *United States Competition Policy in Crisis, 1890–1955*, 94 Minn. L. Rev. 311 (2009).

2. *See, e.g.*, Carl Kaysen & Donald F. Turner, Antitrust Policy: An Economic and Legal Analysis (1959); Joe S. Bain, Industrial Organization (1959); Joe S. Bain, Barriers to New Competition: Their Character and Consequences in Manufacturing Industries (1956).

3. Eastman Kodak Co. v. Image Tech. Servs., Inc., 504 U.S. 451, 479 n.29 (1992).

4. *See, e.g.*, Ward Bowman, Jr., *Tying Arrangements and the Leverage Problem*, 67 Yale L.J. 19 (1957); *see also* Richard A. Posner, *The Chicago School of Antitrust Analysis*, 127 U. Pa. L. Rev. 925 (1979).

5. These views were consolidated and popularized by Robert H. Bork, The Antitrust Paradox: A Policy at War with Itself (1978); *see also* Richard A. Posner, *The Next Step in the Antitrust Treatment of Restricted Distribution: Per Se Legality*, 48 U. Chi. L. Rev. 6 (1981).

6. *See* Ronald H. Coase, *The Nature of the Firm*, 4 Economica (n.s.) 386 (1937); Herbert Hovenkamp, *Coasean Markets*, 31 Eur. J.L. & Econ. 63 (2010). Coase did not invent the idea that the movement or exchange of resources involves a cost that must be considered in policy making. He borrowed heavily from Arthur C. Pigou, whose concept of "costs of movement" included a wide assortment of mobility costs and was broader than Coase's conception of "transaction costs." Further, *Nature of the Firm* itself never spoke of "transaction costs," but rather of "marketing costs." See Herbert Hovenkamp, *Coase, Institutionalism, and the Origins of Law and Economics*, 86 Ind. L.J. 499 (2011); Herbert Hovenkamp, *The Coase Theorem and Arthur Cecil Pigou*, 51 Ariz. L. Rev. 633 (2009).

7. *See* Herbert Hovenkamp, *Antitrust and the Costs of Movement*, __ Antitrust L. J. __ (forthcoming, 2011).

8. Oliver E. Williamson, The Mechanisms of Governance 66, 93–119 (1996).

9. See Christina Bohannan & Herbert Hovenkamp, Creation Without Restraint: Promoting Liberty and Rivalry in Innovation, ch. 11 (2011).

10. *See* Herbert Hovenkamp, The Antitrust Enterprise: Principle and Execution 54–56 (2005).

11. *See* 8 Phillip E. Areeda & Herbert Hovenkamp, Antitrust Law ¶1604 (3d ed. 2010).

12. Oliver E. Williamson, The Economic Institutions of Capitalism 15–42 (1985).

13. Benjamin Klein, Robert G. Crawford & Armen A. Alchian, *Vertical Integration, Appropriable Rents, and the Competitive Contracting Process*, 21 J.L. & Econ. 297 (1978).

14. On this point, see Herbert Hovenkamp, *The Law of Vertical Integration and the Business Firm*, 95 Iowa L. Rev. 863 (2010).

15. On the economics of bilateral monopoly, see Roger D. Blair & Jeffrey L. Harrison, Monopsony in Law and Economics 123–45 (2d ed. 2010).

16. *See* Ronald H. Coase, *The Acquisition of Fisher Body by General Motors*, 43 J.L. & Econ. 15 (2000); *see also* Benjamin Klein, *Vertical Integration as Organizational Ownership: The Fisher Body-General Motors Relationship Revisited*, 4 J. L. Econ. & Org. 199 (1988).

17. Eastman Kodak Co. v. Image Tech. Servs., Inc., 504 U.S. 451, 497 (1992) (Scalia, J., dissenting).

18. *See* Bohannan & Hovenkamp, Creation Without Restraint, *supra* note 9, ch. 2. For a technical analysis, see Giuseppe Dari-Mattiacci & Francesco Parisi, *Substituting Complements*, 2 J. Competition L. & Econ. 333 (2006).

19. *See* Herbert Hovenkamp, *Harvard, Chicago, and Transaction Cost Economics in Antitrust Analysis*, 55 Antitrust Bull. 613, 634–37 (2010); for more technical treatment, see W. Kip Viscusi, Joseph E. Harrington, Jr. & John M. Vernon, Economics of Regulation and Antitrust 238–41 (4th ed. 2005).

20. *See, e.g.*, Robert E. Hall, *The Relation Between Price and Marginal Cost in U.S. Industry*, 96 J. Pol. Econ. 921 (1988).

21. State Oil Co. v. Khan, 522 U.S. 3 (1997); see Herbert Hovenkamp, Federal Antitrust Policy: the Law of Competition and its Practice §11.5c (4th ed. 2011); *see also* 8 Antitrust Law, Ch.16C (3d ed. 2010).

22. *See* 11 Herbert Hovenkamp, Antitrust Law ¶1807 (3d ed. 2011); Bruce H. Kobayashi, *The Economics of Loyalty Discounts and Antitrust Law in the United States*, 1 Competition Pol'y Int'l 115 (2005).

23. For other double marginalization issues that might be addressed by market share discounts akin to exclusive dealing, see Gianluca Faella, *The Antitrust Assessment of Loyalty Discounts and Rebates*, 4J. Competition L. & Econ. 375 (2008); Sreya Kolay, Greg Shaffer & Janusz Ordover, *All-Units Discounts in Retail Contracts*, 13 J. Econ. & Mgmt. Strategy 429 (2004).

24. *See* Erik Hovenkamp & Herbert Hovenkamp, *Exclusionary Bundled Discounts and the Antitrust Modernization Commission*, 53 Antitrust Bull. 517 (2008); Erik Hovenkamp & Herbert Hovenkamp, *Complex Bundled Discounts and Antitrust Policy*, 57 Buffalo L. Rev. 1227 (2009).

25. Carbice Corp. v. Am. Patents Dev. Corp., 283 U.S. 27, 31–32 (1931); Int'l Salt Co. v. United States, 332 U.S. 392 (1947).

26. *See, e.g.*, Static Control Components, Inc. v. Lexmark Int'l, Inc., 487 F. Supp. 2d 861 (E.D. Ky. 2007) (denying summary judgment on claim that printer/cartridge technological tie was unlawful).

27. *See, e.g.*, Queen City Pizza, Inc. v. Domino's Pizza, Inc., 124 F.3d 430, 433 (3d Cir. 1997) (tied product was pizza dough; dismissing complaint based on "lock in" theory of power); Burda v. Wendy's Intern., Inc., 659 F. Supp. 2d 928 (S.D. Ohio 2009) (nonmonopoly franchisor; tied product was hamburger buns; sustaining complaint based on lock in theory of market power); Martrano v. Quizno's Franchise Co., LLC, 2009 WL 1704469 (W.D. Pa. June 15, 2009, unpublished) (nondominant fast food franchisor; tied product was unspecified supplies and services; dismissing complaint for failing to allege appropriate relevant market).

28. *See, e.g.*, Jean Tirole, The Theory of Industrial Organization 175–76 (1988).

29. *See* Mark A. Lemley & Carl Shapiro, *Patent Holdup and Royalty Stacking*, 86 Tex. L. Rev. 1991 (1996). On devices for addressing the problem, see Bohannan & Hovenkamp, Creation Without Restraint, *supra* note 9 at chs. 2, 4–5.

30. *See* Erik N. Hovenkamp & Herbert Hovenkamp, *Tying Arrangements and Antitrust Harm*, 52 Ariz. L. Rev. 925 (2010).

31. *See* Lester G. Telser, *Why Should Manufacturers Want Free Trade?*, 3J.L. & Econ. 86 (1960).

32. *See* 8 Areeda & Hovenkamp, Antitrust Law ¶¶ 1614f, 1615d.

33. *Id.* at ¶ 1604.

34. *See, e.g.*, Toledo Mack Sales & Serv., Inc. v. Mack Trucks, Inc., 530 F.3d 204 (3d Cir. 2008) (dealer cartel).

35. *See* Herbert Hovenkamp, Enterprise and American Law, 1836–1937, at 331–48 (1991) (discussing cartel of retail druggists that used RPM to limit price cutting).

36. *See* Hovenkamp & Hovenkamp, *supra* note 30.

37. Bowman, *supra* note 4.

38. *See* Heaton-Peninsular Button-Fastener Co. v. Eureka Specialty Co., 77 F. 288 (6th Cir. 1896) ("These machines have been placed in the hands of shoe dealers . . . at the actual cost of the machines to the makers, they expecting a profit on their monopoly alone from the sale of fasteners or staples to those having the machine.").

39. Siegel v. Chicken Delight, Inc., 448 F.2d 43 (9th Cir. 1971).

40. *See id.* at 46–47:

> Over its eighteen years existence, Chicken Delight has licensed several hundred franchisees to operate home delivery and pick-up food stores. It charged its franchisees no franchise fees or royalties. Instead, in exchange for the license granting the franchisees the right to assume its identity and adopt its business methods and to prepare and market certain food products under its trade-mark, Chicken Delight required its franchisees to purchase a specified number of cookers and fryers and to purchase certain packaging supplies and mixes exclusively from Chicken Delight. The prices fixed for these purchases were higher than, and included a percentage markup which exceeded that of, comparable products sold by competing suppliers.

41. *See, e.g.*, Gen. Talking Pictures Corp. v. W. Elec. Co., 304 U.S. 175 (1938) (field of use restriction distinguishing commercial and residential users); ProCD, Inc. v. Zeidenberg, 86 F.3d 1447 (7th Cir. 1996) (software licensing agreement distinguishing commercial and noncommercial users); *see also* Christina Bohannan, *IP Misuse as Foreclosure*, 96 Iowa L. Rev. 475 (2011).

42. *See, e.g.*, Xerox Corp. v. Media Sciences, Inc., 660 F. Supp..2d 535, 539 (S.D.N.Y. 2009) (noting that virtually all printer manufacturers tie by selling the printer at a price of cost or less, and place the overcharge in the expendable cartridges).

43. Hovenkamp & Hovenkamp, *supra* note 30.

44. *See, e.g.*, Gen. Talking Pictures Corp., 304 U.S. 175; *see also* 8 Phillip E. Areeda & Herbert Hovenkamp, Antitrust Law ¶¶ 1616e, 1647c5, 1641c (3d ed. 2010).

45. *See* Phillip E. Areeda & Donald F. Turner, *Predatory Pricing and Related Practices Under Section 2 of the Sherman Act*, 88 Harv. L. Rev. 697, 698 (1975); Williamson's principal response, Oliver E. Williamson, *Predatory Pricing: A Strategic and Welfare Analysis*, 87 Yale L. J. 284 (1977); and the reply, Phillip E. Areeda & Donald F. Turner, *Williamson on Predatory Pricing*, 87 Yale L. J. 1337 (1977). The debate and the current position of *Antitrust Law* are developed in 3A Phillip E. Areeda & Herbert Hovenkamp, Antitrust Law, ¶¶ 729, 736 at 106–21, 135–56 (3d ed. 2007).

46. *See, e.g.*, Thomas G. Krattenmaker & Steven C. Salop, *Anticompetitive Exclusion: Raising Rivals' Costs to Achieve Power over Price*, 96 Yale L.J. 209 (1986); Steven C. Salop & David T. Scheffman, *Raising Rivals' Costs*, 73 Am. Econ. Rev. 267 (1983).

47. *See, e.g.*, Richard A. Posner, Antitrust Law 196 (2d ed. 2001) (describing RRC as "not a happy formula"). One prominent Chicago School economist sees much more promise in the theory of RRC, but also difficulties in administration. *See* Dennis W. Carlton, *The Relevance for Antitrust Policy of Theoretical and Empirical Advances in Industrial Organization*, 12 Geo. Mason L. Rev. 47, 50–54 (2003). On the Chicago School and RRC, see Herbert Hovenkamp, *Exclusion and the Sherman Act*, 72 U. Chi. L. Rev. 147, 159–60 (2005).

48. *See, e.g.*, 11 Herbert Hovenkamp, Antitrust Law ¶ 1812 (3d ed. 2011).

49. *See, e.g.*, 9 *id.* ¶¶ 1704, 1709 (foreclosure).

Chapter 6

1. Frank H. Easterbrook, *The Limits of Antitrust*, 63 Tex. L. Rev. 1 (1984).

2. Ronald Reagan, Inaugural Address (Jan. 20, 1981).

3. George J. Stigler, *The Theory of Economic Regulation*, 2 Bell J. Econ. & Mgmt. Sci. 3 (1971); Sam Peltzman, *Toward a More General Theory of Regulation*, 19 J.L. & Econ. 211, 212–13 (1976); Gary S. Becker, *A Theory of Competition Among Pressure Groups for Political Influence*, 98 Q.J. Econ. 371 (1983); George J. Stigler, *The Origin of the Sherman Act*, 14 J. Legal Stud. 1 (1985).

4. For one of the early antitrust-related works in this area on "the economic justifications for exceptions [to antitrust law] to competition policy" see Carl Kaysen & Donald F. Turner, Antitrust Policy: An Economic and Legal Analysis 189 (1959).

5. Easterbrook, *supra* note 1, at 34 (footnote omitted).

6. Dennis W. Carlton & Jeffrey M. Perloff, Modern Industrial Organization 332 (3d ed. 2000).

7. R. Preston McAfee, Hugo M. Mialon & Michael A. Williams, *What Is a Barrier to Entry?*, 94 Am. Econ. Rev. 461 (2004).

8. Cees van Beers & Jeroen C. J. M. van den Bergh, *Perseverance of Perverse Subsidies and Their Impact on Trade and Environment*, 36 Ecological Econ. 475 (2001).

9. Stephen Weymouth, Oligopolists Rule: The Microeconomic Determinants of Lobbying and Political Influence (Oct. 18, 2010) (working paper).

10. D. Daniel Sokol, *Competition Policy and Comparative Corporate Governance of State-Owned Enterprises*, 2009 BYU L. Rev. 1713 (2009).

11. Stigler, *The Theory of Economic Regulation*, *supra* note 3.

12. See Dennis C. Mueller, Public Choice III (2004) for a literature review.

13. Pablo T. Spiller & Mariano Tommasi, *Agency Discretion and Accountability in Regulation*, *in* The New Palgrave Dictionary of Economics and the Law (Peter Newman ed., 1998).

14. 317 U.S. 341 (1943).

15. *Id.* at 344.

16. *Id.* at 345.

17. 445 U.S. 97 (1980).

18. *Id.* at 105 (citations omitted).

19. James C. Cooper & William E. Kovacic, *U.S. Convergence with International Competition Norms: Antitrust Law and Public Restraints on Competition*, 90 B.U. L. Rev. 1555, 1581 (2010); D. Daniel Sokol, *Limiting Anticompetitive Government Interventions That Benefit Special Interests*, 17 Geo. Mason L.

Rev. 119, 141–46 (2009); Capacity Building and Competition Policy Implementation Working Group, International Competition Network, Competition Advocacy in Regulated Sectors: Examples of Success 47–48 (2004).

20. Arnold C. Celnicker, *The Federal Trade Commission's Competition and Consumer Advocacy Program*, 33 St. Louis U. L.J. 379, 391 (1989).

21. Delegation of United States to the Competition Committee, Note Submitted for OECD Roundtable on Evaluation of the Actions and Resources of Competition Authorities 7–8 (May 25, 2007).

22. Bryan Caplan, The Myth of the Rational Voter: Why Democracies Choose Bad Policies (2007).

23. Suzanne Weaver, Decision to Prosecute: Organization and Public Policy in the Antitrust Division (1977); Robert A. Katzmann, Regulatory Bureaucracy: The Federal Trade Commission and Antitrust Policy (1980).

24. The Causes and Consequences of Antitrust: The Public-Choice Perspective (Fred S. McChesney & William F. Shughart II eds., 1995); Thomas J. DiLorenzo, *The Origins of Antitrust: An Interest-Group Perspective*, 5 Int'l Rev. L. & Econ. 73 (1985); Thomas W. Hazlett, *The Legislative History of the Sherman Act Re-Examined*, 30 Econ. Inquiry 263, 267 (1992); George J. Stigler, *The Origin of the Sherman Act*, *supra* note 3.

25. This of course presumes that there is a common understanding of what efficiency means.

26. Fred S. McChesney & William F. Shughart II, *Public Choice Theory and Antitrust Policy*, 142 Pub. Choice 385 (2010).

27. Richard A. Posner, *The Federal Trade Commission*, 37 U. Chi. L. Rev. 47, 48–49 (1969).

28. ICN Competition Advocacy Work Group, International Competition Network, Report on Assessment of ICN Members' Requirements and Recommendations on Further ICN Work on Competition Advocacy 14–15 (2009).

29. *Id.*

30. Niamh Dunne, OECD, Strategies for Competition Advocacy: Background Paper by the OECD Secretariat for the Latin American Competition Forum 14 (2010).

31. Korea Fair Trade Commission, 2009 Annual Report 23–24 (2009).

32. *Id.* at 23.

33. *Id.*

34. *Id.* at 23–24.

35. *Id.* at 24.

36. OECD, Competition Assessment Principles 27 (2010).

37. *Id.*

38. Allan Fels, OECD, Strategies for Competition Advocacy for the Latin American Competition Forum (2010).

39. Robert D. Anderson, William E. Kovacic & Anna Carolina Muller, *Ensuring Integrity and Competition in Public Procurement Markets: A Dual Challenge for Good Governance*, *in* The WTO Regime on Government Procurement: Challenge and Reform (Sue Arrowsmith & Robert D. Anderson eds., 2011).

40. OECD, Collusion and Corruption in Public Procurement: Breakout Sessions, Briefing Note by the Secretariate for the Global Forum on Competition 3 (2010).

41. Fiscalia Nacional Economia, OECD, Strategies for Competition Advocacy: Contribution from Chile for the Latin American Competition Forum 6 (2010).

Chapter 7

While the views expressed in this chapter are the author's own, their formulation has benefited greatly from a thoughtful exchange with Eleanor M. Fox.

1. Timothy J. Muris, *Principles for a Successful Competition Agency*, 72 U. Chi. L. Rev. 165, 170 (2005).

2. D. Daniel Sokol, *Limiting Anti-Competitive Government Interventions That Benefit Special Interests*, 17 Geo. Mason L. Rev. 119 (2009).

3. *See generally* Okeoghene Odudu, The Boundaries of EC Competition Law (2006). On the complexity of the notion of efficiency, *see* Eleanor M. Fox, *The Efficiency Paradox*, *in* How the Chicago School Overshot the Mark: The Effect of Conservative Economic Analysis on U.S. Antitrust 77 (Robert Pitofsky ed., 2008).

4. *See* Anti-Monopoly Law of the People's Republic of China (promulgated by the Standing Comm. Nat'l People's Cong., Aug. 20, 2007), at ch. V.

5. Mark Williams, Competition Policy and Law in China, Hong Kong and Taiwan 140 (2005).

6. Eleanor M. Fox, *An Anti-Monopoly Law for China—Scaling the Walls of Government Restraints*, 74 Antitrust L. J. 173 (2007).

7. *Id.* at 177 and 181.

8. United States v. Topco Assocs., 405 U.S. 596, 610 (1972).

9. 15 U.S.C. §1-7.

10. Muris, *supra* note 1, at 531.

11. Parker v. Brown, 317 U.S. 341 (1943).

12. U.S. Const. art. VI, cl. 2; *see also* Richard Squire, *Antitrust and the Supremacy Clause*, 59 Stan. L. Rev. 77 (2006).

13. Cal. Liquor Dealers v. Midcal Aluminum, Inc., 445 U.S. 97 (1980).

14. For a recent discussion, see the 2006 Memoranda released by the Antitrust Modernization Commission.

15. Federal Trade Commission, *Report of the State Action Task Force*, September 2003.

16. *See, e.g.*, D. Daniel Sokol, *supra* note 2, at 132–33.

17. *Id.* at 185.

18. *See* TFEU at arts. 34, 49, 56, and 63.

19. Case 194/94, CIA Security, 1996 E.C.R. I-2201, ¶ 40.

20. For recent Commission's decisions, *see* http://ec.europa.eu/competition/liberalisation/cases.html (accessed Nov. 4, 2011).

21. As a result, Article 106 TFEU is recognized as having direct effect and can thus be invoked by private parties in front of national courts to challenge the legality of State measures.

22. *See, e.g.*, Case C-475/99, Ambulanz Glöckner, 2001 E.C.R. I-8089, ¶ 24.

23. *See, e.g.*, Case C-209/98, Sydhavnens Sten & Grus, 2000 E.C.R. I-3743, ¶ 56.

24. *See, e.g.*, Case C-451/03, Servizi Ausiliari Dottori Commercialisti, 2006 E.C.R. I-2941, ¶ 23; *see also* Case C-209/98, Sydhavnens Sten & Grus, 2000 E.C.R. I-3743, ¶ 66.

25. *See, e.g.*, Case C-209/98, Sydhavnens Sten & Grus, 2000 E.C.R. I-3743, ¶ 77; *see also* Case C-340/99, TNT Traco, 2001 E.C.R. I-4109, ¶ 52; Case C-475/99, Ambulanz Glöckner, 2001 E.C.R. I-8089, ¶ 57.

26. *See*, respectively, C-258/98, Carra and others, 2000 E.C.R. I-4217, ¶ 13;Case C-41/90, Höfner, 1991 E.C.R. I-1979, ¶ 34; Case C-340/99, TNT Traco, 2001 E.C.R. I-4109, ¶ 46;Case C-475/99, Ambulanz Glöckner, 2001 E.C.R. I-8089, ¶ 40.

27. *See* TFEU Section 1 of Chapter 1 of Title VII.

28. *See*, originally, Case 13/77, SA G.B.-INNO-B.M./Association des détaillants en tabac (ATAB), 1977 E.C.R. 2115.

29. *See, e.g.*, Cases 267/86, Van Eycke, 1988 E.C.R. 4769, ¶ 16; C-2/91, Meng, 1993 E.C.R. I-5751, ¶ 14; C-185/91, Reiff, 1993 E.C.R. I-5801, ¶ 14; C-245/91, OHRA, 1993 E.C.R. I-5851, ¶ 10; C-96/94, Centro Servizi Spediporto, ¶¶ 20–21; C-35/96, CNSD. 1995 E.C.R. I-2883, ¶¶ 53–54; C-35/99, Arduino, 2002 E.C.R. I-1529, ¶¶ 34–35; C-198/01, CIF, 2003 E.C.R. I-8055, ¶¶ 45–46; C-250/03, Mauri, 2005 E.C.R. I-1267, ¶¶ 29–30; C-94/04, Cipolla, 2006 E.C.R. I-11421, ¶¶ 46–47; C-446/05, Doulamis, 2008 E.C.R. I-1377, ¶¶ 19–20; Order of May 5, 2008 in Case C-386/07, Hospital Consulting et al., 2008 E.C.R. I-67, ¶¶ 19–20.

30. Case 229/83, Association des Centres distributeurs Edouard Leclerc and others v. SARL "Au blé vert" and others, 1985 E.C.R. 1, ¶ 15.

31. Opinion of Advocate General Léger in Case C-35/99, Arduino, ¶ 88.

32. Case C-35/99, Arduino, ¶ 41 ; Case C-198/01, CIF, ¶¶ 6–7 *vs.* ¶¶ 77–78.

33. Case C-185/91, Reiff, ¶ 17; *see also* Case C-96/94, Centro Servizi Spediporto, ¶ 23.

34. Case C-35/99, Arduino, ¶ 38; *see also* Case C-185/91, Reiff, at ¶ 18; Case C-35/96, CNSD, ¶ 41.

35. *See* Opinion of Advocate General Jacobs in Joined Cases C-180 to C-184/98, Pavlov, ¶¶ 161–164 Joined; *see also* Opinion of Advocate General Léger in Case C-35/99, Arduino, ¶ 89; Opinion of Advocate General Maduro in Case C-94/04, Cipolla, ¶ 33.

36. Article 101(3) TFEU only allows for market/economically based justifications such as "improving the production or distribution of goods" and "promoting technical or economic progress."

37. European Commission, Commission Decision of May 10, 2007 Pursuant to [Art. 106(3) TFEU] on the Special Rights Granted to La Banque Postale, Caisses d'Epargne and Crédit Mutuel for the Distribution of the livret A and livret bleu.

38. European Commission, Commission decision of October 20, 2004 Pursuant to [Art. 106(3) TFEU] on the German Postal Legislation Relating to Mail Preparation Services (in particular to the access of self-provision intermediaries and consolidators to the public postal network and related special tariffs).

39. Case C-258/98, Carra and others, 2000 E.C.R. I-4217.

40. Case C-209/98, Sydhavnens Sten & Grus, 2000 E.C.R. I-3743.

41. Case C-475/99, Ambulanz Glöckner, 2001 E.C.R. I-8089.

42. A similar reasoning was used by the ECJ in its Judgment of April 29, 2010 in Case C-160/08, Commission v Germany, 2010 E.C.R. I-3713.

43. Case 13/77, SA G.B.-INNO-B.M. v. Association des détaillants en tabac (ATAB), 1977 E.C.R. 2115, ¶ 35.

44. Opinion of Advocate General Maduro in Case C-94/04, Cipolla, ¶¶ 60–75.

45. *See* Leclerc, *supra* note 30.

46. *See*, by analogy, Case C-442/02, CaixaBank France, 2004 E.C.R. I-8961.

47. In *Centro Servizi Spediporto*, the ECJ briefly examined the impact of the tariffs on the free movement of goods but found such impact to be "too uncertain and indirect in order for the [State measure] to be regarded as being such as to hinder trade between Member States." *See* Case C-96/94, ¶ 41 citing Case C-379/92, Peralta, 1994 E.C.R. I-3453, ¶ 24.

48. Case C-35/96, CNSD, ¶¶ 49–50.

49. Case C-198/01, CIF, ¶ 17.

50. As restated by Advocate General Bot in Case C-446/05, Doulamis, ¶¶ 85–86 (emphasis added).

51. *See* Opinion of Advocate General Maduro in Case C-94/04, Cipolla, ¶ 57 and the case law cited there.

52. For a discussion, see D. Daniel Sokol, *supra* note 2, at 123–24.

53. *See*, respectively Case 294/83, Parti écologiste "Les Verts" v European Parliament, 1986 E.C.R. 1339, ¶ 23; *see also* Helen Keller & Alec Stone Sweet, *Assessing the Impact of the ECHR on National Legal Systems*, *in* A Europe of Rights—The Impact of the ECHR on National Legal Systems 686, 686 (Helen Keller & Alec Stone Sweet eds., 2008).

54. Generally, committing to the discipline of trade law is a natural step for states or state entities toward embracing the virtues of the market economy.

55. Odudu, *supra* note 3, at 46–47.

Chapter 8

1. Frank H. Easterbrook, *The Limits of Antitrust*, 63 Tex. L. Rev. 1 (1984).

2. *See, e.g.*, Robert Pitofsky, How the Chicago School Overshot the Mark: The Effect of Conservative Economic Analysis on U.S. Antitrust (2009). In a quotation on the back cover of *How Chicago*, Senator Herb Kohl describes the Chicago School's antitrust as "lifeless."

3. For example, Einer Elhauge attacks Chicago's "one monopoly profit" theory as overstated and its assumption that price discrimination is generally output maximizing as simply wrong. Einer Elhauge, *Tying, Bundled Discounts and the Death of the Single Monopoly Profit Theory*, 123 Harv. L. Rev. 397 (2009).

4. *See* Robert J. Shapiro & Kevin A. Hassett, *The Economic Value of Intellectual Property*, USA for Innovation, Oct. 2005, at 3.

5. Most cartel cases involve fungible intermediate manufactured goods. *See* John M. Connor, *Cartels & Antitrust Portrayed: Private International Cartels from 1990–2008*, available at: http://papers.ssrn.com/sol3/papers.cfm?abstract_id=1467310.

6. Edward Chamberlain, The Theory of Monopolistic Competition 56–64 (5th ed. Harvard University Press 1945)

7. *See* S. Vermont, *The Economics of Patent Litigation*, *in* From Ideas to Assets: Investing Wisely in Intellectual Property 327, 332 (B. Berman ed., 2002); F. M. Scherer, *Firm Size, Market Structure, Opportunity and the Output of Patented Inventions*, 55 Am. Econ. Rev. 1097, 1098 (1965).

8. *See* Daniel A. Crane, *Antitrust Antifederalism*, 96 Cal. L. Rev. 1, 28–32 (2008).

9. I am indebted to Ariel Katz for the comparison of *Feist* and *McGill*. *See* Ariel Katz & Paul-Erik Veel, *Beyond Refusal to Deal: Innovation, Intellectual Property and Competition Policy Across the Atlantic* (draft, on file with author).

10. Feist Publications, Inc. v. Rural Tel. Serv. Co., 499 U.S. 340 (1991).

11. *See* Katz & Veel, *supra* note 9 (discussing antitrust history in *Feist*).

12. *Feist Publications, Inc.*, 499 U.S. at 345.

13. Joined Cases C-241 & C-242/91, Radio Telefs Eirseann (RTE) & Independent Television Publications Ltd (ITP) v. Commission of the European Communities (Magill), 1995 E.C.R. I-00743.

14. This is not to say that the Supreme Court can always choose a policy lever in every individual case, since some are framed only as antitrust or IP cases when they arrive at the Court. Rather, the Court has the power systemically to advance competition values by narrower tailoring of substantive IP rights, which allows it to employ a lighter touch in antitrust cases.

15. *See, e.g.*, Qualcomm, Inc. v. Broadcom Corp., 548 F.3d. 1004, 1025–26 (3d Cir. 2008).

16. *See* Federal Trade Commission, *In the Matter of Rambus Inc.*, Docket No. 9302.

17. Federal Trade Commission, *In re Rambus Inc.*, Opinion of the Commission on Remedy.

18. Federal Trade Commission, Remedy Statement of Commissioner Pamela Harbour Jones; *see also* Federal Trade Commission, Statement of Commissioner J. Thomas Rosch.

19. Guido Calabresi & A. Douglas Melamed, *Property Rules, Liability Rules and Inalienability Rules: One View of the Cathedral*, 85 Harv. L. Rev. 1089 (1972).

20. I develop these points more fully in Daniel A. Crane, *Intellectual Liability*, 88 Tex. L. Rev. 253 (2009).

21. *See, e.g.*, Stewart E. Sterk, *Property Rules, Liability Rules and Uncertainty About Property Rights*, 106 Mich. L. Rev. 1285 (2008); Henry E. Smith, *Intellectual Property as Property: Delineating Entitlements in Information*, 116 Yale L.J. 1742 (2007); Mark A. Lemley & Philip J. Weiser, *Should Property or Liability Rules Govern Information?*, 85 Tex. L. Rev. 783 (2007); Ian Ayres & Eric Talley, *Solomonic Bargaining: Dividing a Legal Entitlement to Facilitate Cosean Trade*, 104 Yale L.J. 1027 (1995); Robert P. Merges, *Of Property Rules, Coase and Intellectual Property*, 94 Colum. L. Rev. 2655 (1994).

22. *See* Crane, *supra* note 20, at 258–69.

23. Louis Kaplow, *The Patent-Antitrust Intersection: A Reappraisal*, 97 Harv. L. Rev. 1813 (1984).

24. *See generally* Crane, *supra* note 20, at 272–74.

25. *Id.* at 280.

26. Mark A. Lemley, *Intellectual Property Rights and Standard-Setting Organizations*, 90 Cal. L. Rev. 1889, 1893 (2002).

27. *See* Albert A. Foer, American Antitrust Institute, *Request for Investigation of Rembrandt, Inc. for Anticompetitive Conduct That Threatens Digital Television Conversion*, Petition to the Federal Trade Commission, March 26, 2008.

28. Rambus, Inc. v. FTC, 522 F.3d 456 (D.C. Cir. 2008).

29. eBay v. MercExchange LLC, 547 U.S. 388 (2006).

30. Verizon Commc'ns, Inc. v. Law Offices of Curtis V. Trinko, 540 U.S. 398, 415 (2004) (citing Phillip Areeda, *Essential Facilities: An Epithet in Need of Limiting Principles*, 58 Antitrust L.J. 841, 853 (1989)).

31. U.S. Dep't of Justice and Federal Trade Comm'n, *Antitrust Enforcement and Intellectual Property Rights: Promoting Innovation and Competition*, at 28 (April 2007).

32. Christina Bohannan & Herbert Hovenkamp, *IP and Antitrust: Reformation and Harm*, 51 B.C. L. Rev. 905, 965 (2010).

33. *See* United States v. Microsoft Corp., No. 98-1232, 2002 WL 31654530 (D.D.C. Nov. 12, 2002).

Chapter 9

1. For a broader discussion of "internal failures," see Neil W. Averitt & Robert H. Lande, *Consumer Sovereignty: A Unified Theory of Antitrust and Consumer Protection Law*, 65 Antitrust L.J. 713 (1997).

2. On the relationship between unfair terms control and competition law see Paolisa Nebbia, *Standard Form Contracts Between Unfair Terms Control and Competition Law*, 31 Eur. L. Rev. 102 (2006);

Thomas Wilhelmsson, *Cooperation and Competition Regarding Standard Contract Terms in Consumer Contracts* 17 Eur. Bus. L. Rev. 49 (2006).

3. Thomas B. Leary, *Competition Law and Consumer Protection Law: Two Wings of the Same House*, 72 Antitrust L.J. 1147 (2005).

4. Fernando Gómez Pomar, *The Unfair Commercial Practices Directive: A Law and Economics Perspective*, 2 Eur. Rev. Cont. L. 4 (2006).

5. *See* Timothy Muris, *The Federal Trade Commission and the Future Development of U.S. Consumer Protection Policy*, Working Paper No. 04-19 (2004).

6. Of course "the core issue, under such a goal, is how to design and apply an optimal system of duties of information and behavior that covers the gaps that market forces are unable to check, and, at the same time, does not interfere with those same driving pressures of competitive markets which, overall, are the major factors in attaining optimality in the relationship between producers and consumers." Gómez Pomar, *supra* note 4, at 5.

7. A commercial practice may also be misleading through omission. The directive does not attempt to define a comprehensive list of information to be positively disclosed in all circumstances, but imposes on businesses the duty not to omit "material" information that the average consumer needs to make an informed decision.

8. One of the reasons leading to entrusting the ICA with powers in that area was that the ICA was already in charge of enforcing the laws on misleading advertising and therefore could already boast a considerable experience in one of the fields covered by Directive 2005/29. Other European countries that have chosen to entrust, in full or in part, the enforcement of Directive 2005/29 to their national competition authorities include, for example, Hungary, Lithuania, and the United Kingdom. Outside Europe, egregious examples are the United States and Australia.

9. AGCM, "Relazione Annuale sull'attività svolta," March 31, 2010.

10. *See* AS201/2000 (opinion of the procedures for the grant on individual licenses for mobile communication systems).

11. *See* AS224/2001 (on Mobile Number Portability).

12. *See* PS333 Telecom—Misleading Retention, decision n. 20122/2009.

13. The ICA has constantly held that the notion of unfair "practice" does not include occasional misconduct: "practice" only includes conduct that is likely to be repeated in an indefinite number of cases.

14. Autorité de la concurrence, Décision n° 09-D-24 du 28 juillet 2009 relative à des pratiques mises en oeuvre par France Télécom sur différents marchés de services de communications électroniques fixes dans les DOM.

15. In the telecom sector, the same type of unfair conduct has also been detected in oligopolistic markets; *see* AS224/2001 (where reference was made to two operators, TIM and Omnintel, who jointly held 80 percent of phone lines).

16. See, among many others, decision no. 18727/2008. The decision was then overturned, mainly for procedural reasons, by a judgment of the Regional Administrative Court (TAR) of Lazio at the beginning of 2009. For an overlap between competition and consumer protection in the energy sector see also AGCM decisions no. 20549/2009 and 18829/2008.

17. Cour d'appel, Paris, May 14, 2009 (The decision was confirmed by the Cour de cassation, Cass. com., July 13, 2010, no. 798).

18. Canal Plus had been granted the right to retransmit the remaining ones.

19. *See* Tribunal de Commerce, Paris, February 23, 2009.

20. Directive 2005/29 is a measure of "maximum harmonization." This means that Member States cannot adopt or maintain in force any domestic provision that is more restrictive than the provisions of the directive itself (such as a blanket prohibition on certain forms of tying). Should this occur, the relevant domestic provision must be considered inapplicable.

21. Autorité de la Concurrence, Opinion No. 09-A-42, On Relations of Exclusivity Among the Activities of Electronic Communication Operators and Activities of Distribution of Contents and Services.

22. There seem to be, in this respect, two major schools of thought: one argues that "consumer welfare" refers to "aggregate welfare" (*see, e.g.*, Joseph Farrell & Michael L. Katz, *The Economics of Welfare Standards in Antitrust*, 2 Competition Pol'y Int'l 3 (2006)), while the other one suggests that

the term should mean "consumer surplus," (*see, e.g.*, John B. Kirkwood & Robert H. Lande, *The Fundamental Goal of Antitrust: Protecting Consumers, Not Increasing Efficiency*, 84 Notre Dame L. Rev. 191, 213 (2008); Steven C. Salop, *Question: What Is the Real and Proper Antitrust Welfare Standard? Answer: The True Consumer Welfare Standard*, 22 Loy. Consumer. L. Rev. 336 (2010)).

23. European Commission, White Paper on Damages Actions for Breach of EC Antitrust Rules, COM(2008) 165, 2.4.2008.

24. This has already been done in Italian law, where a recent amendment to the Consumer Code has introduced under art. 140 bis (as inserted by Law No. 244/2007) the possibility for certain consumer organizations to bring actions for damages caused by a wide range of misconducts, including infringements of competition law as well as consumer law.

25. CLEF, Background Paper: Competition and Unfair Commercial Practices.

26. European Commission, Paper on Consumer Collective Redress, COM(2008) 794 final.

Chapter 10

The views expressed in this chapter are our own and do not purport to reflect those of the FNE (Chilean Competition Agency). We acknowledge Gael Yeomans for invaluable research assistance.

1. *See* Ronald Dworkin, Taking Rights Seriously 22 (1977); H. W. R. Wade & C. F. Forsyth, Administrative Law 250 et seq. (9th ed. 2004); Stephen G. Breyer, Richard B. Stewart, Cass R. Sunstein & Matthew L. Spitzer, Administrative Law and Regulatory Policy: Problems, Text, and Cases 227 (5th ed. 2002); Frank H. Easterbrook, *The Limits of Antitrust*, 63 Tex. L. Rev. 1 (1984).

2. Easterbrook, *supra* note 1, at 2.

3. *Id.*

4. Although the meaning of courts and tribunals differ in each jurisdiction, we treat them here as synonyms and refer to them indistinguishably.

5. Breyer et al., *supra* note 1.

6. Alison Jones & Brenda Sufrin, EC Competition Law: Text, Cases and Materials 1147 (3d ed. 2008).

7. It may also fulfill other roles, such as advocacy or even decision making in the area of mergers. We do not consider these aspects in this chapter.

8. In the case of a specialized body, the incentives the design creates with respect to the agency are similar to those described below for specialized reviewing courts with respect to the primary decision maker.

9. Some commentators have wrongly made this assumption. *E.g.* Ronald M. Levin, *Identifying Questions of Law in Administrative Law*, 74 Geo. L.J. 1, 43 (1985).

10. Indeed, day-to-day business does not transform the court into an expert but helps it to specialize. For this reason, it is a mistake that some legislation requires adequate *expertise* (for example, the Council Directive, Framework Directive 2002/21, art. 4 (EC), which indicates that the appeal body, which may be a court, "shall have the appropriate expertise to enable it to carry out its functions effectively").

11. Because, as Jaffe once pointed out, "It is not merely the presence of expertness, but the wide-reaching and systematic character of agency regulation which tends to choke out the normal jurisdiction of the courts" (Louis L. Jaffe, *Primary Jurisdiction*, 77 Harv. L. Rev. 1037, 1040–41 (1964).

12. Stephen H. Legomsky, Specialized Justice: Courts, Administrative Tribunals, and a Cross-National Theory of Specialization 22 (1990).

13. The reference to "degrees of deference" is common in the literature on both sides of the Atlantic. In the United Kingdom, see Paul Craig, Administrative Law 615 (2008); A. L. Young, *In Defence of Due Deference*, 72 Mod. L. Rev. 554 (2009). In the United States, see Emerson H. Tiller, *Controlling Policy by Controlling Process: Judicial Influence on Regulatory Decision Making*, 14 J.L. Econ. & Org. 114, 117 (1998); Stephen Breyer, *Judicial Review of Questions of Law and Policy*, 38 Admin. L. Rev. (1986).

14. Indeed, the same analysis may in principle apply to questions of policy.

15. Tom De la Mare, *Regulatory Judicial Review: The Impact of Competition Law* ¶ 14 (paper presented at the 2007 ALBA conference).

16. Three of these models correspond to the classification made by Trebilcock and Iacobucci: a "bifurcated judicial model," a "bifurcated agency model," and the "integrated agency model." *See*

Michael J. Trebilcock & Edward M. Iacobucci, *Designing Competition Law Institutions: Values, Structure, and Mandate*, 41 Loy. U. Chi. L.J. 455, 459–64 (2010).

17. The administrative model seems to be the rule. This is the model followed, for example, by most competition regimes in Latin America. Note that the U.S. Federal Trade Commission (FTC) only *appears* to follow this model. In reality, from the passage of the Sherman Act in 1890 until the creation of the FTC in 1915, all antitrust cases were brought and decided only in court proceedings, and the great majority of antitrust cases are still decided by the federal courts. Thus, the body of American antitrust doctrine is *entirely* judge made. As a result, the courts have not deferred to the sometimes contrary decisions of the FTC in antitrust. Instead, they have treated the FTC in antitrust matters as if it were just another federal district court. For a dramatic illustration of this, see the Supreme Court's opinion in *California Dental Ass'n v. FTC*, 526 U.S. 756 (1999).

18. General Court decisions, on points of law, can be scrutinized by the ECJ.

19. Certain activities are subject to prosecution under the criminal law of Canada and hence are not subject to the decision of the Competition Tribunal. Criminal offenses include conspiracies (as well as the implementation in Canada of collusive arrangements entered into outside of Canada), bid rigging, multilevel marketing, and certain misleading advertising and telemarketing practices.

20. Further examples include South Africa (Competition Commission and the Competition Tribunal, plus a specialized Competition Appeal Court) and Israel (Israel Antitrust Authority and the Antitrust Tribunal).

21. Competition Act, 1998, c. 41 §§ 46–47, sched. 8 (U.K.).

22. *Id.* There are a few exceptions where the appeal is not on the merits. When the statute creates such exceptions, the issue may still be challengeable by way of judicial review in the Administrative Court. Competition Act, 1998, c. 41 §§ 46(g)–(h), 47(b)–(c). We do not deal with other areas of the CAT's jurisdiction.

23. Joined Cases C-189/02 P, C-202/02 P, C-205/02 P to C-208/02 P & C-213/02 P, Dansk Rørindustri A/S & Others v. Comm'n, 2005 E.C.R. I-5425, ¶ 170.

24. As Jerry L. Mashaw summarizes in his classic study on the subject, "[i]n a legal culture largely oriented toward court enforcement of individual legal rights, 'administration' has always seemed as antithetical to 'law' as 'bureaucracy' is to 'justice.' Law focuses on rights, administration on policy." *See* Jerry L. Mashaw, Bureaucratic Justice: Managing Social Security Disability Claims 1 (1983).

25. Peter Cane, Administrative Tribunals and Adjudication 142 (2009).

26. As Cane, *supra* note 25, summarizes, "implementation tends to favour the promotion of social objectives whereas adjudication tends to favour the promotion of individual interests."

27. Council Regulation 1/2003, art. 7(1), 2002 O.J. (L 1) (EC).

28. For a full review of the EU competition arrangements, see Wouter P. J. Wils, *The Combination of the Investigative and Prosecutorial Function and the Adjudicative Function in EC Antitrust Enforcement: A Legal and Economic Analysis*, 27 World Competition: L. & Econ. Rev. 201(2004); and Wouter P. J. Wils, *The Increased Level of EU Antitrust Fines, Judicial Review, and the European Convention on Human Rights*, 33 World Competition: L. & Econ. Rev. (2010).

29. See Council Regulation 1/2003, *supra* note 27, on the implementation of the rules on competition laid down in Articles 81 and 82 of the Treaty Regulation 1/2003, and Commission Regulation 773/2004 (EC), relating to the conduct of proceedings by the Commission pursuant to Articles 81 and 82 of the EC Treaty (Text with EEA relevance).

30. *See* Commission Decision 2001/462, 2001 O.J. (L 162/21) (EC) on the terms of reference of hearing officers in certain competition proceedings (the hearing officer mandate).

31. Sophie Germont & Ole Andresen, *Public Enforcement by the Commission: A Strategic Perspective*, *in* EC Competition Law: A Critical Assessment 675, 701(Giuliano Amato & Claus-Dieter Ehlermann eds. 2007).

32. As Jones & Sufrin, *supra* note 6, at 1190, explain, the idea behind creating the post of the hearing officer "was to inject an element of disinterested objectivity into the Commission's decision-making process."

33. Wils, *Combination*, *supra* note 28, at 3.

34. Eleanor M. Fox, *Antitrust and Institutions: Design and Change*, 41 Loy. U. Chi. L.J. 473, 482 (2010).

35. Treaty on the Functioning of the European Union, art. 263, 2008 O.J. (C 115).

36. Jones & Sufrin, *supra* note 6, at 1252.

37. *Id.*

38. Law Decree 211 of 1973 (the competition statute), art. 6.

39. In addition to the five judges, the TDLC has a staff of six professionals, lawyers and economists, headed by the Secretary of the Tribunal.

40. The Third Chamber on Constitutional Matters hears the competition cases. These cases, however, represent a very small share of this chamber's workload; rather, the bulk of it comprises cases involving administrative law.

41. Defined in article 27.2 of the DL 211 (the Chilean Competition Law).

42. Corte Suprema, Consulta de Subtel sobre participación de concesionarios de telefonía móvil en conurso público de telefonía móvil digital avanzada, Rol 4797-2008, Decision of January 27, 2009, C. 6°.

43. Corte Suprema, FNE y Banco de Chile con Falabella y otros, Rol 2339-2008, Decision of August 13, 2008, C. 17°.

44. Corte Suprema, Voissnet con Empresa de Telecomunicaciones de Chile S.A., Rol 6236-2006, Decision of July 4, 2007, C. 29°.

45. Corte Suprema, Demanda de OPS Ingeniería Ltda. y Otros contra Telefónica Móviles de Chile S.A., Rol 8077-2009, Decision of July 7, 2010, C. 17°.

46. Corte Suprema, FNE contra Compañía Chilena de Fósforos S.A., Rol 277-2010, Decision of June 2, 2010, C. 22° (emphasis added) ("Que en lo referente a la determinación de la multa—objeto de impugnación de los tres recursos de reclamación—este Tribunal, coincidente con lo razonado por la sentencia recurrida, *considera que la multa debe implicar a CCF al menos un costo mayor al beneficio esperado de haber establecido las barreras artificiales al mercado acreditadas en esta sentencia*").

47. For example, in a recent case the Supreme Court stated: "The mentioned conclusions set forth in said decision, on examination of their grounds and the elements of judgement on which they rely, and considering, moreover, the rigor of the pursuant deliberations, determine that this Court also concludes that the charged actions cannot be considered as constituting an infringement of article 3, letter b) or c) of [DL 211]" (Corte Suprema, Rol 2591-2007, Decision of October 24, 2007. The corresponding TDLC decision is Asociación de Químicos Farmacéuticos de Farmacias Independientes de Chile, Decision of April 26, 2007, Judgment 51/2007.)

48. Corte Suprema, FNE contra Air Liquide Chile S.A. y otros, Rol 5057-2006, Decision of January 22, 2007, C. 6°; Corte Suprema, Asociación de Exportadores de Chile AG contra Ultramar Agencias Marítimas S.A. y otros, Rol 3395-2006, Decision of December 28, 2006, C. 9°–15°.

49. Corte Suprema, FNE contra Isapre ING S.A. y otros, Rol 4052-2008, Decision of January 28, 2008, C. 15°.

50. *Id.*, C. 11°–12°.

51. Corte Suprema, Producción Química y Electrónica Quimel S.A. contra James Hardie Fibrocementos Limitada, Rol 3449-2006, Decision of November 29, 2002, C. 6°.

52. Corte Suprema, Rol 2339-2008, Decision of August 13, 2008. *See also* Corte Suprema, Rol 5505-2008; Corte Suprema, Rol 5937-2008.

53. Competition cases, which are heard by the Third Chamber on Constitutional Matters, represent a very small share of this chamber's workload. The bulk of cases involve administrative law.

Chapter 11

1. John Vickers, *Central Banks and Competition Authorities: Institutional Comparisons and New Concerns* (BIS Working Paper No. 331, Nov. 2010).

2. George Yarrow, Beesley Lecture, Institute of Directors, London, What Is Next for Utility Regulation? (Sept. 16, 2010). (BIS Working Paper No. 331, Nov. 2010).

3. ICN, Seminar of Competition Agency Effectiveness (2009).

4. Vince Cable, U.K. Secretary of State, Address at the CBI Conference, London, Education at the Heart of Growth (Oct. 25, 2010).

5. OECD, Competition Advocacy: Challenges for Developing Countries.

6. OECD, OECD Global Forum on Competition, Russian Federation—The Objectives of Competition Law and Policy and the Optimal Design of a Competition Agency, at 2, OECD Doc. No. CCNM/GF/COMP/WD(2003)2 (Jan. 9, 2003).

7. *Id.*

8. ICN, Seminar on Competition Agency Effectiveness, Summary Report (Jan. 2009) [hereinafter ICN Seminar].

9. *Id.*

10. Vickers, *supra* note 1 at 19 ("Whether or not the evidence gathered in a case shows to the requisite standard of proof that an agreement or conduct breached a competition law prohibition can raise questions about, among other things, evidence gathering, factual inference, rights of defence, the standard of proof, and not least how to interpret the statutory and case law itself.").

11. Case T-201/04, Microsoft Corp. v. Comm'n, 2007 E.C.R. II-3601 (Ct. First Instance), ¶¶ 87, 380–81, 391, 421, 457, 526, 530, 534, 557, 618, 649, 665, 683.

12. Competition authorities also engage in other forms of advocacy with consumers and consumer groups, with the business community, with academics, and with the press. This is done to publicize the goals and the importance of competition and the role of the competition authority. These advocacy programs are complementary to advocacy with the government and aimed at developing a competition culture in the country. However, as this second form of advocacy is less important for the purpose of our argument, it will not be extensively commented upon and we will focus on advocacy with the government.

13. OECD, OECD Global Forum on Competition, Republic of Korea—Advocacy Role of the Korea Fair Trade Commission in Regulatory Reform, at 4, OECD Doc. No. CCNM/GF/COMP/WD(2001)23 (Oct. 10, 2001).

14. Competition Advocacy, *supra* note 5.

15. *Id.*

16. ICN Seminar, *supra* note 8.

17. Kazuhiko Takeshima, Chairman of the Japan Fair Trade Commission, Address at the ICN Annual Conference, Mérida, Mexico, The Position of Competition Authorities Within Government (June 23–25, 2003).

18. It is worth noting that the independence of competition authorities, even in their adjudicative functions, can be the source of tensions with the executive.

19. DG Competition Management Plan 2010, May 12, 2010.

20. Paloma Martinez-Lage, *Spain's New Competition Act*, 3 Revue Concurrences 174, 174–80 (2007).

21. OECD, OECD Global Forum on Competition, Optimal Design of a Competition—Note by the OECD Secretariat, at 10-1, OECD Doc. No. CCNM/GF/COMP(2003)2 (Feb. 3, 2003).

22. Takeshima, *supra* note 17, at 1–2.

Chapter 12

1. Frank H. Easterbrook, *The Limits of Antitrust*, 63 Texas L. Rev. 1 (1984).

2. Nicholas Economides & Ioannis Lianos, *The Quest for Appropriate Remedies in the EC Microsoft Cases: A Comparative Appraisal*, *in* Microsoft on Trial: Legal and Economic Analysis of a Transatlantic Antitrust Case 393 (Luca Rubini ed., 2010).

3. Carl Shapiro, *Microsoft: A Remedial Failure*, 75 Antitrust L.J. 739 (2009).

4. Keith N. Hylton, *Remedies, Antitrust Law and Microsoft: Comment of Shapiro*, 75 Antitrust L.J. 773 (2009); and the articles published in the special issue Symposium: Remedies for Dominant Firm Misconduct, 76 Antitrust L.J. 11 et seq., (2009).

5. United States v. Microsoft Corp., 87 F. Supp. 2d 30 (D.D.C. 2000).

6. William H. Page & Seldon J. Childers, *Software Development as an Antitrust Remedy: Lessons from the Enforcement of the Microsoft Communications Protocol Licensing Requirement*, 14 Mich. Telecomm. Tech. L. Rev. 77, 114 (2007).

7. *See EU Seeks Big Drop in Microsoft Market Share*, Reuters, Sept. 17, 2007.

8. Brunswick Corp. v Riegel Textile Corp., 752 F.2d 261, 267 (7th Cir. 1984).

9. Case 322/81, NV Nederlandsche Banden Industrie Michelin v. Comm'n (*Michelin I*), 1983 E.C.R. 3461, ¶ 70 (Eur. Ct. Justice); Case 85/76, Hoffman-La Roche & Co. v. Commission, 1979 E.C.R. 461, ¶ 91 (Eur. Ct. Justice); and Case C-95/04, British Airways plc v. Commission, 2007 E.C.R. I-2331, ¶ 66 (Eur. Ct. Justice): Article 102 TFEU "refers to conduct *which is such as to influence the structure of a market* where, as a result of the very presence of the undertaking in question, the

degree of competition is already weakened." British Airways, 2007 E.C.R. I-2331, ¶ 66 (emphasis added).

10. Communication from the Commission, Guidance on the Commission's Enforcement Priorities in Applying Article 82 EC Treaty to Abusive Exclusionary Conduct by Dominant Undertakings, 2009 O.J. C 45/7, ¶ 19.

11. Commission Notice on Remedies Acceptable Under the Council Regulation (EC) No 139/2004 and Under Commission Regulation (EC) No 802/2004, 2008 O.J. C 267/1.

12. *See* OECD, *Policy Roundtables: Remedies and Sanctions in Abuse of Dominance Cases*, (2006); Nicholas Economides & Ioannis Lianos, *A Critical Appraisal of Remedies in the E.U. Microsoft Cases*, 2010 Colum. Bus. L. Rev. 346 (2010).

13. Harry First, *Netscape Is Dead: Remedy Lessons from the Microsoft Litigation* 31 (NYU Law & Econ. Research Paper Series, Working Paper No. 08–49, 2008).

14. A term first employed in the context of restitution by Professor Peter Birks, *Three Kinds of Objection to Discretionary Remedialism*, 29 U.W. Australia L. Rev. 1 (2000), who was a fervent critic of "discretionary remedialism."

15. Simon Evans, *Defending Discretionary Remedialism*, 23 Sydney L. Rev. 463, 463 (2001). For a general discussion, *see* Darryn Jenson, *The Rights and Wrongs of Discretionary Remedialism*, Singapore J. Legal Stud. 178 (2003).

16. Charles Alan Wright, *The Law of Remedies as a Social Institution*, 18 U. Det. L.J. 376, 376 (1955).

17. *Id.*

18. Peter Birks, *Rights, Wrongs, and Remedies*, 20 Oxford J. Legal Stud. 1, 3 (2000).

19. Kellis E. Parker, Modern Judicial Remedies: Cases and Materials 10 (Little, Brown 1975); *see also* Birks, *supra* note 14.

20. Christopher C. Langdell, A Brief Survey of Equity Jurisdiction 19 (The Harvard Law Review Association 1904).

21. John Austin, Lectures on Jurisprudence or the Philosophy of Positive Law 762 (Robert Campbell ed., John Murray 5th ed. 1885).

22. Kit Barker, *Rescuing Remedialism in Unjust Enrichment Law: Why Remedies Are Right*, 57 Cambridge L.J. 301, 319 (1998).

23. Birks, *supra* note 14, at 7.

24. *Id.* at 10.

25. *Id.* at 17.

26. *Id.* at 23.

27. On the classification of the legal system in regimes of private and public governance, see Anthony Ogus, Costs and Cautionary Tales: Economic Insights for the Law 71–86 (2006).

28. For example, the breach of a contract might be efficient because the profit of the breach would exceed the profit from completion of the contract. See, for instance, Charles J. Goetz & Robert E. Scott, *Liquidated Damages, Penalties and the Just Compensation Principle: Some Notes on an Enforcement Model and A Theory of Efficient Breach*, 77 Colum. L. Rev. 554 (1977); Richard A. Posner, Economic Analysis of Law 120 (2003).

29. Barker, *supra* note 22, at 320.

30. *Id.* at 323.

31. *Id.*

32. Richard A. Posner, *The Concept of Corrective Justice in Recent Theories of Tort Law*, 10J. Legal Stud. 187, 201 (1981) (noting that "in [the economic theory of law], laws is a means of bringing about an efficient [in the sense of wealth maximizing] allocation of resources by correcting externalities and other distortions in the market's allocation of resources). The idea of rectification in the Aristotelian sense is implicit in this theory.") For a criticism of this view of the Aristotelian theory of corrective justice, see Bill Shaw & William Martin, *Aristotle and Posner on Corrective Justice: The Tortoise and the Hare*, 9 Bus. Ethics Q. 651 (1999).

33. It is interesting here to compare the almost unlimited discretion for imposing remedies under this conception with the limited scope of the liability if one uses the concept of causation. *See* Steven Shavell, *An Analysis of Causation and the Scope of Liability in the Law of Torts*, 9J. Legal Stud. 463 (1980).

34. The issue is more complicated in competition law (as in all areas of commercial law) as one should also examine the question of the efficient allocation or mix of deterrence between the corporation and individuals acting on its behalf.

35. Keith N. Hylton, *Punitive Damages and the Economic Theory of Penalties*, 87 Geo. L.J. 421 (1998).

36. Gary S. Becker, *Crime and Punishment: An Economic Approach*, 76J. Pol. Econ. 169 (1968).

37. William M. Landes, *Optimal Sanctions for Antitrust Violations* 50 U. Chi. L. Rev. 652, 656 (1983).

38. Wouter P. J. Wils, *Optimal Antitrust Fines: Theory and Practice*, 29 World Competition 183, 190 (2006).

39. John Gardner, *What Is Tort Law For? Part 1. The Place of Corrective Justice*, 30 L. & Phil. 1, 30 (2011).

40. Herbert Hovenkamp, *Antitrust's Protected Classes*, 88 Mich. L. Rev. 1 (1989).

41. Wils, *supra* note 38, at 183.

42. Gardner, *supra* note 39, at 26, 29.

43. *See* Stephen Perry, *On the Relationship Between Corrective and Distributive Justice*, *in* Oxford Essays in Jurisprudence 237, 238 (Jeremy Horder ed., 4th series, Oxford Univ. Press 2000); Dennis Klimchuk, *On the Autonomy of Corrective Justice*, 23 Oxford J. Legal Stud. 49 (2003).

44. Klimchuck, *supra* note 43, at 52.

45. *Id.*

46. *Id.* at 53.

47. Steven Walt, *Eliminating Corrective Justice*, 92 Va. L. Rev. 1311 (2006).

48. Larry A. Alexander, *Causation and Corrective Justice: Does Tort Law Make Sense?*, 6 L. & Phil. 1, 7 (1987).

49. Peter Benson, *The Basis of Corrective Justice and Its Relation to Distributive Justice*, 77 Iowa L. Rev. 515 (1992).

50. *Id.* at 530–31.

51. *Id.* at 531.

52. *Id.* at 532.

53. Jules L. Coleman, Risks and Wrongs 348 (Cambridge University Press 1992).

54. Perry, *supra* note 43.

55. *Id.* at 259.

56. *Id.* at 246.

57. *See* A. Douglas Melamed, *Afterword: The Purposes of Antitrust Remedies*, 76 Antitrust L.J 359 (2009).

58. Take illegal gains away from the law violators and "restore those monies to the victims" constitutes a principal goal of competition law remedies. Robert Pitofsky, *Antitrust at the Turn of the Twenty-First Century: The Matter of Remedies*, 91 Geo. L.J. 169, 170 (2002).

59. Eleanor M. Fox, *Remedies and the Courage of Convictions in a Globalized World: How Globalization Corrupts Relief*, 80 Tul. L. Rev. 571, 573 (2005).

60. Council Regulation No. 1/2003, 2003 O.J. (L 1/1) (EC). See also, on the distinction between remedies and sanctions, OECD, Remedies and Sanctions in Abuse of Dominance Cases 18 (2006) ("Typically, remedies aim to stop a violator's unlawful conduct, its anticompetitive effects, and their recurrence, as well as to restore competition. Sanctions are usually meant to deter unlawful conduct in the future, to compensate victims, and to force violators to disgorge their illegal gains.").

61. *See also*, OECD, *supra* note 12.

62. Douglas Laycock, Modern American Remedies: Cases and Materials 2 (Little, Brown 1994).

63. Michael Tilbury, Michael Noone & Bruce Kercher, Remedies: Commentary and Materials 1 (LBC Information Services 3d ed. 2000).

64. In this case, consumer welfare or consumer sovereignty will be proxies of consumer harm.

65. See the Opinion of AG Kokott in Case C-8/08, *T-Mobile Netherlands BV and Others*, Feb. 19, 2009, ¶¶ 58, 71 (defending the view that the objective of EU competition law is to "protect competition as such" because this is of benefit, not only for consumers but for "the public at large.") In Case C-8/08, *T-Mobile Netherlands BV and Others*, June 4, 2009, ¶ 38, the Court of Justice of the EU accepted that "Article 81 EC [now Article 101 TFEU], like the other competition rules of the Treaty,

is designed to protect not only the immediate interests of individual competitors or consumers but also to protect the structure of the market and thus competition as such" but did not adopt the position of AG Kokott with regard to the ultimate beneficiaries of the principle of competition, thus suggesting that a possible interpretation of the aims of EC competition law is the avoidance of a long-term consumer harm.

66. In industries with significant network effects, even in the absence of anticompetitive actions, the natural equilibrium is neither perfect competition nor an egalitarian market structure. Markets with strong network effects, such as the market for operating systems of PCs, are "winner-take-most" markets with significant market share and profits inequality as well as high concentration. Thus, the "but for" world that would have existed in the absence of anticompetitive actions is one of very significant inequality. Attempting to impose the perfectly competitive egalitarian environment of a nonnetwork industry can lead to lower social benefits. *See* Nicholas Economides, *The Economics of Networks*, 14 Int'l J. Indus. Org. 675 (1996); Nicholas Economides, *Competition Policy in Network Industries: An Introduction*, *in* The New Economy and Beyond: Past, Present and Future (Dennis Jansen ed., 2006).

67. *See* United States v. Microsoft Corp., 253 F.3d 34, 103 (D.C. Cir. 2001) (citation omitted).

68. For the distinction between markets and hierarchies, see Oliver E. Williamson, Markets and Hierarchies: Analysis and Antitrust Implications: A Study in the Economics of Internal Organization (Free Press, 1975); Oliver E. Williamson, The Mechanisms of Governance (Oxford Univ. Press, 1996).

69. Communication from the Commission, Guidance on the Commission's Enforcement Priorities in Applying Article 82 EC Treaty to Abusive Exclusionary Conduct by Dominant Undertakings, 2009 O.J. C 45/7.

70. For a discussion, see Economides & Lianos, *supra* note 12.

71. *See* Commission Decision, Case COMP/C-3/39.530, Microsoft (Dec. 16, 2009), (hereinafter EU "Microsoft II decision"); Microsoft's commitments are included in the Annex of the Commission's decision (hereinafter "Commitment"). Microsoft made additional commitments on interoperability between rivals' software and its own, including Windows, Windows Server, Office, Exchange, and SharePoint.

72. The screen will allow each consumer to set the default browser of his or her choice and allow the consumer to uninstall Internet Explorer.

73. Press Release, Microsoft, Annex A (July 24, 2009), (detailing how this will be implemented in Windows 7).

74. Press Release, Microsoft, Proposed Commitment ¶ 8 (July 24, 2009).

75. *Id.* at ¶ 9.

76. Matthew Newman, *Microsoft Is Said to Be in Talks to Settle EU Cases*, Bloomberg, July 7, 2009. Microsoft intended to produce and distribute, only in Europe, a special edition of Windows 7 called Windows 7 E, which would not have Internet Explorer or any other browser preinstalled, adopting the removal approach of the Windows XP N remedy imposed by the Commission in the first Microsoft case, as the sole version of Windows in Europe. *See* Commission Decision Case COMP/C-3/37.792—Microsoft, 2007 O.J. (L32/23).

77. *See also,* Wils, *supra* note 38.

78. *See* Case T-170/06, Alrosa Co. Ltd v. Commission, 2007 E.C.R. II-2601, ¶ 102; Case T-338/94, Finnboard, 1998 E.C.R. II-1617, ¶ 242; Case T-76/89, RTE and ITP v. Commission, 1991 E.C.R. Ii-757, ¶ 93; Case T-7/93, Langnese-Iglo v. Commission, 1995 E.C.R. II-1533, ¶ 209; Case T-9/93, Schöller v. Commission, 1995 E.C.R. II-1611, ¶ 163.

79. *See* Joined Cases C-189/02 P, C-202 P, C-205-208/02 P, C-213/02 P, Dansk Rørindustry and others, 2005 E.C.R. I-5425, ¶ 243.

80. Case T-170/06, Alrosa v. Commission, 2007 E.C.R. II-2601, ¶¶ 105–06; Appeal Case C-441/07 P.

81. *Id.* at ¶ 156. See, however, the contrary position of Advocate General Kokkott in Case C-441/07 P, Commission v. Alrosa, ¶ 62.

82. Case C-441/07, European Commission v. Alrosa Company Ltd., June 29, 2010, not yet reported.

83. *Id.* at ¶¶ 38, 48.

84. Case T-260/94, Air Inter v. Commission, 1997 E.C.R. II-997; Case T-65/98, Van den Bergh Foods v. Commission, 2003 E.C.R. II-4653, ¶ 201; Case T-170/06, Alrosa v. Commission, ¶ 98.

85. Opinion of Advocate General Kokkott in Case C-441/07 P, ¶ 46.

86. Case C-331/88, The Queen v. Minister of Agriculture, Fisheries and Food and Secretary of State for Health, ex parte: Fedesa and others, 1990 E.C.R. I-4023, ¶ 13.

87. Case T-170/06, *Alrosa v. Commission*, ¶ 99.

88. Tracy A. Thomas, *Proportionality and the Supreme Court's Jurisprudence of Remedies*, 59 Hastings L.J. 73 (2007); E. Thomas Sullivan & Richard S. Frase, Proportionality Principles in American Law: Controlling Excessive Government Actions (Oxford University Press, 2008). *See also* State Farm Mut. Auto. Ins. Co. v. Campbell et al., 538 U.S. 408 (2003) where the U.S. Supreme Court has declined to adopt a strict ratio test for punitive damages, but has suggested that the punitive-to-actual ratio should rarely be in double digits (i.e., exceed a 9:1 ratio).

89. On the importance of categorization in the context of Article 82 EC, see Ioannis Lianos, *Categorical Thinking in Competition Law and the "Effects-Based" Approach in Article 82 EC, in* Article 82 EC: Reflections on Its Recent Evolution (Ariel Ezrachi ed., Hart Publishing, 2009).

90. *See* Thomas O. Barnett, *Section 2 Remedies: What to Do After Catching the Tiger by the Tail*, 76 Antitrust L.J. 31, 36 (2009) ; Gregory J. Werden, *Remedies for Exclusionary Conduct Should Protect and Preserve the Competitive Process*, 76 Antitrust L.J. 65, 65 (2009), "[r]emedies for exclusionary conduct should arise 'organically out of the theory of the case'" (citing Lawrence A. Sullivan, Handbook of the Law of Antitrust 146 (1977)).

91. *Microsoft*, 253 F.3d at 80.

92. Per Hellström et al., *Remedies in European Antitrust Law*, 76 Antitrust L.J. 43, 58 (2009).

93. *Id.* at 59.

94. *Id.*

95. *Id.* The authors' reasoning is based on an internal contradiction. They advance that remedies may go beyond mirroring the abuse but at the same time they qualify their statement by recognizing that the remedy "should not undermine the infringer's incentive to compete on the merits." However, this is not very different from advancing that the remedy should mirror the abuse. Indeed, if the dominant firm competes on the merits, there is no abuse.

96. A broader theory of abuse (and consumer harm) under Article 102 TFEU that would have a direct link with the remedies sought could be one option to deal with the problem in this case. Sector inquiries with the possibility of imposing effective remedies, market investigation references, or a provision equivalent to § 5 of the FTC Act could also be adequate tools.

97. Brunswick Corp. v. Riegel Textile Corp., 752 F.2d 261, 267 (7th Cir. 1984).

98. Case T-170/06, *Alrosa v. Commission*, ¶ 131.

99. *Id.* ¶ 103.

100. *Id.* ¶ 141.

101. *Id.* ¶ 145 (referring to point 70 of the statement of objections sent by the Commission).

102. *Id.* ¶ 146.

103. Case C-441/07, European Commission v. Alrosa Company Ltd., June 29, 2010, not yet reported, ¶ 67.

104. One could compare the approach of the Court of Justice of the EU with that adopted by the U.K. Competition Appeal Tribunal (CAT) in a series of recent cases reviewing the remedies imposed by the U.K. Competition Commission in a number of market investigation reference decisions, under Part IV of the Enterprise Act of 2002. The CAT went beyond examining the rationality of the remedy to inquire further into the weight attached to the relevant considerations and thus explicitly linked the remedy with the consideration of the "adverse effect on competition" (AEC) through the means of a proportionality test. The test includes some quantitative and qualitative analysis and requires that the remedy "(1) must be effective to achieve the legitimate aim in question (appropriate), (2) must be no more onerous than is required to achieve that aim (necessary), (3) must be the least onerous, if there is a choice of equally effective measures, and (4) in any event must not produce adverse effects which are disproportionate to the aim pursued," Tesco Plc v. Competition Commission, 2009 CAT 6, ¶ 137. *See also* BAA Limited v. Competition Commission, 2009 CAT 35, ¶ 261.

105. For a useful and broad compilation of a bibliography on remedies, see Eleanor M. Fox & Paul Sirkis, Antitrust Remedies: Selected Bibliography and Annotations (American Antitrust Institute, Working Paper No. 06-01, 2005). In Europe, most literature has focused on merger remedies, an area where the Commission has published guidelines: Commission Notice on rRemedies Acceptable Under the Council Regulation (EC) No 139/2004 and Under Commission Regulation (EC) No 802/2, 2008 O.J. C267/1.

106. *See* Lianos, *supra* note 89.

107. As it is clear from the recent *Intel* decision of the European Commission, however, "[a]lthough not indispensable for finding an infringement under Article 82 of the Treaty according to the case law," the efficient competitor analysis is only "one possible way of showing whether Intel's rebates and payments were capable of causing or likely to cause anticompetitive foreclosure." *See*, Case COMP/C-37.990, Intel, Commission Decision ¶ 925 (May 13, 2009) (summary at 2009 O.J. (C227) 13).

Chapter 13

1. *See, e.g.*, Maurice E. Stucke, *Behavioral Economists at the Gate: Antitrust in the Twenty-First Century*, 38 Loy. U. Chi. L.J. 513 (2007).

2. Christopher R. Leslie, *Trust, Distrust, and Antitrust*, 82 Tex. L. Rev. 515, 524–27 (2004).

3. *Id.* at 546–99.

4. Patricia M. Doney, Joseph P. Cannon & Michael R. Mullen, *Understanding the Influence of National Culture on the Development of Trust*, 23 Acad. Mgmt. Rev. 601 (1998).

5. Geert Hofstede, Culture's Consequences: Comparing Values, Behaviors, Institutions and Organizations Across Nations 359 (2001).

6. Paul Sheard, *Keiretsu, Competition, and Market Access*, *in* Global Competition Policy 506, 506–07 (Edward E. Graham & J. David Richardson eds., 1997).

7. *Id.* at 526–28.

8. *See, e.g.*, Steven J. Kachelmeier & Mohamed Shehata, *Culture and Competition: A Laboratory Market Comparison Between China and the West*, 19J. Econ. Behav. & Org. 145 (1992). This study found that, apart from some minor differences, Mainland Chinese on the one hand and Americans and Canadians on the other hand exhibit the same profit-maximizing behavior in a highly stylized single-seller, single-buyer bargaining setting. The bargaining strategies adopted by both groups do not reveal any systematic differences. This remains true even in public information markets, where the payoffs to the buyers and sellers from each bargain are known to both groups. This refutes the presumption that Chinese may be less willing to be seen as driving hard bargains and taking overt advantage of others.

There is every reason to believe that the differences are even smaller between Chinese and Westerners today than in 1992, when the study was conducted. Economic reforms had only been in place in China for thirteen years at the time and capitalist thinking may not have been as deeply ingrained in its citizens then than it is now.

9. Eva Green, Jean-Claude Deschamps & Dario Paez, *Variation of Individualism and Collectivism Within and Between 20 Countries*, 36J. Cross Cultural Psychol. 321, 332 (2005).

10. *Id.* at 330–32.

11. Luigi Guiso, Paola Sapienza & Luigi Zingales, *Does Culture Affect Economic Outcomes?*, 20J. Econ. Persp. 23, 27–28 (2006).

12. *Id.* at 26 ("Adam Smith viewed his arguments in *A Theory of Moral Sentiments* as intertwined with his arguments in *The Wealth of Nations*.").

13. *Id.* at 27.

14. *Id.*

15. *Id.* at 27.

16. The study has been updated since and expanded in scope.

17. *See, e.g.*, David Yau-Fai Ho & Chi-Yue Chiu, *Component Ideas of Individualism, Collectivism, and Social Organization—An Application in the Study of Chinese Culture*, *in* Individualism and Collectivism: Theory, Method, and Applications 137 (Uichol Kim et al. eds., 1994).

18. Shalom H. Schwartz, Cultural Value Orientations: Nature & Implications of National Differences 12, available at: http://www.tau.ac.il/law/cegla3/tax/Schwartz%202008.pdf.

19. *Id.* at 6.
20. Ho & Chiu, *supra* note 17, at 143–44.
21. Jae-Ho Cha, *Aspects of Individualism and Collectivism in Korea, in* Individualism and Collectivism: Theory, Method, and Applications 157 (Uichol Kim et al. eds., 1994).
22. Richard Whitley, Business Systems in East Asia: Firms, Markets and Societies 166–217 (1992).
23. Doney, Cannon & Mullen, *supra* note 4, at 607.
24. *Id.* (providing a literature review).
25. Charles W. Hill, International Business: Competing in the Global Marketplace 67 (1997).
26. Geert Hofstede, Culture's Consequences: International Differences in Work Related Values 21 (1984).
27. Schwartz, *supra* note 18, at 4.
28. *Id.*
29. *Id.*
30. *Id.* at 5.
31. Hofstede, *supra* note 26, at 98.
32. Schwartz, *supra* note 18, at 8.
33. *Id.* at 8.
34. *Id.*
35. *Id.*
36. *Id.* at 9.
37. Hofstede, *supra* note 26, at 161.
38. Rui Baptista, *Culture, Institutions and Government Attitudes Towards New Firm Entry, in* Discussion Papers on Entrepreneurship, Growth and Public Policy 9 (2004).
39. Schwartz, *supra* note 18, at 9.
40. *Id.* at 62.
41. Baptista, *supra* note 38, at 10.
42. Hofstede, *supra* note 26, at 225.
43. Schwartz, *supra* note 18, at 7.
44. *Id.*
45. One key question to understanding the dynamics in a collectivist society is what defines the in-groups. In most of these societies, the in-groups have traditionally been based on family or clan. Yet the boundaries of in-groups have evolved over time. Cha observes that in Korea, family and clan have lost significance while school has become an increasingly important in-group. Younger Koreans tend to value school connections more so than family ties. This may reflect a shift of the country from an agrarian society to a modern industrial economy. When agricultural production, which tends to be family based, was the main economic activity, family ties were economically valuable. As manufacturing and services replaced agriculture as the main economic activities, family members moved to the cities for employment opportunities. Extended families and clans broke down. Classmates at schools and universities became the ones who could offer the most valuable business connections.
46. Hofstede, *supra* note 26, at 297.
47. *Id.*
48. *Id.*
49. Schwartz, *supra* note 18, at 8.
50. *Id.*
51. Hofstede, *supra* note 26, at 359.
52. Doney, Cannon & Mullen, *supra* note 4, at 604.
53. *Id.* at 605.
54. *Id.*
55. *Id.* at 606.
56. *Id.*
57. *Id.*
58. *Id.* at 606.
59. *Id.* at 610.
60. *Id.* at 610.

61. *Id.* at 611.
62. *Id.* at 612.
63. Guiso, Sapienza & Zingales, *supra* note 11, at 31.
64. *Id.* at 30.
65. *Id.*
66. Andreas Stephan, *Cartel Laws Undermined: Corruption, Social Norms and Collectivist Business Cultures*, 37 J.L. & Soc. 345, 361 (2010).
67. A fact relatively unknown outside of China is that one's geographical origin within China matters a lot. Chinese tend to feel stronger emotional ties with fellow Chinese from the same province or locality.
68. Stephan, *supra* note 66, at 362.
69. *Id.*
70. Ki Jong Lee, *Cultures and Cartels: Cross-Cultural Psychology for Antitrust Policies*, 21 Loy. Consumer L. Rev. 33 (2008).
71. *Id.* at 6–7.
72. Lee, *supra* note 70, at 9.
73. *Id.*
74. Stephan, *supra* note 66, at 354–59.
75. Akinori Uesugi, *How Japan Is Tackling Enforcement Activities Against Cartels*, 13 Geo. Mason L. Rev. 349, 355 (2005).
76. *Id.*
77. *Id.* at 355–56.
78. *Id.* at 356.
79. *Id.* at 362.
80. *Id.*
81. Reading Industries v. Kennecott Copper Corp., 631 F.2d 10 (2d Cir. 1980).
82. Sheard, *supra* note 6, at 521–25.
83. Whitley, *supra* note 22, at 167–83.
84. Green, Deschamps & Paez, *supra* note 9, at 326.
85. *Id.*

Chapter 14

This work was supported by the National Research Foundation of Korea Grant funded by the Korean Government (NRF-2011-330-B00092).The author acknowledges the comments received on statistical analysis from Professor Yun Jeong Choi at Kyung Hee University.

1. Cheong Wa Dae, *Press Release: Trilateral Cooperation Vision 2020*, Korea.net: Gateway to Korea, May 30, 2010, available at: http://www.korea.net/news.do?mode=detail&guid=47111.
2. So-hyun Kim, *Korea, Japan, China to launch cooperation secretariat in 2011*, Korea Herald, May 30, 2010.
3. David J. Gerber, Law and Competition in Twentieth Century Europe: Protecting Prometheus 347 (1998).
4. On the synchronized model of harmonized law and enforcement networks for the Association of Southeast Asian Nations (ASEAN), see Lawan Thanadsillapakul, *The Harmonization of ASEAN Competition Laws and Policy and Economic Integration*, 3 Rev. Dr. Unif. 25, 25–26 (2004).
5. Geert Hofstede, Culture's Consequences: Comparing Values, Behaviors, Institutions, and Organizations Across Nations (2003). On the thumbnail introduction to Hofstede's cultural value dimension (CVD) framework, see Ki Jong Lee, *Culture and Competition: National and Regional Levels*, 21 Loy. Consumer L. Rev. 33, 34–36 (2008).
6. Hofstede, *supra* note 5, at 500, Exhibit A5.1.
7. *Id.* at 62.
8. *Id.* at 502, Exhibit 5.3.
9. Lee, *supra* note 5, at 39.
10. *Id.* at 47.
11. World Economic Forum, The Global Competitiveness Report 2001–2002 at 167–68, 413 (2002).

12. Michael W. Nicholson, *An Antitrust Law Index for Empirical Analysis of International Competition Policy*, 4 J. Competition L. & Econ. 1009, 1016–18 (2008).
13. *Id.* at 1018–22.
14. World Economic Forum, *supra* note 11, at 413, Table 8.07.
15. *Id.* at 1014, 1022–23.
16. Hofstede, *supra* note 5, at 98.
17. Global Competition Review, The 2003 Handbook of Competition Enforcement Agencies (2003).
18. Nicholson, *supra* note 12, at 1018, Table 3.
19. *Id.* at 1022, Table 5.
20. *Id.* at 1024.
21. Spencer Weber Waller, *The Internationalization of Antitrust Enforcement*, 77 B.U. L. Rev. 343, 355 (1997).
22. Hofstede, *supra* note 5, at 62.
23. On the structural legacies from the centrally planned economy and the efforts to overcome them in China, see Ignacio De León, *Institutional Analysis of Competition Policy in Transition and Developing Countries: The Lessons from Latin America*, 3 Wash. U. Global Stud. L. Rev. 405, 421–24 (2004).
24. Abbott B. Lipsky Jr., *The Global Antitrust Expulsion: Safeguarding Trade and Commerce or Runway Regulation*, 26 Fletcher F. World Aff. 68 (2002) (putting great emphasis on the popular support for the issues of international antitrust).
25. *See, e.g.*, Hofstede, *supra* note 5, at 36.
26. *See, e.g.*, Lawrence E. Harrison, *Promoting Progressive Cultural Change*, *in* Culture Matters: How Values Shape Human Progress 296 (Samuel P. Huntington & Lawrence E. Harrison eds., 2001).
27. Lee, *supra* note 5, at 47–52.
28. On the indigenous roots of European competition laws, see Gerber, *supra* note 3, at chapters II–V.
29. For classical research on Kaegjoo, the commission agencies of the Joseon Dynasty, see Won Sun Park, Kaejoo (1968).
30. On the Meiji Restoration as an illustration of self-imposed cultural transformations in Japan, see Lan Cao, *The Ethnic Question in Law and Development*, 102 Mich. L. Rev. 1044, 1071 (2004).
31. Waller, *supra* note 21, at 396–97.

Chapter 15

1. Ignacio De León, An Institutional Assessment of Antitrust Policy: The Latin American Experience 11 (2009).
2. Julián Peña, *Competition Policies in Latin America, Post-Washington Consensus*, *in* Handbook of Research in Trans-Atlantic Antitrust 732, 732 (Philip Marsden ed., 2006).
3. De León, *supra* note 1, at 586.
4. *Id.* at 50.
5. Moisés Naím, *Does Latin America Need Competition Policy to Compete?*, *in* Competition Policy, Deregulation, and Modernization in Latin America 2, 2 (Moisés Naím & Joseph Tulchin eds., 1999).
6. Alfredo Bullard, *El Regreso del Jedi (O de la discrecionalidad en la aplicación de las Normas de Libre Competencia)*, 47 Themis (2005).
7. *Id.*
8. OECD, *Competition Law and Policy in Peru: A Peer Review*, *in* Competition Law and Policy in Latin America 323, 323 (2006).
9. Secretaria de Acompanhamento Econômico, Parecer Técnico N° 196, October 7, 2002, at 38.
10. Comisión Nacional De Defensa de la Competencia, Concentration Report 542, August 12, 2010.
11. Gabriel Ibarra, Límites a la Política de la Competencia 11–12 (2008).
12. *Id.* at 14.
13. The Economist, *Efficiency Drive*, *A Special Report on Latin America*, September 9, 2010.
14. OECD, Competition Policy and the Informal Economy 11 (2009).
15. Inter-American Development Bank, La Era de la Productividad: Cómo Transformar las Economías desde sus Cimientos 177 (Carmen Pagés ed., 2010).

16. OECD, *supra* note 14, at 21.
17. Clarín, August 6, 2005.
18. CNDC Concentration Report 542, March 15, 2006.
19. Franceschini analyzed the market effects of different divestment decisions ordered by CADE in Brazil and reached the conclusion that the effects were either neutral or negative to the markets. *See* José Inácio Franceschini, *Conditions Imposed by the CADE to the Clearance of Mergers: A Mistaken Paradigm*, *in* 19 Boletín Latinoamericano de Competencia 62 (2004).
20. De León, *supra* note 1, at 533.
21. Gabriel Castañeda, *Comments on Bruce M. Owen's Paper: Competition Policy in Latin America* (Center for International Development. Stanford Institute for Economic Policy Research. Stanford, 2003).
22. José Inácio Franceschini, *Private Competition Enforcement: Is There Room for CADE?*, 1st Antitrust Spring Conference, IBA-IBRAC. Rio de Janeiro, May 12–13, 2005.
23. *Id.*

Index

Note: Page numbers followed by *f* or *t* indicate figures or tables.

Accountability, independence of competition authorities and, 164–166, 273n10
Administrative Council for Economic Defense (CADE), 242, 248, 250, 282n19
Administrative law model, of judicial scrutiny, 146–151, 147*t*, 148*t*
Advocacy. *See* Competition advocacy
Agencias Navieras case, 153
Aggressive practices, consumer protection and, 130
Airtours v. Commission, 45
AKZO v. Commission, 48–49
All-or-none supply issue, monopsony law and, 55, 57–60, 261n10
Alrosa v. Commission, 195, 197–199
Ambulanz Glöckner, 111
American Recovery and Reinvestment Act (ARRA), 171
AM Patagonia case, 155
Andreangeli, Arianna: essay by, 22–36; references to, 2–3
Anticompetitive government regulation, 83–98; competition advocacy, 88–90; competition advocacy, prioritization, 94–97; competition advocacy, public choice pushback, 91–94, 93*t*; Easterbrook and, 83–85; economic theory of regulation and, 86–88, 91–92
Antitrust Paradox, The (Bork), 20
Antitrust standing, monopsony law and, 61–62, 261n20
Appellate review, 144–145
Arduino, 107, 108, 109, 112
Areeda, Phillip, 49, 79, 125
Argentina, 238, 242, 243, 245, 247, 248, 250
Asia. *See* Culture-competition correlation, in Northeast Asia
Australia, 95, 162, 231
Autonomy versus embeddedness, as cultural value, 210
Autorité de la Concurrence, France, 162

Banking sector, consumer protection law and, 133
Baptista, Rui, 210–211
Barker, Kit, 182
Barriers to entry, anticompetitive government regulation and, 85–86, 88
Benson, Peter, 186–187
Bohannan, Christina, 125
Bolivia, 238
Bork, Robert, 20
Brazil, 238, 242, 245, 250
Brooke Group Ltd. v. Brown & Williamson Tobacco Corp., 49, 59
Bulan v. Moldova, 30
Bullard, Alfredo, 242
BundesKartellamt, Germany, 162

Cable, Vince, 161
Calabresi, Guido, 20, 122
California Retail Liquor Dealers Ass'n v. Midcal Aluminum, Inc., 88, 102–103, 107
Canada: anticompetitive government regulation, 97; institutional models of judicial scrutiny, 146–148, 148*t*, 271n19
Canadian Competition Bureau (CB), 146
Cannon, Joseph P., 213
Carbice Corp. v. Am. Patents Dev. Corp., 73–74
Carra, 111
Castañeda, Gabriel, 247
Centro Servizi Spediporto, 108, 112, 267n47
Cha, Jae-Ho, 208, 279n45

Chamberlain, Edward, 118
Cheng, Thomas K.: essay by, 205–220; references to, 10
Chicago School antitrust tradition, 117, 267n3; attitude toward culture, 207; Coase, market superiority, and judicial error, 2, 15–20, 254n21; Easterbrook and, 18–21; transaction cost economics contrasted, 66–67, 69–70, 78, 80
Chicken Delight franchise, 78, 263n40
Chile, 238, 248; anticompetitive government regulation, 97; institutional models of judicial scrutiny, 146, 147, 148*t*, 151–156, 271n19
China: Anti-Monopoly Law, 101–102; cartels, 205–206; cultural values, 208, 214, 216, 278n8; vertical restraints, 206. *See also* Culture-competition correlation, in Northeast Asia
Chiu, Chi-Yue, 208
Chung Ho-Yul, 158
CIF, 108, 113
Cipolla, 109, 112
Clark, Herbert, 208
CNSD, 108, 112
Coase, Ronald: Chicago School belief in superiority of markets and mistaken views of courts, 2, 15–20, 254n21; transaction cost economics and, 67, 262n6
Coleman, Jules, 187
Collectivism. *See* Individualism versus collectivism
Collusive monopsony, 61–62
Colombia, 238
Competition advocacy, 88–90; independence of competition authorities and, 166–169, 273n12; prioritization, 94–97; public choice pushback, 91–94, 93*t*; spending on, 93–94, 93*t*
Competition and Consumer Commission, Australia, 162
Competition authorities, 158–176; accountability and independence, 164–166; advocacy, 166–172, 273n12; advocacy's limits, 173–175; case for independence from government and business, 159–161; characteristics of independent, 161–164; reinforcement of powers of, 172–173
Competition General Directorate of the European Commission (DG Comp), 162, 168, 171–172
Competition Tribunal (CT), Canada, 146, 271n19
Compulsory licenses, ECHR and, 29–35
Consumer protection law, 127–137; competition law contrasted, 127–128; competition law's intersections with, 128–129, 269n6; as complement to competition law, 135–137; unfair commercial practices and France Telecom, 133–134, 269n20; unfair commercial practices and Italian Competition Authority, 129–135, 269nn7,8,13,16
Cooperative buying, monopsony law and, 62–63
Corrective justice, distributive justice and remedies, 185–188
Costa Rica, 238
Cost of movements concept, 262n6
Council Regulation (EC) No 1/2003, 2, 23, 28–29, 32; remedies and, 189–190, 194
Court of Justice of the EU, due process standards and, 26–27, 30, 32
Crane, Daniel A.: essay by, 117–126; references to, 8
Cultural values, 205–220; abuse of dominance, 218–219; behavioral economics assumptions, 205–206, 278n8; cartels, 206, 212, 214–216; definitions of culture, 208–209; horizontal restraints, 216–218; scientific studies of economics, 206–208; specific cultural values, 209–212; trust, 212–213; vertical restraints, 206, 218
Culture-competition correlation, in Northeast Asia, 221–235; antitrust law and culture, 228–229, 229*t*, 230*t*; competition agency effectiveness and culture, 223, 226, 227*t*; implications, 230–232; previous findings, 222–223, 224–225*t*; promotion of, 232–234; resource inputs into policy, 226–227, 228*t*

De Beers, 198
Deference and nondeference approaches to judicial scrutiny, 142, 145, 147–148, 147*t*, 148*t*, 154–156, 154*t*
De León, Ignacio, 237, 238, 247
Deschamps, Jean-Claude, 207, 219
Deterrence, remedies and, 184–185
Director, Aaron, 2, 15–16, 18
Discretionary remedialism: corrective justice, 187–188; defined, 179; effects-based approach and remedial proportionality, 199–201; primary and secondary rights, 180–183; remedial proportionality, 194–199
Distributive justice, corrective justice and remedies, 185–188

Dominican Republic, 238
Doney, Patricia M., 213
Double jeopardy, ECHR and Court of Justice, 28–29, 35
Doulamis, 107, 112
Due process, ECHR and, 27–29

Easterbrook, Frank, 18–21, 83–85, 89, 117, 141, 177
Eastman Kodak Co. v. Image Tech. Servs., Inc., 71, 77–78
eBay v. MercExchange, 124
Economic efficiency, corrective justice and, 183–185, 274n32
Economics. *See* Legal techniques, for importing economics into law; Monopsony; Transaction cost economics (TCE)
Economic theory of regulation (ETR), 86–88, 91–92
Ecuador, 238
Egalitarianism versus hierarchy, as cultural value, 210
El Salvador, 245
European Commission (EC): competition advocacy in, 94; consumer protection law, 136–137. *See also* European Convention on Human Rights (ECHR)
European Competition Network (ECN), 23, 28, 29, 35
European Convention on Human Rights (ECHR), 22–36; enforcement and due process issues, 24–29; European Commission's powers and, 22–24; intellectual property and compulsory licensing issues, 29–36; rule of law and corporate entities, 4–25
European Court of Justice (ECJ): dominant position and, 41; trade law discipline and, 110–115; Treaty on the Functioning of the European Union and, 104–109
Exclusionary distribution requirements, transaction cost economics and, 80
Experience, of reviewing courts, 143
Expertise, of reviewing courts, 143, 270n10

Fair, reasonable, and nondiscriminatory (FRAND), intellectual property law and, 123–124
False negatives (Type II prosecutorial errors), 19–20, 117
False positives (Type I prosecutorial errors), 19–21, 117
Federal Trade Commission (FTC), 90, 103, 121–122, 124, 162, 171, 271n17
Feist Publications v. Rural Telephone Services, 119–120
Feminity. *See* Masculinity versus femininity
First, Harry, 179
Fiscalía Nacional Económica (FNE), Chile, 146
Fox, Eleanor, 101–102
France, 166, 168, 173, 175. *See also* France Télécom
Franceschini, José Inácio, 250
France Télécom, 49, 132, 133–134, 161, 269n20
France Télécom v. Commission, 132–134
Franchises, transaction cost economics and, 77–79
Funke v. France, 26

Gardner, John, 184–185
Gerard, Damien M. B.: essay by, 99–116; references to, 5–6, 88
Germany, 162
Global Competition Review, 223, 226
Government intervention, financial crisis and competition authorities, 170–171
Government restraints. *See* Anticompetitive government regulation; State action
Green, Eva, 207, 219
Group boycotts, monopsony law and, 64
Guanxi, 216
Guiso, Luigi, 207, 213

Hall, Edward, 208
Hall, Mildred, 208
Harmony. *See* Mastery versus harmony, as cultural value
Harrison, Jeffrey L.: essay by, 54–65; references to, 4
Hayek, Friedrich, 15, 24
Health care reform, in the United States, 95
Herfindahl-Hirschmann Index (HHI), 244, 246
Hierarchy versus egalitarianism, as cultural value, 210
Hill, Charles, 208
Ho, David, 208
Hofstede, Geert, 207–212, 219, 222, 230, 231, 279n45
Horizontal market division, monopsony law and, 64, 65
Hospital Consulting, 108
Hovenkamp, Herbert: essay by, 66–80; references to, 4–5, 125, 185
Human rights. *See* European Convention on Human Rights (ECHR)
Hur, Joseph Seon, 158

Ibarra, Gabriel, 244–245
Impala judgment, 45

IMS Health GmbH & Co v. NDC Health GmbH & Co, 34, 35
Indirect purchaser doctrine, monopsony law and, 61–62, 261n20
Individualism versus collectivism: cultural-competition correlation and, 222–223, 224–225*t*, 226, 226*t*, 227*t*, 228*t*, 230–231, 230*t*; as cultural value, 209, 211, 213, 214–215, 217, 218, 219
Inflation, in Latin America, 246
INNO/ATAB. See *SA G.B.–INNO-B.M. v. Association des détaillants en tabac (ATAB)*
Intellectual property laws, 117–126; advantages of remedial structures, 121–124; ECHR and, 29–36; market power and substantive rights, 118–121; natural fault line, 124–126; share of economy characterized by intellectual property, 117
International Competition Network (ICN), 89, 93, 160–161, 164–165, 170
In the Matter of Rambus Inc., 121–122, 124
Int'l Salt Co. v. United States, 73–74
Isapres case, 153, 154
Italian Competition Authority, consumer protection law and, 129–135, 269nn7,8,13,16
Italy: telecom sector, 131–132; transport industry, 134–135

James Hardie case, 154
Japan: competition advocacy, 94; cultural values, 206, 208, 216, 218. *See also* Culture-competition correlation, in Northeast Asia
Japan Fair Trade Commission, 175–176
Jenny, Frédéric: essay by, 158–176; references to, 7–8
Journal of Law & Economics, 15–16, 18–19
Judicial errors: Chicago School and, 17–19, 20; Easterbrook's analysis of, 19–21
Judicial review, 144–145
Judicial scrutiny, allocation of power and, 141–157; application to Chile, 146–147, 151–156, 271n19; four models of, 146–151, 147*t*, 148*t*; institutional variables, 142–146

Kaplow, Louis, 123–124
Keiretsu, 206
Kim Dong-Su, 158
Korea, 94–95, 158, 208, 279n45. *See also* Culture-competition correlation, in Northeast Asia
Korean Fair Trade Commission (KFTC), 94–95, 158, 168

Latin America, limits of competition law in, 236–251; cultural limits, 237–241; economic limits, 244–246; institutional limits, 246–250; political limits, 241–244
Leclerc case, 112
Lee, Ki Jong: essay by, 221–235; references to, 10, 214–215
Legal techniques, for importing economics into law, 39–53; legal tests, 41, 44–45; linking relevant facts to legal category, 41, 46–47; predation example, 48–50; presumptions and, 50–53; properties for interpreting law, 40–41; rearranging relevant facts, 41, 43–44; stating legal relevance of facts, 41–42
Leniency programs, cultural values and cartel enforcement, 215–216
Liability rules, intellectual property law and, 122–123
Lianos, Ioannis: essay by, 177–201; references to, 8–9
Licensing. *See* Intellectual property laws
Liggett v. Brown and Williamson Tobacco, 59
Limits of Antitrust, The (Easterbrook): anticompetitive government regulation and, 83–85, 141; Chicago School antitrust tradition and, 18–21

Magill. See *Radio Telefs Eirseann (RTE) & Independent Television Publications Ltd (ITP) v. Commission of the European Communities*
Market definition, legal relevance and, 41–42, 259n2
Masculinity versus femininity: cultural-competition correlation and, 222–223, 224–225*t*, 226*t*, 227*t*, 228*t*, 230*t*; as cultural value, 209, 211, 213, 214, 215, 217, 219
Mashaw, Jerry L., 271n24
Mastery versus harmony, as cultural value, 210, 211–212, 214, 215, 217, 218, 219
McGee, John, 16
Melamed, Douglas, 20, 122
Meng, 107, 112
Mexico, 238, 242, 248
Microsoft v. Commissioner, 3, 33–34, 36, 125–126, 166
Misleading practices, consumer law and, 130
Modernisation Regulation, of European Commission, 23, 28, 29, 32, 35
Monopsony, 54–65, 261n1; all-or-none supply issue, 55, 57–60, 261n10; antitrust standing, 61–62, 261n20; cooperative buying, 62–63; general issues, 63–65; monopsony theory, 55–57, 56*f*, 57*f*, 261n4;

Weyerhaeuser Co. v. Ross-Simmons Hardwood Lumber Co., 54, 58–60, 65
Mont Pelerin Society, 15
Montt, Santiago: essay by, 141–157; references to, 7
Mullen, Michael R., 213
Muris, Timothy, 99

Namenwirth, Zvi, 208
National Commission for the Defense of Competition (CNDC), Argentina, 243, 245, 248
National Competition Authorities (NCAs), 23, 28–29
National Institute for the Defense of Competition and Intellectual Property (INDECOPI), Peru, 242
Nature of the Firm, The (Coase), 18, 67, 262n6
Nebbia, Paolisa: essay by, 127–137; references to, 6–7
New Zealand, 94, 231
Nicholson, Michael, 223, 228–229
Nondeference. *See* Deference and nondeference approaches to judicial scrutiny
Northwest Wholesale Stationers, Inc. v. Pacific Stationery and Printing Co., 63

Obama, Barack, 95
Odudu, Okeoghene, 115, 116
O'Halloran and Francis v. United Kingdom, 26, 27
OHRA, 107, 112
Oliogopsony, 61–62
Orange Foot, 133–134, 269n20
Organisation for Economic Co-operation and Development (OECD), 49–50, 162, 164, 169–170, 171, 174, 245
Orkem v. Commission, 26
Oxigeno case, 153

Paez, Dario, 207, 219
Palmer v. BRG of Georgia, Inc., 64
Panama, 245
Parallel jurisdiction, ECHR and Court of Justice, 28–29, 35
Parity of the Economic Marketplace, The (Director), 19
Parker v. Brown, 88, 102–103
Pavlov, 109
Peña, Julián: essay by, 236–251; references to, 10
Perry, Steven, 187–188
Peru, 242, 247
Petrobras, 242
Pigou, A. C., 17, 18, 262n6
Posner, Richard, 46, 47
Power distance: cultural-competition correlation and, 222–223, 224–225*t*, 226–227, 226*t*, 227*t*, 228*t*, 230–231, 230*t*; as cultural value, 209, 210, 217
Predation: legal techniques for importing economics into law and, 41, 42, 44, 46–50, 53; monopsony law and, 59–60; transaction cost economics and, 79–80
Price discrimination, transaction cost economics and, 76–79
Priest, George L.: essay by, 15–21; references to, 2
Problem of Social Cost, The (Coase), 17–20
Property rules, intellectual property law and, 122–123
Property Rules, Liability Rules and Inalienability (Calabresi and Melamed), 20
Protectionism, cultural limits in Latin America and, 237–241
Public restraints. *See* Anticompetitive government regulation

Radio Telefs Eirseann (RTE) & Independent Television Publications Ltd (ITP) v. Commission of the European Communities, 120
Raising rivals' costs (RRC), 79–80, 85–86
Reagan, Ronald, 84
Reasonable and nondiscriminatory (RAND), intellectual property law and, 123–124
Reclamación, 151–153, 156
Reiff, 108, 112
Remedies, 177–201; aim of, 189–191, 275n65, 276n66; distributive justice and corrective justice, 185–188; economic efficiency and distributive justice, 183–185, 274n32; effects-based approach and remedial proportionality, 199–201; liabilities and, 177–180; primary and secondary rights issues, 180–183; remedial proportionality, 194–199; for TFEU violations, 191–194, 192*f*
Resale price maintenance (RPM), 73, 75–76, 103

SA G.B.-INNO-B.M. v. Association des détaillants en tabac (ATAB), 106, 112
Sapienza, Paola, 207, 213
Scalia, Antonin, 71
Schwartz, Shalom, 208, 209, 210, 211, 219
Sector regulation, anticompetitive government regulation and, 87–88
Seigel v. Chicken Delight, Inc., 78, 263n40
Self-incrimination, ECHR and Court of Justice, 26–27, 35

Sherman Antitrust Act, 20, 21, 46, 102–103, 125
Short-term versus long-term orientation: cultural-competition correlation and, 222–223, 224–225*t*, 226*t*, 227*t*, 228*t*, 229, 230*t*, 231; as cultural value, 212, 218
Sibony, Anne-Lise: essay by, 39–53; references to, 3
Small but Significant and Nontransitory Increase in Price (SSNIP), 246
Smith, Adam, 207
Smith Kline and French Laboratories v. the Netherlands, 30–31, 35
Sokol, D. Daniel: essay by, 83–98; references to, 5
Spain, 94, 173
Specialization, of reviewing courts, 143–144, 146
Standard Oil case, 16
Standard setting organizations (SSOs), intellectual property law and, 123–124
Standing. *See* Antitrust standing, monopsony law and
State action, 99–116; competition law system's limits and, 101–109; trade law as disciplining approach, 100, 110–116
State Oil Co. v. Khan, 73
State-owned enterprises (SOEs), anticompetitive government regulation and, 85–86
Stephan, Andreas, 214, 216
Structuralism paradigm, contrasted to transaction cost analysis, 66–67, 69–70, 78, 80
Sydhavnens Sten & Grus, 111

Tacit collusion, culture and, 217
Takeshima, Kazuhiko, 175
Tapia, Javier: essay by, 141–157; references to, 7
Telecom sector, consumer law and, 131–134, 161, 269n15
Territorial divisions, monopsony law and, 64, 65
Tetra Laval v. Commission, 51–52
TFEU (Treaty on the Functioning of the European Union), 2, 23, 29–36; consumer protection law, 131–132; remedies, 178–179, 189–190, 191–194, 192*f*, 199–201; state action to restrict competition, 104–109; trade law discipline, 110–115
Trade law discipline, state action and, 110–116
Transaction cost economics (TCE), 66–80; Chicago School position and structuralism contrasted, 66–67, 69–70, 78, 80; private contracting and, 75–79; raising rivals' costs and, 79–80; theory of, 67–69; tying and double marginalization, 67, 73–75, 79
Transport industry, consumer law and, 134–135
Trentalia, 134–135
Tribunal de Defensa de la Libre Competencia (TDLC), Chile, 146–147, 151–156
Trinko. See *Verizon Commc'ns, Inc. v. Law Offices of Curtis V. Trinko*
Trust, culture and, 212–213, 214, 217, 218
Turkish Competition Authority, 164
Turner, Donald, 49, 79
Tying: intellectual property law, 123; monopsony law, 64–65; transaction cost economics, 67, 73–75, 79

Uncertainty avoidance: cultural-competition correlation and, 222–223, 224–225*t*, 226*t*, 227, 227*t*, 228*t*, 230–231, 230*t*, 233; as cultural value, 209, 210–211, 215, 218
United Kingdom: competition advocacy in, 94; competition authorities, 172–173
United States: competition advocacy in, 94; state action as limit to competition, 102–103, 109. *See also* Federal Trade Commission (FTC)
United States v. Microsoft, 178, 193–194, 196, 276nn71,76
United States v. Topco, 64, 65
Uruguay, 238
U.S. Supreme Court: adoption of Chicago School approach to antitrust, 20; *Standard Oil* case, 16

Varney, Christine A., quoted, 21
Venezuela, 238
Verizon Commc'ns, Inc. v. Law Offices of Curtis V. Trinko, 125
Vertical restraints, culture and, 218
Vickers, John, 159, 166, 273n10

Wanadoo judgment, 48, 49–50
Washington Consensus, 236, 237–238
Weber, Robert, 208
Weyerhaeuser Co. v. Ross-Simmons Hardwood Lumber Co., 54, 58–60, 65
Whitley, Richard, 208, 218
Williamson, Oliver, 79

Yarrow, George, 159–160

Zingales, Luigi, 207, 213

Global Competition Law and Economics

Ioannis Lianos and D. Daniel Sokol, editors

Competition law and economics—known in the United States as antitrust—is an area of cutting-edge academic work with significant policy implications. Once confined to the United States and a few other countries, antitrust has taken off as an area of study in a relatively short period of time. More than 100 jurisdictions now have competition laws. Increasingly, enforcement activities abroad have far-reaching implications for any antitrust regime. Moreover, developments in economic thinking have helped to reformulate attitudes in both academic and policy circles. This book series is at the forefront of the development of new ideas and approaches within the field.